*Naresh Sehgal*

*Santa Clara*

# Ja

## and Servlets

# Java Server and Servlets

## Building Portable Web Applications

PETER ROSSBACH AND HENDRIK SCHREIBER

An imprint of Pearson Education

Harlow, England • London • New York • Reading, Massachusetts • San Francisco • Toronto
Don Mills, Ontario • Sydney • Tokyo • Singapore • Hong Kong • Seoul • Taipei • Cape Town
Madrid • Mexico City • Amsterdam • Munich • Paris • Milan

PEARSON EDUCATION LIMITED

Head Office:
Edinburgh Gate
Harlow CM20 2JE
Tel: +44 (0)1279 623623
Fax: +44 (0)1279 431059

London Office:
128 Long Acre
London WC2E 9AN
Tel: +44 (0)20 7447 2000
Fax: +44 (0)207 240 5771

Website: www.awl.com/cseng/

_____

First published in Great Britain in 2000

© Pearson Education Limited 2000

Copyright © 1999 by Addison Wesley Longman Verlag GmbH. All rights reserved. First published in the German language under the title *Java Server und Servlets* by Addison Wesley Longman Verlag GmbH, München.

The rights of Peter Rossbach and Hendrik Schreiber to be identified as Authors of this Work have been asserted by them in accordance with the Copyright, Designs and Patents Act 1988.

ISBN 0-201-67491-2

*British Library Cataloguing in Publication Data*
A CIP catalogue record for this book can be obtained from the British Library.

*Library of Congress Cataloging in Publication Data*
Rossbach, Peter, 1965–
    [Java server und Servlets. English]
    Java server and servlets: building portable wed applications / Peter Rossbach and Hendrik Schreiber.
        p.  cm.
    Translation of: Java servers und servlets.
    Includes bibliographical references and index.
    ISBN 0–201–67491–2 (pbk.: alk. paper)
        1. Java (Computer program language) 2. Web servers. I. Schreiber, Hendrik, 1973-
        II. Title.

QA76.73.J38R68 2000
005.2'276- -dc21                                                                        00–022939

The programs in this book have been included for their instructional value. The publisher does not offer any warranties or representations in respect of their fitness for a particular purpose, nor does the publisher accept any liability for any loss or damage arising from their use.

Many of the designations used by manufacturers and sellers to distinguish their products are claimed as trademarks. Pearson Education Limited has made every attempt to supply trademark information about manufacturers and their products mentioned in this book. A list of trademark designations and their owners appears on page vi.

10  9  8  7  6  5  4  3  2  1

Typeset by M Rules.
Printed and bound in the United States of America.

*The Publishers' policy is to use paper manufactured from sutainable forests.*

For Regina
P.R.

*"Life is Vegas."*
H.S.

## Acknowledgements

The publishers wish to thank Sun Microsystems, Inc. for permission to reproduce an extract from Sun's 'Java™ Servlet Specification, V2.2' in Appendix C. This material is copyright 1998–2000 Sun Microsystems, Inc. All rights reserved. Used by permission. Sun, Sun Microsystems, the Sun Logo, Java, Java Foundation Classes, Java Server Development Kit, Java Server Pages, JavaScript, JDBC Kona and Servlet API, and all Sun-based and Java-based marks are trademarks or registered trademarks of Sun Microsystems in the United States and other countries.

## Trademark notice

# Contents

# About the authors

**Peter Rossbach**, who has a degree in computing science, has worked with object-oriented analysis, design and programming since 1990, and tests the methods by putting them into practice. He is particularly interested in developing decentralized information systems. The architecture of robust systems and the process of developing them have given him and his team a few tough nuts to crack. He is particularly concerned with designing and creating frameworks and integrating relational databases with the world of objects. Since 1997 Peter Rossbach has been concentrating on using Java for Web applications. He was brought to writing through leading the development of a distributed content management system for commerce and banking, which now supplies more than 500 sites with up-to-date information.

With this experience behind him, he has now founded his own company, whose business is the creation of products and projects for Java-based e-commerce solutions.

**Hendrik Schreiber** always wanted to be a writer: something between Paul Auster and John Steinbeck. But then his computer got infested with Java and turned itself into a virtual machine. So in the end he finished up as 'just' a specialist author. As with other highly infectious diseases, it is not possible to look back and identify the day that he was infected. However, what is certain is that it happened in August 1996, and that it was a network infection. Only a year later, the first servlets were discovered on his computer. Since then, Hendrik Schreiber has expended all his energy on developing Web applications and servers. Part of this work involves the creation of the Java-based script language objectHTML. Another part involves the servlet-enabled Web server jo!

In the meantime, Hendrik Schreiber works as a contract developer and studies Journalism and Computing Science at Dortmund University in his spare time. It used to be the other way round, but that was when he wanted to be a writer.

# Preface

This book is supposed to be about servlets. When we began developing our first servlet-based application in Autumn 1997, we were forced to accept that there was no printed literature on the subject. Admittedly, a very active group formed in the Web and particularly in a variety of mailing lists – but we were still kept waiting for printed material. The Apache JServ project developed one 0.9.x version after the other (`http://java.apache.org`), Sun launched the Java Web Server on the market and IBM followed up with ServletExpress, the early fore-runner of today's Websphere. At the same time, Live Software came along and made a big impression with their plug-in JRun. But all this time, there was still nothing put down, black on white – apart from a few short articles in the relevant technical publications (Heid 1997, Rossbach and Schreiber 1997).

After our first attempts we rapidly came to realize that the pure servlet API promised small and beautifully formed solutions for just such problems, but would not help us achieve a major breakthrough. This led to the birth of the first idea for extending the API, which we later christened *Servlet Method Invocation (SMI)*. This extension, based on the servlet API, made it possible for us to build robust and configurable applications.

Then, one thing came after another: we needed a configuration manager, and object-related mapping for databases, and then we wrote our own servlet engine, jo!. We had created a framework, the WebApp framework. During development we laid a great deal of value on keeping all components as flexible as possible. Only a few of the dependencies within the WebApp framework are really hard-coded. Most of them are detached via interfaces. You can read more about this design principle in Part II of this book.

Owing to all these activities, the actual servlet programming was pushed ever further into the background, in favour of ideas concerning the application and server architecture, a powerful layer for saving object networks and applications for the framework. For this reason, the book may give the impression, in some places, that it explains a few things about a large number of subjects, but never does anything in depth. Our objection to that impression is that the book definitely does one thing: it explains how to build Web-based applications. The fact remains that you need certain ingredients, such as servlets, a servlet engine, an extension such as SMI and a persistence layer, to do so.

We believe that you need all these elements, together, to be able to work efficiently. What use is it, to write a great mail servlet, if you cannot integrate it in your application? What use can you have for program code that includes SQL statements that are almost impossible to maintain? What do you do if your application suddenly has to have its own, more convenient and easy-to-use client and should no longer work only with Web browsers? You can respond to all these questions calmly if you have taken a critical look at a few issues when you began developing your software –

and not just with servlet programming in its natural state and 'raw' JDBC (Java DataBase Connectivity).

The framework presented in this book is certainly no wonder cure. However, it can help you to develop better applications. Even if you never use it, you will get a feel for the problems you have to overcome.

There are now a few good books about servlet programming (Moss 1998, Hunter and Crawford 1998). Even though the first part of this book covers servlet programming, it is not a pure servlet book. It is a book about the architecture and the building of servlet-based applications.

## The software for the book

As this subject develops very rapidly and the life of software and the documentation that goes with it generally appears to be getting shorter, we decided not to include a CD-ROM with this book. Instead, there is a Web site for the book. http://www.webapp.de. We recommend that you download the WebApp framework from the website, so you can work through and understand the example applications yourself.

## Notation in UML

In all three parts we have used diagrams to give you a clear view of the design and processes. The notation we used is UML (Unified Modelling Language) 1.0 (Oestereich 1998). To create the diagrams we used Rational Rose for Java.

## Questions and suggestions

We welcome open dialogue about this book and the servlet scene. For this purpose we have created the mail address book@webapp.de. Please send us your thoughts, suggestions, inspirations and ideas for improvements. They will be heartily welcomed.

## Our thanks

We would like to thank our colleagues in FACTUM Projektentwicklung und Management GmbH, Phillip Ghadir, Michael Jürgens, Wolfgang Neuhaus, Frank Peske, Henning Steiner and Axel Terfloth, for their willingness to again and again correct and comment on yet another chapter. We also thank all members of the intraNEWS team who created a distributed information system based on a servlet-based application server with us, during a period of 14 months, for their ideas and their hard work. At the end of the day they played an important role in motivating us to write this book.

We owe a special thank you to Frank Wegmann for his accurate and constructive criticism. Owing to his perfectionism, we were able to see many things in the proper light for the first time.

In addition we would like to thank Ulrich Büttgen who put earlier versions of the framework and the book under the microscope and gave us valuable advice.

Furthermore we give our thanks to our reader, Susanne Spitzer, for her uncomplicated way of working with us and the freedom that she gave us when we were creating this book. It has become a rather different Java book and we hope that it will be rewarded with success.

## Peter Rossbach

I would like to thank my family. Special thanks to my wife, Regina Potthoff, for her patience and the encouraging support she gave me during difficult phases. To my daughters Josephine and Vivienne for the incalculable joy and refreshing change they gave me. Josephine has given us her name for the jo! servlet engine and her helpful words of consolation – 'Everything will be all right!' – pushed me to finish the book.

## Hendrik Schreiber

I want to thank everyone who helped me write this book – especially Barbara, Rolf, Marc, Bernd and Enke. Without their support, understanding and patience, and a few nights in the 'Keller' and 'Soundgarden', this book would never have been created.

Bochum, Dortmund 1999

# Basis

The first part of this book deals with the basics of server and servlet programming in Java. Chapter 1 begins with an explanation of the simplest basic concepts both of the World Wide Web, and of Java sockets and threads. This is intended to provide a gradual introduction into the main subject matter, to give a little of the historical background and to bring the processes and techniques a little closer. Although we start from the beginning in some places, this chapter is not an introduction to the Java programming language (Cornell and Horstmann 1996, Campione and Walrath 1997), any more than the later chapters in the book.

In Chapter 2 we show how to develop a simple Web server, and use this to give a deeper insight into the processes between the Web browser and Web server. The primary concern here is to show how easy it is to create a server with Java. To do this we introduce the principle of the service handler architecture. Alongside this you will learn quite a lot about HTTP, which is the Web's transfer protocol.

In Chapter 3 we give you a more comprehensive explanation of the servlet API with all its possible uses. The various interfaces and classes of the programming interface are dealt with in greater detail. We also give you a few tips on how to build robust servlets. Along with the smaller examples which are spread through the text, at the end of Chapter 3 you will see examples of servlets for standard applications. These are a mail servlet, a database servlet and a guest book. After reading this chapter you should be able to program servlets quickly and effectively. Being able to do this is the basic skill needed in the second and third parts of this book.

# Fundamentals 1

To start with, we would like to give a brief introduction to the basic technical fundamentals. If you already know about HTML, HTTP and CGI, you can confidently miss out the sections about them. To understand the following sections, you have to be an expert in Java threads and sockets. If that is no problem for you, you can start looking at programming your first server right away, in the next chapter.

## 1.1 Hypertext Markup Language

*Hypertext Markup Language (HTML)* was developed by Tim Berners-Lee at CERN in Geneva, from 1989 onwards, to make it easier for the scientists working there to access information. At that time, Berners-Lee said that it was easier to find something in a non-linear, non-hierarchical information system such as hypertext than in a hierarchically structured branching catalogue (Berners-Lee 1989). Consequently, HTML – essentially an application of the *Standard Generalized Markup Language (SGML ISO 8879)* – was soon developed at CERN.

An HTML document (Listing 1.1) consists of a header and a body. The header contains the title and other meta-information while the body stores the content of the document. Tags are used to assign a characteristic to a section. For example, the text between the tag `<body>` and the tag `</body>` has the characteristic of being the body of the HTML document. From this we can already see that there is usually a starting tag and a final tag, You can recognize the final tag by the forward slash after the 'less than' character.

Listing 1.1: Example HTML document

```
<html>
  <head>
    <title>This title appears in the title row of the browser
    </title>
  </head>
```

```
<body>
    <h1>This is a first-level header</h1>
    Here, any text could be inserted.
    It could contain <em>emphasized</em> passages,
    <b>bold</b> or also <i>italic</i>.
</body>
</html>
```

`<body>`, just like `<em>` (for emphasized), for example, is a logical tag which means that it does not exactly define how the text that is present is to be displayed. As a result, a text marked with `<em>` might be displayed with underlining, or bold, or in another colour, by a browser. How does not matter, the main thing is that the text is emphasized. Complementing these *content-based* tags there are also *physical* tags. Examples of these tags include bold, underlined or italic (`<b>`, `<u>` or `<i>`).

As the *World Wide Web (WWW)* was originally intended only as a simple way to access information and not as a graphical medium, the HTML coders preferred to use the content-based tags. But soon layouters discovered the WWW, and to use the Web via a graphical interface, the designers needed more control. The company Netscape was only too happy to give them it. Over time, with its Navigator browser, Netscape introduced tables, frames and other extensions which made it much easier to create accurate layouts. The Web became a graphical medium – much to the regret of those who had no graphical user interface and had to view the world through a $80 \times 25$ character screen.

Yet it was not only the layouters who had their desires. The HTML designers also wished they had a bit more functionality in some places. For this reason, the programmers working for Netscape developed *LiveScript*, which was later renamed *JavaScript* for marketing reasons. Microsoft in its turn built interpreters for its own in-house script languages *VBScript* and *JScript* into its browser.

The uncontrolled explosion of proprietary HTML extensions continued to grow. At the same time the guardian of the HTML standard, the *World Wide Web Consortium (W3C)*, worked hard on making the language more flexible while promoting the separation of logical and physical tags. The result is *Cascading Style Sheets (CSS)*. With their help, HTML programmers can tag their code logically and still instruct the browser to format individual elements on a page in a very specific way. Unfortunately, there is a great variation in the extent to which the different browsers support CSS. The same applies for the *Document Object Model (DOM)* which is supposed to help influence the appearance of a page, using script languages. Equally, browser support for the extensible markup language *XML (Extensible Markup Language)* combined with *XSL (Extensible Stylesheet Language)* is as yet anything but widespread.

According to the *Web Standards Project (WASP,* http://www.webstandards.org), an organization that fights for compliance with standards, incompatibilities among different browsers and variations from the W3C standard cause around 25% extra costs for the development of a Web site.

Developers for the WWW now come across various versions of three script languages, the fourth HTML version and wide differences in support for CSS, DOM,

XML and XSL. This should be reason enough to get more involved with programming on the server side. That is exactly what we want to do in this book.

## 1.2  Hypertext Transfer Protocol

Just like HTML, the Hypertext Transfer Protocol (HTTP) was developed by Tim Berners-Lee and his colleagues at CERN in 1989. Its main purpose is to transfer data, and therefore it is not just restricted to texts, as you might assume from its name. HTTP is a protocol at application level, it is status-free, to a certain extent object-oriented and works on the basis of a simple request/response scheme.

Most simple HTTP servers only know the commands GET, HEAD and POST. They use GET and the entry of a *Uniform Resource Identifier (URI)* to request the resources of a server. Using POST they can send data to a URI, and HEAD simply supplies the header of a resource, which is accessed via a URI. This reveals an essential structural feature of HTTP responses: they always consist of a header, which is mostly followed by a body.

In a header of this kind, the type of data transferred by HTTP is one of the things that is encoded. For this purpose, MIME (Multipurpose Internet Mail Extension) identifiers are used. They are defined in RFC (Request For Comment) 2045 (`http://www.cis.ohio-state.edu/htbin/rfc/rfc2045.html`). For example, HTML has the key 'text/html'. GIFs (Graphics Interchange Format) are identified by 'image/gif'. Other important information located in the header includes cookies (Section 3.8.4) and the date that an object was last changed.

Currently, most browsers and servers only handle Version 1.0 of the protocol (Berners-Lee *et al.* 1996). Some servers, including the freeware server *Apache* and the *Java Web Server* by JavaSoft, can already manage the next version, HTTP 1.1 (Fielding *et al.* 1999). One of the main advantages of the new version is the ability to send one request over a Transmission Control Protocol (TCP) connection and to receive the appropriate responses over the same connection. In contrast, in HTTP 1.0 a new connection is created for each object that is to be loaded. This leads to inefficient use of resources, particularly for Web sites with a lot of pictures or frames.

To avoid problems with upgrading, HTTP is backwards-compatible. You will find a detailed discussion of the differences between HTTP 1.0 and HTTP 1.1 in (Krishnamurthy *et al.* 1998).

## 1.3  Common Gateway Interface

HTTP mainly specifies the transportation of objects. However, a mechanism by which the transported data reach an application is not defined in HTTP. For this reason, the *Common Gateway Interface (CGI)* developed by the NCSA (National Center for Supercomputing Applications) was the only way through the HTTP server to a program, for a long time.

Web servers that use the CGI usually have a directory called CGI-BIN (BIN = binary, i.e. executable). Therefore you can find scripts or little C programs in this directory. Now, when a client sends a request to the URI of one of these programs, the reaction of the Web server is to spawn a new process and make available to this process all the data in the request as well as some environment variables. The outputs of the program that is started are sent back to the client as a response, provided they have been written to the standard output (stdout).

The nice thing about this, as a starting point, is that the application process is cleanly separated from the server process. There really are two different, independent programs. This means that CGI programs can be written in any language and do not crash the server. In addition, there is no proprietary API (application programming interface), which might change from one server version to the next. The developers are even largely independent of the server itself, provided this contains a CGI.

However, there is a big disadvantage to set against these advantages: CGI requires a great deal of resources. For each request, a new process has to be created, initialized when it is started and then removed after use. Let us suppose that this application is resource-hungry, and needs five seconds to run on a system that is currently experiencing low load levels. What happens if a thousand requests pour in to this computer in a minute should be fairly clear.

Naturally, this problem has been known for some time. For this reason, *FastCGI* was developed. The main advantage of it is that, for each application, a process is only started once. This process lives for as long as the Web server is running. Another advantage is the way in which the application is informed of the request variables. CGI sends the required data as environment variables, over pipes, whereas FastCGI uses a single full duplex connection. This not only has advantages in terms of speed, but also makes it possible for the FastCGI application to run on a different computer from the Web server. If this is required, a TCP connection is used. Otherwise a full duplex pipe is used. Essentially, FastCGI applications are nothing other than servers.

## 1.4 Java

The Java language became known in 1996 through small programs, so-called *Applets*, that can be integrated in Web pages. They were the start of Java's triumphal march: there is no computer magazine or developers' conference that has not discussed Java at some time or other. The media are dominated by the hype, but so far there are only a few products for the mass market. No doubt, this is largely due to the fact that the first *AWT (Abstract Windows Toolkit)*, the classes library for programming applications with graphic user interfaces (GUI), has turned out to be rather rudimentary. In the meantime Sun has added the Java Foundation Classes, whose Swing components considerably improve the API.

The slow speed of the first interpreter was certainly a hindrance. Now, however, good JIT (Just in Time) compilers are available, and processor performance continues to improve, so slow speed is no longer a convincing argument to prevent the use of Java. In Java 2 the automatic memory management system (Garbage Collection) has been completely re-worked and, with Sun's hotspot technology, promises additional improvements in speed.

Although there has been little activity so far in the area of Java applications with GUI, there are now a lot of applications that make use of the in-built network and multithreading capability. Java is intended for client/server applications and most especially for middleware technologies such as CORBA (Common Object Request Broker Architecture). The most important concepts for this purpose are sockets and threads.

## 1.4.1 Sockets

In order to be able to communicate over an IP (Internet Protocol) network, you need a description of the communication's end point. In Java this is called a socket. Basically there are two socket types: a TCP socket and a UDP (User Datagram Protocol) socket. The main difference between the two protocols is their reliability.

TCP guarantees that the data packets actually arrive, and even do so in the right sequence. UDP on the other hand does not ensure that all transmitted data packets (or datagrams) arrive, or that they arrive in the right sequence. For this reason, UDP is typically used for real-time applications such as the Internet radio. In these cases it is not so important that every individual data packet arrives; it is more important that most of the packets arrive on time. As the administrative effort that is required for TCP is not needed for UDP, you gain a bit of speed, but this process is less suitable for transmitting files, as then every bit matters[1]. Here we use the more reliable TCP.

In Java, TCP sockets are created using the `java.net.Socket` class and UDP sockets are created using the `java.net.DatagramSocket` class.

The special thing about Java sockets is that they are easy to use. For example, all you need to create a connection to the Yahoo Web server is this single line of code:

```
Socket mySocket = new Socket ("www.yahoo.com", 80);
```

The only parameters we need for the constructor are the Internet address of the remote computer and the port on which the Web server waits for a connection. By convention this is port 80, for a WWW server. Using different constructors you can define the Internet address either as a character string (`java.lang.String`) or as a `java.net.InetAddress` type object. In each case, the port is an `int` value.

So that an instance of the `java.net.Socket` class can be used to communicate, it has the `getOutputStream()` and `getInputStream()` methods. Once a connection has been created, a program can use `read()` and `write(int b)` to read data from the associated streams and write to them, just as it would do with a file.

The example program below, `SimpleWebClient` (Listing 1.2) accepts the address of a WWW page as a start parameter, reads the page and writes it to the standard output. This is very easy to achieve: after the usual parameter parsing, the program instantiates a socket. With the associated output stream it executes the appropriate HTTP command, loads the response via the input stream and outputs it to the screen.

1. Of course, it is also possible, if you implement error correction, re-transmission etc. But why reinvent something if there is already a very good solution called TCP? If you still want to find out how it is done, see Stevens (1990), 465ff.

Listing 1.2: The `SimpleWebClient` class

```
package de.webapp.Examples.HttpClient;

import java.net.Socket;
import java.io.OutputStream;
import java.io.InputStream;
import java.io.IOException;

public class SimpleWebClient {
public static void main[String args()] {
  String host;
  String file;

  if (args.length != 1) {
    System.out.println("Usage : java SimpleWebClient <URL without protocol
name>");
    System.out.println("Example: java SimpleWebClient
www.yahoo.com/index.html");
    System.exit(0);
  }
  int delimiterIndex = args[0].indexOf('/');
  if (delimiterIndex == -1) {
    // if there is no '/' in the argument,
    // assume only the host name is involved
    // and request '/' as a file
    host = args[0];
    file = new String("/");
  }
  else {
    // Split host and file name.
    host = args[0].substring(0, delimiterIndex);
    file = args[0].substring(delimiterIndex);
  }
  try {
    // Create connection to port 80 on the host.
    Socket socket = new Socket(host, 80);
    // Obtain socket's output stream.
    OutputStream out = socket.getOutputStream();
    // Assemble command.
    String command = new String("GET " + file + " HTTP/1.0\r\n\r\n");
    // Write HTTP GET command.
    out.write(command.getBytes());
    // Ensure that the command is really sent
    // and does not get left in a
    // temporary buffer.
    out.flush();
    // Obtain socket's input stream.
```

```
        InputStream in = socket.getInputStream();
        int aByte;
        // Read from the input stream until its end is
        // reached. During the read, write every character
        // to the standard output.
        while ((aByte = in.read()) != -1) {
          System.out.write(aByte);
        }
        // Release resources.
        out.close();
        in.close();
        socket.close();
      }
      // If errors have occurred, write them
      // to the standard output.
      catch (IOException ioe) {
        System.out.println(ioe.toString());
      }
    }
  }
} // End of the class
```

Incidentally, the Telnet program works in a very similar way. The only difference is that, in Telnet, all inputs and outputs are routed to the standard input and output and it is capable of interpreting terminal commands.

As shown above, SimpleWebClient is ideal for initiating a connection. However, to do so you need a communication partner. In the example this is any Web server which simply waits for a client to try and create a connection to it. If this succeeds, it accepts commands, executes them and sends the result back.

To program this functionality in Java you need a java.net.ServerSocket. When you instantiate it, you assign a port to it and call its accept() method. This causes the ServerSocket instance to wait for a connection request. When a connection is created, the accept() method returns a Socket object. Like all Socket objects, this also has the characteristics described above. A Web server that is programmed in Java should also obtain an input stream from the Socket object it has just reached, and attempt to read an HTTP command and execute it. Then, it would have to write the result in the Socket object's output stream.

Of course, that is not everything that a Web server does. Another important feature of a Web server is its ability to process several requests almost simultaneously. You will find more about this in the next section.

## 1.4.2  Threads

When network applications are being programmed it is often the case that you would like to carry out two or more tasks at once, such as loading a picture from a server (see java.awt.Images) – which can take quite a long time – and accepting user entries. If you want to implement both these things, you can take one of four approaches. You can:

**1** Write loop constructs, in which both tasks are carried out, but which are difficult to understand;

**2** Integrate an equally unclear and cryptic interrupt control function in your program;

**3** Spawn an extra process for loading the picture;

**4** Spawn a thread for loading the picture.

Options one and two are likely to be the fastest, provided they are well implemented. However, they are generally difficult to understand and therefore hard to upgrade and extend. If the execution time is unimportant, which should be the case when loading a picture from the Net, it makes more sense to use the multitasking capability of the operating system. This is just the case when you spawn a process. Basically, the programmer then starts a small program that carries out the required task and reports back when it has finished. Unless you use tricks like split memory blocks, it can be a bit difficult to deliver the picture to the calling process. Furthermore, a process change creates a considerable load for the operating system, as the entire processor status of the process that is to be left has to be saved, and the processor status of the process that is to be started has to be loaded. If too many processes are running on a computer, it soon starts spending more effort on managing processes than on executing them.

Threads solve all these problems. Using them you can place program parts, whose job is to carry out tasks independently of each other, in different code blocks (threads). All these program parts can be executed almost simultaneously, communicate with each other using cleverly thought-out mechanisms and use split memory blocks (or objects or variables). As all threads run within a process, no time-intensive process change is necessary. Threads offer the programmer a way of achieving multitasking within a program, just as processes do within an operating system, but without the baggage that is redundant for this application. Threads are also called lightweight processes, for this reason.

Just like sockets, threads are not a discovery of the Java programming language – but can be used simply, effectively and therefore productively in Java. In Java a new thread is made by generating an instance of the `java.lang.Thread` class. You can create special functionality simply by inheriting from this base class:

```
class MyApplication extends java.lang.Thread {
 ...
}
```

The tasks that a thread is to carry out must be encoded in the `public void run()` method:

```
class MyApplication extends java.lang.Thread {
   ...
 public void run() {
   ...
   }
 }
```

To start a thread you simply call the `public void start()` method:

```
MyApplication myApp = new MyApplication();
myApp.start();
```

Within `start()` the thread's `run()` method is called automatically. A thread is then ended when the `run()` method has been completely executed. If the `run()` method contains an endless loop, the thread only terminates when the *Virtual Machine (VM)* is stopped.

You can also use `stop()` to stop a thread. However, this method is so brutal that, in Java 2, Sun recommend that you do not use it (i.e. it is 'deprecated'). The reason is that objects in the `run()` method suddenly give up using all monitors that they are currently holding. As a result, objects that were in a transaction that was protected by synchronize now lose this protection and appear in an inconsistent state for other objects.

## Thread status

Threads can have one of four statuses (Fig. 1.1):

- new;
- runnable;
- blocked;
- dead.

A new thread is a thread that has not yet been started, and a dead thread is a thread whose `run()` method has terminated. The other two statuses are not so easy to explain.

A thread is described as runnable if it has been started. Runnable does not mean, though, that the thread has actually been run. It is the job of the operating system and the virtual machine to actually run a thread. Even when it has been run, it still has the status 'runnable'. A thread keeps this status until it either dies or is blocked. A block can be due to one of these three causes[2]:

- The `wait()` method has been called.
- The `sleep()` method has been called.
- The thread calls a method that blocks the input or output.

The main difference between `wait()` and `sleep()` is that, when `wait()` is used, the thread stops using all monitors, but when `sleep()` is called, the sleeping thread keeps all monitors. When the two methods are cancelled or interrupted, the thread becomes runnable once more. The same applies when a blocking input or output method is called.

---

2  In Java 2 the `suspend()` and `resume()` methods are deprecated because they can cause a dead-lock. For this reason we will not go into them in more detail here.

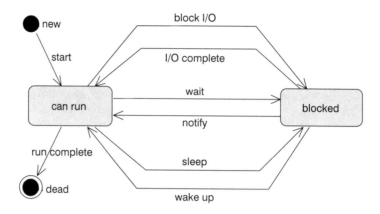

**Figure 1.1**  Status change diagram for the `java.lang.Thread` class

### Runnable interface

Occasionally you would like to execute classes like a thread but can no longer derive them from `Thread` because they already inherit from another class. In this case you should implement the `java.lang.Runnable` interface. To do so, you simply need to add a `run()` method to the class.

```
class MyRunnableApplication extends AnyClass
implements java.lang.Runnable {
   ...
 public void run() {
   ...
   }
}
```

To execute an instance of this class like a thread, it needs to be passed to a thread in the constructor. Then, this thread is started, just like any other. The only difference is that instead of calling its own `run()` method it calls the `run()` method of the Runnable object.

```
class MyRunnableApplication extends AnyClass
implements java.lang.Runnable {
   public static void main (String args[]) {
      MyRunnableApplication myApp = new MyRunnableApplication();
      Thread myThread = new Thread(myApp);
      MyThread.start();
   }
   ...
   public void run() {
   ...
   }
}
```

That completes our explanation of the fundamentals of using Java threads. In this book, we do not want to go into the special problems of developing Java programs that run in parallel. Instead we will just take a look at a few special cases at the appropriate points. If you want to find out more about this subject, which is without doubt very interesting, we recommend you read the book by Doug Lea (1997).

# HTTP Server 2

n this section we want to program a simple HTTP server. This will not involve a complete or elegant HTTP implementation. Our main aim is to build up our basic understanding of a server's structure, and of HTTP.

## 2.1 The minimalist implementation

Our first server will only understand one HTTP command, the GET command. Also, it will only be able to execute it once. Admittedly, that is not very high-level performance for a server, but it is ideal as a first example.

Once it is started, our server listens on the predefined port, 8080, until a client creates a connection to that port. Of course, HTTP servers normally listen on port 80. However, this port is reserved for the system administrator on Unix systems. We chose port 8080 so that you could also use and understand this example on a Unix computer, without any problems.

You can test the server with a normal Web browser such as Netscape Navigator, Microsoft Internet Explorer, Opera or Lynx. To do so, enter the URL http://<host-name>:8080/. So that the server can also return something, you should make sure that there is a file called index.html in your working directory, as the server interprets requests relative to the current directory.

If your browser has created a connection with the server, the accept() method returns a socket. From this socket we get an input stream, which we access via a Reader. We transfer the socket's output stream using a BufferedOutputStream, as streams that are buffered in Java transfer data much more efficiently. Then we read the first line from the input stream. The first line should contain the request. So we can check what happens, we output the line.

To let us execute the request, we use a java.util.StringTokenizer to split it into three parts: the command, the URI and the protocol that we are using. If these are not three tokens, or the first token is not a GET command, we output an error message and cancel. If everything is all right, we access the name of the requested file from token number two and add it to our server's document root directory path (docRoot). As the requested file name always begins with a forward slash, in accordance with RFC 2616 (http://www.rfc-editor.org/rfc/rfc2616.txt), this can be done without problems. If there is nothing left, or only a directory name, we use the file name 'index.html' as the default. Then, the sendDocument() method copies the requested file into the socket's output stream.

Listing 2.1: Class OneShotHttpd

```java
package de.webapp.Examples.HttpServer;

import java.io.*;
import java.net.*;
import java.util.*;

public class OneShotHttpd {

public final static int HTTP_PORT = 8080;

public static void main(String argv[]) {
  try {
    ServerSocket listen = new ServerSocket(HTTP_PORT);
    Socket client = listen.accept();
    BufferedReader is = new BufferedReader(
      new InputStreamReader(client.getInputStream()));
    DataOutputStream os = new DataOutputStream(client.getOutputStream());
    String request = is.readLine();
    System.out.println("Request: " + request);
    StringTokenizer st = new StringTokenizer(request);
    if ((st.countTokens()==3) && st.nextToken().equals("GET")) {
      request = st.nextToken().substring(1);
      if (request.endsWith("/") || request.equals(""))
        request += "index.html";
      sendDocument(os, request);
    }
    else
      System.err.println ("400 Bad Request");
    is.close();
    os.close();
    client.close();
  }
  catch (IOException ioe) {
    System.err.println("Error: " + ioe.toString());
  }
}

public static void sendDocument(DataOutputStream out, String file)
    throws IOException {
  try {
        BufferedInputStream in = new BufferedInputStream (new
FileInputStream(file));
```

```
      byte[] buf = new byte[1024];
      int len;
      while ((len = in.read(buf, 0, 1024)) != -1) {
        out.write(buf, 0, len);
      }
      in.close();
    }
    catch (FileNotFoundException fnfe) {
      System.err.println ("404 Not Found");
    }
  }
}
} // End of class
```

If you repeat the request to OneShotHttpd (Listing 2.1) via the browser, you get an error message, because the server has not been found. To improve this situation we want to extend the program so that it can serve several requests. Only minimal changes are needed to extend the program in this way.

## 2.2 Serving requests simultaneously

Unlike OneShotHttpd, SimpleHttpd (Listing 2.2) inherits from java.lang.Thread instead of from java.lang.Object. In the static main() method, OneShotHttpd always listens on port 8080, but as soon as a connection is made, SimpleHttpd is instantiated with the socket that has been found as an argument. Owing to an endless loop, this process is repeated each time there is a new request. It is purely and simply used to accept the connection. The actual work is done by the generated instances of the class SimpleHttpd, to which the socket is transferred (Fig. 2.1). Therefore, the static main method acts as an acceptor and every instance of the class SimpleHttpd acts as a handler.

First, the current socket is assigned to the instance variable s in the constructor. Then the start() command is used to start the SimpleHttpd thread. In the run() method we find a large part of the same code again, which had previously been used in the main() method. The sendDocument() method is totally unchanged. This is how SimpleHttpd is created from OneShotHttpd:

Listing 2.2: Class SimpleHttpd

```
package de.webapp.Examples.HttpServer;

import java.io.*;
import java.net.*;
import java.util.*;

public class SimpleHttpd extends Thread {

protected Socket s = null;
public final static int HTTP_PORT = 8080;
```

```java
public static void main(String argv[]) {
  try {
    ServerSocket listen = new ServerSocket(HTTP_PORT);
    while (true) {
      SimpleHttpd aRequest = new SimpleHttpd(listen.accept());
    }
  }
  catch (IOException e) {
    System.err.println("Error: " + e.toString());
  }
}
public SimpleHttpd(Socket s) {
  this.s = s;
  start();
}

public void run() {
  try {
    BufferedReader is = new BufferedReader(
      new InputStreamReader(s.getInputStream()));
    DataOutputStream os = new DataOutputStream(s.getOutputStream());
    String request = is.readLine();
    System.out.println("Request: " + request);
    StringTokenizer st = new StringTokenizer(request);
    if ((st.countTokens()==3) && st.nextToken().equals("GET")) {
      request = st.nextToken().substring(1);
      if (request.endsWith("/") || request.equals(""))
        request += "index.html";
      sendDocument(os, request);
    }
    else
      os.write ("400 Bad Request\r\n".getBytes());
    is.close();
    os.close();
    s.close();
  }
  catch (IOException ioe) {
    System.err.println("Error: " + ioe.toString());
  }
}
protected void sendDocument(DataOutputStream out, String request)
    throws IOException {
  ...
}
} // End of class
```

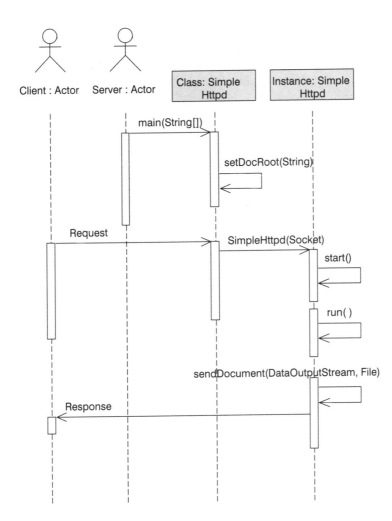

**Figure 2.1** `SimpleHttpd` flow diagram

## 2.3 A bit more security, please

`SimpleHttpd` provides us with a very simple multithreaded Web server which can understand the GET command. It can respond to as many requests as you like, simultaneously and successively. Unfortunately it responds to almost every request, even those it would be better not to respond to. Instead, a request with the following format should lead to the production of an error message:

```
http://<hostname>:8080/../../../../../etc/passwd
```

Otherwise, you could use any Web browser to get to any file on the computer. To prevent this, we must ensure that no file is supplied that is located below the document root directory. This can be done by resolving all relative references in the path of the requested file (/path/../file.dat corresponds to /file.dat) and determining the absolute path of the document root directory as well as of the requested file. These canonical paths are unique for each file system. Thus, if the path of the requested file does not begin with the path of the document root directory, this is an unauthorized request. Therefore we need to make two small changes to our server.

As the canonical path of the document root directory always stays the same, we only determine it once and store it in a class variable. Usefully, the class java.io.File has the method getCanonicalPath(), which determines just the path that we need.

```
...
protected static String canonicalDocRoot;
...
public static void main(String argv[]) {
    ...
    docRoot = new File(".");
    canonicalDocRoot = docRoot.getCanonicalPath();
    ServerSocket listen = new ServerSocket(HTTP_PORT);
    ...
}
```

Now, every time there is a request, there must be a comparison to check whether the requested file path begins with the canonical path of the document root directory. This is done in the run() method.

```
public void run() {
    ...
    if (filename.endsWith("/") || filename.equals(""))
        filename += "index.html";
    File file = new File(filename);
    if (file.getCanonicalPath().startsWith(canonicalDocRoot))
        sendDocument(os, file);
    else
        System.err.println("403 Forbidden");
    ...
}
```

Now, if a request is made for a file that is below the document root directory, the server writes an error message to the standard error output (stderr).

## 2.4  Status codes

Our server is now working quite well, but unfortunately it is far from conforming to the HTTP standard. The protocol defines that the first line of every response should contain the HTTP version, a status code and a short message (reason phrase). These three parts must be separated by blanks. In addition, a carriage return and line feed (CRLF) should be appended. For example:

```
HTTP/1.0 200 OK\r\n
```

To keep things simple we write the protocol version to a class variable, and we also create a few constants for the status codes. Furthermore, it makes sense to store the current status code in an instance variable (`statusCode`) which can be accessed via suitable `get` and `set` methods. In this way we can initialize `statusCode` with the constant `SC_OK`, "200 OK" and simply overwrite it with `setStatusCode(String)` if a change is made to the code.

The method `sendStatusLine(DataOutputStream)` sends the protocol name, the current status code and then appends the constant CRLF (`"\r\n"`).

```java
public final static String CRLF = "\r\n";
public final static String PROTOCOL = "HTTP/1.0 ";
public final static String SC_OK = "200 OK";
public final static String SC_BAD_REQUEST = "400 Bad Request";
public final static String SC_FORBIDDEN = "403 Forbidden";
public final static String SC_NOT_FOUND = "404 Not Found";
protected String statusCode = SC_OK;

protected void setStatusCode(String statusCode) {
   this.statusCode = statusCode;
}

protected String getStatusCode() {
   return statusCode;
}

protected void sendStatusLine(DataOutputStream out)
     throws IOException {
   out.writeBytes(PROTOCOL + getStatusCode() + CRLF);
}
```

Finally we just have to add a suitable call to the method `sendDocument`:

```java
protected void sendDocument(DataOutputStream os, File file)
     throws IOException {
   try {
      BufferedInputStream in = new BufferedInputStream (new
        FileInputStream(file));
      sendStatusLine(os);
      setHeader("Content_Length", (new Long (file.length())).to String());
      setHeader("Content_Type", guessType (file.getPath));
      ...
      sendHeader(os);
      os.writeBytes(CRLF);
      ...
   }
}
```

We have deliberately added the call to sendStatusLine after the file is opened so that, if there is an error, a different status code can be sent instead of SC_OK. We then write CRLF to the OutputStream because, according to the HTTP specification, there must be an extra CRLF between the header and body (remainder) of the response.

Using the status codes that are now present, it is easy to improve the error-handling. Finally the client also wants to be informed of errors. For this purpose we write the method sendError.

```
protected void sendError(String statusCode, DataOutputStream out)
    throws IOException {
  setStatusCode(statusCode);
  sendStatusLine(out);
  out.writeBytes(
      CRLF
    + "<html>"
    + "<head><title>" + getStatusCode() + "</title></head>"
    + "<body><h1>" + getStatusCode() + "</h1></body>"
    + "</html>"
  );
  System.err.println(getStatusCode());
}
```

Now, we must also replace the calls to System.err.println with corresponding calls to sendError.

## 2.5  Header data

Besides the status line, the response's header can and should contain additional information that should be sent back to the client. Firstly, this includes the general data such as the name of the server and the current time. Secondly it is data about the requested object such as its size, or date and time of last change. However, in every case key value pairs are involved. For this reason, the obvious choice for a data structure is a hash table. Besides the data structure we also need methods that can be used to access it, as well as a method for outputting all header data in the right format. In our server, these tasks are carried out by the getHeader(), setHeader() and sendHeader() methods.

```
protected Hashtable myHeaders = new Hashtable();
protected void setHeader(String key, String value) {
  myHeaders.put(key, value);
}
protected String getHeader(String key) {
  return (String)myHeaders.get(key);
}

protected void sendHeader(DataOutputStream out)
    throws IOException {
```

```
      String line;
      String key;
      Enumeration e = myHeaders.keys();
      while (e.hasMoreElements()) {
          key = (String)e.nextElement();
          out.writeBytes(key + ": " + myHeaders.get(key) + CRLF);
      }
  }
```

The header data need to be sent to the client before the requested object is sent. For this reason, the call to sendHeader() comes before the file is written.

```
protected void sendDocument(DataOutputStream os, File file)
      throws IOException {
    try {
      BufferedInputStream in = new BufferedInputStream (new
      FileInputStream(file));
      sendStatusLine(os);
      setHeader("Content-Length", (new Long(file.length())).toString());
      setHeader("Content-Type", guessType(file.getPath));

      ...
      sendHeader(os);
      os.writeBytes(CRLF);
      ...
}

protected static Properties typeMap = new Properties();

public String guessType(String filename) {
    String type = null;
    int i = filename.lastIndexOf(".");
    if (i > 0)
      type = typeMap.getProperty(filename.substring(i));
    if (type == null)
      type = "unknown/unknown";
    return type;
}
```

One of the most important header values is the Content type, as it helps the browser decide how to display an object. HTML objects are displayed differently from PDF files. For this reason, the MIME type of the requested data is coded in the Content type. Usually this can be derived from the file extension. This is just what we do with the method guessType(String), in which the file extension suffix is used as a key for a java.util.Properties object. First, this Properties object needs to be loaded. This happens in the main method. It must contain key value pairs with the following formats:

```
.html=text/html
.htm=text/html
```

```
.txt=text/plain
.gif=image/gif
.jpeg=image/jpeg
.jpg=image/jpeg
...
```

We are sure that developing this simple server has made the basics of the Hypertext Transfer Protocol clear. The server fulfils a couple more functions than are defined in HTTP 0.9, but is still far from complying with the full implementation of HTTP 1.0. In fact it can only deliver files, and ignores all other HTTP commands. In the next chapter we will find out how you can use servlets to extend the functionality of a server far beyond the mere delivering of files.

Below is the entire listing, to give you a complete overview of the server:

Listing 2.3: Class SimpleHttpd2

```java
package de.webapp.Examples.HttpServer;

import java.io.*;
import java.net.*;
import java.util.*;

public class SimpleHttpd2 extends Thread {
protected Socket s = null;
protected static File docRoot;
protected static String canonicalDocRoot;

public final static int HTTP_PORT = 8080;
public final static String CRLF = "\r\n";
public final static String PROTOCOL = "HTTP/1.0";

public final static String SC_OK = "200 OK";
public final static String SC_BAD_REQUEST = "400 Bad Request";
public final static String SC_FORBIDDEN = "403 Forbidden";
public final static String SC_NOT_FOUND = "404 Not Found";

protected static Properties typeMap = new Properties();
protected String statusCode = SC_OK;
protected Hashtable myHeaders = new Hashtable();

public static void main(String argv[]) {
  try {
    typeMap.load(new FileInputStream("mime.types"));
    docRoot = new File(".");
    canonicalDocRoot = docRoot.getCanonicalPath();
    ServerSocket listen = new ServerSocket(HTTP_PORT);
    while (true) {
      SimpleHttpd2 aRequest = new SimpleHttpd2(listen.accept());
    }
  }
```

```java
      catch (IOException e) {
        System.err.println("Error: " + e.toString());
      }
  }

  public SimpleHttpd2(Socket s) {
     this.s = s;
     start();
  }

  public void run() {
     try {
        setHeader("Server", "SimpleHttpd2");
        BufferedReader is = new BufferedReader(
           new InputStreamReader(s.getInputStream()));
        DataOutputStream os = new DataOutputStream(s.getOutputStream());
        String request = is.readLine();
        System.out.println("Request: " + request);
        StringTokenizer st = new StringTokenizer(request);
        if ((st.countTokens()==3) && st.nextToken().equals("GET")) {
           String filename = docRoot.getPath() + st.nextToken();
           if (filename.endsWith("/") || filename.equals(""))
              filename += "index.html";
           File file = new File(filename);
           if (file.getCanonicalPath().startsWith(canonicalDocRoot))
              sendDocument(os, file);
           else
              sendError(SC_FORBIDDEN, os);
        }
        else {
           sendError(SC_BAD_REQUEST, os);
        }
        is.close();
        os.close();
        s.close();
     }
     catch (IOException ioe) {
        System.err.println("Error: " + ioe.toString());
     }
  }

  protected void sendDocument(DataOutputStream os, File file)
       throws IOException {
     try {
        BufferedInputStream in = new BufferedInputStream (new
        FileInputStream(file));
        sendStatusLine(os);
```

```java
      setHeader("Content-Length", (new Long(file.length())).toString());
      setHeader("Content-Type", guessType(file.getPath()));
      sendHeader(os);
      os.writeBytes(CRLF);
      byte[] buf = new byte[1024];
      int len;
      while ((len = in.read(buf, 0, 1024)) != -1) {
        os.write(buf, 0, len);
      }
      in.close();
    }
    catch (FileNotFoundException fnfe) {
      sendError(SC_NOT_FOUND, os);
    }
  }

  protected void setStatusCode(String statusCode) {
    this.statusCode = statusCode;
  }

  protected String getStatusCode() {
    return statusCode;
  }

  protected void sendStatusLine(DataOutputStream out)
      throws IOException {
    out.writeBytes(PROTOCOL + getStatusCode() + CRLF);
  }

  protected void setHeader(String key, String value) {
    myHeaders.put(key, value);
  }

  protected void sendHeader(DataOutputStream out)
      throws IOException {
    String line;
    String key;
    Enumeration e = myHeaders.keys();
    while (e.hasMoreElements()) {
      key = (String)e.nextElement();
      out.writeBytes(key + ": " + myHeaders.get(key) + CRLF);
    }
  }

  protected void sendError(String statusCode, DataOutputStream out)
      throws IOException {
    setStatusCode(statusCode);
    sendStatusLine(out);
    out.writeBytes(
```

```
      CRLF
      +"<html>"
      +"<head><title>" + getStatusCode() + "</title></head>"
      +"<body><h1>" + getStatusCode() + "</h1></body>"
      +"</html>"
    );
    System.err.println(getStatusCode());
}

public String guessType(String filename) {
    String type = null;
    int i = filename.lastIndexOf(".");
    if (i > 0)
      type = typeMap.getProperty(filename.substring(i));
    if (type == null)
      type = "unknown/unknown";
    return type;
}

} // End of class
```

# Servlets 3

The services provided by conventional Web servers are mainly restricted to the delivery of files. For this reason, if more complex services are required, a powerful interface is needed between the actual application and the HTTP server. Three basic types are used:

- Common Gateway Interface (CGI): This interface, developed by the NCSA, works on the basis of a simple method. A client requests an object from the Web server. This starts a program as an external process and sends its output back to the client (Section 1.3).

- Proprietary server APIs: Netscape and Microsoft supply the *NSAPI (Netscape Server Application Programming Interface)* and *ISAPI (Internet Server Application Programming Interface)* to provide their Web servers with their own API. Using this programming interface you can integrate programs directly with the server. They are initialized when the server is started up. As they usually run in the same process as the server, there is no need to waste resources changing processes when the program is run. Compared with CGI this results in considerable improvements in speed. Unfortunately this method also has a major disadvantage: it needs only one integrated program to go down to make the whole server crash. Microsoft has recognized this problem and now supplies the *Internet Information Server (IIS)* version 4.0, with which you can run Web-based applications in separate processes.

- Servlet API: Sun developed this application programming interface to provide Java programs on the server with a simple and flexible basis on which to run. Like CGI, the programmer can use the API to access environment variables and write the response to the request in a stream. In addition to that, the API provides cookie support and session management. It is left open whether the application on the server runs in the same process as the server or a different process. If you want to split the processes, you can always do this easily with CORBA, RMI (Remote Method Invocation) or by integrating Enterprise Java Beans (EJB).

In this chapter we will dedicate ourselves to servlet programming. The necessary classes are provided in the `javax.servlet` and `javax.servlet.http` packages, in the *Java Servlet Development Kit (JSDK)* which you can download from Sun's Web server (`http://java.sun.com/products/servlet/index.html`). There you will also find the *Java Server Web Development Kit (JSWDK)*, Version 1.0 of which was available when this book went to print. Unlike the JSDK, the JSWDK also includes a Java Server Pages implementation (JSP) and is therefore a complete development platform.

When this book went to print the final version, 2.2, was not available, so all the details here about the servlet API 2.2 refer to the public release of 19 August 1999. We hope that there are no major changes in the final version.

## 3.1 Introduction

First we want to describe the communication process between a user and a Web application (Fig. 3.1). When users surf the Web, they click on links with the mouse. This prompts the browser to send a request to a server. The *Uniform Resource Locator (URL)*, which is the address of the requested object, is contained in the HTML code used in the request:

```
<a href="http://www.MySite.de/aFile.html">link</a>
```

If a user clicks on a link of this kind, the browser sends an HTTP GET command to the server, so that the server loads the requested object in the browser and displays it. This explains what happens, from the client's point of view.

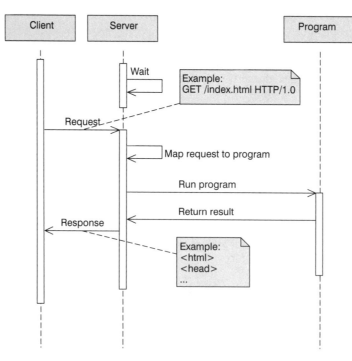

**Figure 3.1** Interaction between client and server

For the server the process looks like this: a client creates a connection with the port on which the server is waiting for HTTP commands. The server reads the command, tries to execute it and sends back the result or, if there is an error, it sends back a suitable error message. All messages are defined in the HTTP specification RFC 2616 (`http://www.rfc-editor.org/rfc/rfc2616.txt`).

We are only interested in how commands are executed (run). If the object requested with the `GET` command is a file, the server must simply read it, assign an appropriate header to it, and then send it to the browser. However, if the URL is actually a program, the server must execute this program and send its outputs to the client. If the server includes a servlet engine, this provides you with a way of integrating your own Java code at exactly this point.

## 3.2 Servlet engines

Now there is a suitable servlet engine for nearly every server. To work with, and understand, the majority of the examples in this book, all you need is the engine *jo!* which you can find in the WebApp framework at `http://www.webapp.de/`. If you now want to integrate a servlet engine in the Web server you already have running, we recommend you use the engines *JServ* from the Apache Group (`http://www.apache.org`, `http://java.apache.org/`) or *JRun* from Live Software (`http://www.livesoftware.com/`). Both are available in the Net and are constantly upgraded. JServ works only with the Apache Web server, but JRun is available for a whole series of servers. These include the Apache Web server (NT and Unix), Microsoft Personal Web Server 4.x, Microsoft Internet Information Server 3.x/4.x, Netscape FastTrack and Enterprise server 3.x (NT and Unix) and also the StarNine WebSTAR 3.x (Mac).

Besides JServ and JRun there is a whole range of other commercial and freeware engines, and also servers that include an engine, whose exact characteristics we do not want to give in detail here. Below is a short list of the most important ones:

- *Java Web server* from JavaSoft (`http://jserv.java.sun.com/products/webserver/`)
- *Jigsaw* by the World Wide Web Consortium (`http://www.w3.org/Jigsaw/`)
- *Websphere* (formerly servlet*Express*) from IBM (`http://www.software.ibm.com/webservers/`)
- *WebExpress* from WebLogic (`http://weblogic.beasys.com/`)
- *ServletExec* from New Atlanta (`http://www.newatlanta.com/`)
- *Jetty* from Mortbay (`http://www.mortbay.com/software/Jetty.html`)

You will find a list on the Sun Web site, if you use this URL: `http://java.sun.com/products/servlet/runners.html`. This list is constantly kept up to date.

## 3.3 'Hello World'

The usage described below is a well-worn cliché, and the servlet technology is not really a new programming language, but only an API, but even so, we do not want to miss out on using *the* classic to begin with: our first servlet is supposed to display 'Hello World' in the user's browser.

As you can see in Fig. 3.2, our class `HelloWorld` inherited from `javax.servlet.GenericServlet`. This is not absolutely necessary, but convenient. Servlets are not defined by a superclass, but by the `javax.servlet.Servlet` interface. This interface requests that only a class that contains the methods `init(ServletConfig)`, `service(ServletRequest, ServletResponse)`, `destroy()`, `getServletConfig()` and `getServletInfo()` can call itself a servlet. `GenericServlet` achieves all these methods and a few more besides. It is therefore

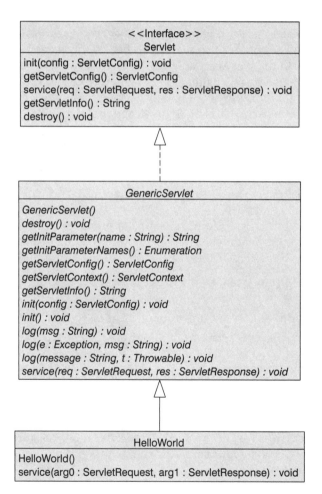

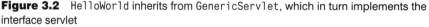

**Figure 3.2** `HelloWorld` inherits from `GenericServlet`, which in turn implements the interface servlet

sensible to inherit from this class and, if necessary, to overwrite methods. This is at least true for the service() method, as it has been declared abstract in GenericServlet. To stop our first example from being unnecessarily complicated, we have limited ourselves to overriding this method, and no others, in HelloWorld.

### 3.3.1 The heart of every servlet: the service() method

Every time the server receives a request for a servlet, the server prompts the servlet engine to call the servlet's service() method. Logically enough, this method is therefore the ideal place for sending out our greetings to the world. In the case of the ServletResponse object, it is helpful to us that the method is transferred by the engine when it is called. Among other things, ServletResponse also has the central methods setContentType(String) and getOutputStream().

As we want to display 'Hello World' in HTML in a browser, we must stick to the rules and let the browser know that our reply is in HTML. We do this by setting the MIME type of the answer to HTML by using setContentType("text/html") equals 'text/html'. This prompts the servlet's engine to add the line 'Content-type: text/html' in the header. As the header is the first thing to be sent to the browser, setContentType() should be called before there is any output. You can differ from this rule only if the engine you use stores the output in a memory buffer before actually sending the data to the client. More information on this in Section 3.5.4.

Before we can output anything at all, we must acquire an OutputStream for the ServletResponse object. We can do this with the getOutputStream() method. However, the stream obtained is not a normal java.io.OutputStream, but a derivative of it, a javax.servlet.ServletOutputStream.

The OutputStream class, which in any case is fairly abstract, has been extended so that ServletOutputStream provides print () and println () methods for both primitive data types (boolean, char, double, float, int and long) and for String objects, which make it much easier to use the stream. In particular, the resulting HTML code is made much easier to read, owing to the Carriage Return and Line Feed, CRLF, which is added when println () is called.

So, once we have obtained a ServletOutputStream, we call its println method and print 'Hello World'. As you can see in Listing 3.1, we deliberately do not flush any buffer that may be present for the stream or close the stream. This is possible, but is not necessary, as the servlet engine does this for us.

Listing 3.1: Hello World servlet

```
package de.webapp.Examples.Servlet;

import javax.servlet.GenericServlet;
import javax.servlet.ServletException;
import javax.servlet.ServletResponse;
import javax.servlet.ServletRequest;
import javax.servlet.ServletOutputStream;
import java.io.IOException;
```

```
public class HelloWorld extends javax.servlet.GenericServlet {
public void service(ServletRequest req, ServletResponse res)
    throws ServletException, IOException {
  // set MIME type to "text/html".
  res.setContentType("text/html");
  // obtain servletOutputStream of the ServletResponseObject
  servletOutputStream out = res.getOutputStream();
  // write "Hello World" in the servletOutputStream.
  out.println("Hello World");
}
} // End of class
```

### 3.3.2 Translating, installing, testing

So that you can test servlets quickly, JSDK 2.1 contains a simple server which can handle servlets. You can use the file `default.cfg` to configure it. You will find the parameters you need in Table 3.1.

**Table 3.1** JSDK 2.1 server configuration parameters

| Parameter | Meaning |
|---|---|
| server.port | Port that the server is to use. Default is 8080. |
| server.docbase | Directory in which the files and servlets are located. You can set this parameter relative to the current directory or as a complete URL. |
| server.hostname | Name of the server. This parameter is optional. |
| server.inet | Internet address of the server. This parameter is optional. |
| server.tempdir | Directory for temporary files. |
| server.webapp.<webapp name>.mapping | Defines the mapping of a URI in a Web application. If the URI of a request begins with this parameter, the request is assigned to the defined Web application. |
| Server.webapp.<webapp name>.docbase | Base directory of a Web application. You can set a directory relative to the current path or as a complete URL. |

Before we start the engine we still have a couple of things to do. First we want to compile `HelloWorld`. To do this, ensure that the jar file `servlet.jar` is located in the class path. If this is the case, servlets, like all other classes, can also be translated with the Java compiler `javac`, including `HelloWorld`.

To start the engine, at least two configuration files need to be processed. In `servlets.properties` the servlet is registered with the engine. In `mappings.properties` the mapping of URIs on servlets is defined. Both files are located in the JSDK or JSWDK subdirectory `/webpages/WEB-INF/`.

In `servlets.properties`, you must enter the class names and, if required, initialization arguments for all servlets that are to be started by the engine (Listing 3.2). In addition to that, a name is assigned to each servlet. This name must be unique within the `servlets.properties` file. In some engines it is also used as part of the URL that can be used to call the servlet after the engine has started.

Listing 3.2: `Servlets.properties` example file

```
# "servlets.properties" example file
#
# <Name>.code=<class name>(class or class.class)
# <Name>.initparams=comma-separated
# list of <Name=Value> pairs that
# the servlet can access via API calls.
#

# HelloWorld servlet
HelloWorld.code=de.webapp.Examples.Servlet.HelloWorld

# OtherServlet
Other.code= OtherServlet
Other.initparams=argument1=arg1, argument2=arg2
```

Once we have registered our servlet, we must then define the mapping of a URI on our servlet. To do this we use the file `mappings.properties`. It contains assignments of file extensions such as, for example, `.jsp`, to a servlet that has previously been defined in `servlets.properties` (Listing 3.3).

Listing 3.3: `Mappings.properties` example file

```
# "mappings.properties" example file
#
# <Path>=<servletname>
# <file extension >=<servletname>
#

# assign /HelloWorld to the servlet HelloWorld
/HelloWorld=HelloWorld
# assign URIs with the file extension .jsp to the servlet JSPServlet
jsp=JSPServlet
```

Once we have defined all the important parameters, we can now start the server with the `startserver` command.

Now, any Web browser can be used to call the `HelloWorld` servlet via the URL `http://<ServerAddress>:8080/HelloWorld`. To do so, `<ServerAddress>` must be replaced by the name or the IP address of the computer on which the server has been started.

To start the WebApp Frameworks engine jo!, you may first need to modify the `/webapp/projects/jo/etc/server.cfg` file. Here, enter the port via which the jo! engine is to be reached. Note that, in Unix systems, the port 80 is reserved for administrators.

For the most part, the structure of the `servlets.properties` file is the same as the structure of the file with the same name in the servlet runner. Note that, here, the URI mapping on servlets is also created in the `servlets.properties` file.

To start jo! you use a script in the `/webapp/projects/jo/bin` directory called jostart, or jostart.bat in Windows systems. If the class path has not already been set correctly, you can correct this in the script.

As you have no doubt just realized, you do not configure servlets the same way in all engines. Help came with Version 2.2 of the servlet API, which introduced the deployment descriptor, which described all configuration data in a defined format. You will find the deployment descriptor's DTD (Document Type Definition), with comments, in Appendix C.

## 3.4 Life cycle of servlets

Now that we have programmed and tried out our first servlet, we must take a closer look at the life cycle of servlets. The documentation for javax.servlet.Servlet tells us that the life of a servlet, once it has been instantiated by the servlet engine, is split into three phases (Fig. 3.3):

**1** Initialization by call to the init(ServletConfig) method.

**2** As many calls as required to service(ServletRequest, ServletResponse).

**3** Release by destroy().

These methods are called from the servlet engine. Time-consuming and one-off tasks should be included in the init(ServletConfig) method. service(Servlet Request, ServletResponse) should contain all the program parts which are to be executed each time the servlets are called. Finally, in destroy(), you carry out any clean-up work that may be needed. It is useful to close database connections, or save persistent data, there.

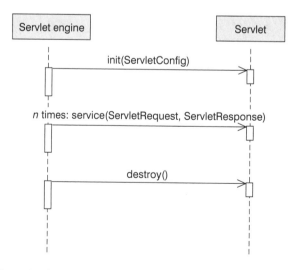

**Figure 3.3** Life cycle of a servlet

## 3.4.1  Bean counter

We want to create a counter servlet as an example (Listing 3.4). To set its initial value, our servlet should read the counter value from a file. Each time the servlet is called, the value is increased by 1 and output. If the servlet engine considers it necessary to remove our servlet from the memory, the counter value is to be saved in a file.

Listing 3.4: The `PersistentCounter` class

```java
package de.webapp.Examples.Servlet;

import javax.servlet.GenericServlet;
import javax.servlet.ServletException;
import javax.servlet.ServletResponse;
import javax.servlet.ServletRequest;
import javax.servlet.ServletOutputStream;
import javax.servlet.ServletConfig;
import java.io.IOException;
import java.io.FileInputStream;
import java.io.FileOutputStream;
import java.io.DataInputStream;
import java.io.DataOutputStream;

public class PersistentCounter extends javax.servlet.GenericServlet {
protected String myFilename;
protected int myCount = 0;
public void init(ServletConfig conf) throws ServletException {
   super.init(conf);
   // Read file name
   myFilename = getInitParameter("counterFile");
   // Set default file name
   if (myFilename == null) {
     myFilename = new String("counter.txt");
   }
   // Read counter value
   try {
     FileInputStream fileIn = new FileInputStream(myFilename);
     DataInputStream dataIn = new DataInputStream(fileIn);
     myCount = dataIn.readInt();
     dataIn.close();
   }
   catch (IOException e) {
     // Do nothing.
   }
}
public void service(ServletRequest req, ServletResponse res)
     throws ServletException, IOException {
```

```
        // Set MIME type to equal "text/html"
        res.setContentType("text/html");

        // Get ServletOutputStream of the servlet response
        // object
        ServletOutputStream out = res.getOutputStream();
        // Increment counter ...
        myCount++;

        // ... and output current value
        out.println("This servlet has been called"+ myCount +"times.");
    }

    public void destroy() {
        // Write counter level.
        try {
            FileOutputStream fileOut = new FileOutputStream(myFilename);
            DataOutputStream dataOut = new DataOutputStream(fileOut);
            dataOut.writeInt(myCount);
            dataOut.close();
        }
        catch (IOException e) {
            // Output error message if required.
            System.err.println("Could not save counter level: "+e.toString());
        }
    super.destroy();
    }

    } // End of the class
```

To start the servlet, the `servlets.properties` file must contain the following entry:

```
...
# Bean counter servlet
Bean_counter.code=de.webapp.Examples.Servlet.PersistentCounter
Bean_counter.initparams=counterDatei=Bean_counter.txt
...
```

The `mappings.properties` file should contain the following entry:

```
...
# Bean counter servlet
/Bean_counter=Bean_counter
...
```

After your servlet engine is started the servlet should be available under the address `http://<hostname>:<port>/Bean_counter`.

### 3.4.2 Initialization

During initialization we use `getInitParameter(String)` to get the file name of the file from which we want to read the counter value. To do this, `getInitParameter(String)` accesses the initialization parameters that have been entered in the `servlets.properties` file. If the method responds with `null`, this means that the initialization parameters have not been entered. In this case we set a default file name (`counter.txt`) so that the servlet can still be used.

To continue to be able to access the file name, we save it in the `myFilename` instance variable. Then we read an integer from the file and assign it to the `myCount` instance variable. For simplicity's sake we shall ignore all `IOExceptions`.

The prerequisite for saving the counter value in an instance variable is that only one instance of this servlet exists. In accordance with the servlet specification this must be the case only if a distributed environment is not involved. At present, however, most servlet engines only work with one instance per servlet. In addition, since servlet API 2.2, servlets that have been optimized for distributed environments must be marked as such.

### 3.4.3 Service

In comparison with `HelloWorld` the changes are minimal. Our counter variable is increased by 1 and the sentence 'This servlet has been called X times' is output.

### 3.4.4 Release

In order to rescue the counter value, even after our servlet has come to the end of its life, we save the value in the file whose name we discovered during initialization. If something goes wrong here we can write a short message in the standard error output. To call the `destroy()` method as a test, you can call the `stopserver` script in JSDK/JSWDK.

## 3.5 Run-time environment

Until now we have limited ourselves to 'pure' servlet programming and not paid much attention to the environment. Only with the `getInitParameter(String)` method have we glanced briefly above and beyond the servlet. But now for something completely different.

### 3.5.1 Configuration with `ServletConfig`

As we have already described, the `init(ServletConfig)` method is called to initialize a servlet. To do so, an object of the `javax.servlet.ServletConfig` type is transferred as an argument. The `ServletConfig` interface provides methods which make it possible to access the initialization parameter and a `ServletContext` object (Table 3.2).

**Table 3.2** Methods of the `ServletConfig` interface

| Method | Meaning |
| --- | --- |
| `String getInitParameter(String name)` | Returns the corresponding initialization argument from the `servlets.properties` file. |
| `Enumeration getInitParameterNames()` | Supplies a list of all parameter names (see Java API documentation: `java.util.Enumeration`). |
| `ServletContext getServletContext()` | Returns the `ServletContext` object of the servlet (more about this in the next section). |
| `String getServletName()` | Returns the name with which the servlet was registered in the servlet engine. |

It is a prerequisite that each servlet engine must provide each servlet with a `ServletConfig` object – otherwise it would be impossible to call it up correctly. In addition it makes sense for you to implement the interface in your own servlets, to simplify access to initialization parameters and the context. This is what happens in the `GenericServlet`.

## 3.5.2 Interface to the engine: `ServletContext`

Just like `ServletConfig`, the `javax.servlet.ServletContext` is an interface that must be implemented from one class of the servlet engine. The context is the environment in which a servlet is executed. From servlet API 2.2 onwards, this environment is also known as a *Web application*. Each servlet instance has one specific context, which it can access using the `ServletConfig` object. Table 3.3 shows an overview of the interface methods.

You use `ServletContext` to find out all the environment's characteristics and also to use some environment-specific services. It is important that you understand precisely what this environment is, and how it is restricted.

Servlet engines that provide their services for various domains (virtual hosts) have always given each domain its own context. Since the release of servlet API 2.1, `ServletContext` is now no longer just used for various hosts but is also mapped in the URI space on an individual host. For this reason, it is possible that a servlet with the URI `/context1/myServlet` has a different context from a servlet with the URI `/context2/myServlet` (Fig. 3.4). The specification also makes it clear that the granularity of the contexts is at least as large as that of the virtual host. A server with several virtual hosts must also provide each host with at least one context of its own. In doing so the URL space taken up by a context must not be larger than that of its host.

In principle it is possible to access one context from another using the `getContext(String URIPath)` method, if the context or the servlet is not subject to specific restrictions. This is the case, for example, if a servlet runs in a special security environment (sand box), which restricts access to the server's resources. If the

**Table 3.3** The ServletContext interface

| Method | Meaning |
|---|---|
| String getInitParameter(String name) | Returns an initialization parameter for this context. |
| Enumeration getInitParameterNames() | Returns a list of all keys for initialization parameters. |
| ServletContext getContext(String URI) | Returns a suitable context for the URI. If no suitable context is found or the servlet is not authorized to request it, the method returns null. |
| int getMajorVersion() | Returns the main version of the servlet API which is supported by the server. Therefore 2 is returned for Version 2.1. |
| int getMinorVersion() | Returns the subversion of the servlet API, which is supported by the server. For Version 2.1. 1 is therefore returned. |
| String getMimeType(String filename) | Finds out the MIME type of a file and returns this or null, if it is unknown. |
| String getRealPath(String virtual path) | Returns the real path of a file. |
| URL getResource(String URI) | Returns a URL object for a URI. |
| URL getResource(String URI, Locale loc) | Returns a localized URL object for a URI. |
| InputStream getResourceAsStream(String URI) | Returns a stream for a resource. |
| InputStream getResourceAsStream(String URI) | Returns a stream for a localized resource. |
| RequestDispatcher getRequestDispatcher(String URI) | Returns a suitable RequestDispatcher for a URI or null, if none is present. The URI must be entered relative to the ServletContext base and start with a forward slash (/). See also ServletRequest.getRequestDispatcher(). |
| RequestDispatcher getNamedDispatcher(String name) | Returns a suitable RequestDispatcher for a servlet name or null, if there is no servlet or registered Java server page present with the name entered. |
| String getServerInfo() | Returns the name and version of the server. |
| void log(String message) | Writes a message to the central log file. |
| void log(String message, Throwable t) | Writes a message and a throwable object or its stacktrace to the central log file. |
| void log(Exception e, String message) *deprecated* | Writes a message and an exception object or its stack trace to the central log file. |
| Object getAttribute(String name) | Tells you the attributes of the servlet engine which are not specifically covered by ServletContext interface methods. |
| void setAttribute(String name, Object o) | Sets an attribute of this context. |
| void removeAttribute(String name) | Deletes an attribute of this context. |
| Servlet getServlet(String name) *deprecated* | Returns a reference for a servlet. This method should no longer be used. Newer engines return null. |
| Enumeration getServletNames() *deprecated* | Returns a list of all servlet names. Newer engines supply an empty enumeration object. |
| Enumeration getServlets() *deprecated* | Returns a list of all servlets. Newer engines supply an empty enumeration object. |

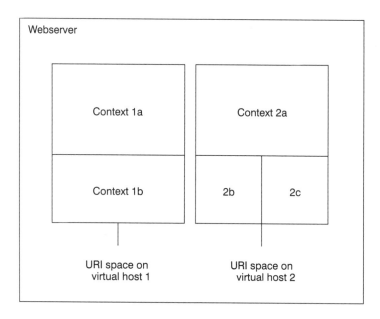

**Figure 3.4** One virtual host can contain several separate ServletContexts. However, one ServletContext cannot extend over more than one host.

URI path does not correspond to a context, or if the servlet is not allowed to access the context, the method returns null.

Now that we know what a context looks like, we are going to have a closer look at its services. One extremely important service is the access to resources. The getResource(String URI) method returns a URL object that makes it possible to access resources independently of a file system. The engine has the task of translating the URI you enter in a URL. In this case it no longer matters where the resource is actually located or whether it is a file on a remote server in a Java archive (Jar) or something completely different. The only thing that is important is whether the location can (or cannot) be described with a URL.

To make it easier and more convenient to use resources, the context also offers the getResourceAsStream(String URI) method. However, if you use this method, meta-information such as the length and type of the resource is lost. Both methods were introduced in Version 2.1 as a logical extension to the locally restricted getRealPath() method. All three methods are classically used in file servlets. File servlets analyze the query and simply deliver a file from the file system (just as a Web server does).

In Version 2.2 of the API two additional variants joined the getResource() methods: getResource(String URI, Locale loc) and getResource AsStream-(String URI, Locale loc). Both methods return a localized version of the resource, if this is available. If it is not, you will receive null as the returned value. In order to use both methods, you must mark local resources as such. There are two ways of doing this.

Let us say that one of your Web application files is called index.html. In order to access the German version of this file, you must save it with the name index_de.html in the same directory. If you also have a French version, you must call this file index_fr.html, and so on. The language abbreviations must be those defined in ISO 639 (http://www.ics.uci.edu/pub/ietf/http/related/iso639.txt). The format used to assign these names is also described in greater detail in the java.util.PropertyResourceBundle documentation.

The second way of accessing localized versions of your resources is by using the deployment descriptor (Appendix C). Here you can enter your own directory tree in the appropriate place for a particular language. Then individual file names do not have to be changed.

Another important method of the context was introduced in Version 2.1. This is getRequestDispatcher(String URI). Using this method you can call or bind other server resources. This can be used for almost any of the resources provided by the server. These include, among others, servlets, Java Server Pages (JSP), files or CGI scripts. We will describe the RequestDispatcher in greater detail in Section 3.9.

getRequestDispatcher() makes it possible to use a procedure that was the standard way of doing things before Version 2.0. You could request a reference on a servlet via the now obsolete getServlet(), getServlets() or getServlet Names() methods. You could then call its service() method. This procedure involved a significant danger, because there was no way of finding out the status of the servlet you requested. It was therefore quite possible to call the service() method of servlets which had already been deleted or even those that had not been installed at all.

This procedure was also often used to access the instance variables of other servlets in order to share objects. This foolhardy procedure has also become obsolete since the release of Version 2.1 of the API. Alongside getAttribute(String), the setAttribute(String, Object) and removeAttribute(String) methods were also introduced. These now make it possible for groups of servlets to share and use objects without encountering any problems.

The servlet engine also sets at least one context attribute. This is a temporary directory, which conceals itself as a java.io.File object with the name javax.servlet.context.tempdir.

The last characteristic of the context we are to mention is the centralized log service. You can use log(String) and log(String, Throwable) (previously: log(Exception, String)) to write data very easily to a central log file. Furthermore, you can use GenericServlet (Fig. 3.2) as an easy way of accessing both methods.

### 3.5.3 Request object: ServletRequest

In addition to configuring the servlets with ServletConfig and accessing the server or the servlet engine with ServletContext, the servlet API with the ServletRequest interface also allows you to access the characteristics of a request. Many of the methods provided by the ServletRequest supply values that correspond to classic CGI variables. These are listed in Table 3.4.

**Table 3.4** Methods with CGI equivalent

| Method | CGI equivalent | Meaning |
|---|---|---|
| int getContentLength() | CONTENT_LENGTH | Gives the length of the request data or − 1, if this is not known |
| String getContentType() | CONTENT_TYPE | Corresponds to the MIME type of the request, or null, if this is not known |
| String getProtocol() | SERVER_PROTOCOL | Protocol with version number. The following format is used here: <Protocol>/<main version>.<sub-version> |
| String getScheme() | − | Sets the scheme according to which the URL, on which the request is based, is formed. Examples: http, ftp, https. |
| String getServerName() | SERVER_NAME | Host name of the server |
| int getServerPort() | SERVER_PORT | Server's port number |
| String getRemoteAddr() | REMOTE_ADDR | Client's IP address |
| String getRemoteHost() | REMOTE_HOST | Client's host name |

In addition there are a few methods that are vital for working with servlets (Table 3.5). The first is servlet ServletInputStream getInputStream(). The InputStream that this method returns is primarily designed to read binary data. It is used, for example, for transferring files using FTP (File Transfer Protocol) or when uploading files. If you are sure that only text data are to be transferred, you should consider opting for Reader getReader() so you can use a reader instead of the stream. In contrast to streams, the reader and writer introduced with JDK 1.1 (see JDK documentation, package java.io) are able to deal with character set encoding correctly. It does not matter whether you now access a stream or reader: once you have done one, you cannot do the other. If, despite this, you call both methods an IllegalStateException is triggered.

In addition to providing raw access via either a stream or a reader, each ServletRequest also provides methods for accessing parameters. In this case, parameters mean key value pairs which can be sent to the server via a request string, using GET or via a form, using POST. The corresponding methods used to access parameters are called String[] getParameterValues(), String getParameter (String name) and Enumeration getParameterNames(). Be careful how you use String getParameter(String name): if more than one value is assigned to a key and you use getParameter(String name) you will receive only one value. For this reason this method was to be removed from the servlet API. However, because of the protests of many developers, Sun has reintroduced this method. If you are sure that you want to transfer only one value, it is much easier to work directly with a string than always having to access an array. If several parameters with the same name are transferred, getParameter(String name) supplies the first one. However, take care, this has only been the case since Version 2.2. From Version 2.2 onwards it is also defined that, when String[] getParameters() is called, the

**Table 3.5**  Methods with no CGI equivalent

| Method | Meaning |
| --- | --- |
| Object getAttribute(String name) | Returns the value of a request-specific attribute which is not already covered by other methods. If there is no attribute present with the name you entered, the method returns null. |
| void setAttribute(String name, Object o) | Sets an object as an attribute of this request. This is particularly useful for nested servlets (see RequestDispatcher). Attributes whose key begins java, javax, sun or com.sun are reserved and should not be used. |
| String getCharacterEncoding() | Returns the character set encoding of the request body back or null, if none is coded. |
| ServletInputStream getInputStream() throws IOException | Returns a stream for reading the binary data of the request body. |
| String getParameter(String name) | Returns an individual value from a parameter or null, if this does not exist. |
| Enumeration getParameterNames() | Returns a list of all parameter names in this request. |
| String[] getParameterValues(String name) | Supplies an array with all the values of this parameter or null, if the parameter does not exist. |
| BufferedReader getReader() throws IOException | Supplies a reader which can read the text from the request body. |
| Locale getLocale() | Shows the preferred language of the client. This information is usually taken from the Accept-Language header. |
| Enumeration getLocales() | Returns a list of the preferred languages in ascending order of preference. |
| boolean isSecure() | Shows whether the request was transferred using a secure connection such as SSL. If so, and this is a server that runs on Java 2, the corresponding certificate is contained in the attribute with the javax.servlet.request.X509Certificate key. |
| RequestDispatcher getRequestDispatcher(String URI) | Returns a suitable RequestDispatcher for a URI or null, if none is present. The URI may be relative to the currently displayed resource and must not start with a /. See also ServletContext.getRequestDispatcher(). |
| String getRealPath(String virtual path) *deprecated* | Transforms a virtual path into a real path. This method has been replaced by the method with the same name in ServletContext. |

parameters transferred using GET are arranged before the parameters transferred using POST. Therefore, if there is a request using POST with a request string Greeting=Hallo and this is followed by Addressee=World, String[] getParameterValues() returns Hallo as the first parameter value and World as the second parameter value.

Listing 3.5 provides an example of how you can output parameters and their values:

Listing 3.5: Parameter output code extract

```
public void showParameters(ServletRequest req, ServletResponse res)
    throws ServletException, IOException {
  // First obtain an OutputStream,
  servletOutputStream out = res.getOutputStream();
  // then the parameter name.
  Enumeration e = req.getParameterNames();
  while (e.hasMoreElements()) {
    String name = (String)e.nextElement();
    // Output each name ...
    out.println(name + ":");
    String[] values = req.getParameterValues(name);
    // ... and if present, all its values.
    if (values != null) {
      for (int i=0; i < values.length; i++)
        out.println(values[i]);
    }
  }
}
```

In addition to the parameters, a request object can have other attributes. You can find out about these by using the Object getAttribute(String name) method. These are usually attributes which are set by the servlet engine for specific requests. For example, the attribute javax.net.ssl.cipher_suite contains the name of the SSL encoding suite, if SSL classes (Secure Socket Layer: a process for encrypting network data to make it more secure) by Sun have been used. There are other attributes of this kind. They share the characteristic that, for their name prefix, they use the package name of those classes over which they distribute information.

From Version 2.1 of the API onwards there is also an Enumeration getAttributeNames() method which returns a list of all attribute names. Previously we unavoidably had to stumble around in the dark. The void setAttribute(String name, Object o) method was also introduced. This is particularly useful if the request is to be transferred using a RequestDispatcher and you want to add other information before it is transferred.

### 3.5.4 ServletResponse: response object

The ServletResponse interface is the counterpart to ServletRequest. The methods that make it possible to send updated data back to the client are encapsulated

**Table 3.6** The `ServletResponse` interface

| Method | Meaning |
| --- | --- |
| `String getCharacterEncoding()` | Returns the character set encoding in use. |
| `ServletOutputStream getOutputStream()` `throws IOException` | Supplies a `ServletOutputStream`. |
| `PrintWriter getWriter() throws` `IOException` | Returns a `PrintWriter` for writing text. |
| `void setContentLength(int length)` | Sets the response length. |
| `void setContentType(String type)` | Sets the MIME type of the response. |
| `int getBufferSize()` | Returns the size of the buffer used. |
| `void setBufferSize(int size)` | Sets the buffer size. |
| `boolean isCommitted()` | Shows whether the buffered output data has already been finally sent to the client. |
| `void flushBuffer()` | Empties the buffer and sends the data to the client. |
| `void reset()` | Deletes all tasks and header values which have already been written, if `isCommitted()` returns incorrect. If this is not the case, an `IllegalStateException` is triggered. |
| `void setLocale(Locale loc)` | Sets the Header Content language according to the pre-set locale (location). |

there (Table 3.6). We have already given several examples of how you can receive a stream here, just like in `ServletRequest`. The corresponding method is called `ServletOutputStream getOutputStream()`. In the same way, `PrintWriter getWriter()` returns a corresponding writer. You should use this for writing texts. Once again, you cannot use both methods at the same time. `ServletResponse` also has several methods which influence the output buffer and the header.

If you know the length of the response, you set it using `setContentLength(int length)`. This is not strictly necessary in most cases, but we recommend you do so to improve performance. Only if this header is set can you set up persistent connections with browsers that have not yet implemented HTTP/1.1. For example, Netscape Navigator 4.7 still does not speak HTTP/1.1.

But even if the client speaks HTTP/1.1 it does not ensure that you can save yourself the trouble of setting the response length. This is only possible in two situations without paying a time penalty. Either your servlet engine buffers the response to determine its length, or it splits up the response into what are known as chunks. Chunked encoding is defined in HTTP/1.1 (Fielding *et al.* 1999, 24 ff.) and enables you to maintain persistent connections without knowing the content length.

To test whether your engine can carry out chunked encoding or uses the buffer, simply connect to your server via Telnet and request the `HelloWorld` servlet described in Section 3.3 in the following way:

```
telnet <servername> <port><enter>
GET /HelloWorld HTTP/1.1<enter>
Host: <servername>:<port><enter>
<enter>
```

In the response you can easily see which protocol your server speaks, whether it has `ContentLength` or `TransferCoding` and has set the key word 'chunked'.

From Version 2.2 of the API onwards, you can use a program to control how the output data is buffered. Use `void setBufferSize(int size)` to set the buffer size and learn about it with `int getBufferSize()`. In this case you should realize that the servlet engine does not necessarily set the value you want as the buffer size. Your entry is really only a wish in this situation. The actual buffer size is returned as a return value by the `int getBufferSize(int size)` method. This can sometimes be larger than the value you want. You must also take note that you must set the buffer size before you write any data using `ServletOutputStream` or `Writer`, otherwise an `IllegalStateException` is triggered.

Using a buffer gives a certain sense of convenience. With it you can re-delete tasks that have already been executed and header values that you have already set by calling up `reset()`, at least for as long as `isCommitted()` is false. How long that is depends in turn on the buffer size and which tasks have already been executed. `flushBuffer()` finally forces all buffered data to be written immediately.

In most cases you must call `setContentType(String type)` explicitly. If you do not, the basic MIME type 'text/plain' is used. It is important that you set the MIME type before you finally send any output to the client. If a buffer is not used explicitly, this is usually the case when the first output is created.

Using `setLocale(Locale)` you can set the Content-Language header according to the language of your output data. This also immediately sets an appropriate character set for the language. You will find more information about localization in Section 3.10. Finally `String getCharacterEncoding()` returns the character coding used here (for example ISO–8859–1).

## 3.6 Servlet exceptions

Of course, even servlets are not immune to errors or incorrect configurations. However, to guarantee reliable performance you can trigger the `init` method as well as the `service` method in addition to the `IOException` of a `javax.servlet.ServletException`.

You should always do this if a servlet cannot solve a problem itself. Usually the underlying problem is itself an exception, which is encapsulated in a `ServletException`. For this reason there are the corresponding constructors which accept `Throwable` objects as arguments:

- `public ServletException()`
- `public ServletException(String message)`
- `public ServletException(String message, Throwable reason)`
- `public ServletException(Throwable reason)`

In order to access the `Throwable` that is triggering, the exception also recognizes the `Throwable getRootCause()` method.

**Table 3.7**  UnavailableException methods and constructions

| Method | Meaning |
| --- | --- |
| int getUnavailableSeconds() | Shows the time at which the servlet is expected to be no longer available. If the servlet is permanently no longer available this method returns –1. |
| boolean isPermanent() | Shows whether the servlet is permanently no longer available. |
| Servlet getServlet() *deprecated* | Returns the affected servlet. This method should no longer be used. Since API 2.2 it returns null. |
| UnavailableException(Servlet servlet, String message) *deprecated* | Constructor which should no longer be used. |
| UnavailableException(int seconds, servlet servlet, String message) *deprecated* | Constructor which should no longer be used. |

In addition to the normal ServletException, the API recognizes another exception, the UnavailableException. UnavailableException, which is based on ServletException, tells the servlet engine that the servlet is not available, either for a certain period of time, or permanently.

The servlet engine must be informed of a long-lasting interruption if the servlet is no longer able to carry out its operations without the server being restarted. A temporary interruption is signalled if the problem can also be solved at run-time. This class of problems includes, for example, interruptions to external services, which are reliant on a servlet. These include databases, among others.

In Version 2.2 the UnavailableException has two new constructors:

- public UnavailableException(String message)
- public UnavailableException(String message, int secounds)

You can access the data specified in them by using the methods shown in Table 3.7. The methods and constructors shown as deprecated (their use is not recommended) should not be used from Version 2.2 of the API onwards.

## 3.7  Thread security

If, when programming servlets, you want to keep all the threads at your fingertips, you must be aware that, in some situations, a servlet's service() method will call several threads at the same time. There are also usually fewer servlet instances than threads, which run this servlet simultaneously. In actual fact, a servlet is normally only instantiated *once*. This means that unprotected classes and instance variables could be changed from thread A to thread B during execution. This relationship can easily lead to inconsistencies.

### 3.7.1 Problems with the ability to run concurrently

Take as an example the `ConcurrentCalculation` servlet (Listing 3.6) which first calculates the total of the two instance variables, then a difference. Between these two calculation steps it calls up a method which waits for approximately three seconds. In the meantime it writes the values of the instance variables a and b to the log file. If you now call the servlet, wait for the output and then call it up again, you see the following log entry:

```
Init
Service Start
a=10
b=0
Service End
Service Start
a=16
b=16
Service End
destroy
```

However, if you do not wait for the output of the first call and then call the servlet again immediately, you see this log entry:

```
init
Service Start
a=10
Service Start
a=16
b=6
Service End
b=10
Service End
destroy
```

After each of these two calls the servlet is therefore in different states, i.e. (16,16) or (16,10). The simplest way of avoiding this unpredictable relationship would be to define the `service()` method as `synchronized`. This would prevent two threads from accessing it at the same time. However, we strongly recommend that you *do not* do this.

Listing 3.6: The `ConcurrentCalculation` servlet

```
package de.webapp.Examples.Servlet;

import javax.servlet.*;
import java.io.IOException;
import java.io.PrintWriter;

public class ConcurrentCalculation extends javax.servlet.GenericServlet {
int a = 4;
```

```
int b = 10;

public void service(ServletRequest req, ServletResponse res)
        throws ServletException, IOException {
    log("Service Start");
    // First calculation
    a = a + 6;
    log("a=" + a);
    // wait...
    waitABit();
    // Second calculation
    b = a - b;
    log("b=" + b);
    log("Service End");
    // Output in browser
    res.setContentType("text/html");
    PrintWriter out = res.getWriter();
    out.println("Calculation complete.");
}

public void waitABit {
    try {
        synchronized (this) {
            wait (3000);
        }
    } catch (InterruptedException ignore) {}
}
} // End of the class
```

As so often happens, the simplest option is unfortunately not the best. In this case it would actually be the worst. If `service()` `synchronized` is declared, this is a safe method but slows down execution considerably. It is better to synchronize only those program parts where problems can actually occur. These are the code passages in which resources are used and manipulated. They are available for several threads, especially the instance and class variables of servlets, files, or database or network connections. In contrast, local data or parameters should not be synchronized, because this slows down the execution of the servlets unnecessarily.

### 3.7.2  One after the other: SingleThreadModel

Another way of ensuring thread security is by using the `javax.servlet.SingleThreadModel` interface. This is an interface which is used only to mark a class and does not specify any methods. If a servlet implements this interface, it tells the servlet engine that no more than one thread may ever execute this servlet's `service()` method at a time. However, in order to guarantee shorter response times, servlet engines usually create a pool of servlet instances. Incoming requests can therefore always be served by an instance whose `service()` method is not currently being executed by another thread.

The disadvantage of this method is the increase in time and effort used to manage the pool and its significantly higher memory requirements. Anyone who writes memory-intensive servlets would do better to concern themselves with real synchronization. In addition `SingleThreadModel` servlets are not able to distribute your data via instance variables. The counters described in Section 3.4.1 would therefore not function in this case. You should also ensure that your servlet engine recognizes the interface before you rely on it.

### 3.7.3 Secure release

If a servlet engine releases a servlet (for example to clear space in memory), it usually calls up `destroy()` after all `service()` calls have been completed, or, at the latest, after a period of time defined in the configuration has passed. This means that servlets which are carrying out time-consuming tasks must themselves ensure that they are not unloaded before all the tasks have been completed, or that occupied resources such as, for example, database connections are not released again.

Listing 3.7: The LongRunner class

```
package de.webapp.Examples.Servlet;

import javax.servlet.*;
import java.io.IOException;

public class LongRunner extends javax.servlet.GenericServlet {
private int serviceCounter = 0;
private boolean shuttingDown = false;
protected long _PollInterval = 500;

protected void beforeService() {
   serviceCounter++;
}

protected void afterService() {
   serviceCounter--;
}

protected int getNumServices() {
   return serviceCounter;
}

protected void setShuttingDown(boolean flag) {
   shuttingDown = flag;
}

protected boolean getShuttingDown() {
   return shuttingDown;
}

public void service(ServletRequest req, ServletResponse res)
     throws ServletException, IOException {
```

```
    beforeService();
    try {
      // Insert the actual
      // service code or
      // super.service(req, res) here;
    }
    finally {
      afterService();
    }
  }

  public void destroy() {
    setShuttingDown(true);
    while (getNumServices() > 0) {
      synchronized (this) {
        try {
          wait(_PollInterval);
        }
        catch (InterruptedException e) {
          // insert exception handler here if required
        }
      }
    }
    super.destroy();
  }

} // End of the class
```

In our LongRunner example (Listing 3.7) we therefore save the number of serv-
ice() calls in the private instance variable serviceCounter. serviceCounter is
increased in the beforeService() method or reduced in the afterService()
method. As their names imply, these methods are called before and after the actual
service code. We have encapsulated them in a try block, and by using finally can
ensure that afterService() will also be called in an exceptional situation.

So that you can define in the service code whether the servlet engine attempts to
unload the servlet, we also introduce the boolean shuttingDown flag. This is initialized by false and set to true when destroy() is called. Via boolean
getShuttingDown(), running threads can determine whether destroy() was
called and access the appropriate measures if required.

After shuttingDown has been set to true, you can use int getNumServices()
to check whether one or more threads are executing service(). If not,
super.destroy() is called immediately. Otherwise, the servlet engine waits for
the period defined in long_PollInterval and then carries out another check to see
whether service() is being executed by at least one thread. This process repeats
until the number of running threads is zero.

In practical terms this allows the structure of LongRunner also to apply its behaviour later to existing servlets. To do so, LongRunner must simply inherit from the

servlets concerned and the service() method named super.service (ServletReqest, ServletResponse) needs to be called in the try block. The only disadvantage is that getShuttingDown() is, of course, not accessible from the superclass.

## 3.8 HTTP-specific servlets

All the examples described above were fairly general and not really HTTP-specific. In order to be able to use HTTP, the servlet must analyze the request that was sent by the browser to a servlet. The first thing we are interested in is which HTTP command was actually sent. Then we shall look at the environment variables and the session tracking.

### 3.8.1 HttpServlet

With the javax.servlet.http.HttpServlet class Sun has provided developers with a comfortable starting point for their own HTTP-specific servlets. Although it is a descendant of GenericServlet, the service() method has another function here and should not be overwritten. The HTTP command used by the client is defined in it and an appropriate method is called. It usually supports the commands GET, POST, HEAD, PUT, DELETE, OPTIONS and TRACE. The corresponding methods have the same name as the HTTP commands but also have a 'do' prefix (e.g. doGet(), doPost()). With the exception of OPTIONS and TRACE, all methods return the HTTP error message '400 – BadRequest' to the client, if they have not been overwritten.

Therefore, in order to write a servlet that reacts to the GET command, the doGet() method must be overwritten. The same applies for POST, PUT and DELETE. doHead(), doOptions() and doTrace() can also be overwritten, but usually the standard implementation is fully sufficient. This is particularly true for doHead(). For example, as soon as doGet() is overwritten the HttpServlet also understands HEAD. This is because HEAD basically does the same as GET, with the difference that the body of the document is not sent with it.

Listing 3.8 shows a simple servlet which supports the GET, HEAD, POST, OPTIONS and TRACE methods. Here, only the doGet() and the doPost() methods have to be overwritten explicitly. When GET or POST is used for a call, a message appears in the browser window to confirm which method was called.

Listing 3.8: The SimpleHttpServlet class

```
package de.webapp.Examples.Servlet;

import javax.servlet.http.*;
import javax.servlet.*;
import java.io.IOException;
import java.io.PrintWriter;
```

```
public class SimpleHttpServlet extends javax.servlet.http.HttpServlet {
/** doGet() method */
public void doGet(HttpServletRequest req, HttpServletResponse res)
      throws ServletException, IOException {
  res.setContentType("text/html");
  PrintWriter out = res.getWriter();
  out.println("You have called this servlet via the Get method.");
}

/** doPost() method */
public void doPost(HttpServletRequest req, HttpServletResponse res)
      throws ServletException, IOException {
  res.setContentType("text/html");
  PrintWriter out = res.getWriter();
  out.println("You have called this servlet via the Post method.");
}
} // End of the class
```

If you look closely at SimpleHttpServlet you will notice that, instead of the normal javax.servlet.ServletRequest and the javax.servlet.Servlet Response object, a javax.servlet.http.HttpServletRequest and a javax.servlet.http.HttpServletResponse object are transferred. We shall describe this in more detail in the next two sections.

## 3.8.2  HttpServletRequest

As the name suggests, javax.servlet.http.HttpServletRequest is the HTTP-specific extension of a ServletRequest. Like ServletRequest, HttpServletRequest is also an interface which must be implemented by one of the servlet engine's classes. In addition to the methods from ServletRequest it mainly has methods that query the specific characteristics of a HTTP request. Just like in ServletRequest, CGI programmers will recognize most of the methods, because they are very similar to the CGI environment variables. Table 3.8 shows an overview of the available HTTP-specific methods with the CGI equivalent. Table 3.9 lists the remaining methods.

The following central equation applies to the most important path methods:

getRequestURI() = getContextPath() + getServletPath() + getPathInfo()

Here you must be aware that the RequestURI can be URL-coded. In addition to this, the following also applies:

getPathTranslated() = getRealPath(getPathInfo())

The interface also makes it easier to access the header of an HTTP request via the appropriate methods. For example, Enumeration getHeaderNames() reports a list of all header names. Enumeration getHeaders(String) returns a list of all header fields which have the same header name. String getHeader(String), int getIntHeader(String) and long getDateHeader(String) return the first

**Table 3.8** HTTP-specific methods with CGI equivalents

| Method | CGI equivalent | Meaning |
|---|---|---|
| `String getAuthType()`<br>`String getMethod()`<br>`String getPathInfo()` | `AUTH_TYPE`<br>`REQUEST_METHOD`<br>`PATH_INFO` | Returns the authentication type or `null`.<br>Shows the query method, i.e. `GET` or `POST`.<br>Returns the optional part of the query path between servlet path (see `getServletPath()`) and query string or `null`, if no extra information follows the servlet path. Example: `http://host/servlets/myServlet/optionalPath?QueryString` would result in `/optionalPath`. |
| `String getPathTranslated()` | `PATH_TRANSLATED` | Converts the virtual path `PATH_INFO` into a real path. Example: `http://host/servlets/myServlet/optionalPath?QueryString` could result in `/usr/local/htdocs/optionalPath`. If no optional path has been entered, this method returns `null`. |
| `String getQueryString()`<br>`String getRemoteUser()` | `QUERY_STRING`<br>`REMOTE_USER` | Supplies the query string part of the Request URI or `null`.<br>The user name, if identified via HTTP authentification, or `null`. See also `getRemoteUserPrincipal()` and `isRemoteUserInRole()`. |
| `String getServletPath()` | `SCRIPT_NAME` | Returns the part of the URI which refers to the servlet. If a servlet was mapped to `/servlet/myServlet` and the called URI is called `/servlet/myServlet/extraInfo`, the servlet path is the same: `/servlet/myServlet`. If the servlet is mapped to the file extension `.shtml` and the URI is `/path/file.shtml` the servlet path corresponds to this. However, this only applies if the context path is empty – otherwise this must also be removed. |

**Table 3.9** Methods of the `HttpServletRequest` without a CGI equivalent

| Method | Meaning |
|---|---|
| `Cookie[] getCookies()` | Returns a list of all the cookies in this query. If no cookies exist, an empty array is returned. |
| `long getDateHeader(String name)` | Returns the value of the requested header field in milliseconds since 1 January 1970 GMT. If the header field does not exist, this method returns -1. |
| `Enumeration getHeaders (String name)` | Returns all values with the same header name in the form of a list. For example, the Cache-Control header may occur several times. |
| `String getHeader(String name)` | Returns the first value of the requested header field or `null`, if the field does not exist. |
| `Enumeration getHeaderNames()` | Returns a list of the header field names in this query. |
| `int getIntHeader(String name)` | Returns the value of the requested header field as a scalar integer. If the header field does not exist, this method returns -1. |
| `String getContextPath()` | Path of the current context. |
| `boolean isRemoteUserInRole(String role)` | Shows whether an authenticated user has been assigned a particular role. See also `getRemoteUser()`. |
| `Principal getRemoteUserPrincipal()` | Returns the principal object of an authenticated user. |
| `String getRequestedSessionId()` | Returns the `SessionID` of this request. |
| `String getRequestURI()` | Returns the URI contained in the query line. This does not include a query string even if one is present. |
| `HttpSession getSession()` | Returns the associated session, or creates it if it does not already exist. |
| `HttpSession getSession (boolean create)` | Returns the associated session, or creates it if it does not already exist and create is true. |
| `Boolean isRequested SessionIdValid()` | Shows whether the session associated with this query is valid. |
| `isRequestedSessionIdFromCookie()` | Shows whether the requested SessionID comes from a cookie. |
| `isRequestedSessionIdFromURL()` | Shows whether the requested SessionID comes from a URL. |
| `isRequestedSessionIdFromUrl()` *deprecated* | In order to maintain a standardized writing approach, it is recommended that, instead of this method, you use `isRequestedSessionIdFromURL()` (see above). |

referenced header field as a string object or scalar. There are also methods which access cookies and sessions or SessionIDs. These are described in a later section.

Our example, `RequestInfoServlet` (Listing 3.9), shows all available environment variables (also from `ServletRequest`) for a query. A similar servlet (SnoopServlet) is also provided as a standard example in JSDK.

Listing 3.9: The RequestInfoServlet class

```
package de.webapp.Examples.Servlet;

import java.io.*;
import java.util.*;
import javax.servlet.*;
import javax.servlet.http.*;

public class RequestInfoServlet extends HttpServlet {
public void doPost (HttpServletRequest req, HttpServletResponse res)
    throws ServletException, IOException {
  // For simplicity's sake we shall call doGet here...
  doGet(req, res);
}

public void doGet (HttpServletRequest req, HttpServletResponse res)
    throws ServletException, IOException {
  // Set the MIME type of the response
  res.setContentType("text/html");
  // Get a Writer.
  Writer out = res.getWriter()
  // Print the HTML header.
  out.write("<html>");
  out.write("<head><title>RequestInfoServlet</title></head>");
  out.write("<body>");
  out.write("<h2>RequestInfoServlet</h2>");
  out.write("<b>Requested URL: </b>");
  out.write (HttpUtils.getRequestURL (req).toString () + "<br>");
  out.write("<h2>environment variables</h2>");
  out.write("<b>Method: </b>" + req.getMethod() + "<br>");
  out.write("<b>Protocol: </b>" + req.getProtocol() + "<br>");
  out.write("<b>Request URI: </b>" + req.getRequestURI() + "<br>");
  out.write("<b>Servlet path: </b>" + req.getServletPath() + "<br>");
  out.write("<b>Path info: </b>" + req.getPathInfo() + "<br>");
  out.write("<b>Translated path: </b>" + req.getPathTranslated() + "<br>");
  out.write("<b>Query string: </b>" + req.getQueryString() + "<br>");
  out.write("<b>Length: </b>" + req.getContentLength() + "<br>");
  out.write("<b>MIME type: </b>" + req.getContentType() + "<br>");
  out.write("<b>Server name: </b>" + req.getServerName() + "<br>");
  out.write("<b>Server port: </b>" + req.getServerPort() + "<br>");
  out.write("<b>User: </b>" + req.getRemoteUser() + "<br>");
```

```
    out.write("<b>Client address: </b>"+ req.getRemoteAddr() + "<br>");
    out.write("<b>Client host name: </b>" + req.getRemoteHost() + "<br>");
    out.write("<b>Authentication scheme: </b>" + req.getAuthType() + "<br>");
    out.write("<h2>Header data</h2>");
    Enumeration e = req.getHeaderNames();
    if (e.hasMoreElements()) {
      while (e.hasMoreElements()) {
        String name = (String)e.nextElement();
        out.write("<b>" + name + ": </b>"+ req.getHeader(name) + "<br>");
      }
    }
    out.write("<h2>Servlet-Parameter</h2>");
    e = req.getParameterNames();
    while (e.hasMoreElements()) {
      String name = (String)e.nextElement();
      String vals[] = (String []) req.getParameterValues(name);
      if (vals != null) {
        out.write("<b>" + name + ": </b>");
        for (int i = 0; i<vals.length; i++)
          out.write(vals[i] +"");
        out.write("<br>");
      }
    }
    out.write("<p></body></html>");
  }
} // End of the class
```

### 3.8.3 HttpServletResponse

In addition to innumerable status and error codes (RFC 2616, Section 10) the
HttpServletResponse interface has only a few methods. These are primarily used
to return these specific codes to a client, as well as setting and querying header data.
Table 3.10 provides an overview.

Without exception, the status codes are public static final int variables
whose names begin with 'SC_' for status code. An HTTP status message is appended.
Practically all of these variables are filled with the HTTP status code as a value.

Examples are:

```
public static final int SC_OK = 200;
public static final int SC_NOT_FOUND = 404;
```

If you want to return a status message to the client which differs from the usual 200
(for example: '302 MOVED TEMPORARILY'), you can do so using the setStatus(int
sc) method. It is useful to use one of the predefined constants as the status code – previously you could also enter a message text. Now, it is no longer recommended that
you use the method for entering a message text (the method is deprecated).
setStatus() should only be used if no errors are present. Status codes whose first

**Table 3.10** `HttpServletResponse` methods

| Method | Meaning |
|---|---|
| `void addCookie(Cookie cookie)` | Sets a cookie. |
| `boolean containsHeader(String name)` | Shows whether the response contains a particular header field. |
| `String encodeRedirectURL(String url)` | Codes a `SessionID` in a URL which is intended for the `sendRedirect()` method. |
| `String encodeRedirectUrl(String url)` *deprecated* | In order to maintain a standardized writing approach, it is recommended that, instead of this method, you use `encodeRedirectURL(String url)`. |
| `String encodeURL(String url)` | Codes a SessionID in a URL. |
| `String encodeUrl(String url)` *deprecated* | In order to maintain a standardized writing approach, it is recommended that, instead of this method, you use `encodeURL(String url)`. |
| `void sendError(int statusCode) throws IOException` | Sends an error message to the client. |
| `void sendError(int statusCode, String message) throwsIOException` | Sends an error message to the client. The message is sent as body text with the response. |
| `void sendRedirect(String url)` | Sends the HTTP command `Moved Temporarily` to the client. Since Version 2.2 the URL entered no longer has to be absolute. |
| `void setDateHeader(String name,long date)` | Sets the named header field. The date should be entered in milliseconds since 1 January 1970 GMT. |
| `void addDateHeader(String name, long date)` | Adds the named header field to the header. The date should be entered in milliseconds since 1 January 1970 GMT. |
| `void setHeader(String name, String value)` | Sets a header field. If a header with the same name has already been set, this is overwritten. |
| `void addHeader(String name, String value)` | Adds a header field to the header, without overwriting existing values. |
| `void setIntHeader(String name, int value)` | Sets a scalar integer as a header field. |
| `void addIntHeader(String name, int value)` | Adds a scalar integer as a header field. |
| `void setStatus(int statusCode)` | Sets the status code of this response. |
| `void setStatus(int statusCode, String message)` *deprecated* | Sets the status code of this response. The message is returned as the body text of the response to the client. |

digit is a 4 (client error) or 5 (server error) should be sent using the `sendError(int sc)` and `sendError(int sc, String msg)` methods. These not only set the status code, but also in each case send an HTML page with a short description of the error to the client.

You can also add other attributes to each response to the client. To do this, you use the `setHeader(String key, String value)`, `addHeader(String key, String value)`, `setIntHeader(String key, int value)`, `addIntHeader(String key, int value)`, `setDateHeader(String name, long date)` or `addDate-Header(String name, long date)` methods. Use `boolean contains-Header(String name)` to see whether a header value has already been set. When you set a header value again, the old value is overwritten.

In addition, `HttpServletResponse` (with the `sendRedirect(String location)` method) allows the browser to send to another URL. For this purpose, the two following lines are simply executed:

```
setStatus(SC_MOVED_TEMPORARILY);
setHeader("Location", location);
```

This enables the browser to load the URL contained in `location`. However, both `sendRedirect()` and `sendError()` have the side effect that all previously carried-out tasks are deleted, replaced accordingly and sent. This is, of course, possible only if `isCommitted()` still returns false. If not, an `IllegalStateException` is also triggered. If you still output data after you have called up one of these methods, it will be ignored.

In addition to the methods described above, `HttpServletResponse` contains other methods for handling cookies and sessions. We shall describe these in greater detail in the sections that follow.

### 3.8.4 Cookies

In applications such as online shops it is necessary to gather user-specific information during purchasing. Otherwise it would be impossible to use virtual shopping baskets (Chapter 12). Unfortunately HTTP is a connection- and status-free protocol. For this reason it is difficult to definitively assign two consecutive requests to one user. Although you could evaluate the client's IP address, there is still the danger that several users may be sharing one IP address. Possible reasons for this are, for example, IP masquerading or dynamic IP address assignment by an Internet service provider. Cookies help sort this out. They are snippets of information which the client saves when requested to by a server and returns to the server each time the client calls up a Web page on this server. This provides a reasonably reliable way for a client to be identified by a server. However, this procedure is by no means secure! Without a better authentification procedure or without a secure connection, for example via SSL, it leaves you vulnerable to many types of deception.

The servlet API supports the use of cookies in accordance with RFC 2109 (`http://www.cis.ohio-state.edu/htbin/rfc/rfc2109.html`) quite comfortably. Using the `HttpServletResponse` interface `addCookie(Cookie aCookie)` method you can set a cookie. The `HttpServletRequest` interface `Cookie[]`

getCookies() method supplies an array of all the cookies sent by the client. The javax.servlet.http.Cookie class itself is merely a data structure whose attributes you can set and query using the get and set methods. By far the most important of these attributes are Name and Value which must also be entered in the Cookie(String name, String value) constructor.

You can set a few other attributes in addition to the name and the value. Normally the cookies from a client are only returned to the server that set them. Using setDomain(String domain) you can extend the number of servers to which the cookies are sent, in a domain. You can also add comments to cookies, influence their duration and set a security flag which shows that the cookie may be returned to the server only via a secure connection.

In our example CookieCounterServlet (Listing 3.10) we first want to request an array of the cookies that have been sent. If no cookies were sent via this request, this array equals 0. If this is not the case, we search through the cookie names until we find our cookie. When we find it, we save it in the myCookie variable. If we do not find it, or if no cookies were sent, we instantiate a new cookie. Then we use getValue() to read our cookie's value and increase it by 1. Then we use addCookie(myCookie) to set the new cookie and then output the counter value with write(...).

Listing 3.10: The CookieCounterServlet class

```
package de.webapp.Examples.Servlet;

import javax.servlet.http.*;
import javax.servlet.*;
import java.io.*;

public class CookieCounterServlet extends HttpServlet {
public void doGet(HttpServletRequest req, HttpServletResponse res)
    throws ServletException, IOException {
  // Set MIME type to "text/html".
  res.setContentType("text/html");

  // Get a Writer.
  Writer out = res.getWriter();

  // Get cookies.
  Cookie[] cookies = req.getCookies();
  Cookie myCookie = null;

  // Find the right cookie.
  int i = 0;
  if (cookies != null) {
    while (myCookie == null && i < cookies.length) {
      if (cookies[i].getName().equals("CookieCounterServlet.number"))
        myCookie = cookies[i];
      i++;
    }
```

```
    }
    // If our cookie could not be found,
    // instantiate a new one.
    if (myCookie == null)
      myCookie = new Cookie("CookieCounterServlet.number", "0");
    // Find out counter level and increase it.
    Integer number = new Integer(new Integer(myCookie.getValue()).intValue()
 + 1);
    // Set new counter level in cookie.
    myCookie.setValue(number.toString());

    // Set the cookie in the response.
    res.addCookie(myCookie);

    // Output message at the client.
    out.write("You have called this servlet " + number.toString() + "time(s).");
  }
} // End of the class
```

If we call the servlet with a browser, this message appears as required:

```
You have called this servlet 1 time(s).
```

At each additional call this value increases by 1. If you now close the browser and then start it again, the counter starts again at one. This is because browsers delete normal cookies when the program ends. A cookie can only outlive a browser if you explicitly set its duration to greater than zero by using setMaxAge(int expiry). In this case, expiry shows the maximum duration of the cookie in seconds. If you set a negative value, the cookie behaves normally. If you set a zero, the cookie is deleted.

In addition to the restrictions described above, the following limitations also apply to cookies:

- A browser cannot store more than 300 cookies.
- A cookie may only be 4 kbyte in size.
- Only 20 cookies may be used per domain or per server. This means that a maximum of 40 cookies can be sent to one server (20 per domain plus 20 per server).

Despite these restrictions, we must not underestimate the quantity of data that can be sent in cookies. Data volumes of 160 kbyte per request may occur. In extreme cases, for example for an HTML page with several pictures, the quantities of data to be transported may reach megabyte size. For this reason you must really ask yourself whether it makes sense to store such large amounts of data in cookies. It is more efficient to save a reference to the data which is present on the server in the cookie. The server already recognizes all the data contained in the cookie and why should you load the network with unnecessary data if a pointer is enough to do the job? Very often, this pointer is also a sessionID.

### 3.8.5 Sessions

A session is a coherent sequence of requests and responses between client and server. Because HTTP is a connection-free protocol, an identification must be sent along with each query and response to identify that several requests belong together. As described above, this is possible with cookies. Another option is to rewrite all the URLs contained in a Web page in such a way that they contain an identifier (a sessionID). This procedure is called URL rewriting.

#### *Basic session support*

Both options are supported by the servlet API. There are also corresponding methods both in the `HttpServletRequest` interface and in `HttpServletResponse`. The API also provides the `javax.servlet.http.HttpSession` interface which contains methods which ensure ease of handling for sessions.

Listing 3.11: The `SessionServlet` class

```
package de.webapp.Examples.Servlet;

import javax.servlet.http.*;
import javax.servlet.*;
import java.io.*;
import java.util.Date;

public class SessionServlet extends HttpServlet {
/**
Outputs values that belong with the session.
*/
public void doGet(HttpServletRequest req, HttpServletResponse res)
    throws ServletException, IOException {
  // Get a session. If none is present,
  // instantiate a new one.
  HttpSession session = req.getSession(true);

  // Set MIME type equals "text/html".
  res.setContentType("text/html");

  // Get a Writer.
  Writer out = res.getWriter();
  // Output title.
  out.write("<h2>SessionServlet</h2>");

  if (session == null) {
    // Report if no session could be reached.
    out.write("Could not reach a session.");
    return;
  }
  // Output SessionID.
```

```
        out.write("<b>Session-ID: </b>" + session.getId() + "<br>");
        // Has the session just been created?
        out.write("<b>Session is new: </b>" + session.isNew() + "<br>");
        // When was the session created?
        out.write("<b>Session created: </b>"
            + new Date(session.getCreationTime()) + "<br>");
        // When was the session last accessed?
        out.write("<b>Last accessed: </b>"
            + new Date(session.getLastAccessedTime()) + "<p>");
        // Which URL was used to access this servlet?
        String requestURL = HttpUtils.getRequestURL(req).toString();
        out.write("<b>Requested URL: </b>" + requestURL + "<br>");
        // What does this URL look like, encoded?
        String encodedURL = res.encodeUrl(requestURL);
        out.write("<b>Encoded URL: </b>" + encodedURL + "<br>");
        // What does this URL look like, encoded, if it
        // is supposed to act as a redirect?
        String redirectURL = res.encodeRedirectUrl(requestURL);
        out.write("<b>Encoded redirect URL: </b>" + redirectURL + "<p>");

        if (req.isRequestedSessionIdFromCookie()) {
            // If the session has been read from a cookie,
            // the reload URL does not need to be encoded.
            out.write("This SessionID has been read from a cookie.<p>");
            out.write("<a href='" + requestURL + "'>Reload</a>");
        }
        else {
            if (req.isRequestedSessionIdFromUrl())
            // Note only output if the SessionID really has
            // been reconstructed from the URL.
            out.write("This SessionID has been reconstructed from the URL.<p>");
            // Even so, always output an encoded URL.
            out.write("<a href='" + encodedURL + "'>Reload</a>");
        }
    }
} // End of the class
```

Our SessionServlet (Listing 3.11) gives an insight into the most important session
mechanisms. First of all HttpSession getSession(true) is used to obtain an
HttpSession object. The true argument ensures that a new object is instantiated
if one is not already present. The HttpSession getSession() method has the
same effect, but is only implemented from API Version 2.1 onwards. If you have to
create a new object, the boolean isNew() method returns the value true, otherwise it returns false. Here you should be aware that there are two situations which
may lead to a session being declared 'new'. One situation is that this may be a user's
first request. However, the second situation may be that the client does not support
cookies and no URL rewriting has been used. In this case the servlet engine shows

each client query as new because a `sessionID` has never been returned to it. In practice this means either that the consistent use of URL rewriting is required, which can require a lot of effort, or that you do not bind larger resources to new sessions. Added to this is the recommendation that, in public Web sites at least, a servlet engine should be used which makes it possible to restrict the maximum number of active sessions. Potential attackers could otherwise easily send the executing virtual machine (VM) into the realms of `OutOfMemoryException`. Another more cumbersome way of protecting yourself is to keep track of the number of created sessions yourself and, if attacked, simply not to create any new sessions.

One other condition to ensure that a session runs smoothly is to call up the `HttpSession getSession(boolean create)` method at least once before anything is written to the output stream.

The received session object has characteristics such as the creation date, last access etc. (Table 3.11), which we can output. In addition our servlet still shows what the called URL looked like. To get an insight into what a rewritten URL might look like, we shall reproduce this one (Fig. 3.5).

### Session as a data structure

You cannot use a session successfully until you have assigned objects to it. No one can achieve anything by just using the ID on its own. `HttpSession` has the methods `Object getAttribute(String name)`, `Enumeration getAttributeNames()`, `setAttribute(String name, Object value)` and `removeAttribute(String name)` for this purpose. Prior to servlet API 2.2 these methods were still called `Object getValue(String name)`, `String[] getValueNames()`, `putValue(String name, Object value)` and `removeValue(String name)`.

This means a session is actually a time-restricted valid data structure which is similar to a hash table with an expiry date. If a session is not used for a while and the expiry date is exceeded, it becomes invalid. Therefore, the `HttpSession` object and its values can no longer be accessed. This is useful because there is no implicit way of telling the session that it has ended. You cannot, and should not, rely upon users logging off. After all, the network might go down or the client computer might crash and the servlet engine would not even notice. This is why you need a timeout mechanism. Usually the maximum survival period of a non-active session is 30 minutes. A low-priority thread regularly checks to see whether a session has to be declared invalid.

If a session goes down while it is being used, you can use the `isRequested SessionIdValid()` method of the `HttpServletRequest` object to check whether the sent `sessionID` is still valid.

### Not 'til death do us part

It is useful if the objects bound to the session can be informed when they are bound and unbound. This is particularly advantageous for restricted or shared resources such as database connections or for memory-intensive object networks. The latter can be explicitly released if you no longer require them. To do this, objects can implement the `javax.servlet.http.HttpSessionBindingListener` interface. If they do so, the

**Table 3.11** HttpSession methods

| Method | Meaning |
|--------|---------|
| `long getCreationTime()` | Shows when this session began. The date should be entered in milliseconds since 1 January 1970 GMT. |
| `String getId()` | Returns the session ID assigned by the server. |
| `long getLastAccessedTime()` | Shows the last time the session was accessed prior to the current request. If the session is new, this method returns −1. |
| `boolean isNew()` | Shows whether this session is new. |
| `int getMaxInactiveInterval()` | Shows how long this session still remains valid without being accessed before it is automatically declared invalid by the servlet engine. The time is specified in seconds. |
| `void setMaxInactiveInterval (int seconds)` | Sets how long this session still remains valid without being accessed before it is automatically declared invalid by the servlet engine. The time is specified in seconds. |
| `Object getAttribute(String name)` | Returns an object saved in the session. |
| `Enumeration getAttributeNames()` | Returns a list of the names of all the attributes stored in a session. |
| `void setAttribute(String name, Object value)` | Creates an object using the name entered in the session. |
| `void removeAttribute(String name)` | Removes the attribute with the name entered, if this is present. |
| `void invalidate()` | Marks the session as invalid. All subsequent accesses to its methods cause `IllegalStateExceptions`. |
| `Object getValue(String name)` *deprecated* | Old version of `Object getAttribute(String name)` |
| `String[] getValueNames()` *deprecated* | Old version of `Enumeration getAttributeNames()` |
| `void putValue(String name, Object value)` | Old version of `void setAttribute(string name, object value)` |
| `void removeValue(String name)` | Old version of `void removeAttribute(String name)` |
| `HttpSessionContext getSessionContext()` *deprecated* | From Version 2.2 onwards, returns a dummy object, which has no functionality. |

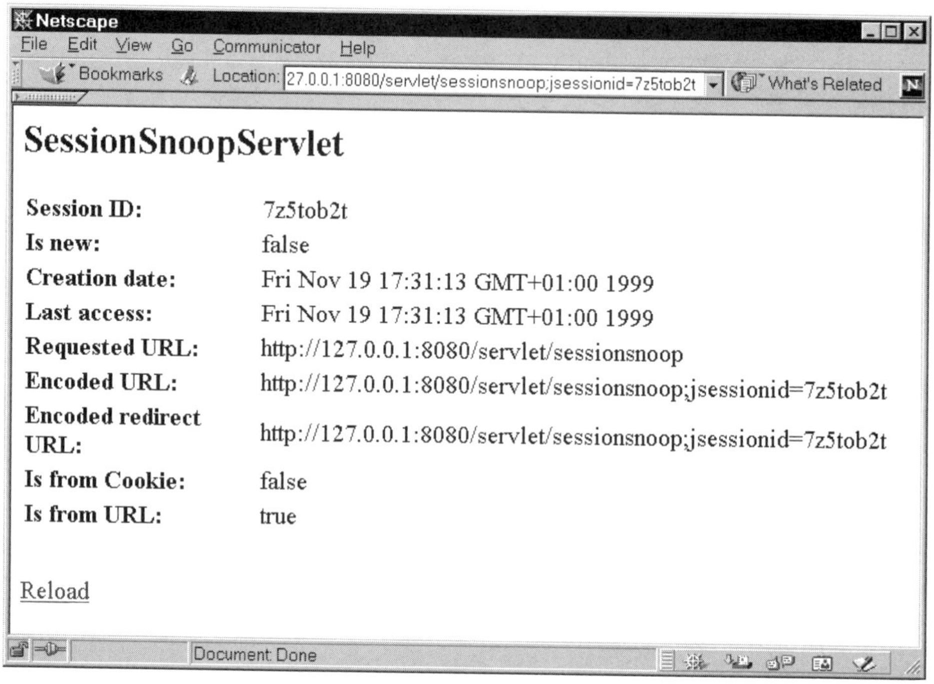

**Figure 3.5** SessionServlet output

valueBound(HttpSessionBindingEvent event) method is called if the object is bound, and the valueUnbound(HttpSessionBindingEvent event) method is called if the object is unbound. The HttpSessionBindingEvent event object transferred when you do this contains not only the source, but also the source name and the session to which the HttpSessionBindingListener is bound or unbound.

Listing 3.12: The SessionBindingServlet class

```
package de.webapp.Examples.Servlet;

import javax.servlet.http.*;
import javax.servlet.*;
import java.io.*;
import java.util.Date;

public class SessionBindingServlet extends HttpServlet {
public void doGet(HttpServletRequest req, HttpServletResponse res)
    throws ServletException, IOException {
  // Get a session. If no session is present,
  // instantiate a new one.
  HttpSession session = req.getSession(true);
```

```java
// As usual, set MIME type to "text/html" and get a Writer.
res.setContentType("text/html");
Writer out = res.getWriter();
// Output title.
out.write("<h2>SessionServlet2</h2>");

if (session == null) {
  // Report if no session could be reached.
  out.write("Could not reach a session.");
  return;
}
// Get the ID.
String sessionID = session.getId();

// Get servlet's own name.
String servletName = req.getContextPath() + req.getServletPath();

// check whether the session should expire.
// For simplicity's sake the only test is whether
// there is a query string.
if (req.getQueryString() != null) {
  session.invalidate();
  out.write("Session"+ sessionID +"has been deleted.<p>");
  out.write("<a href='" + servletName
    + "'>Create new session.</a>");
  return;
}

// Test if the session is new.
if (session.isNew()) {
  out.write("Session"+ sessionID
    +"has been successfully created.<p>");
  out.write("<a href='" + servletName
    + "'>Create big object.</a>");
  return;
}

// Query big object by session.
BigObject bigObject =
  (BigObject)session.getAttribute("bigObject");
if (bigObject == null) {
  // As there is no BigObject yet, instantiate one ...
  bigObject = new BigObject(getServletContext());
  // ... and bind it to the session.
  session.setAttribute("bigObject", bigObject);
  out.write("Big Object created and saved in session"
    + sessionID +".<p>");
  out.write("<a href='" + servletName
```

```
        + "'>Use Big Object.</a>");
      return;
    }
    // Use BigObject.
    bigObject.useMe();
    out.write("Big Object from session"+ sessionID
      +"has been used.<p>");
    out.write("<a href='" + servletName
      + "'>Re-use Big Object.</a><p>");
    out.write("<a href='" + servletName +
      "?expire'>Let session expire.</a>");
  }

} // End of the class

/** Dummy object which implements HttpSessionBindingListener. */
class BigObject implements HttpSessionBindingListener {
/** ServletContext which we need for logging. */
protected ServletContext context = null;

/** Here we only set the ServletContext. */
public BigObject(ServletContext context) {
  this.context = context;
}

/** Dummy method */
public void useMe() {
  log("Big Object has been used.");
}

/** Is called when an instance of this object is
bound to a session. */
public void valueBound(HttpSessionBindingEvent event) {
  String sessionID = event.getSession().getId();
  log("Big Object bound to session"+ sessionID
    + ".");
}

/** Is called when an instance of this object is
unbound from a session. */
public void valueUnbound(HttpSessionBindingEvent event) {
  String sessionID = event.getSession().getId();
  log("Big Object unbound from session"+ sessionID
    + ".");
}

/** Utility for logging */
public void log(String msg) {
  context.log("BigObject:"+ msg);
```

```
  }
} // End of the class
```

The example `SessionBindingServlet` (Listing 3.12) demonstrates how this is done. During the first call, a session is created, during the second a `BigObject` is instantiated and bound to the session via `setAttribute(String name, Object value)`. At the third call the user can use the object, at the fourth the object can be used again or the session allowed to expire. In this case the log file contains data to show if the object was bound, unbound or used.

The fact that there is a sequence of possible actions emphasizes that communications between client and server now have a status. A problem only occurs if the client (browser) does not accept cookies. The session then always appears to be new. For this reason we also do not create the `BigObject` until we are sure that the client supports cookie-based sessions. This is precisely what happens if the session is no longer new. If we did not do this, the resource-hungry `BigObject` would be instantiated anew for each client request and would be wide open to misuse.

We could, of course, also simply use URL rewriting. However, because URL rewriting requires a lot of effort, especially for larger applications (as each individual URL has to be changed), cookies seemed the easier option even if some browsers do not support cookies or refuse to accept them.

## 3.9  Diverting using `RequestDispatcher`

The `javax.servlet.RequestDispatcher` interface is used to bind a server's resources into a servlet, or to divert a query. This was introduced in Version 2.1 of the API. In this context 'resources' mean everything offered by the server for external access, e.g. servlets, files, CGI scripts. If, for example, the file contained in the URI `/index.html` is to be bound into the output of a servlet, a `RequestDispatcher` for this URI must first be requested from the servlet engine.

```
RequestDispatcher aDispatcher =
ServletContext.getRequestDispatcher("/index.html");
```

Here it is important that the URI is specified relative to the base of the `ServletContext`, if the dispatcher is requested via a `ServletContext`. If a context is therefore mapped on the `/myContext` URI, `getRequestDispatcher("/index.html")` finally references the URI `/myContext/index.html`. It behaves in a similar fashion if you request the dispatcher via the `ServletRequest` method with the same name. The only difference is that here the URI does not have to begin with a `/`, but can also be interpreted relative to the current request.

```
RequestDispatcher aDispatcher =
aServletRequest.getRequestDispatcher("LoginServlet?Name=Writer");
```

In both cases you can transfer arguments via a query string. These are arranged in front of the original request parameters, by the servlet container, for the duration of an include() or forward() call.

The getNamedDispatcher("aServletName") was introduced in servlet API 2.2 so that you do not have to struggle with URIs. You can use this method to request a RequestDispatcher for a named resource. This is usually a servlet or a Java server page, whose name the engine already knows.

Once you have received the RequestDispatcher, you can call its include(ServletRequest, ServletResponse) method, to include the output of /index.html in your own response. This procedure is particularly useful if a page consists of several elements. It is often a good idea to write identical page components, such as headers and footers, in extra files and then let the servlet add them automatically:

Listing 3.13: Example of RequestDispatcher.include() code

```
public void service(ServletRequest req, ServletResponse res)
   throws IOException, ServletException {
   res.setContentType("text/html");
   getServletContext().getRequestDispatcher("/header.html").include(req, res);
printBody(...);
   getServletContext().getRequestDispatcher("/footer.html").include(req,
res);
}
```

To ensure that the process runs smoothly, all the resources you include can access the Writer and the OutputStream servlet of the ServletResponse object. The setting of headers will be ignored.

Sometimes it is a good idea to be able to access the paths that led to the inclusion of a servlet from that bound servlet. For this purpose the servlet engine paths are stored as attributes in the request object. The corresponding attribute keys are:

```
javax.servlet.include.request_uri
javax.servlet.include.context_path
javax.servlet.include.servlet_path
javax.servlet.include.path_info
javax.servlet.include.query_string
```

In comparison to include(ServletRequest, ServletResponse) the forward(ServletRequest, ServletResponse) method has a slightly different significance. It can be used to transfer a request and not merely to bind the output of another resource. This is useful if, for example, the logic part of a process is to be separated from the display of its result. In this way, one servlet can carry out database operations while another carries out the formatted output of datasets. To transfer the datasets, you should attach them to the request with the ServletRequest.setAttribute(String, Object) method:

Listing 3.14: Example of RequestDispatcher.forward() code

```
public void service(ServletRequest req, ServletResponse res)
    throws IOException, ServletException {
    req.setAttribute("dbresult", getDBResult());
    getServletContext().getRequestDispatcher("/displayer").forward(req, res);
}
```

In contrast to `include()`, `forward()` enables you to set the header fields of the called resources. The prerequisite for this is that the called servlet has not yet finally sent any data to the client. `ServletResponse.isCommitted()` must therefore be false. If this is not the case, an `IllegalStateException` is triggered.

## 3.10  When in Rome, write like the Romans

In view of the global market-place, the internationalization of products is becoming ever more important. With Version 2.2 of the servlet API, Sun has given this even greater emphasis. There are two difficulties to overcome in this area: different languages and different character sets.

First we want to consider the character set problem. Let us assume that we have been given a lucrative order from a large Japanese company. How, you wonder, am I to encode my tasks in Japanese characters? After you have given this some considerable thought, without any result, here is the solution: unfortunately the character set is not set explicitly, but implicitly via the `setContentType(String content-type)` method of the response object. In fact, to do so, a character set is specified after the MIME type. Therefore, if you want to write Japanese, you must set the following content type:

```
text/html; charset=Shift_JIS
```

The same applies to all other character sets. If you do not specify a character set, ISO-8859-1 (Latin-1) is used automatically. This is a character set that is suitable for most western European languages, but will probably not be much use to your Japanese customers. Once you have set the content type, you can obtain an appropriate `PrintWriter` via `ServletResponse.getWriter()`.

In contrast, encoded data are read completely automatically. If you have requested a reader via `ServletRequest.getReader()`, this should be able to decode the data correctly as long as this has been correctly implemented by your servlet engine's manufacturer.

Now to the language problem. Unfortunately there is still no such thing as a fully automatic, reasonably priced translation system whose quality and speed is such that we need not translate texts manually. For this reason it often happens that otherwise identical files are present in several languages. As already described in the section about `ServletContext`, you can easily access these files in different languages via `URL getResource(String uri, Locale loc)`. If you now still want to inform the client that your output is in English or German, for example, you must set the corresponding Content-Language header:

```
HttpServletResponse.setHeader("Content-Language", "en"); // english
HttpServletResponse.setHeader("Content-Language", "de"); // german
```

If you find this too awkward, there is an alternative. Simply call up the `ServletRequest.setLocale(Locale loc)` method with the `Locale` of your choice and the servlet engine automatically sets the correct `Content-Language` header and character set. You should, of course, do this before you request a writer via `getWriter()`.

## 3.11 Real-life servlets

Now that we have explained the servlet API in sufficient detail we introduce three specially selected servlets to demonstrate how they are used in real life. The first one is a database servlet, followed by a mail servlet and a guest book.

### 3.11.1 Database servlet

Our aim here is to develop a very simple interface for a relational database. The only requirement placed on the database is the existence of a Java Database connectivity (JDBC) driver. Via the servlet, a user should be able to execute Structured Query Language (SQL) commands and display their results. A consequence of this is that the servlet must display an entry form when it is first called. Once the form has been sent off, the result should appear. In addition we want the form to be displayed again so that a new command can be executed immediately.

So far so good for the obvious requirements. When we implement them we encounter others. Typically, databases allow only a limited number of connections. In addition, setting up a connection takes a considerable amount of time and effort. For this reason, our servlet is to use only one connection for all queries. This connection is created during initialization and is dismantled when destroyed.

By doing this we have implicitly determined that the connection parameters must be defined in the servlet properties. For this reason, during initiation, our `JDBCServlet` (Listing 3.16) reads the `driverClass`, `url`, `user` and `password` parameters. The corresponding entries in the `servlets.properties` file look like this:

Listing 3.15: `servlets.properties` extract for a `JDBCServlet` which is 'solidly' bound to the Open Database Connectivity (ODBC) data source via the ODBC bridge produced by Sun

```
# JDBC servlet
jdbc.code=de.webapp.Examples.Servlet.JDBCServlet
jdbc.initArgs=user=aUser,password=userPassword,url=jdbc:odbc:solid,
driverClass=sun.jdbc.odbc.JdbcOdbcDriver
...
```

Using the data the servlet attempts to create a connection in the init() method. If it succeeds, the connection is stored for later use in the myConnection instance variable. If something goes wrong a ServletException is triggered.

Then the servlet requests the connection for any SQL warnings which may have occurred and, if required, writes them to the log. In the same way it learns about the connection metadata which is then stored in the myDatabaseMetaData instance variable. Now the JDBCServlet is ready for use.

During each subsequent call to the servlet, we check whether a query was sent as well. If this is not the case, we output only the HTML header, the connection metadata (URL and database driver name), the form and an HTML footer. However, if a query was also sent, between the metadata and form we also call the executeRequest method, which outputs the query. Then we test what type of SQL expression is involved. JDBC principally differentiates between reading, writing and other accesses. Once the type of command is identified, it is executed via the corresponding method.

To tell the user what is happening, the relevant feedback message is output. In the case of a SELECT expression this is a table (Fig. 3.6). In the case of writing accesses a message tells you how many datasets were changed. If you carry out other commands, this results in a message telling you if they have succeeded or failed.

Because the database connection we are using is a valuable resource, we have to tidy up after ourselves, if the servlet is destroyed. For this reason, destroy() closes the database connection and sets both instance variables myConnection and myDatabaseMetaData to null. To ensure that this happens if anything goes wrong when closing the connection, both these last definitions are present in a finally block.

Listing 3.16: The JDBCServlet class

```
package de.webapp.Examples.Servlet;

import java.io.*;
import java.util.*;
import java.sql.*;
import javax.servlet.*;
import javax.servlet.http.*;
import java.math.BigDecimal;

public class JDBCServlet extends HttpServlet {

/** Stops the database connection*/
protected Connection myConnection = null;
/** Database metadata */
protected DatabaseMetaData myDatabaseMetaData = null;
/** servlet info */
public String getServletInfo() {
   return "JDBCServlet";
}
```

**Figure 3.6**  Screenshot of a JDBC servlet

```
public void init(ServletConfig aConfig)
    throws ServletException {
  super.init(aConfig);
  String url = getInitParameter("url");
  String driverClass = getInitParameter("driverClass");
  String user = getInitParameter("user");
  String password = getInitParameter("password");
  if (url == null
    || driverClass == null
    || user == null
    || password == null)
      throw new ServletException("Missing init parameter\nURL:"
        + url + "\nDriverClass:"+ driverClass + "\nUser: "
        + user + "\nPassword:"+ password);
  try {
    // Load driver.
    Class.forName(driverClass);
    // Create connection.
    myConnection = DriverManager.getConnection(url, user, password);
    // Output warnings.
    checkForWarning(myConnection.getWarnings());
    // Get metadata.
```

```java
        myDatabaseMetaData = myConnection.getMetaData();
    }
    catch (Exception e) {
      throw new ServletException(e.toString());
    }
}

public void doGet(HttpServletRequest req, HttpServletResponse res)
        throws ServletException, IOException {
    res.setContentType("text/html");
    PrintWriter writer = res.getWriter();
    printHTMLHeader(writer);
    printMetaData(writer);
    String query = req.getParameter("query");
    if ( query != null
        && (!query.equals(""))) {
        executeQuery(writer, query);
    }
    printRequestForm(writer, req.getRequestURI());
    printHTMLFooter(writer);
}

protected void printRequestForm(PrintWriter writer, String servletPath)
      throws IOException {
    // Remove QueryString if present.
    int i = servletPath.indexOf('?');
    if (i != -1) servletPath = servletPath.substring(0, i);
    writer.println("<form method='get'action='"+servletPath+"'>");
    writer.println("Query : <input type=text size=30 name='query'>\n");
    writer.println(" <input type=submit value='Execute'>");
    writer.println("</form>");
}

protected void printMetaData(PrintWriter writer)
      throws IOException {
    try {
      if (myDatabaseMetaData != null) {
        writer.println("URL :"+ myDatabaseMetaData.getURL());
        writer.print("Driver:"+myDatabaseMetaData.getDriverName());
        writer.println(" -"+myDatabaseMetaData.getDriverVersion());
      }
    }
    catch (SQLException ex) {
      printException(ex, writer);
    }
}
```

```java
protected void printHTMLHeader(PrintWriter writer)
    throws IOException {
  writer.println("<html>");
  writer.println("<head><title>JDBCServlet</title></head>");
  writer.println("<body>");
  writer.println("<h2>JDBCServlet</h2>");
  writer.println("<pre>");
}

protected void printHTMLFooter(PrintWriter writer)
    throws IOException {
  writer.println("</pre>");
  writer.println("</body>");
  writer.println("</html>");
}

/** Executes the query. */
protected void executeQuery(PrintWriter writer, String query)
    throws IOException {
  // Display query.
  writer.println("Query :"+ query);
  try {
    Statement statement = myConnection.createStatement();
    query = query.trim();
    String lowerQuery = query.toLowerCase();
    if (lowerQuery.startsWith("select")) {
      showResultSet(statement.executeQuery(query), writer);
    }
    else if (lowerQuery.startsWith("insert")
      || lowerQuery.startsWith("delete")
      || lowerQuery.startsWith("update")) {
        writer.println(statement.executeUpdate(query)
          +"Data records successfully changed.");
    }
    else {
      writer.println("Execution "
        +(statement.execute(query)?" was successful.":" failed."));
    }
    statement.close();
  }
  catch (Exception ex) {
    printException(ex, writer);
  }
}

private void checkForWarning(SQLWarning warn)
    throws SQLException {
```

```
  if (warn != null) {
    log("*** A warning has occurred ***");
    while (warn != null) {
       log("SQLState:"+ warn.getSQLState()
          + "\nMessage :"+ warn.getMessage()
          + "\nVendor :"+ warn.getErrorCode());
       warn = warn.getNextWarning();
    }
  }
  else {
    log("*** Database connection created ***");
  }
}

/** Display the result as a table. */
private void showResultSet(ResultSet rs, PrintWriter writer)
    throws SQLException, IOException {
  if (rs == null) return;
  // The metadata are used to provide the column descriptions.
  ResultSetMetaData rsmd = rs.getMetaData();
  int numCols = rsmd.getColumnCount();
  writer.println("</pre>");
  writer.println("<table border=1 cellspacing=0 cellpadding=3>");
  writer.println("<tr>");
  // Output table column labels.
  for (int i=1; i<=numCols; i++) {
    writer.println("<th>" + rsmd.getColumnLabel(i) + "</th>");
  }
  writer.println("</tr>");
  // Output data...
  while (rs.next()) {
    writer.println("<tr>");
    // ...for each line of results:
    for (int i=1; i<=numCols; i++) {
       formatElement(rs, rsmd.getColumnType(i), writer, i);
    }
    writer.println("</tr>");
  }
  writer.println("</table>");
  writer.println("<pre>");
  rs.close();
}

/** Display an element */
private void formatElement(ResultSet rs, int dataType,
  PrintWriter writer, int col)
    throws SQLException, IOException {
```

```
      // Now format the data according to data type.
    switch (dataType) {
       case Types.BINARY:
       case Types.VARBINARY:
       case Types.LONGVARBINARY:
          byte[] binary = rs.getBytes(col);
          writer.println("<td>" + new String(binary, 0) + "</td>");
          break;
       default:
          writer.println("<td>" + rs.getObject(col).toString()+"</td>");
    }
}
/** Close the database connection that was being used*/
public void destroy() {
  try {
    if (myConnection != null) {
      myConnection.close();
      log("*** The database connection '" + myConnection.toString()
         + "' has been closed ***");
    }
  }
  catch (Exception e) {
    log("*** Error in closing database connection:"
       + e.toString() +"***");
  }
  finally {
    myConnection = null;
    myDatabaseMetaData = null;
  }
}

private void printException(SQLException ex, PrintWriter writer){
  writer.println("*** SQLException has occurred ***<p>");
  while (ex != null) {
    writer.println("SQLState:"+ ex.getSQLState() + "<br>");
    writer.println("Message:"+ ex.getMessage() + "<br>");
    writer.println("Vendor:"+ ex.getErrorCode() + "<br>");
    ex = ex.getNextException();
  }
}

private void printException(Exception ex, PrintWriter writer) {
  writer.println("*** An exception has occurred ***<p>");
  writer.println(ex.toString());
}
}
```

## 3.11.2  Mail servlet

Feedback forms have long been a vital item on each Web site. Often, beavering away in the background, is a little script that communicates with a mail server and transfers comments to the person in charge, via email. This can, of course, also be easily carried out with a servlet.

Our example servlet (Listing 3.17) should carry out a more general task, which is to send mails via any SMTP (Simple Mail Transfer Protocol) host. This means that we have to get a couple of items of data about the user: SMTP host, sender, address, subject and message. To make the whole process a little more comfortable you can choose to have the five parameters transferred to the servlet as initialization arguments.

Listing 3.17: The SMTPServlet class

```java
package de.webapp.Examples.Servlet;

import java.io.*;
import java.util.*;
import javax.servlet.http.*;
import javax.servlet.*;
import javax.mail.*;
import javax.mail.internet.*;

/** servlet that can send emails over SMTP. */
public class SMTPServlet extends HttpServlet {

/** Default SMTP host */
protected String myHost = null;

/** Default To-address */
protected String myTo = null;

/** Default From-address */
protected String myFrom = null;

/** Default Subject*/
protected String mySubject = null;

/** Default message*/
protected String myBody = null;

/** Sets the default values*/
public void init(ServletConfig aConfig)
     throws ServletException {
  super.init(aConfig);
  myHost = getInitParameter("host");
  myTo = getInitParameter("to");
  myFrom = getInitParameter("from");
  mySubject = getInitParameter("subject");
  myBody = getInitParameter("body");
}
```

```
/** Outputs the form in which the user enters the message. */
public void doGet(HttpServletRequest req, HttpServletResponse res)
        throws ServletException, IOException {
  res.setContentType("text/html");
  PrintWriter writer = res.getWriter();
  String actionPath = removeQueryString(req.getRequestURI());
  String host = req.getServerName();
  writer.println("<html>");
  writer.println("<head>\n<title>SMTPServlet</title>\n</head>");
  writer.println("<body>");
  writer.println("<h2>SMTPServlet</h2>");
  writer.println("<pre>");
  writer.println("<form action='" + actionPath + "' method='post'>");
  if (myHost == null)
    writer.println("Host    : <input name='host' type=text maxlength=100
size=50 value='" + host + "'>");
  if (myFrom == null)
    writer.println("From    : <input name='from' type=text maxlength=100
size=50>");
  if (myTo == null)
    writer.println("To      : <input name='to' type=text maxlength=100
size=50>");
  if (mySubject == null)
    writer.println("Subject : <input name='subject' type=text maxlength=100
size=50>");
  if (myBody == null)
    writer.println("          <textarea name='body' wrap='soft' cols='50'
rows='10'></textarea>\n");
  writer.println("          <input type='submit' value='Send'>");
  writer.println("</form>");
  writer.println("</pre>");
  writer.println("</body>");
  writer.println("</html>");
}

/** Sends the email */
public void doPost(HttpServletRequest req, HttpServletResponse res)
        throws ServletException, IOException {
  res.setContentType("text/html");

  // Your address
  String actionPath = removeQueryString(req.getRequestURI());
  PrintWriter writer = res.getWriter();

  // Write HTML header etc.
  writer.println("<html>\n<head>\n<title>SMTPServlet</title>\n</head>");
  writer.println("<body>");
```

```
writer.println("<h2>SMTPServlet</h2>");

// Load parameters.
String from = myFrom==null?req.getParameter("from"):myFrom;
String to = myTo==null?req.getParameter("to"):myTo;
String subject = mySubject==null?req.getParameter("subject"): mySubject;
String body = myBody==null?req.getParameter("body"):myBody;
String host = myHost==null?req.getParameter("host"):myHost;
if (host == null)
  host = req.getServerName();
if ( from == null
  || to == null
  || subject == null
  || body == null) {
    writer.println("At least one required parameter is missing.<p>");
}
else {
  // Get a mail session.
  Properties props = new Properties();
  props.put("mail.smtp.host", host);
  Session session = Session.getDefaultInstance(props, null);
  try {
    // Assemble the message object.
    StringTokenizer st = new StringTokenizer(to, ",;");
    int length = st.countTokens();
    InternetAddress[] toAddresses = new InternetAddress[length];
    for (int i=0; st.hasMoreTokens(); i++) {
      toAddresses[i] = new InternetAddress(st.nextToken());
    }
    Message msg = new MimeMessage(session);
    msg.setFrom(new InternetAddress(from));
    msg.setSubject(subject);
    msg.setRecipients(Message.RecipientType.TO, toAddresses);
    msg.setContent(body, "text/plain");

    // Send
    Transport.send(msg);
    writer.println("The message has been sent.<p>");
  }
  catch (MessagingException mex) {
    writer.println("A message occurred when the message was being
sent:<br><blockquote>"
        + mex.toString() + "</blockquote><p>");
  }
}
writer.println("<a href='" + actionPath + "'>New message</a>");
writer.println("</body>\n</html>");
```

```
    }

    protected static String removeQueryString(String aURI) {
        int i = aURI.indexOf('?');
        if (i != -1) aURI = aURI.substring(0, i);
        return aURI;
    }

    } // End of the class
```

The initialization arguments are contained in the servlets.properties file (Listing 3.18). In the same way, during initialization our servlet uses init() to read the parameters with the names host, to, from, subject and body and assigns the values of the corresponding instance variables.

Listing 3.18: Extract of possible servlets.properties for an SMTPServlet

```
...
# Mail servlet
mail.code=de.webapp.Examples.Servlet.SMTPServlet
mail.initArgs=host=my.host.de

# Feedback servlet
feedback.code=de.webapp.Examples.Servlet.SMTPServlet
feedback.initArgs=host=my.host.de,from=webapp.user,to=webapp@webapp.de,
subject=Criticism

...
```

If the servlet is now called via the GET method, a form appears in the user's browser window. Here the user must enter the missing information (Fig. 3.7). When they click on the Send button this returns the completed form to the servlet via POST. The tasks in the servlet are also clearly distributed: doGet() is merely used for display, doPost() actually does the work.

Once the remaining HTML lines have been written, the servlet loads the five required parameters. If no default value has been preset, the servlet uses HttpServletRequest.getParameter() to access the query's values. The host is also set to match the server name if it was not defined either in the request or the default values. If, after this, one parameter is still unfilled, an error message is returned to the browser.

If everything has gone according to plan, a mail session object is created for the host you entered and a message object is created and sent. With the support of the JavaMail API (available from JavaSoft: http://www.javasoft.com) this is very simple. Only the remaining four parameters must be transferred to the message object. Then it only remains to call Transport.send(Message).

Depending on how many parameters were predefined, the servlet can also be used as a universal mailer or feedback form.

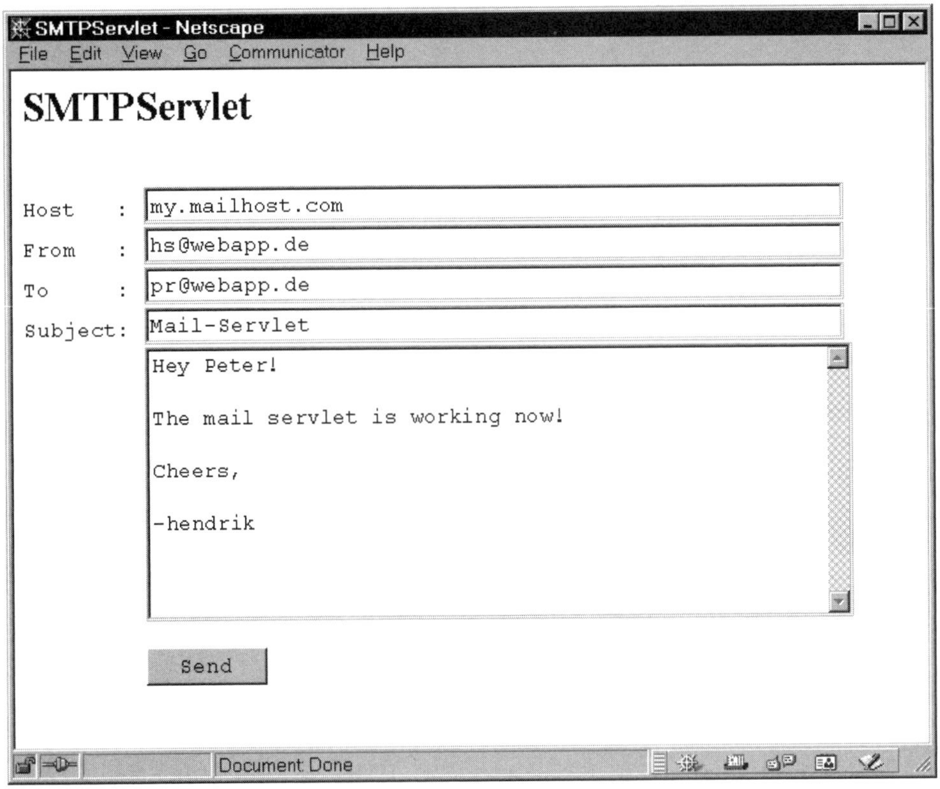

**Figure 3.7** Mail servlet, which has no pre-initialization

## 3.11.3 Guest book

These are the poetry albums of WWW: guest books, which are predominantly to be found on private homepages and are mostly filled with a lot of nonsense. Despite this they enjoy uninterrupted popularity and are regarded as one of the standard applications on the net. You can, of course, also implement them by using servlets.

Our guest book will fulfil all the usual functions. A form will allow users to enter comments along with their name and email address (Fig. 3.8). The 25 most recent entries in the guest book (in chronological order) will also be displayed on the same page. In addition to the author's name and address, each entry will show a time stamp and a number.

We must save our guest book to ensure that it still contains all the entries even after the server has been restarted. Because it involves a manageable quantity of data, and guest books do not usually possess a search function, we do not have to use a database and can therefore save the data on the local hard drive. The simplest way of doing this is to use Java's serialization mechanism.

When you start Guestbook (Listing 3.20) the first thing you must do is to load a guest book, assuming that one already exists. So that different instances of the servlet can display different books, we transfer the file name as an file initialization

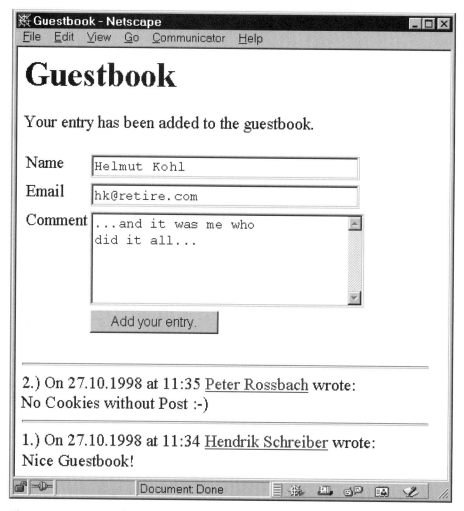

**Figure 3.8** Output of the guest book servlet

argument (Listing 3.19) and save it in the instance variable `myFile`. Now we only have to read the file. To do this, we open an `ObjectInputStream` in the `init()` method and read the `myEntries` vector. Later, the new comments will also be entered in this vector.

Listing 3.19: Possible `servlets.properties` extract for guest book

```
...
# Guestbook example
guestbook.code=de.webapp.Examples.Servlet.Guestbook
guestbook.initparams=file=johns-guestbook.serialized
...
```

If the servlet is to be destroyed, we first have to save the book. For this reason we open our `myFile` guest book file again in the `destroy()` method and write the `myEntries` vector via an `ObjectOutputStream` to this file. For this to function, the vector's elements must implement the `java.io.Serializable` interface.

But what kind of elements are they? It is a good idea to encapsulate each entry in an object. This leads us to the `GuestbookEntry` class. This has the relevant attributes Name, Email, Comment and Creation Date and is also able to output these in HTML via `toHTMLString()`. This class also implements the `Serializable` interface.

So, we have now sorted out loading and saving. Now we only have to explain how the service is provided. Just like in `SMTPServlet` we use the `GET` method to display the data and the `POST` method to do the work. In the same way, only the entry form and the guest book entries are displayed in `doGet()`. To do this, the `printForm(PrintWriter, String)` and `printEntries(PrintWriter, Http ServletRequest)` methods are called.

In the form, the servlet URI is entered as an `action` attribute and defined as the `POST` method. Although, according to the specifications, the `getRequestURI()` method returns the URI without a query string, this method has been incorrectly implemented in some engines (for example in JRun 2.1). For this reason, the servlet must call the `removeQueryString(String)` utility method in order to be compatible.

In addition to the actual display, the `printEntries()` method also has a scrolling mechanism in case the book has too many entries to display them on one page. The maximum number of entries per page is set to 25 in the `entriesPerPage` instance variable. In order to implement this mechanism, we have to know the entry from which the next 25 entries are to be displayed. This `offset` must also be transferred each time the servlet is called. If it is not transferred, it will start again at null. To use the scroll mechanism a reference with a correspondingly higher or lower `offset` must be displayed. This takes place in the `printEntries` method directly before the actual output of the entries, which takes place in a simple loop.

You will notice that the `printEntry` code is synchronized with the `myEntries` vector. This happens to prevent the vector being changed by other threads when it is outputting. This would severely disrupt the display algorithm.

The `doPost()` method is called if the form received via `doGet()` was sent by the client. This method has the job of adding an entry to the guest book. The `addEntry(PrintWriter, HttpServletRequest)` method is called for this purpose. The transferred parameters are read here and it attempts to instantiate a `GuestbookEntry` object. As the `GuestbookEntry` constructor triggers an `IllegalArgumentException` when faced with incorrect or missing parameters, it is easy to issue an appropriate message if errors occur. If everything goes smoothly, we can add the entry to the book and display the form and the entries.

Listing 3.20: Guestbook servlet

```
package de.webapp.Examples.Servlet;

import javax.servlet.http.*;
import javax.servlet.*;
```

```java
import java.io.*;
import java.util.*;
import java.text.*;

public class Guestbook extends HttpServlet {

/** Guestbook entries */
protected Vector myEntries = new Vector();
/** Guestbook file */
protected File myFile;
/** Entries per page*/
protected int entriesPerPage = 25;

public void init(ServletConfig aConfig)
      throws ServletException {
  super.init(aConfig);

  // Read file name.
  String myFilename = getInitParameter("file");
  // Set default.
  if (myFilename == null) {
    myFilename = new String("guestbook.serialized");
  }
  myFile = new File(myFilename);

  // Read guestbook if the file exists.
  if (myFile.exists()) {
    try {
      FileInputStream fileIn = new FileInputStream(myFile);
      ObjectInputStream objectIn = new ObjectInputStream(fileIn);
      myEntries = (Vector)objectIn.readObject();
      objectIn.close();
    }
    catch (Exception e) {
      log("Failed to read"+ myFilename + "."+ e);
    }
  }
}

public void doGet(HttpServletRequest req, HttpServletResponse res)
      throws ServletException, IOException {
  // Set MIME type equals "text/html".
  res.setContentType("text/html");
  PrintWriter out = res.getWriter();
  printHeader(out);
  printForm(out, req.getRequestURI());
  printEntries(out, req);
  printFooter(out);
}
```

```
public void doPost(HttpServletRequest req, HttpServletResponse res)
      throws ServletException, IOException {
   // Set MIME type equals "text/html".
   res.setContentType("text/html");
   PrintWriter out = res.getWriter();
   printHeader(out);
   addEntry(out, req);
   printFooter(out);
}

public void destroy() {
   try {
      FileOutputStream fileOut = new FileOutputStream(myFile);
      ObjectOutputStream objectOut = new ObjectOutputStream(fileOut);
      objectOut.writeObject(myEntries);
      objectOut.flush();
      objectOut.close();
   }
   catch (Exception e) {
      log("Failed to write guestbook to"+ myFile.toString() + "."+
e.toString());
   }
   super.destroy();
}

protected void printHeader(PrintWriter out) throws IOException {
   out.println("<html>");
   out.println("<title>Guestbook</title>");
   out.println("<body>");
   out.println("<h1>Guestbook</h1>");
}

protected void printFooter(PrintWriter out) throws IOException {
   out.println("</body>");
   out.println("</html>");
}

protected void printForm(PrintWriter out, String submituri) throws
IOException {
   int offset
   try {
      offset = Integer.parseInt(req.getParameter("offset"));
   }
   catch (NumberFormatException nfe) {
      offset = 0;
   }
   out.println("<form method='post' action='" + removeQueryString(submituri)
+ "'>");
```

```
      out.println("<input type=hidden name='offset' value='" + offset + "'>");
      out.println("<table border=0>");
      out.println("<tr><td valign=top>Name</td>");
      out.println("<td><input type='text' name='name' size=30
maxlength=60></td></tr>");
      out.println("<tr><td valign=top>Email</td>");
      out.println("<td><input type='text' name='email' size=30
maxlength=80></td></tr>");
      out.println("<tr><td valign=top>Comment</td>");
      out.println("<td><textarea name='comment' rows=5 cols=30
wrap='virtual'></textarea></td></tr>");
      out.println("<tr><td> </td><td><input type='submit' value='Add your
entry.'></td></tr>");
      out.println("</table>");
      out.println("</form>");
  }

  protected void printEntries(PrintWriter out, HttpServletRequest req)
      throws IOException {
    synchronized (myEntries) {
      // Paging
      int offset;
      try {
        offset = Integer.parseInt(req.getParameter("offset"));
      }
      catch (NumberFormatException nfe) {
        offset = 0;
      }
      if (myEntries.size() > entriesPerPage) {
        if (offset > 0) {
          int previous = offset - entriesPerPage;
          out.println("<a href='" + removeQueryString(req.getRequestURI())
          + "?offset=" + previous + "'>[previous page]</a> ");
        }
        if (offset + entriesPerPage < myEntries.size()) {
          int next = offset + entriesPerPage;
          out.println("<a href='" + removeQueryString(req.getRequestURI())
          + "?offset=" + next + "'>[next page]</a>");
        }
      }
      // Print entries.
      for (int i=offset; i<myEntries.size() && i < offset+entriesPerPage;
i++) {
        GuestbookEntry entry = (GuestbookEntry)myEntries.elementAt(i);
        int number = myEntries.size()-i;
        out.println("<hr>");
```

```
      out.println(Integer.toString(number) + ".)"+ entry.toHTMLString());
    }
  }
}

protected void addEntry(PrintWriter out, HttpServletRequest req)
    throws IOException {
  String name = req.getParameter("name");
  String email = req.getParameter("email");
  String comment = req.getParameter("comment");
  try {
    GuestbookEntry entry = new GuestbookEntry(name, email, comment);
    myEntries.insertElementAt(entry, 0);
    out.println("Your entry has been added to the guestbook.<p>");
    printForm(out, req.getRequestURI());
    printEntries(out, req);
  }
  catch(IllegalArgumentException iae) {
    out.println("At least one field is missing or incorrect.<br>");
    out.println("Please try again.<p>");
    printForm(out, req.getRequestURI());
  }
}
protected static String removeQueryString(String aURI) {
  int i = aURI.indexOf('?');
  if (i != -1) aURI = aURI.substring(0, i);
  return aURI;
}
} // End of the class

class GuestbookEntry implements Serializable {

/** Name of the person making the entry*/
protected String myName;
/** E-mail address of the person making the entry */
protected String myEmail;
/** Comment */
protected String myComment;
/** Date created*/
protected Date myCreationDate;

/** No-argument constructor */
public GuestbookEntry() {}

public GuestbookEntry(String name, String email, String comment) {
  if (name == null) throw new IllegalArgumentException();
  myName = name;

  if (email == null) throw new IllegalArgumentException();
```

```
       if (email.indexOf("@") == -1) throw new IllegalArgumentException();
       myEmail = email;

       if (comment == null) throw new IllegalArgumentException();
       myComment = comment;

       myCreationDate = new Date();
    }
    public String toHTMLString() {
       SimpleDateFormat formatter = new SimpleDateFormat ("'On' dd.MM.yyyy 'at'
HH:mm");
       return formatter.format(myCreationDate) +"<a href='mailto:"
          + myEmail + "'>" + myName + "</a> wrote:<br>" + myComment;
    }
    } // End of the class
```

## 3.12 Security

You cannot avoid the subject of security if you want to program real applications as well as simple servlets. Generally speaking, there are four aspects of this subject:

- Authentification: a user must prove his or her identity to the server and vice versa.
- Access control: only a specific group of users are permitted to access resources.
- Integrity: ensures that the data are not in any way changed while being transferred.
- Confidentiality: ensures that third parties cannot eavesdrop on the data while they are being transferred.

All four points are present in one or other API methods or in the deployment descriptor. First, let us have a look at the options for authentification.

### 3.12.1 Authentification

Would you tell everyone your credit card number? Of course not. You give your credit card numbers to those people or companies whom you trust, or at least those who appear to be trustworthy. The same applies in the net, only you cannot, unfortunately, see the people you are dealing with. To ensure that you pass on your credit card number only to someone you trust, this person must identify (authenticate) themselves. The reverse happens with programs at login. To have the right to use the program you must prove to the system (by using a password) that you are who you claim to be. Authentification is also a fundamental prerequisite for commercial and computer security. The servlet API supports three authentification procedures:

- HTTP basic authentification;
- HTTP digest authentification;
- HTTPS client authentification.

HTTP basic and HTTP digest authentification are both defined in HTTP/1.1 (RFC 2617). Whereas the basic variant passwords are transferred in more or less clear text, which is easy to eavesdrop on or manipulate, the digest version encodes the password and is hard to manipulate. However, it can still be eavesdropped upon. In addition, digest authentification is still not supported by all commonly used browsers.

If you want to protect yourself against eavesdroppers, you should turn to other procedures, such as Virtual Private Networks (VPN) or HTTPS (HTTP via SSL). The encoding in these is secure enough that you can rely on otherwise insecure procedures such as HTTP basic authentification. If you find that even typing in a login and password is too insecure, you can also request, in the case of SSL, an X.509 certificate, which unambiguously identifies the client. This procedure is called HTTPS client authentification. In the case of an SSL connection using Java 2 an object of the `java.security.cert.X509Certificate` type is stored as the `javax.servlet.request.X509Certificate request` attribute.

However, all these procedures have a disadvantage: they just do not look good. If you want to influence the login dialogue, you must switch to using normal HTTP forms with all their insecurities. Unfortunately, the procedure for this was not sufficiently specified at the time this book went to print. So we have no alternative other than to refer you to the servlet API specification, which should by now contain a precise description of this procedure.

### 3.12.2 Program-based security

Even after successful authentification, the problem of security is usually not completely solved. At least you now know who is sitting on the other end of the connection. However, it is not yet certain what kind of rights this person has. Basically there are two ways of finding this out: by configuration or by program-based measures. The latter is made possible via the methods provided by `HttpServletRequest`. These methods are:

```
String getRemoteUser()
boolean isUserInRole(String role)
java.Security.Principal getUserPrincipal()
boolean isSecure()
```

Let us have a closer look at these methods. If the user has been authenticated in one way or another, `getRemoteUser()` returns the login name. If he or she has not been authenticated the method returns `null`. In this case `getUserPrincipal()` also returns `null` and `isUserInRole()` is false. So much for the simple scenarios. To describe the methods in greater detail we first have to to explain a couple of terms. We shall start with the role.

You can assign uniquely identifiable, handling objects to a role. These may be, for example, users, groups and even clients, which are connected to your server via a particular network segment. You can assign such roles as 'employee', 'administrator' or 'programmer'. Just as in real life, people take on various roles. A 'programmer' can theoretically also be an 'administrator', which may lead to a conflict of roles in a practical sense, but is more likely to be a sociological problem. The fact remains that roles are linked to different privileges. Furthermore, roles can be mapped to individual users as well as to groups.

This leaves us in the happy situation that, although you can use existing user and group data to manage privileges within a Web application, you do not have to use them one-to-one. The role provides a more far-reaching level of abstraction, particularly if you want to install different Web applications, for which different usage restrictions are defined.

In practice you assign a role to existing users and groups and grant this role certain privileges within your application. Whereas the first assignment is carried out in your servlet engine and depends on the manufacturer, you can carry out the second assignment in the deployment descriptor.

We still have to explain the term `Principal`. You can best compare a `Principal` with a legal entity. In a court of law, a limited company or a sports club can be handled just like a person made of flesh and blood. You can regard a `Principal` in the same way.

Here is an example: Jane and Peter both have a login on their employer's computer system. Because this is an advanced system based on Java 2, an object is present for both people with the `java.security.Principal` interface. This object represents them in the application. However, Jane lives in Birmingham and Peter lives in Boston. And as fate has it, the privileges for people from Birmingham are different from those from Boston. There is also a 'Birmingham' group and a 'Boston' group. Both groups are in turn represented in the application by a `Principal`. As part of a restructuring program, the company decides to introduce teleworking. The 'administrator', who is also naturally enough represented within the application by a `Principal` object, has therefore installed a Web interface based on servlet API 2.2. It becomes evident that Jane also requires the Boston privileges so that she can work effectively over the Web. However, this should apply only to Web access. The 'administrator' therefore assigns the 'BostonNetworkAccess' role to the 'Boston' group and the user 'Jane'. It only assigns the 'BirminghamNetworkAccess' to the 'Birmingham' group.

If the `getUserPrincipal()` method is now called in the program, the corresponding `Principal` object is returned so long as the user has been authenticated. In this case it is always the `Principal` object that matches most closely that is returned. So in the case of Peter this is not the 'Boston' object, but the `Principal` object that matches Peter perfectly, i.e. the corresponding user object.

Sometimes you may want to check in the program not only whether someone has logged in according to their privileges but also which role they are currently using. You use the `isUserInRole()` method to do this. This shows whether the user is in a particular role.

Assume that our 'administrator', introduced above, is not only the master of system crash and restart, but is at the same time a dyed-in-the-wool 'Bostonian'. 'Bostonians' are of course trustworthy people, but there are some things they should really leave to the 'administrator'. For this reason their privileges are more restricted in comparison with those of the 'administrator'. If the 'administrator' logs in now, it may happen that they do so on a page that does not require extra privileges. However, if they then navigate to a page that is available only to the 'administrator', the program has to check whether they are authorized to use this page. This could be achieved by calling `HttpServletRequest.isUserInRole('Administrator')`.

Finally, it may be that some of the 'administrator' operations are only permitted via a protocol that is protected from eavesdroppers or manipulation. To ensure this using programming methods, you can use the `isSecure()` method of the request. This tells you whether the request was transferred via a secure protocol.

### 3.12.3  Declarative security

All well and good, but on-going provision of security using programming methods requires rather a lot of effort. For this reason, you can use the deployment descriptor as a simple and manageable alternative means of configuring security measures.

For this purpose you can enter a collection of your Web application's resources, for which certain security conditions apply. You will find an example of this in the next section.

## 3.13  Web applications

Have you ever tried to port a CGI-based application from one operating system with one particular server to another operating system on another server? If the servlet engine manufacturer complies with the specifications you can do this simply via servlets and Java Server Pages from Version 2.2 of the servlet API. The Web application concept is what makes this possible. It ensures that servlets, Java Server pages, classes, files and other resources are bound together in a Web archive (war) and can therefore be very easily installed (Plug'n'Play) on a system which conforms to 2.2.

The essential prerequisite for this is a standardized configuration method. This is provided by the deployment descriptor which you can find in the `web.xml` file in the `/WEB-INF` directory.

A Web archive has the following structure:

```
/index.html
/revenues.jsp
/feedback.jsp
/images/logo.gif
/images/howtofindussketch.gif
/WEB-INF/web.xml
/WEB-INF/lib/logic.jar
```

```
/WEB-INF/classes/com/mycompany/servlets/MyServlet.class
/WEB-INF/classes/com/mycompany/util/MyUtility.class
```

The /WEB-INF/lib/ directory contains the Java ARchive (jar) that the application requires. All the remaining classes or resources which must be present in the application's class path are found in /WEB-INF/classes/. All the other files of the Web archive are resources which are supplied to the user on request.

The following information is coded in the deployment descriptor:

- Initialization parameters of the ServletContext.
- Session configuration.
- Definitions of servlet and Java Server pages.
- Servlet and Java Server page mappings.
- MIME type mappings.
- Welcome file list.
- Error pages.
- Security.

You will find a more detailed definition of the descriptor specified in XML (and therefore the commented DTD) in Appendix C. Here, we shall only discuss some important points as an example. By the time you read this manual we hope there will be tools with graphical user interface which will save you the effort of coding a descriptor by hand.

### 3.13.1    Minimal deployment descriptor

In order to install a HelloWorld servlet as described in Section 3.3, a minimal deployment descriptor has to look like this:

Listing 3.21: Minimal deployment descriptor for HelloWorld

```
<!DOCTYPE web-app PUBLIC "-//Sun Microsystems, Inc.//DTD Web Application
1.2//EN" "http://java.sun.com/j2ee/dtds/web-app_2_2.dtd">
<web-app>
  <servlet>
    <servlet-name>HelloWorld</servlet-name>
    <servlet-class>de.webapp.Examples.Servlets.HelloWorld</servlet-class>
  </servlet>
  <servlet-mapping>
    <servlet-name>HelloWorld</servlet-name>
    <url-pattern>/HelloWorld</url-pattern>
  </servlet-mapping>
</web-app>
```

As usual in XML documents, the DTD is defined in the first line. This line is therefore obligatory. It is followed by the equally obligatory basic brackets consisting of the start tag <web-app> and the end tag </web-app>. Within these brackets there is the definition of your Web application. As in Section 3.3, in `<servlet>` `...</servlet>` we now define a servlet by a name and a class. Then we define an assignment of the named servlet to a URL pattern (`<url-pattern>...</url-pattern>`). In contrast to the many assignments that are, we hope, no longer in use when you read these lines, this mapping is clearly defined.

- URL patterns that start with a forward slash (`'/'`) and end with a forward slash followed by an asterisk (`'/*'`) describe a path mapping. This means that even URLs that are longer than patterns, but that start in the same way apart from the asterisk, will match this pattern. In this way the asterisk functions as a wildcard.
- URL patterns that start with an asterisk followed by a full stop (`'*.'`) represent an extension mapping. URLs that end in the same way, apart from the asterisk, match this pattern.
- URL patterns that consist only of a forward slash (`'/'`) match if no other option matches (default mapping).
- All other patterns must correspond exactly to the requested URL in order to match.

Of course, one URL can satisfy several of these patterns. For this reason there is a definite sequence in which the servlet engine has to use the patterns. It first searches for an exact match. If no pattern matches exactly, it searches for the longest valid path mapping. If this is also not present it searches for a valid extension mapping. In this case only the last dot within a URL is involved. Other points within the URL are ignored. If no match is found here either, the default mapping finally gets a look in. This is usually implicitly predefined by the engine's file servlet.

### 3.13.2 Deployment descriptor for advanced users

This example is a bit more complicated.

Listing 3.22: Example of a deployment descriptor

```
<!DOCTYPE web-app PUBLIC "-//Sun Microsystems, Inc.//DTD Web Application
2.2//EN" "http://java.sun.com/j2ee/dtds/web-app_1_2.dtd">
<web-app>
  <display-name>A simple application</display-name>
  <icon>
    <small-icon>/images/smallApplicationsIcon.gif</smallicon>
    <large-icon>/images/largeApplicationsIcon.gif</large-icon>
  </icon>
  <description>Description of an example application which doesn't actually
  do anything.</description>
  <context-param>
    <param-name>webmaster</param-name>
    <param-value>webmaster@webapp.de</param-value>
  </context-param>
  <servlet>
    <servlet-name>Example</servlet-name>
```

```
            <servlet-class>de.webapp.Examples.Servlets.Example</servlet-class>
            <init-param>
                <param-name>fineExample?</param-name>
                <param-value>jo!</param-value>
            </init-param>
        </servlet>
        <servlet-mapping>
            <servlet-name>Example</servlet-name>
            <url-pattern>/Example</url-pattern>
        </servlet-mapping>
        <mime-mapping>
            <extension>pdf</extension>
            <mime-type>application/pdf</mime-type>
        </mime-mapping>
        <welcome-file-list>
            <welcome-file>index.jsp</welcome-file>
            <welcome-file>index.html</welcome-file>
        </welcome-file-list>
        <error-page>
            <error-code>404</error-code>
            <location>/errors/fileNotFound.html</location>
        </error-page>
        <error-page>
            <exception-type>java.io.FileNotFoundException</exception-type>
            <location>/errors/fileNotFound.html</location>
        </error-page>
    </web-app>
```

When designing a deployment descriptor you must ensure that it can be easily processed by tools with a graphical user interface. From there you can assign meta-information such as a name (<display-name>...</display-name>) and a description (<description>...</description>) to the deployment descriptor of your Web application. It is also equally easy to use icons to give the abstract application a face (<icon>...</icon>). Alongside these soft parameters, which are not essential to the functioning of the application, there are, of course, also hard ones.

To transfer the ServletContext initialization parameter, you must set it with the <context-param>...</context-param> tag. You can set the initialization arguments for servlets in a similar way.

Our example contains files in .pdf format. As we are not sure whether the server recognizes the MIME type for .pdf, we have to register it. We do this via the marking <mime-mapping>...</mime-mapping>. With the help of <welcome-file-list>...</welcome-file-list> we can specify which files are to be supplied if the client does not specifically request one. The sequence of the files specified here is the same as that used during a search.

Finally we come to <error-page>...</error-page>. This gives you the means of handling errors in an extremely elegant application-specific way. Alternatively you can specify either an exception type (`<exception-type>...</exception-type>`) or an HTTP error code (`<error-code>...</error-code>`). If either of these situations occurs, the resource specified in `<location>...</location>` is displayed instead of the usual error message. If this is an active resource such as a Java server page, it can access the following request attribute, if this is appropriate:

```
javax.servlet.error.status_code
javax.servlet.error.exception_type
javax.servlet.error.message
```

### 3.13.3  Deployment descriptor for secure applications

In our next example we shall describe a deployment descriptor for a 'secure' application.

Listing 3.23: Deployment descriptor of a secure application

```
<!DOCTYPE web-app PUBLIC "-//Sun Microsystems, Inc.//DTD Web Application
1.2//EN" "http://java.sun.com/j2ee/dtds/web-app_1_2.dtd">
<web-app>
   <display-name>A secure application</display-name>
   <security-role>
      <role-name>Administrator</role-name>
   </security-role>
   <servlet>
      <servlet-name>SecureServlet</servlet-name>
      <servlet-class>de.webapp.Examples.Servlets.SecureServlet</servlet-
class>
      <security-role-ref>
         <role-name>admin</role-name> <!-- the role name that is used in the
code -->
         <role-link>Administrator</role-link> <!--the configuration name of
a security role -->
      </security-role-ref>
   </servlet>
   <servlet-mapping>
      <servlet-name>SecureServlet</servlet-name>
      <url-pattern>/admin</url-pattern>
   </servlet-mapping>
   <web-resource-collection>
      <web-resource-name>RestrictedArea</web-resource-name>
      <url-pattern>/admin</url-pattern>
      <url-pattern>/internal/*</url-pattern>
      <http-method>GET</http-method>
      <http-method>POST</http-method>
      <user-data-constraint>
         <transport-guarantee>CONFIDENTIAL</transport-guarantee>
```

```
        </user-data-constraint>
        <auth-constraint>
          <role-name>Administrator</role-name>
        </auth-constraint>
     </web-resource-collection>
   </web-app>
```

In contrast to the deployment descriptors we have already discussed, a security role is defined in this one in `<security-role>...</security-role>`. There are references to this security role from two places. The first reference is located in the `<security-role-ref>...</security-role-ref>` marking of the `servlet`. Here the security role is assigned an alias which is used in the code. In our example the reference refers to the role `<role-link>Administrator</role-link>` and the alias `<role-name>admin</role-name>`.

The second reference to the security role is located in `<web-resource-collection>... <auth-constraint><role-name>Administrator</role-name></auth-constraint></web-resource-collection>`. It tells you that the resources defined via `<web-resource-collection>...</web-resource-collection>` are subject to the authentification structure of the Administrator role. You can specify which resources are involved by using `<url-pattern>...</url-pattern>` and `<http-method>...</http-method>`. If you were not to specify a method here, the restrictions would apply to all the methods. In addition, in the item `<user-data-constraints>...</user-data-constraints>`, a certain quality of communication is requested via `<transport-guarantee>CONFIDENTIAL</transport-guarantee>`. In addition to CONFIDENTIAL, other possible values are NONE and INTEGRAL (unfalsified transfer).

Although our three examples are really pretty comprehensive they have by no means exhausted the possibilities of the deployment descriptor. In addition to those things we have already described there are still a few more to deal with. These include, among others, how the Java 2 Enterprise Edition (J2EE) accesses resources. However, this would be to wander away from the subject of this book, although we regard the J2EE concept as successful and far-reaching.

# WebApp-Framework

U sing a specifically adapted framework is a vital prerequisite for being able to create Web-based applications quickly and effectively. In this part of the book we introduce the basic elements required for a framework for a Web-based application server and explain how they are created. The resulting WebApp framework (Fig. II.1) is available as a package on the `http://www.webapp.de` website, which accompanies the book.

Three topics are important when developing Web-based applications:

1. the Web server's programming interface;

2. the application layer;

3. how to generate HTML.

We have used the servlet API (which is described in detail in Chapter 3) as the interface for the Web server. As the application layer we used the part of a Web application that contains the application logic. This specifically does not include the user interface, because although this is needed for process control, it does not carry the application and it should be possible to use different user interfaces. For this reason a separate, third area is used to describe how HTML is generated.

This part of the book covers all these three areas. As an introduction we start with the basic application services required for configuration and protocolling. These are described in Chapters 4 and 5. This is followed, in Chapter 6, by basic information on how to create powerful servers. For this purpose, a reusable foundation for thread management was developed. In Chapter 7 we use the server package as the basis for designing the servlet engine jo!. Here you get a detailed insight into jo!'s architecture which allows you to build up your knowledge of servlet technology. The same applies to Chapter 8. Here we develop SMI (Servlet Method Invocation). This is an extension of the Servlet API. SMI allows you to create a highly configurable, modular application architecture, more or less behind a servlet. In Chapter 9 we go into exhaustive detail about the object-oriented encapsulation of relational databases for the use of company data. The `Persistence` service described here is one of the pillars of the framework, because it allows easy-to-program database access. In the last chapter of this part of the book we describe the possibilities offered for dynamic HTML

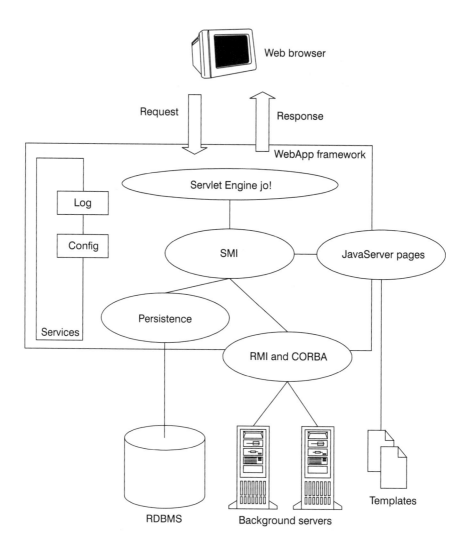

**Figure II.1** Architecture of the WebApp framework

generation. We introduce the quickly evolving techniques that are currently available, in particular Java Server pages.

Now that you have an overview of the contents of this second part of the book, a few things can be discussed about the WebApp framework. What do you expect from a framework that is used to construct Web-based applications? It should, of course, be extremely flexible, be able to suit various areas of application and still cover as many areas of application as possible. By working through a few short steps,

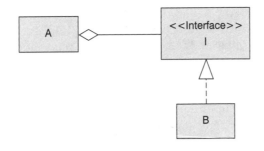

**Figure II.2** Decoupling of the design using interfaces

the framework should allow you to create a reliable, extendible application or at least a part of an application. To ensure this, it must be possible to modify the framework as required. One vital characteristic is therefore its configurability. In order to guarantee this, the WebApp framework has the `ConfigManager` configuration manager. This is used to read configuration data which plays a decisive role in how the application behaves.

Despite this, the purpose of individual framework parts is, of course, predefined. You cannot use configurations from a database layer to create a graphics package. If this happens, something critical has gone wrong at the design stage. Frameworks or parts of a framework should always serve a specific purpose. This usually happens in a particular way. Parts of the framework need other parts. Just as the framework itself must have a defined interface, all parts of the framework should also communicate via defined interfaces. In Java this can be carried out in an extremely elegant manner by the intensive use of interfaces. You define what an object must be able to do, and how it does it can remain a secret. Interfaces make it possible to exchange, improve and extend parts of the framework without a great deal of fuss (Fig. II.2).

In addition to interfaces, the WebApp framework makes extensive use of another of Java's features: generic binding makes it possible to integrate application parts in the program when they are needed, at run-time.

For example: Object A requires the capabilities of another object, to complete a task. A knows that an object which has implemented interface I can fulfil this task. The only thing it therefore needs is an instance of a class that implements interface I. If it knows the relevant class name, A can use the `java.lang.Class.forName(String)` method to obtain a class object. In turn, the `Class` object has the `newInstance()` method with which it can create instances of Class B at run-time.

The trick here, in frameworks, is to work as far as possible with objects of the type of one particular interface, instead of explicitly using the type of the class that the interface implements. In this way you can use configurations to define retrospectively which class should actually be used. So that you do not have to do entirely without formal checks, a type check is carried out by using type conversions (Castings). At the end of the day, it must be possible to convert each class that is created into an interface type.

Large parts of the WebApp framework implement this design principle. The framework behaviour is defined in interfaces. The actual implementation in classes is simply shown as an example and could also be carried out in another way. This is the only way to guarantee the highest possible levels of flexibility. Naturally, this must be matched by intelligent implementation of defaults. It is wonderful to be able to change everything, but even better when everything is already just the way you want it. For this reason, most components have standard, default settings which make configuration much, much easier.

# Configuration management

# 4

In the WebApp framework most components can be configured using the ConfigManager. This concerns different configurations: for example, the configuration manager is not only used to manage simple application data such as the IP address of a server, or a user's settings, but also configuration data that are required to create an application. This is the case, for example, if a suitable class is required for an interface. Configurability is a central issue for the WebApp framework.

The configuration manager should be able to reply to all the important configuration questions for the components in the framework and applications. A result of this is that there can be only one configuration manager per system (JVM), and it must be accessible and available from all points in the framework. It also means that no sensitive information should be managed using the configuration manager.

Of course, it should be possible not only to read the configuration data, but also to write it. When doing so, the format and memory location should essentially be freely selectable. However, there should be a standard format in which information can be stored hierarchically and in a modular way. It should be possible to inform observers as soon as configuration data changes. In addition, the ConfigManager should support comfortable defaulting (the use of default values).

To sum up, the ConfigManager must therefore satisfy the following requirements:

- easy accessibility;
- no restriction to particular memory locations or storage media, but instead access via URL;
- support for hierarchical data structures;
- non-format-specific;
- use of defaults.

## 4.1 Easy accessibility

To ensure that ConfigManager is accessible and unique, it is implemented as a singleton (Gamma *et al.* 1996). The singleton pattern ensures that there is only ever one instance of a class. In addition, an easily accessible access point to this instance is also provided. To achieve this, the class is declared `private` to the constructor. As a result, only the class itself can call the constructor. This call must be carried out via a method that has been declared `static`. If, when you call the static method for the first time, you store the generated instance in a class variable, then next time the method is called, a check can be made to see if it has already been called before. If so, the instance referenced by the class variable is returned, otherwise a new instance is generated and stored in the class variable (Listing 4.1). To ensure that two almost simultaneous calls to the method do not prevent each other from working, it is important that the checking of the class variable and, if relevant, the instantiation, are located in a synchronized block. However, in order to avoid the resource-intensive call to the synchronized block whenever possible, we shall now check if it is really necessary to use it at all.

Listing 4.1: Singleton that ensures safe operation of threads

```
public class Singleton {
  private static Singleton mySingleton = null;
  private Singleton () {}
  public static Singleton getInstance() {
    if (mySingleton == null) { // must we execute the synchronized block?
      synchronized (Singleton.class) {
        if (mySingleton == null) { // check there is still no instance yet
          mySingleton = new Singleton ();
        }
      }
    }
    return mySingleton;
  }
}
```

The `ConfigManager` implements exactly this principle – with the small difference that the constructor and class variable are not `private` but `protected`, to make it easier to extend it later, through inheritance. Therefore, an instance of the `ConfigManager` can be accessed from every point in a program, via the `ConfigManager.getConfigManager()` class method.

## 4.2 No restriction to particular memory locations or storage media

When `getConfigManager()` is called for the first time, the configuration manager's configuration file is read. This file is called, by convention, `Registry.cfg`. In it are stored the base data required to make it easy to access other configuration data. Naturally, the most important factor is the location of the configuration files. After all, only files whose location is known, can be read. This also applies to the `ConfigManager`'s configuration file.

Just like many other programs, the Java virtual machine (JVM) can be started with additional parameters. The syntax is `java -Dkey=value ... myClass`. Via the `-D` attribute, system characteristics can be set which can be accessed by the `System.getProperty(String key)` method. During its instantiation the `ConfigManager` reads the characteristic with the key name `CFGROOT` and expects to find there the name of the directory in which the `Registry.cfg` file is located. To support central administration, this can be a URL (but without a file name). `-DCFGROOT=http://my.ConfigHost.de/` is therefore just as valid an entry as `-DCFGROOT=/usr/local/myconfigurations/` or `-DCFGROOT=c:\config\`. If no protocol is set, the `ConfigManager` assumes that a local file is involved and automatically inserts the protocol indicator `file://` in front of the file name.

If no suitable system attribute has been passed on at the start, the `ClassLoader.getSystemResource("Registry.cfg")` method is used to investigate the class path to find the required file. If this search is unsuccessful, it is continued in the current working directory. Finally, a `ConfigDataSourceException` is initiated, if the configuration file could not be found.

## 4.3  Hierarchical data structures

Now we have explained how the `ConfigManager` obtains its configuration, we are going to take a closer look at the contents of this configuration. To do so, we will go over what the `ConfigManager` is meant to do again. An application – as an example, we will call it 'OnlineShop' – should obtain its configuration in the easiest way possible. The `ConfigManager` must therefore have a `getConfiguration ("OnlineShop")` method. When this method is called, it should check in its configuration file, to see whether there is an entry for 'OnlineShop' and, if so, return the appropriate configuration to the application. What could an entry of this kind look like?

Naturally it must have a name which is used to store it. In our case this is 'OnlineShop'. The entry itself must primarily contain information about where the configuration that is needed is located. Therefore, it would be useful to have a path as well as a file name. Furthermore, it can be useful to interpret the path as absolute, relative to the working directory or relative to the `Registry.cfg` file. An attribute would also be desirable for this purpose. Below you can find the typical structure of a `Registry.cfg` file:

Listing 4.2: Simple `Registry.cfg` file

```
{
  OnlineShop = {
    PATH = "OnlineShopPath"
    FILE = "OnlineShop.cfg"
    RELATIVE2CFGROOT = true
  }
}
```

The PATH value sets the base path for all files that belong to this configuration. The default is the current working directory. FILE stands for a default file which is read if no other specific file is requested. RELATIVE2CFGROOT sets whether the path is to be interpreted relative to Registry.cfg or relative to the current working directory. If PATH is absolute, the RELATIVE2CFGROOT attribute is irrelevant. Its default value is therefore false.

The format of Registry.cfg can be read with the ConfigManager package's ConfigFileReader class. We explain how that happens in the next section. It is important to remember that even the configuration of the ConfigManager alone contains hierarchies. A sample attribute (OnlineShop) can possess a large number of details (PATH, FILE, etc.) which can in turn theoretically have other details available to them. It must be possible to nest configuration data in many ways, to ensure that specific data can be accessed via a navigation path. This also makes it possible to obtain a list of all attributes of 'OnlineShop'. Without an explicit hierarchy this would be more complicated.

So that it can access a particular configuration the ConfigManager has the getConfiguration() method. Accordingly, getConfiguration("OnlineShop") returns the configuration 'OnlineShop' to the caller. This is the default configuration file that is specified in FILE. If another file is requested, its name must be passed on as the second argument. A call then consists of getConfiguration ("OnlineShop", "otherconfiguration.cfg").

For each instance, both methods return the Configuration class (Fig. 4.1). Configuration has some similarities with the java.util.Properties class. For

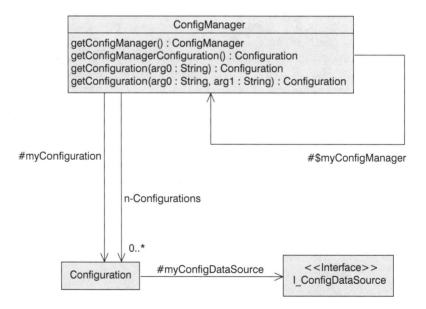

**Figure 4.1** Relationships between ConfigManager, Configuration and I_ConfigDataSource

example, the Configuration class also has methods for reading and writing persistent data, and methods for setting and reading individual values. In addition, each instance of Configuration can have a second instance assigned to it, which contains the default values.

So much for common features. The main differences between them lie in the way they access individual elements and save all the data. In contrast to Properties, Configuration explicitly supports hierarchical structures. The getElement(String aPath) method can be used to access a particular element via a path. This elements can be a String, Boolean, Integer, Double, Vector or a Hashtable. The access path is formed from the keys for the encapsulated hashtables and the lists of vectors contained. The elements of the path must be separated by commas or semicolons. Therefore, OnlineShop's FILE attribute can be accessed in the following way: getElement("OnlineShop;FILE").

## 4.4  ConfigFileReader file format

The ConfigFileReader file format provides us with an example implementation of the requirements described above. It allows us to represent data structures such as Hashtable and Vector, and to nest them. To do so, the following conventions must be complied with:

- Each configuration file is either a hashtable or a vector.
- Hashtables begin and end with a curly bracket.
- Hashtable keys must comply with the conventions for Java variable names.
- Hashtable values consist of an unlimited number of character strings, whole numbers or floating point numbers, the two truth values true and false or else Hashtables or Vectors, delimited by quotation marks.
- The keys and values in the tables are separated by an equals sign.
- Between values and keys a separator character (comma, semicolon) can be inserted.
- Vectors begin and end with parentheses '()' and contain no vector elements or an umlimited number.
- Vector elements must be separated from each other by a blank space, tab, line feed character, carriage return character, comma or semicolon.
- Vector elements consist of an unlimited number of character strings, whole numbers or floating point numbers, the two truth values true and false or else Hashtables or Vectors, delimited by quotation marks.

You will find the formal definition of the file format in Appendix A. Listing 4.3 shows an example file in ConfigFileReader format.

Listing 4.3: Example configuration file for the ConfigFileReader

```
{
    key1 = "oneString" // Comment
```

```
/*
 * multi-line
 * comment
 */
key2 =
    {
        secondLevelKey1 = "oneString"
        secondLevelKey2 = 12.5 // Decimal fraction
        secondLevelKey3 = 42 // Integer
        secondLevelKey4 = true // Boolean
        secondLevelKey5 = false // Boolean
        secondLevelKey6 =
            (
               "Element1", "Element2", 5
               // the third element is an integer,
               // the commas are optional
            )
    }
  key3 = #include("anotherFile.cfg")
}
```

The following call would be necessary to access the vector's `Element1` value via a `Configuration` object:

```
aConfiguration.getElement("key2;secondLevelKey6;0");
```

The following call would return `Element2`:

```
aConfiguration.getElement("key2;secondLevelKey6;1");
```

In addition, `ConfigFileReader` supports modular construction of configurations via the `#include` command. It can be inserted in a file instead of a vector element or hash table value. After the command a URL must be added in brackets and quotation marks. Relative URLs are always interpreted relative to the file in which they are located.

As `Configuration` does not explicitly support modular file structures, these are lost when data is saved. As a result, one single file may be produced from many, under certain circumstances.

## 4.5  Flexible file format

The `ConfigFileReader` format provides us with a very flexible file format. However, we should not assume that all configuration data are always to be stored using exactly this format. For this reason, it makes sense to abstract from the file format. Accordingly, the `ConfigFileReader` class is not permanently bound to `Configuration`, but instead separated by the `I_ConfigDataSource` interface (Fig. 4.2).

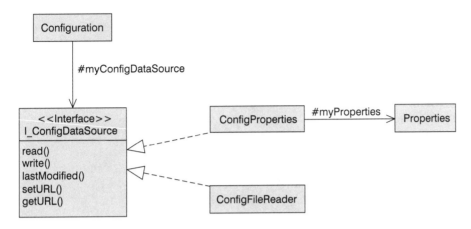

**Figure 4.2**   I_ConfigDataSource and its implementations ConfigFileReader and ConfigProperties

The interface (Listing 4.4) defines that a class that implements I_ConfigDataSource must be able to write to, and read, Configuration. The storage location is defined via a URL. Furthermore, it must be possible to query the date that it was last changed. How a class fulfils these requirements is left up to it. Besides saving to a file you could also link to a database, for example.

Listing 4.4: The I_ConfigDataSource interface

```
package de.webapp.Framework.ConfigManager;

import java.net.*;

public interface I_ConfigDataSource {
/** Reads the data source and returns the result as an object */
public Object read() throws ConfigDataSourceException;
/** Writes a configuration object */
public void write(Configuration configuration) throws
ConfigDataSourceException;
/** Tells you when the data source was last changed */
public long lastModified();
/** Sets the URL for the data source*/
public void setURL(String aURL) throws MalformedURLException;
/** Returns the URL for this data source*/
public URL getURL();
}
```

In the ConfigManager package there are two classes that implement the interface (Fig. 4.2). One of them, ConfigProperties, is simply a thin wrapper round the java.util.Properties class. Accordingly it only supports character strings and no real hierarchical structures. The other, ConfigFileReader, fulfils all the requirements mentioned above. Furthermore, owing to the #include directive, it is capable of reading configurations that consist of several files.

To use a particular implementation of I_ConfigDataSource, there are several possibilities. First, you can explicitly define the class name as an attribute of a Registry.cfg file entry. You do so using the DATASOURCECLASSNAME attribute. Otherwise, the Configuration class can recognize which I_ConfigDataSource is to be used on the basis of the file extension. Here, the ConfigProperties class is the default for files with the file extension properties and ConfigFileReader for all others. Other mappings can be managed using appropriate methods from the Configuration class.

For this reason, addConfigDataSourceClass(String, Class) registers a I_ConfigDataSource class for a file extension. Using removeConfigData SourceClass(String), a mapping of this sort can be removed again. As both methods are static, these settings apply to all instances of Configuration.

## 4.6 Use of defaults

Often, the differences between configurations for the same application are only marginal. Therefore it makes sense to be able to fall back on a default configuration. For this purpose, the configuration manager offers a simple mechanism. In addition to the attributes FILE, PATH etc. you can use DEFAULTS to give a reference to another configuration (Listing 4.5). The returned Configuration object then contains a Configuration object from another configuration as its default configuration. If an element is not present in its own configuration object, the default configuration object is accessed automatically. This can, in turn, have a default object and so on. In using this procedure, you must ensure that no endless loops are formed.

A Registry.cfg file of this kind might look like this:

Listing 4.5: CDShop configuration that accesses a default configuration

```
{
    DefaultOnlineShop = {
        PATH = "DefaultOnlineShopPath"
        FILE = "DefaultOnlineShop.cfg"
        RELATIVE2CFGROOT = true
    }
    CDShop = {
        PATH = "CDShopPath"
        FILE = "CDShop.cfg"
        RELATIVE2CFGROOT = true
        DEFAULTS = "DefaultOnlineShop"
    }
}
```

In addition, as in the Properties class, a default value can be set for every call to getElement(). This value is returned if the no value is assigned to the key, either in the configuration itself, or in any default configuration that may be present. The complete signature is called Object getElement(String path, Object default).

## 4.7 Configuration object

Besides the normal way of accessing configuration data, the `Configuration` class also offers other characteristics and methods that make work much easier. The most important method is definitely `setElement(String, Object)` which, similarly to `getElement(String)`, makes it possible to change a value in the configuration. You can use the `write()` method to save a changed configuration.

Using the `setAutoReload(boolean)` method you can switch a configuration into a mode that checks whether there has been a change to the configuration, before every attempt to access that configuration. If this is the case, it is reloaded automatically. In addition, it is possible to register configuration observers with the configuration. To do so you use the `addObserver(Observer)` method, which `Configuration` inherits from the `java.util.Observable` class. Every time there is a change to the configuration, all registered `java.util.Observers` are informed.

This check to see whether the configuration is up to date can also be carried out automatically at set periods. To do so, you simply have to call the `startPeriodicObservation()` method. `setCheckInterval(long)` sets the time in milliseconds that is to pass between each check, `getCheckInterval()` returns the set time and `stopPeriodicObservation()` stops the automatic observation.

# Protocol Service  5

n a framework, besides central administration using a configuration service, it is indispensable to be able to trace back the program messages as well. For this, you need a protocol service. Just like the `ConfigManager`, this service must also be easy to access and have a simple interface. Finally, you do not want to struggle with complicated commands when programming, you simply want to write one line in a file.

The WebApp framework has a simple protocol service that you can find in the `de.webapp.Framework.Log` package. Unlike `ConfigManager`, the `Log` class is not implemented as a singleton, as it is very unlikely that it would be inherited from `Log`. In order to make it easily available, `Log` has only those statistical methods that can be divided into three different categories:

- Protocolling methods: `Log.log(...)`.
- Methods that establish whether you need to protocol: `Log.isLog(...)`.
- Methods for adjusting the accuracy of the protocol (log level): `setLogLevel (...)` and `setLogLevelDefault(...)` or `getLogLevel(...)`, `getLogLevel Default(...)`.

## 5.1  Basics

Often, not all of the output should be protocolled – in the case of an error search it is sometimes possible that there is not enough output. Therefore, it is essential to have a mechanism to control the accuracy of the protocol messages. You control this in `Log` via the log level, which you can change as much as you want. The integer constants are already defined for different log levels (Table 5.1) in the `C_Log` interface. However, these are only recommendations. Basically, you can use all the levels between 0 and the system-dependent constants `Integer.MAX_VALUE`.

**Table 5.1** Log level constants from C_Log

| Constants | Value | Meaning |
|-----------|-------|---------|
| NOLOG | 0 | No protocolling |
| ERROR | 1 | Protocol mistakes |
| MODULE | 2 | Protocol module messages |
| METHOD | 3 | Protocol method messages |
| FORTYTWO | 42 | Protocol just about everything |

Using the Log.log(Object, int) method you can protocol the message of a specific log level. The first parameter specifies the message and the second one specifies the log level. If there is only one message specified and the log level is not set specifically, the message will then be protocolled with the log level that has been set by the setLogLevelDefault(int) method. The corresponding method display is called Log.log(Object).

In order to control the log level from which to protocol a message, you have to use the setLogLevel(int) method. For example:

```
setLogLevelDefault(C_Log.MODULE);
setLogLevel(C_Log.METHOD);
Log.log("Message without LogLevel");
Log.log("Message with LogLevel", C_Log.FORTYTWO);
```

Here, the standard log level (LogLevelDefault) for messages is C_Log.MODULE. The current log level is C_Log.METHOD. If a program now attempts to transmit a protocol message without log level via Log.log("Message without Loglevel"), this will be protocolled, as the current log level is higher than the standard log level.

If a message is transmitted via Log.log("Message with Loglevel", C_Log.FORTYTWO), this will be not protocolled, as C_Log.FORTYTWO shows a lower log level than the real log level C_Log.METHOD. The message will therefore be suppressed.

## 5.2 To log or not to log?

Unfortunately, the character string operations in Java with the String class are very resource-hungry. If you use the concatenation operator to assemble different character strings ("String1" + "String2"), the two objects will be junked and a third one will be generated. In the short run, this is a lot of effort and in the long run it creates too much work for the automated memory clean-up (garbage collection). We should avoid those operations as much as possible. For this reason, Log also has the method Log.isLog(). It allows you to establish whether protocolling is required, before constructing a message.

While Log.isLog() shows whether the current log level is higher than C_Log.NOLOG, Log.isLog(int) specifies whether the message of a certain level should be protocolled or not. In practice, that means that the Log calls have to be coded in the following way:

```
if (Log.isLog(C_Log.METHOD)) {
    String message = "Something has happened with"+ name +
    reason +"might be the reason. But it might also be:"+
    otherreason + ","+ yetanotherreason;
    Log.log(message, C_Log.METHOD);
}
```

name, reason, otherreason and yetanotherreason are the character strings that in a very labour-intensive way achieve the construction of message. By using isLog() to save the code block, this construction, which requires a lot of processing and memory capacity, is only carried out when it is really needed. The length of the construction time can be improved by using StringBuffers instead of Strings.

## 5.3 Configuration of protocol service

If all the protocol messages were included in the standard output, it would be rather confusing. Therefore, you can create different protocol files.

While the Log class is initializing, a configuration file is analyzed for this purpose. This will be drawn from the ConfigManager. To make this possible, you must have an entry with the name Log in the Registry.cfg file (Listing 5.1). If there is no corresponding entry, all the outputs are made in the standard error stream.

Listing 5.1: Example extract from Registry.cfg file

```
{
    Log = {
        FILE = "log.cfg";
        RELATIVE2CFGROOT = true ;
    };
    ...
}
```

The different protocols are defined in the log.cfg file. To restrict the number of parameters that have to be entered to as few as possible, the file is divided into two parts. First, you have to set the basic values and default values. Secondly, you can overwrite them for different protocols.

Listing 5.2: Example configuration file for the protocol service

```
{
    // PART I
    LOGROOT = "../logs"
    RELATIVE2CFGROOT = true
    LEVEL = 4
```

```
DEFAULTLEVEL = 1
FILE = "default.log"

// PART II
LOGS = {
  jo = {
    FILE = "jo_event.log"

  }
  jo_access = {
    FILE = "jo_access.log"
    RELATIVE2LOGROOT = true

  }
  AdminService = {
    LEVEL = 1
    DEFAULTLEVEL = 1
  }
}
}
```

In the first part the parameters set the log level and the place where the output is made. If no file is specified, the output is automatically made in the standard error stream. If a file is specified by the FILE attribute, you can enter a path with LOG-ROOT, which will be used as the root directory for all protocol files. You can then use RELATIVE2CFGROOT to define the location of LOGROOT relative to the Registry.cfg file.

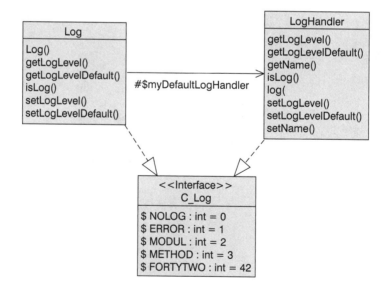

**Figure 5.1** Delegation to a LogHandler

The entries in the second part are similar. Basically, you use all the settings from the first part as initial default values. Here, you do not need to specify all the parameters for each protocol. The possible parameters are RELATIVE2LOGROOT, FILE, LEVEL and DEFAULTLEVEL. If the RELATIVE2LOGROOT is not specified and yet a file is specified, it will be interpreted in relation to the specified log root directory.

In order to write a message in a particular protocol, you have to specify the protocol. Otherwise, you will use the standard protocol. For example:

```
if (Log.isLog(C_ERROR, "jo")) Log.log("Message", C_Log.ERROR, "jo");
```

This program line writes a message in the protocol jo. Accordingly, there are versions for all the methods that accept the name of a protocol as the last argument.

In the implementation of the protocol service, this functionality is achieved by delegating it to a LogHandler (Fig. 5.1). A LogHandler is provided for each defined protocol. In order to document errors in the Log class, this class also has a standard LogHandler.

## 5.4 Protocolling with format

```
D:\repository\webapp\bin>Adminservice
ConfigManager: Reading '../etc/ConfigManager.cfg' ...
[12.11.1998 00:44:51] - AdminService: Trying to bind service to port 9090.
[12.11.1998 00:44:52] - AdminService: Bound service to 0.0.0.0/0.0.0.0:9090
[12.11.1998 00:44:52] - AdminService: Listening...
[12.11.1998 00:44:53] - jo: Trying to bind service to port 8080.
[12.11.1998 00:44:53] - jo: Bound service to 0.0.0.0/0.0.0.0:8080
[12.11.1998 00:44:53] - jo: Listening...
[12.11.1998 00:44:53] - jo: Built context doc.
[12.11.1998 00:44:53] - jo: Built context default.
[12.11.1998 00:44:53] - jo: Added model HelloWorld to context default
[12.11.1998 00:44:53] - jo: Added model bean counter to context default
[12.11.1998 00:44:53] - jo: Added model simpleservlet to context default
[12.11.1998 00:44:53] - jo: Added model jdbc to context default
[12.11.1998 00:44:53] - jo: Added model fileImport to context default
[12.11.1998 00:44:53] - jo: Added model request to context default
[12.11.1998 00:44:53] - jo: Added model smtp to context default
[12.11.1998 00:44:53] - jo: Added model session to context default
[12.11.1998 00:44:53] - jo: Added model file to context default
[12.11.1998 00:44:53] - jo: Added model file to context doc
[12.11.1998 00:44:53] - jo: Added model StudentDBServlet to context default
[12.11.1998 00:44:53] - jo: Added model odbc to context default
[12.11.1998 00:44:53] - jo: Added model guestbook to context default
[12.11.1998 00:44:53] - jo: Added model persistence counter to context default
[12.11.1998 00:44:53] - jo: Added model OnlineShop to context default
```

**Figure 5.2** Protocol output at the start of AdminServices

In order to protocol not only character strings, but also an exception or some other different object, all the log methods accept Object as a parameter. Throwable objects are given special treatment: they are protocolled automatically with their StackTrace. ServletExceptions, SQLExceptions, InvocationTarget Exceptions and I_WebAppExceptions that may have encapsulated Throwables are treated in the same way. If you only want to protocol the Throwable's message, you have to call the toString() method:

```
Throwable myThrowable = new Throwable("Error");
// with StackTrace
Log.log(myThrowable);
// or without
Log.log(myThrowable.toString());
```

As a standard, all protocol outputs will begin with a date, time and protocol name. Following that, you will find the actual message (Fig. 5.2).

In many cases, this format is not desirable, for example in the case of the log files of a Web server (Fig. 5.3). Usually, in this case, you use the Common Log Format (CLF), which accurately specifies what has to stand in the protocol file, and in which sequence.

In order to achieve this, you can transfer the log() method when you call a pattern character string. The corresponding signatures are as follows:

```
void log(Object[] args, String aPattern, int aLevel, String aLog)
void log(Object[] args, String aPattern, String aLog)
void log(Object[] args, String aPattern, int aLevel)
```

The pattern used has to correspond to the conventions of the java.text.MessageFormat class (see JDK API documentation). The standard pattern is "[{0, date} {0,time}] – {1}: {2}".

```
D:\repository\webapp\bin>jostart
ConfigManager: Reading '../etc/ConfigManager.cfg' ...
auster.ping.de - - [21/Nov/1998:17:26:24 +0100] "GET /servlet/HelloWorld HTTP/1.0" 200 -
auster.ping.de - - [21/Nov/1998:17:26:26 +0100] "GET /servlet/HelloWorld HTTP/1.0" 200 -
auster.ping.de - - [21/Nov/1998:17:26:29 +0100] "GET /servlet/request HTTP/1.0" 200 -
auster.ping.de - - [21/Nov/1998:17:26:33 +0100] "GET /servlet/bean counter HTTP/1.0" 200 -
auster.ping.de - - [21/Nov/1998:17:26:34 +0100] "GET /servlet/bean counter HTTP/1.0" 200 -
auster.ping.de - - [21/Nov/1998:17:26:37 +0100] "GET /servlet/session HTTP/1.0" 200 -
auster.ping.de - - [21/Nov/1998:17:26:41 +0100] "GET /servlet/session?JSID%3D91166559767870 HTTP/1.
" 200 -
auster.ping.de - - [21/Nov/1998:17:26:46 +0100] "GET /servlet/session HTTP/1.0" 200 -
auster.ping.de - - [21/Nov/1998:17:26:47 +0100] "GET /servlet/session HTTP/1.0" 200 -
auster.ping.de - - [21/Nov/1998:17:26:52 +0100] "GET /servlet/session2 HTTP/1.0" 200 -
auster.ping.de - - [21/Nov/1998:17:26:54 +0100] "GET /servlet/session2 HTTP/1.0" 200 -
auster.ping.de - - [21/Nov/1998:17:26:55 +0100] "GET /servlet/session2 HTTP/1.0" 200 -
auster.ping.de - - [21/Nov/1998:17:26:56 +0100] "GET /servlet/session2?verfallen HTTP/1.0" 200 -
auster.ping.de - - [21/Nov/1998:17:26:58 +0100] "GET /servlet/session2 HTTP/1.0" 200 -
auster.ping.de - - [21/Nov/1998:17:27:03 +0100] "GET /servlet/guestbook HTTP/1.0" 200 -
auster.ping.de - - [21/Nov/1998:17:27:05 +0100] "POST /servlet/guestbook HTTP/1.0" 200 -
auster.ping.de - - [21/Nov/1998:17:27:07 +0100] "POST /servlet/guestbook HTTP/1.0" 200 -
auster.ping.de - - [21/Nov/1998:17:27:12 +0100] "GET /servlet/smtp HTTP/1.0" 200 -
auster.ping.de - - [21/Nov/1998:17:27:16 +0100] "POST /servlet/smtp HTTP/1.0" 200 -
auster.ping.de - - [21/Nov/1998:17:27:23 +0100] "GET /servlet/smtp HTTP/1.0" 200 -
```

**Figure 5.3**  Output in Common Log Format

# Server Toolkit 6

I n Chapter 2, we dealt with the development of a simple HTTP server. There we
provided a basic introduction using the HTTP example. Now we are going to look
into the underlying concepts in more detail.

Usually we divide a server architecture into two parts: the service and one or more
handlers (Fig. 6.1). The service generally accepts a connection or a data package, so
that it can pass them on to a handler. This carries out the requested service. The service normally provides the handler with the environment variables and different
general attributes or services. The `de.webapp.Framework.Server` package contains various interfaces and classes that define or implement this behaviour.

The package provides a platform with which you can program a server in the
shortest time possible. This is achieved by the fact that classes from the package need
only have the application protocol-specific parts added to them.

## 6.1 Basic interfaces

First there is the `I_Service` interface. It defines all the important features of a service from the name, version, port and IP address to the possible attributes such as the
class name of its handler. In addition, the interface contains management methods
to start the service, to stop it, and then to restart it. It also defines the handler management.

The `I_Handler` corresponding to `I_Service` contains methods for accessing the
relevant service and its attributes. There is also a `destroy()` method, which makes
it possible for the service to release the handler and any of its bound resources.

**Figure 6.1**   Service/handler relationship

## 6.1.1 Service provision

You can assign the methods of services (Table 6.1) to different categories. There are simple attribute methods that only announce fixed features of the service. These include getName(), getMajorVersion(), getMinorVersion(), getBindAddress() and getPort(). The getAttribute(), setAttribute() and getAttributeNames() methods play a special role, as they provide access to a data structure that can change substantially at run-time under some circumstances.

You can define the run-time behaviour by using another type of method. These include start(), stop(), restart() and isAlive().

Finally, there are methods for handler management. Handler management means the mechanism that makes sure that a connection (if you use TCP as the network protocol) or a datagram (if you use UDP) is available for a handler. You could obviously instantiate a new handler for each datagram or each connection, as we did in Chapter 2. But, because we want to increase the call-handling capacity of our server, we shall not do that.

Starting a thread is very resource-intensive in Java. Between calling the start() and the run() methods of a thread you have to carry out a certain amount of administration work. Unfortunately, you cannot reduce this initialization effort, but we can reuse an already initialized thread. We shall explain how it works in Section 6.4.2. As handlers are usually implemented as threads it means that the service has to have a recycleHandler() method in addition to a getHandler() method.

In order to increase the output of your service, we shall also maintain a handler pool. A pool can be identified by the characteristic that you can add to it similar elements and that you can do so without entering a key. In addition, each pool has a limited capacity (see de.webapp.Framework.Utilities.I_Pool). If you want to have a little more control over this pool, you can use the following methods, which are part of the service: setMaxHandlerThreads() and setMinHandlerThreads() as well as the corresponding get methods.

Now you understand how the handler is managed, we shall take a closer look at how it is instantiated. It should be possible for our service to use all the handlers that implement the I_Handler interface, as described in Section 6.1.2. That means that we must be able to set the class names, and I_Service takes care of that via the setHandlerClassname() and getHandlerClassname() methods. If we want to ensure correct instantiation, the given handler class has to have an argument-free constructor.

## 6.1.2 Definition of the handler interface

Unlike the service interface, the handler interface (Table 6.2) is relatively modest. It only permits access to the service, the service attributes and the life-cycle methods init() and destroy().

init() must be called before the handler is used in any fashion. You have to call the destroy() method when the handler is no longer in use. The method makes sure that all resources that had been tied up by the handler get released again.

**Table 6.1**  The de.webapp.Framework.Server.I_Service interface

| Method | Meaning |
| --- | --- |
| Object getAttribute(String name) | Returns a service attribute. |
| Enumeration getAttributeNames() | Returns a list of the attribute names. |
| InetAddress getBindAddress() | Supplies the Internet address where this service has been bound. |
| I_Handler getHandler() throws HandlerException | Provides a handler. If something then goes wrong, a HandlerException will be started. |
| String getHandlerClassname() | Provides the class name of the handler. |
| int getMajorVersion() | Returns the major version number of the service. A service of version 2.1 must return a 2. |
| int getMaxHandlerThreads() | Reports the maximum number of active handler threads. |
| int getMinHandlerThreads() | Reports the minimum number of threads available in the pool. |
| int getMinorVersion() | Returns the service's sub-version number. A service of version 2.1 must return a 1. |
| String getName() | Returns the name of the service. |
| int getPort() | Returns the port number of this service. |
| int getSoTimeout() | The maximum time in milliseconds that the socket used is blocked during input/output operations. |
| boolean isAlive() | Shows whether the service is running. |
| void recycleHandler(I_Handler handler) | Takes a handler thread back into the pool. |
| void restart() throws ServerException | Restarts the service. Usually, you simply call stop() and start(). |
| void setAttribute(String name, object o) | Sets an attribute. |
| void setBindAddress(InetAddress aBindAddress) | Sets the IP address, to which the service is bound. You can only set the address when the service is not running. |
| void setHandlerClassname(String class name) | Sets the class name for the handler that is to be instantiated. |
| void setMaxhandlerThreads(int number) | Sets the maximum number of active handler threads. |
| void setMinHandlerThreads(int number) | Sets the minimum number of threads ready in the pool. |
| void setName(String name) | Sets the name of the service. |
| void setPort(int aPort) | Sets the port, at which the service is to listen. You can only set it when the service is not running. |
| void setSoTimeout(int time) | Sets the maximum time in milliseconds that the socket used is blocked during input/output operations. |
| void start() throws ServerException | Starts the service. |
| void stop() throws ServerException | Stops the service. |

**Table 6.2**   The `de.webapp.Framework.Server.I_Handler` interface

| Method | Meaning |
|---|---|
| `void destroy()` | Specifically releases any resources tied up by this handler. |
| `I_Service getService()` | Returns the service of this handler. This must first be set via `init()`. |
| `Object getServiceAttribute(String name)` | Proxy method that accesses the service's attributes. |
| `void init(I_Service)` | Initializes this handler. |
| `void setServiceAttribute (String name, Object o)` | Proxy method that allows you to set an attribute of a service. |

## 6.2   UDP and TCP services

Neither of the interfaces defines the method that they use to communicate. That is largely due to the fact that in `java.net` package no abstract superclass or interface for TCP sockets and UDP sockets has been implemented. In order to forward the data from the service to its handler, you have to define an `I_TCPService` and an `I_TCPHandler` as well as an `I_UDPService` and an `I_UDPHandler`. In both cases, you then add the protocol-specific methods.

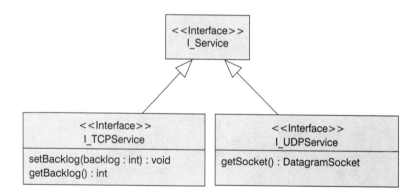

**Figure 6.2**   Relationship between `I_TCPService`, `I_UDPService` and `I_Service`

The only way that `I_TCPService` extends `I_Service` is by adding backlog methods (Fig. 6.2). The queue of incoming connections is called a backlog. `I_TCPService` has methods that set or query the maximum length of the queue. If a queue is full and a client is attempting to create a connection, the connection will be refused.

As UDP is a connection-free protocol, there can be no backlog for connections. Instead of this, you could integrate methods for manipulating the transmission and

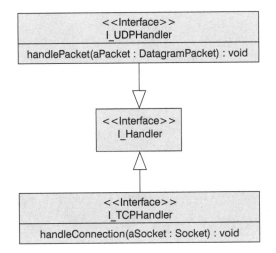

**Figure 6.3**  Relationship between `I_TCPHandler`, `I_UDPHandler` and `I_Handler`

reception memory buffers in the interface. However, these methods are also available via the applied `DatagramSocket`, to which the `I_UDPService` interface grants access via the `getSocket()` method. Therefore, we are not going to resort to them now.

The `I_UDPHandler` and `I_TCPHandler` interfaces always contain just one method. In the case of an `I_UDPHandler`, this is called `handlePacket (DatagramPacket)`. In the case of `I_TCPHandler` it is called `handleConnection(Socket)`.

## 6.3  Interaction between service and handler

Even when the interfaces are different, the communication algorithm (Fig. 6.4) is nevertheless the same:

**1** Establish a connection with a client or receive a datagram.

**2** Using `getHandler`, provide a handler for this connection. This handler must already be initialized.

**3** Call the `handleConnection(Socket)` or `handlePacket(DatagramPacket)` method.

**4** Respond to the client with `handleConnection(Socket)` or `handlePacket (DatagramPacket)`.

**5** The handler that has been called calls the service's `recycleHandler(I_Handler)` method. After that the handler has no more to do.

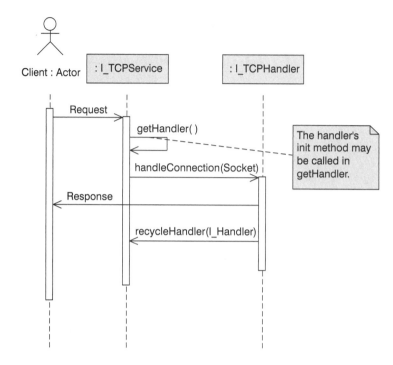

**Figure 6.4**  Flow diagram of a TCP service

## 6.4  Handler recycling

The most interesting part of the server package is definitely handler management. As Section 6.1.1 revealed, it is worth reusing handlers that have already been initialized. For this reason we want to take a closer look at how this is achieved in the Service, Handler, TCPService and TCPHandler classes.

### 6.4.1  Service view

If the service receives a request, it uses getHandler() to request an initialized handler. As this process is the same for TCP and UDP, it does so in the Service class. The recycleHandler(I_Handler) method can also be found in this class (Listing 6.1).

In order to understand what getHandler() offers, we first have to describe the HandlerPool class. The pool takes responsibility for a great part of the management of the handler (Fig. 6.5). You can obtain a handler from the pool via the methods get() and add(Object) and you can return them to the pool in the same way. In addition, you can register them with the pool handler or check how many registered handlers there are by using the countRegisteredHandlers() method. In this way we always have an overview of how many handlers there are. The clear() method removes all the handlers from the pool and calls their destroy() methods.

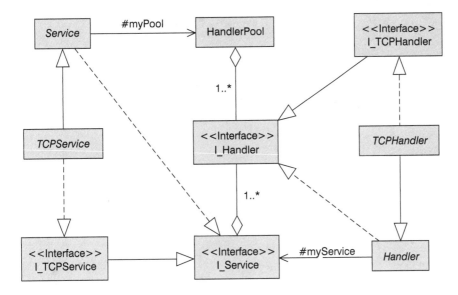

**Figure 6.5**  Connections between interfaces and classes in the server package

Now let us go back to the getHandler() method. Next we shall use myPool.get() to try to obtain an already initialized handler from a pool. If we succeed, we can return the handler we obtained. If we are not so lucky, we have to test whether the number of registered handlers is still smaller than the allowed maximum number of handler threads. If this is so, we can instantiate a new handler, initialize it via init() and register it in the pool.

As registerHandler(I_Handler) influences the result of countRegistered-Handlers(), this part must be located in a section that is synchronized with the pool.

If the maximum number of handlers has been instantiated and registered, we have to wait using myPool.wait() until a handler adds itself to the pool again. We do this by calling the recycleHandler(I_Handler) method. So that we are told when a handler is available again, we add a call to myPool.notify() after the handler is added to the pool using myPool.add(I_Handler).

Listing 6.1: The methods getHandler() and recycleHandler(I_Handler) from de.webapp.Framework.Server.Service

```
/** contains the handlers*/
protected HandlerPool myPool = new HandlerPool();

public I_Handler getHandler() throws HandlerException {
   I_Handler aHandler = null;
   aHandler = (I_Handler)myPool.get();
   if (aHandler != null) return aHandler;
   synchronized (myPool) {
```

```
      if (myPool.countRegisteredHandlers()<= getMaxHandlerThreads()) {
        try {
          aHandler =
  (I_Handler)Class.forName(getHandlerClassname()).newInstance();
          aHandler.init(this);
          myPool.registerHandler(aHandler);
        }
        catch (Exception e) {
          throw new HandlerException(e);
        }
        return aHandler;
      }
      while ((aHandler = (I_Handler)myPool.get()) == null) {
        try {
          myPool.wait();
        }
        catch (InterruptedException ie) {}
      }
    }
    return aHandler;
  }

  public void recycleHandler(I_Handler aHandler) {
    synchronized (myPool) {
      myPool.add(aHandler);
      myPool.notify();
    }
  }
}
```

If you obtain a handler via getHandler(), it is already initialized, but not activated yet. In the TCPService class, the I_Handler is typecast into an I_TCPHandler, in order to call its handleConnection(Socket). A similar thing happens in UDPService – here you call the handlePacket(DatagramPacket) of an I_UDPHandler.

In Listing 6.2 you will find the entire process from the creation of a connection to the calling of a handler. The extract originates in the TCPService class which, just like Service and UDPService, implements the Runnable interface. Therefore, the extract contains a run() method. In addition, it contains an init() method. In the Service start() method (which has not been listed), both methods are called, one after the other.

## Initialization

Now a ServerSocket is instantiated in the init() method. If no address is defined, to which the service is to be bound, all the available addresses will be targeted. This will be shown in the log output, where there will be the address 0.0.0.0. Then the SO_TIMEOUT is set. This is the maximum length in milliseconds that the socket blocks during write and read operations. Once this time has expired, the java.io.InterruptedIOException is initiated.

## Service phase

Once the socket has been initialized, you call the run() method. Its main component is a while loop in which the incoming connections are accepted and passed on to the handler.

This loop needs to handle three exceptions. First, a HandlerException, as is initiated by getHandler() if no handler can be obtained. In this case you have to close the socket so that it does not carry on running. The second possible exception is InterruptedIOException, which we have already mentioned. If this is initiated, we call the handleSoTimeout() method of the Service superclass. It makes sure that the pool is reduced to the smallest number of handlers possible. This is handy when the service has received no requests for a long time.

That just leaves SocketException. It is initiated, among other times, when the ServerSocket.close() method is called, while it uses accept() or receive() to wait for data. A call like this can be made deliberately when the service has to be stopped. Therefore we log an error only when the flag stopped equals false.

## Stopping the service

Altogether there are three possibilities for breaking the loop and therefore stopping the service:

**1** An exception inside the loop is not handled.

**2** The socket is closed and stopped is true.

**3** The SO_TIMEOUT has expired and stopped is true.

In each case you still need to do a little more work. The stopped flag must be set to true, the pool needs to be cleared and the socket needs to be closed. That happens in the finally block.

Listing 6.2: init() and run() methods from de.webapp.Framework.Server.TCPService

```
public synchronized void init() throws IOException, ServerException {
    super.init();
    if (Log.isLog(getName())) {
        if (getBindAddress() != null)
            Log.log("Attempt to bind service: " + getBindAddress() + ": " +
getPort(), getName());
        else
            Log.log(Attempt to bind service: " + getPort() + ".", getName());
    }
    myServerSocket = new ServerSocket(getPort(), getBacklog(),
getBindAddress());
```

```
        // set Blocking-Timeout
        myServerSocket.setSoTimeout(getSoTimeout());
        // Set address, if not known before.
        if (getBindAddress() == null) myBindAddress =
    myServerSocket.getInetAddress();
        // Set port, if not known before.
        if (getPort() == 0) myPort = myServerSocket.getLocalPort();
        if (Log.isLog(getName())) Log.log("Service has been bound" +
    getBindAddress() + ": " + getPort(), getName());
        if (Log.isLog(getName())) Log.log("Listen...", getName());
    }

    public void run(){
        try {
            I_TCPHandler aHandler;
            Socket aSocket = null;
            while (!stopped) {
                try {
                    aSocket = null;
                    aSocket = myServerSocket.accept();
                    aHandler = (I_TCPHandler)getHandler();
                    aHandler.handleConnection(aSocket);
                }
                catch(HandlerException he) {
                    if (aSocket != null) aSocket.close();
                    if (Log.isLog(getName())) Log.log(he.toString(), getName ());
                }
                catch (InterruptedIOException ie) {
                    handleSoTimeout();
                }
                catch (SocketException se) {
                    // is initiated if the socket is closed during stopping.
                    if (!stopped && Log.isLog(getName())) Log.log(se.getMessage
                    (), getName());

                }
            }
        }
        catch (IOException ioe) {
            if (Log.isLog(getName())) Log.log(ioe.toString(), getName());
            throw new ServerRuntimeException(ioe);
        }
        finally {
            stopped = true;
            myPool.clear();
            try {
                close();
```

```
        }
        catch (IOException ioe) {
          if (Log.isLog(getName())) Log.log(ioe.toString(), getName ());
            throw new ServerRuntimeException("Could not close socket.", ioe);
        }
      }
    }
  }
```

## 6.4.2 Lifespan of handlers

In order to fulfil the service requests, the handler has to have one basic attribute: it has to be reusable. In order to make asynchronous execution possible, the handlers are often created in the form of a thread. However reusing threads is not without its problems. As explained in Chapter 1 (Fig. 1.1), there is no change of condition from 'dead' to 'new'. A thread that has already been used up cannot be resuscitated. If you want to use a thread several times, you must process *several* requests *inside* the run() method. The thread should pause in a resting position between requests.

Listing 6.3 shows the corresponding code extracts from the TCPHandler and Handler classes. To make them clearer to understand, they are printed together.

Listing 6.3: Code extracts from TCPHandler and Handler

```java
// from TCPHandler
protected Socket mySocket = null;

// from Handler
protected I_Service myService = null;
protected boolean stopped = false;

public void init(I_Service aService) {
   if (aService == null)
     throw new IllegalArgumentException("Service must not be null.");
   myService = aService;
   start();
}

// from TCPHandler
public synchronized void handleConnection(Socket aSocket) {
   mySocket = aSocket;
   notify();
}

public void run() {
   synchronized (this) {
     try {
       started = true;
       wait();
     }
```

```
        catch(InterruptedException ie) {   }
      }
    while (!stopped) {
      if (mySocket != null) {
        try {
          service();
        }
        catch (Throwable t) {
          if (Log.isLog(getService().getName())) Log.log(t, C_Log.ERROR,
getService().getName());
        }
        try {
          mySocket.close();
        }
        catch(Exception e) {
        }
        mySocket = null;
        if (!stopped) {
          try {
            synchronized (this) {
              myService.recycleHandler(this);
              wait();
            }
          }
          catch(InterruptedException ie) {
          }
        }
      }
      else {
        try {
          if (!stopped) {
            synchronized (this) {
              wait();
            }
          }
        }
        catch (InterruptedException ie) {
        }
      }
    }
  }

// from Handler
public abstract void service();

public synchronized void destroy() {
  stopped = true;
  notify();
}
```

## Initialization

To start the handler life cycle, you call the init() method. Here, in the instance variable myService, the service is defined and the start() method is called. As the handler inherits from java.lang.Thread it starts the thread. Then we call the run() method. It checks whether the handler has already been stopped. If that is the case, the run() method returns without having done anything – the thread is dead. If the thread is not stopped yet, it checks whether there is a connection. If this is the case, the service() method is called. This is only abstractly defined in the class handler and should be overwritten to create a service. Once the service() has completed its task, the connection closes and mySocket is set to null. The handler is again in a usable status, therefore we may call the service's recycle Handler(I_Handler) method. The next time wait() is called, this sets the handler is set to a waiting state. It is important to note that wait() is also called when no connection is present. This is particularly so directly after initialization.

## Service phase

But how does the handler get its connection? To achieve this, a TCPService has to call a handler's handleConnection(Socket) method. There, the connection is stored in the instance variable mySocket and any threads that may be waiting are informed via notify(). If a handler is in a waiting state, it wakes up and checks whether there is a connection. As this is the situation now, service() processes the information request.

## Stopping handler threads

In order to stop a handler thread, the destroy() method has to be called. It sets the stopped flag to true and calls notify(). If the handler is in a pause state, it is informed, and completes the run() method. If the handler is currently carrying out a request, it stops it and then the run() method. The handler is now 'dead', and cannot be used again.

## 6.5 Echo service

As an example application for the server classes, we will program an echo service. Its characteristic shall be that it uses a TCP connection to read a line and then writes the line back. We finish the connection by the keyword 'bye'.

First we have to instantiate the class TCPService and set the parameters for this service. Fortunately, TCPService has a few methods that make this easier. For example, the main(String[]) method instantiates a TCPService class and sets the name to equal the first command line parameter. Then it calls the start() method of the instance. During start() there is a call to the init() method, which in its turn executes loadConfiguration(). loadConfiguration() finally asks the configuration manager (Chapter 4) for a suitable configuration for the service. It uses the service name as a key. It reads and sets the configuration (Listing 6.4) and then the service starts.

Listing 6.4: EchoService configuration file,
webapp/projects/Examples/Server/EchoService.cfg

```
{
  // Port number
  PORT = 8090
  // maximum number of buffered connections
  BACKLOG = 50
  // maximum number of HandlerThreads
  MAXHANDLERTHREADS = 50
  // minimum number of HandlerThreads
  MINHANDLERTHREADS = 5
  // Class name of the handler
  HANDLERCLASSNAME = "de.webapp.Examples.Server.EchoHandler"
  // Time in ms that must pass without a connection,
  // until the HandlerPool is set to its minimum size.
  SO_TIMEOUT = 30000
  // Major version number
  MAJORVERSION = 0
  // Minor version number
  MINORVERSION = 1
}
```

Finally, we do not need to write a new service class, rather, we only have to create configuration files. At the handler, on the other hand, we have to define the service behaviour and to do so, we must overwrite the service() method. Listing 6.5 shows the very simple implementation of the EchoHandler:

Listing 6.5: The class de.webapp.Examples.Server.EchoHandler

```
package de.webapp.Examples.Server;

import de.webapp.Framework.Server.*;
import java.net.Socket;
import java.io.*;

public class EchoHandler extends TCPHandler {

public void service() {
   try {
     BufferedReader in = new BufferedReader(
       new InputStreamReader(getSocket().getInputStream())
     );
     BufferedWriter out = new BufferedWriter(
       new OutputStreamWriter(getSocket().getOutputStream())
     );
     String line;
     while ((line = in.readLine()) != null
          && !line.toLowerCase().startsWith("bye")) {
```

```
        out.write(line);
        out.newLine();
        out.flush();
      }
    }
    catch (IOException ioe) {
      ioe.printStackTrace();
    }
  }

  } // End of the class
```

To start the service we have to pass on the location of the `Registry.cfg` file to the virtual machine, if it is not in the same directory. In `Registry.cfg` there should be an entry called 'EchoService' that gives a reference to the service's configuration file (Listing 6.6). In the software for the book, all the entries have already been created. In the `/webapp/bin` directory there is a script called `EchoService`, which should make it easier for you to start.

In order to test the echo service, you can set up a connection with the address of the computer via Telnet to run the echo service across. You have to enter 8090 as the port.

Listing 6.6: Possible entry in `Registry.cfg`

```
{
  ...
  EchoService = {
    PATH = "../projects/Examples/Server";
    FILE = "EchoService.cfg";
    RELATIVE2CFGROOT = true ;
  };
  ...
}
```

## 6.6 Metaservice

Perhaps you have noticed that, although you can start the `EchoService` very easily via the `main()` method, no way is provided to stop it properly. As Java does not support the processing of operating system signals, we have to find another way of sending a stop signal to a service. As we have a server package at our disposal, nothing is easier than to write a metaservice via which we can start and stop other services. This is what we are going to do in the next section.

### 6.6.1 Service

If we want to start a service, we have to know the name of its entry in the `Registry.cfg` file as well as its class name. Both should be stored in a configuration file that our `AdminService` reads when it is being initialized. It seems to us to make sense to be able to assign an attribute to services that allows the `AdminService` to include the individual service in start-up. In Listing 6.7 you can see a suitable configuration file:

Listing 6.7: The `AdminService` `services.cfg` configuration file

```
{
  EchoService = {
    Class = "de.webapp.Examples.Server.EchoService";
    AutoStart = true;
  }
  aDifferentService = {
    Class = "aDifferentService";
    AutoStart = false;
  }
}
```

Naturally, only authorized persons should be allowed to start and stop the service. To keep our example simple, we have not attempted to include complex access authorization checks. If we do not want to allow unlimited access to `AdminService` for everyone, we have to check whether the address list contains the IP address of the client whom we always allow to access the service. For the sake of simplicity, we write this list in the server configuration, so the `server.cfg` file for our `AdminService` will look the same as in Listing 6.8:

Listing 6.8: `AdminService` `server.cfg` file

```
{
  PORT = 9090
  BACKLOG = 50
  MAXHANDLERTHREADS = 50
  MINHANDLERTHREADS = 1
  HANDLERCLASSNAME = "de.webapp.Framework.Server.AdminHandler"
  VALID_ADDRESSES = ("localhost","127.0.0.1")
  MAJORVERSION = 0
  MINORVERSION = 1
}
```

Listing 6.9 shows the implementation of `AdminService`. Please note that the class consists of only nine methods.

In order to fulfil the requirements, we need a list of the authorized addresses, a hash table with the active services, and the configuration for the services that are to be started. For starting the services, the configuration must also be read.

As the `init()` method from `TCPService` or `Service` calls `loadConfiguration()` in any case, it makes sense to extend the functionality of `loadConfiguration()`. The additional code checks the list of valid addresses and files and then stores them in the vector `myValidAddresses`. In addition, the `services.cfg` configuration file is read and loaded into `myServiceConfiguration`. So that we are also made aware of any change in the file, we set the `Configuration` object attribute `AutoReload` to true. This ensures that, on each attempt to read an entry in the configuration, there is a check to see if it has been changed. If that is the case, it will be automatically loaded again.

Once the configuration has been loaded via `super.init()` and the `AdminService` has been started, the `AdminService` registers itself in the service's hash table and starts the services with the characteristic `AutoStart`. To do so, it calls the `autoStart()` method, which calls the `startService(String)` for the services that are to be started. The `startService(String)` method will be passed on as a parameter for the name of a service that is to be started. If the named service has not been started yet, it will be instantiated, started and added to the services hash table. `stopService(String)` works in a similar way. Here the named service is removed from the services hash table and its `stop()` method is called, if it is running at all.

`stopAllServices()` finally stops all the services except for `AdminService`. That can only be stopped by calling its own `stop()` method, which calls `stopAllServices()`. In addition to that, the service contains only the `isValidAddress(InetAddress)` method, which checks whether there is an entry for an Internet address in the list of privileged addresses.

Listing 6.9: The `AdminService` class

```
package de.webapp.Framework.Server;

import java.net.*;
import java.util.*;
import java.io.*;

import de.webapp.Framework.Log.*;
import de.webapp.Framework.ConfigManager.*;

/** MetaService */
public class AdminService extends I_JoServletService {
/** Contains the valid login addresses */
protected Vector myValidAddresses = new Vector();
/** Contains the managed services */
protected Hashtable myServices = new Hashtable();
/** Configuration of this service */
protected Configuration myServiceConfiguration = null;
/** Defines if a user is permitted to log themselves in from an address*/
public boolean isValidAddress(InetAddress aAddress) {
   return myValidAddresses.contains(aAddress);
}
/** Initializes this service */
public synchronized void init() throws ServerException, IOException{
   super.init();
   myServices.put(getName(), this);
   autoStart();
}
```

```
/** Stops all managed services and then itself */
public synchronized void stop() throws ServerException {
  stopAllServices();
  super.stop();
}
/** Starts all services that are to be started automatically */
protected void autoStart() throws ServerException {
  Hashtable config = (Hashtable)myServiceConfiguration.getConfigData();
  Enumeration e = config.keys();
  while (e.hasMoreElements()) {
    String name = (String)e.nextElement();
    Hashtable entry = (Hashtable)config.get(name);
    if (Boolean.TRUE.equals(entry.get("AutoStart"))) {
      startService(name);
    }
  }
}
/** Starts a service via its name */
public synchronized void startService(String name) throws ServerException {
  I_Service aService = (I_Service)myServices.get(name);
  if (aService == null) {
    try {
      Class serviceClass = Class.forName(
        (String)myServiceConfiguration.getElement(name + ";Class"));
      aService = (I_Service)serviceClass.newInstance();
      myServices.put(name, aService);
    }
    catch (Throwable t) {
      throw new ServerException("Instantiation error for"+ name, t);
    }
  }
  if (!aService.isAlive()) {
    aService.setName(name);
    aService.start();
  }
  else {
    throw new ServerException("Service"+ name +"running already.");
  }
}
/** Stops a service via its name */
public synchronized void stopService(String name) throws ServerException {
  I_Service aService = (I_Service)myServices.get(name);
  if (aService != null) {
    if (!aService.isAlive()) throw new ServerException("Service"+ name
      +"is not running.");
    aService.stop();
    myServices.remove(name);
```

```
    }
    else {
      throw new ServerException("Service"+ name +"does not exist.");
    }
  }
  /** Stops all services apart from AdminService */
  protected void stopAllServices() throws ServerException {
    Enumeration e = myServices.elements();
    while (e.hasMoreElements()) {
      I_Service aService = (I_Service)e.nextElement();
      if (aService != this && aService.isAlive()) aService.stop();
    }
    myServices.clear();
  }
  /** Loads the configuration */
  public void loadConfiguration() throws ServerException {
    super.loadConfiguration();
    Configuration conf = getConfiguration();
    Vector v = (Vector)conf.getElement("VALID_ADDRESSES");
    myValidAddresses.removeAllElements();
    Enumeration e = v.elements();
    while (e.hasMoreElements()) {
      String aAddress = (String)e.nextElement();
      try {
        myValidAddresses.addElement(InetAddress.getByName(aAddress));
      }
      catch (UnknownHostException uhe) {
        if (Log.isLog(getName())) Log.log("Unknown host:"
          + aAddress, Log.ERRORs, getName());
      }
    }
    ConfigManager cm = ConfigManager.getConfigManager();
    myServiceConfiguration = cm.getConfiguration(getName(), "services.cfg");
    myServiceConfiguration.setAutoReload(true);
  }
  /** Starts the service */
  public static void main(String[] args) throws ServerException {
    AdminService admin = new AdminService();
    if (args.length == 1) {
      admin.setName(args[0]);
    }
    else {
      admin.setName("AdminService");
    }
    admin.start();
  }
} // End of the class
```

## 6.6.2 Handler

Once we have created the general functions of the service with the `AdminService` class, we still need a protocol to be able to address it. This should be created by the handler. Therefore, we need to define it first.

A client should be able to start and stop services. It seems to make sense, therefore, to be able to set up more than one command per connection, for example to stop a service and then to restart it. Also we need a command to close the connection. Basically, we only need three commands for our simple service: `start`, `stop` and `exit`.

While `exit` requires no parameters, in the case of `start` and `stop` you have to enter the name of the service. Each command should be finished by a new line character.

To implement the protocol, we overwrite the `service()` method. First we examine whether the connection was created from one of the authorized addresses. To do so, we use the `AdminSevice's isValidAddress(InetAddress)` method. If the address is not valid, we use `PrintWriter` to issue an error message and close the connection.

If the connection was started from a privileged address, we welcome the user and provide a short description of the usage, by calling the `usage(PrintWriter)` method.

Once the formalities are taken care of, users can start entering commands. To let them do that, a `BufferedReader` opens, from which one line at a time is read via a `while` loop.

Using a `java.util.StringTokenizer` the lines that have been read are now broken up into tokens. If the number of tokens is zero, the next line will be read immediately. If it is one and the token is `exit`, then return is used to leave the `service()` method. In the case of two tokens, it is important to differentiate between the two commands `start` and `stop`. If it is `start`, then the `startService(String)` method of the service is called. There the argument will be passed on as the second token. The `stop` command is used in a similar way – with the minor difference that here the `stopService(String)` method of the service is applied. In both cases, we simply output any initiated `ServerExceptions`.

If the line read contains more than two tokens and does not correspond to the cases discussed above, the `usage()` method is called, and the next line is read.

Listing 6.10: The `AdminHandler` class

```
package de.webapp.Framework.Server;

import java.net.*;
import java.util.*;
import java.io.*;

import de.webapp.Framework.Log.*;

public class AdminHandler extends TCPHandler {

public void service() {
    AdminService service = (AdminService)getService();
```

```java
  try {
      Socket aSocket = getSocket();
      PrintWriter out = new PrintWriter(new
OutputStreamWriter(aSocket.getOutputStream()), true);
      if (!service.isValidAddress(aSocket.getInetAddress())) {
        out.println("You are not allowed to log in.");
      }
      else {
        out.println("Welcome to"+ service.getName() + ".");
        usage(out);
        String line;
        BufferedReader in = new BufferedReader(
          new InputStreamReader(aSocket.getInputStream()));
        while ((line = in.readLine()) != null) {
          if (Log.isLog(service.getName())) Log.log(line,
            Log.MODUL, service.getName());
          Log.log(line, Log.ERROR, service.getName());
          StringTokenizer st = new StringTokenizer(line,"");
          int count = st.countTokens();
          if (count == 0) continue;
          if (count == 1 && line.toLowerCase().equals("exit")) {
            out.println("Bye!");
            return;
          }
          else if (count == 2) {
            String command = st.nextToken().toLowerCase();
            String serviceName = st.nextToken();
            try {
               if (command.equals("start")) {
                  service.startService(serviceName);
                  out.println("Service"+ serviceName +"has been started.");
            }
          else if (command.equals("stop")) {
            service.stopService(serviceName);
            out.println("Service"+ serviceName +"has been stopped.");
            if (serviceName.equals(service.getName())) {
              out.println("Bye!");
              return;
            }
          }
        }
            catch (ServerException se) {
              out.println(se.toString());
            }
          }
          else {
```

```
                usage(out);
            }
        }
        in.close();
    }
    out.close();
}
catch (IOException ioe) {
    if (Log.isLog(service.getName())) Log.log(ioe.toString(),
        Log.ERROR, service.getName());
    }
}

public static void usage(PrintWriter out) {
    out.println("Usage: exit | (start|stop) <servicename>");
}
} // End of the class
```

### 6.6.3  Execution

As the AdminService has a main() method, you can start it exactly the same way as the EchoService, from the command line. In any case, there is a script in the /webapp/bin/ directory with the name AdminService.

For binding itself with the AdminService, the Telnet program provides excellent services. AdminService normally listens on port 9090. If you have no access to high capacity Telnet, you can use instead an AdminClient, which you can start using a script in the same directory.

As the AdminService is used more or less the same way as any other service, you can stop it by using the stop AdminService command. In this case all the other services will also be stopped.

## 6.7  Server construction made easy

The examples show how easy server programming can be when you start on firm foundations. The ServerKit provides these firm foundations:

● ServerKit creates the service/handler pattern.

● Administration is made easy using a metaservice via defined interfaces.

● It achieves high-capacity, configurable thread management.

● The developer also only needs to implement the protocol-specific functionalities.

# Developing the  7
# servlet engine jo!

**N**ow we have used the server package to find out the basics of simple server development, we want to take a closer look into the servlets execution environment. In order to do that, we shall try to understand the basic design of the jo! servlet engine, by looking at its interfaces and some classes. jo! is a Web server, which is fully written in Java. Its servlet engine (see Chapter 3) implements the specification of Servlet API 2.1. In addition, jo! is able to manage hosts (Fig. 7.1), which means it can convert requests to one IP address into requests to different hosts. To makes this possible, the host name is always sent as a header field, in a request.

## 7.1 Basic design

Just as in the server package, we want to derive our design from a classic service handler model. That means that a service object accepts connections. Each connection that is accepted will be forwarded in the form of a Socket object to a handler. This handler is responsible for fulfilling the requested services – in our case, for calling a servlet.

As our server has to support virtual hosts, it is obvious that we should represent these hosts using objects. That means that our service object should know a fair number of host objects. According to the servlet specification, each virtual host should at least have a servlet context. Each servlet context, in turn, can theoretically have an unlimited number of servlets. A servlet instance cannot be assigned to different contexts. Similarly, one context instance can be assigned to a maximum of one host. Therefore, there is always a unique navigation path from a host to a servlet. That produces a basic design, as shown in Fig. 7.2.

The handling of a given request will always follow the same process: first the service has to find the right host, then the right servlet context and finally the requested servlet. If the request can be assigned to a servlet, this will be executed, and the client will be sent a reply.

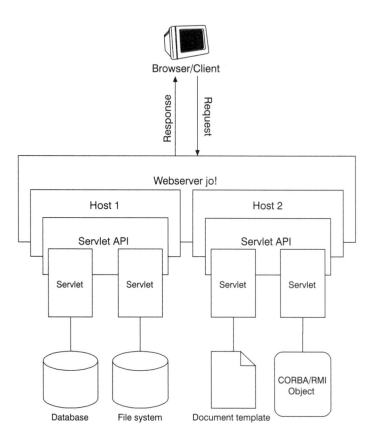

**Figure 7.1**   The architecture of jo!

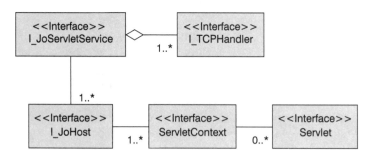

**Figure 7.2**   Basic design of jo!

## 7.2 Design improvement

To be fair to the servlet specification, we need to make some further improvements. That applies especially to the management of servlets and servlet contexts.

### 7.2.1 Servlet model

Servlets have a context, a configuration and a life cycle. All of this must be managed. Therefore, we are now going to have a look at the specification.

It follows from the signature of the `init()` method that each servlet has a `ServletConfig` object. Each `ServletConfig` object, in turn, has a `ServletContext` object. In addition to these explicit features, each servlet has an execution status. It can be carried out simultaneously by different threads. This is important as, according to the specification, a servlet can only be released when no thread is executing it. There is only one exception to this rule: after a waiting period defined by the configuration, the servlet engine can destroy a servlet, even when it is still working.

Therefore it seems to make sense to encapsulate each servlet in an object which manages the servlet's life cycle. This object should be in a position to instantiate, to initialize, to execute and to interrupt a servlet when needed. In the WebApp servlet engine jo! this object is defined by the interface `I_JoServletModel` (Fig. 7.3).

### 7.2.2 Servlet context peer

A further problem arises, concerning the servlet context. Although servlets are always assigned to a context, according to the specification, it should not be possible to obtain a servlet from a context. The `getServlet(String)` method, which is now outdated, should always return `null`, from API Version 2.1 onwards. The

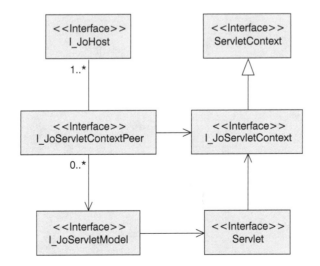

**Figure 7.3** Relationships between `I_JoServletContextPeer` and `I_JoServletContext`, and `I_JoServletModel` and the servlet

specification states explicitly that the servlets should allow no access to other servlets, as it is impossible to later check the status of a servlet. This rule contradicts our basic design which definitely demands servlets from the context.

On the one hand, we need access to the servlets in order to execute them. On the other hand, we have to conceal them from other servlets. To resolve the dilemma we introduce a new class, the servlet context peer. Its task is to manage the servlet models and to make the servlet context available. In this way we can see the context from two points of view. One – via the peer – for the engine, and one for the servlets via `ServletConfig` object.

As we can obtain the context via the peer, but cannot access the peer via the context, this ensures that no servlet has access to another servlet instance (Fig. 7.3).

### 7.2.3 Interaction

Our examination has given us a more precise picture of the processes inside the engine than we had before. As we have already described, the service receives a request, and forwards it to a handler. The handler asks the service for an acceptable host. The host will then be asked what the servlet context peer is. A servlet model is obtained from the peer, and the servlet model's encapsulated servlet is executed. The process is represented in Fig. 7.4.

In the next section we will devote more attention to the tasks of the objects.

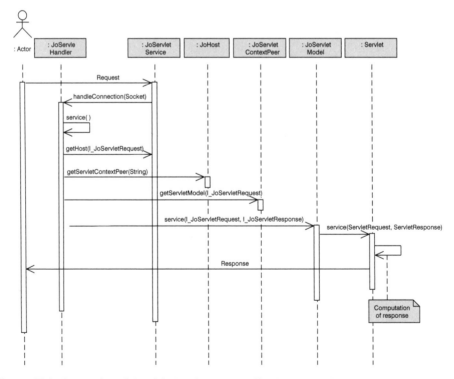

**Figure 7.4** Interaction of the objects when responding to a request

## 7.3  Service

The service object, in addition to its role as defined by the server package, provides server-wide, non-request-specific services and also finds hosts. Our previous explorations and an analysis of the servlet API interfaces lead us to the following list of objects that we need to manage:

- server sockets;
- MIME types;
- hosts.

The server socket serves to receive a connection and is already defined through I_TCPService, from which our I_JoServletService service inherits. This functionality therefore does not need to be implemented again.

The MIME types can be managed with little effort. The service simply needs to be able to assign a file extension to a MIME type. Not so simple, but still manageable, is the mapping of a request to a host. For this, you need to have a getHost(ServletRequest) method available, which accepts a request, uses it as an argument, analyzes which host the request is meant for, and returns the right host object. To achieve that, the service has to have methods that make it possible to add and remove a host.

The collected requests result in the I_JoServletService interface, which is easy to understand (Listing 7.1). This is a further development of I_TCPService:

Listing 7.1: The I_JoServletService interface

```
package de.webapp.Framework.ServletEngine;

import javax.servlet.ServletException;
import java.util.Hashtable;
import de.webapp.Framework.Server.I_TCPService;

public interface I_JoServletService extends I_TCPService {
/** Returns a host for a request */
public I_JoHost getHost(I_JoServletRequest aRequest);
/** Adds a host to the service */
public void addHost(I_JoHost aHost);
/** Removes a host from this service */
public void removeHost(I_JoHost aHost);
/** Adds a MIME type */
public void addMimeType(String aSuffix, String aMimeType);
/** Removes a MIME type */
public void removeMimeType(String aSuffix);
/** Returns a hash table of all registered MIME types */
public Hashtable getMimeTypes();
/** Returns the MIME type of a file name */
public String getMimeType(String aFile);
} // End of interface
```

## 7.4 Host

The main tasks of a host include the management and determination of servlet context peers for a given request. In addition, the host should be able to provide the document root directory, as well as information about the server. This includes, for example, the server name. Furthermore, it should know the name, the host name and also aliases for its host name. The methods for all of these functions are defined in I_JoHost interface (Listing 7.2). In addition to that, the host arranges another resource we have not mentioned so far: the session context.

The session context is responsible for managing all the sessions of a host. Up to Version 2.1 of the servlet API, the specification of the API also included a corresponding interface, but it was met with disapproval, as it gave servlets access to alien HttpSession objects. This is unacceptable on security grounds. Still, the session objects have to be managed. In jo! this is achieved via a host's session context. Neither of the objects are accessible by the servlet in jo!, therefore there is no security problem.

Apart from this, the session context offers great development potential. For instance, there are servlet engines (JRun and Java Web server) that serialize the sessions that have not been used for long, and save them on the hard disk, to save RAM capacity. For a mechanism like that, a more intelligent session management would be required than is provided by jo! Owing to abstraction by interfaces, however, a development of this kind can be installed quickly.

Just like most of the other interfaces in the de.webapp.Framework. ServletEngine package, I_JoHost also has the two life-cycle methods, init() and destroy(). As you cannot define constructors in interfaces, we use the init() method instead for defining the initialization of the object. Usually, a reference to the service object is also passed on here. To release active resources, destroy() should be called. This should happen before an object is passed on to the garbage collection.

Listing 7.2: The I_JoHost interface

```
package de.webapp.Framework.ServletEngine;

import de.webapp.Framework.ConfigManager.Configuration;
import de.webapp.Framework.Server.ServerException;
import java.util.*;

public interface I_JoHost {
/** Initializes this host */
public void init(String aName, String aHostname, Vector aAliases, String
aDocRoot, I_JoServletService aService) throws ServerException;
/** Returns the name of this host */
public String getName();
/** Returns the host name of this host */
public String getHostname();
/** Lists the aliases for the host name*/
public Enumeration getAliases();
```

```
/** Gives the name and version of the server */
public String getServerInfo();
/** Sets the document root directory */
public void setDocumentRoot(String aDocRoot);
/** Returns the document root directory */
public String getDocumentRoot();
/** Returns the appropriate ContextPeer for a URI path */
public I_JoServletContextPeer getServletContextPeer(String aURI);
/** Adds a ContextPeer to the host */
public void addServletContextPeer(I_JoServletContextPeer aPeer);
/** Removes a ContextPeer from the host */
public void removeServletContextPeer(String aName);
/** Returns the SessionContext */
public I_JoSessionContext getSessionContext();
/** Releases all resources */
public void destroy();
} // End of the interface
```

## 7.5 Servlet context peer

The servlet context peer manages the servlet models. Therefore, there must be methods for adding, removing and reaching peer models. In addition, you must be able to access a ServletContext via the peer by using the getServletContext() method. One further characteristic of the context that it is assigned to a URI path. Correspondingly, the servlet context peer must have a getURIPath() method. The complete I_JoServletContextPeer interface is defined in Listing 7.3.

The context peer has life-cycle methods with the same semantics as the host. The only difference is that the init() method can initiate a FactoryException. This happens if an attempt to instantiate a ServletContext object using JoFactory is unsuccessful (more about this in Section 7.8).

Listing 7.3: The I_JoServletContextPeer interface

```
package de.webapp.Framework.ServletEngine;

import de.webapp.Framework.Utilities.FactoryException;

public interface I_JoServletContextPeer {
/** Initializes this ContextPeer */
public void init(String aName, String aURIPath, String aDocRoot, I_JoHost
aHost, I_JoServletService aService) throws FactoryException;
/** Adds a ServletModel to the Peer*/
public void addServletModel(I_JoServletModel aModel);
/** Removes a ServletModel from the Peer */
public void removeServletModel(String aName);
/** Returns the appropriate ServletModel for a request */
```

```
public I_JoServletModel getServletModel(I_JoServletRequest aRequest);
/** Returns the name of this ContextPeer */
public String getName();
/** Returns the URI path of this context */
public String getURIPath();
/** Returns the ServletContext involved*/
public I_JoServletContext getServletContext();
/** Releases all resources */
public void destroy();
} // End of the interface
```

## 7.6 Servlet model

As we have already described, a servlet model should encapsulate each servlet. Therefore, the servlet model should have access to all the data concerning the servlet. With such data, it should be possible for the servlet model to instantiate, initialize, execute and release the servlet. Table 7.1 shows which parameters a servlet model needs to perform administration correctly.

The initialization parameters can be set when the servlet model is generated. The

**Table 7.1** Parameters required by a servlet model

| Category | Necessary parameter |
| --- | --- |
| Initialization parameters | Name, aliases, class name, initialization parameters for a ServletConfig object, ServletContext object, timeout, maximum number of the instances of a SingleThreadModel servlet |
| Execution parameters | ServletRequest and ServletResponse object |
| Internal parameters | Status |

execution parameters are the parameters of a call to service() and internal parameters are, of course, managed internally.

The description is summed up in the I_JoServletModel interface (Listing 7.4):

Listing 7.4: The I_JoServletModel interface

```
package de.webapp.Framework.ServletEngine;

import javax.servlet.*;

import java.util.*;
import java.io.*;
import de.webapp.Framework.Utilities.FactoryException; 2057

public interface I_JoServletModel {
/** Initializes this model */
```

```
public void init(String aClassname,
     Hashtable aInitParameters,
     int aDestroyTimeout,
     int aMaxActiveInstances,
     String aName,
     Vector aliases,
     I_JoServletContext aContext,
     I_JoServletService aService)
        throws FactoryException;
/** Returns the name of the model */
public String getName();
/** Returns a list of the aliases for this model */
public Enumeration getAliases();
/** Sets the maximum number of active instances */
public void setMaxActiveInstances(int max);
/** Returns the maximum number of active instances */
public int getMaxActiveInstances();
/** Sets the time after which the servlet can be forcibly released */
public void setDestroyTimeout(int aTimeout);
/** Returns the time after which the servlet can be forcibly released */
public int getDestroyTimeout();
/** Instantiates the servlet, if this has not yet happened */
public void preload() throws FactoryException, ServletException;
/** Carries out a request */
public void service(I_JoServletRequest aRequest, I_JoServletResponse
aResponse)
        throws IOException, ServletException;
/** Releases the servlet */
public void unload();
/** Shows whether the servlet is ready for use */
public boolean isLoaded();
/** Returns the class name of the servlet */
public String getClassname();
} // End of the interface
```

Here, just like in I_JoServletContextPeer, the init() method can initiate a FactoryException. That happens if an attempt to instantiate a ServletConfig object using JoFactory is unsuccessful (more about this in Section 7.8). Just like the ServletContext object, the ServletConfig object is set at the time the model is initialized. Here the ServletContext object cannot instantiate itself, but is passed on as a parameter, as it is a resource that is divided among various servlet models.

In comparison with the init() method, the service() method is elementary. It should be implemented in such a way that the encapsulated servlet is instantiated and initialized, if that has not already happened. If the model has a ready-to-use servlet instance, then it executes its service().

If you want to end the life cycle of the encapsulated servlet, you can call the unload() method. It should call the destroy() method of all servlet instances referenced by this model. When doing so, it should wait for the amount of time set in the destroy timeout before releasing a servlet that has just been executed.

In order to gain a little more control over the status of the model, it also has the methods preload() and isLoaded(). The preload() method instantiates and initializes a servlet, without executing it. isLoaded() specifies whether the model has at least one ready-to-use instance of the servlet. The getClassname() method returns the class names of the encapsulated servlets. getAliases() returns a list of the rules on the basis of which the servlet is mapped on a URI.

Now we explain the role of the setMaxActiveInstances(int) and getMaxActiveInstances() methods. In the special case that a servlet implements the javax.servlet.SingleThreadModel interface (Section 3.7.2), the servlet model has to be in the position to manage a pool of servlet instances. The size of the pool has to be limited so that memory use can be controlled. Both methods also serve the purpose of controlling the way the pool behaves. If we are not dealing with a SingleThreadModel servlet, both methods are irrelevant.

## 7.7 Handler

The handler is the next step when the service has already established a connection and a request is waiting to be fulfilled. In our case, a request always refers to a servlet. It is therefore appropriate to read the request and then to find and execute the corresponding relevant servlet.

So far, we have considered requests in the abstract. But inside the servlet API we are dealing with a concrete object that is defined by the ServletRequest interface and its extension HttpServletRequest. The same applies to the response sent by the server. It is mapped by the objects ServletResponse or Http-ServletResponse.

It is therefore the handler's task to generate a ServletRequest and a ServletResponse object. The Handler then uses the ServletRequest object to ask the Service for a model. At this point the model's service() method is executed with ServletRequest and ServletResponse as parameters (Fig. 7.4 and Fig. 7.5). As this is a fairly simple process, which easily finds a place in the service() method of a TCPHandler, it is not necessary to define a separate interface for our handler.

The request and reply objects are more interesting. Both require the connection's socket as an initializing parameter. This is necessary to obtain the input and output stream and to get information about other data concerning the connection such as the server name and address, as well as the port number. For this, both need a reference to the service. This is especially necessary to ensure the session management is processed correctly, as this is managed by the host, which is accessible via the service. Similarly, information about log services and similar things can be provided via the service and host. This includes the server name, which should be included in the header of each reply.

While the logical separation of ServletRequest and ServletResponse seems to make sense at first, it causes session management problems. In reality, the

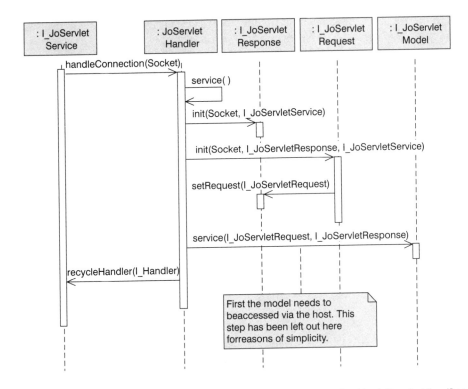

**Figure 7.5** Interaction within the handleConnection(Socket) method in JoServletHandler

request/response model is specified by Sun, and session management functionality was added to it later. To make this possible, it is really imperative that an HttpServletRequest should know its HttpServletResponse and vice versa (Fig. 7.5). Otherwise it would not be possible to use the request object to generate a session as to do so it would be necessary to set a cookie. Even so, URL rewriting could not be achieved by the response object without using session dates that are only available with the help of HttpServletRequest. There are two possible ways to implement this: both interfaces in one class or a separate class for each interface.

As both of the interfaces are very extensive, we have to decided to write two classes. This is not mandatory. For example, version 1.0 of the JServ servlet engine combines the two interfaces in the JServConnection class. However, with over 1700 lines of code, this is very hard to see, read and understand.

## 7.8 JoFactory

Now that we have had an overview of the structure of the most important interfaces of jo!, we want to look briefly at another design element. As already explained in the introductory session to the framework section of this book, in the course of development we laid emphasis on the fact that as many parts of the framework as possible, and therefore of jo!, have been defined by interfaces. Obviously, implementations of these interfaces also exist. However, it is not necessary to use them. In jo! it is particularly easy to exchange the implemented classes of an interface. All you have to do is edit the /webapp/projects/jo/etc/factory.cfg configuration file.

Listing 7.5: The factory.cfg file defines which class is to be used to create each interface

```
// "factory.cfg" file

{
    I_JoServletConfig = "de.webapp.Framework.ServletEngine.JoServletConfig"
    I_JoServletModel = "de.webapp.Framework.ServletEngine.JoServletModel"
    I_JoServletContext = "de.webapp.Framework.ServletEngine.JoServletContext"
    I_JoServletContextPeer =
    "de.webapp.Framework.ServletEngine.JoServletContextPeer"
    I_JoServletRequest = "de.webapp.Framework.ServletEngine.JoServletRequest"
    I_JoServletResponse =
    "de.webapp.Framework.ServletEngine.JoServletResponse"
    I_JoServletService = "de.webapp.Framework.ServletEngine.JoServletService"
    I_JoSession = "de.webapp.Framework.ServletEngine.JoSession"
    I_JoSessionContext = "de.webapp.Framework.ServletEngine.JoSessionContext"
    I_TCPHandler = "de.webapp.Framework.ServletEngine.JoServletHandler"
    I_JoRequestWrapper = "de.webapp.Framework.ServletEngine.JoRequestWrapper"
    I_JoResponseWrapper =
    "de.webapp.Framework.ServletEngine.JoResponseWrapper"
    I_JoRequestDispatcher =
    "de.webapp.Framework.ServletEngine.JoRequestDispatcher"
    I_JoHost = "de.webapp.Framework.ServletEngine.JoHost"
}
```

The factory.cfg file contains a list that consists of aliases and their corresponding class names. If you ask the relevant JoFactory class for an alias, you are given an instance of the class with the class name assigned to it. Basically, all the important classes are instantiated within jo! this way. One of the results of this method is that all the classes have to have an argument-free constructor. Instead, initialization is carried out with an init() method that has already been defined in the interface.

The gain is greater flexibility. For example, if the servlet API changes in such a way that the new version is not compatible with the old one, you need to edit only the configuration file to change the classes to be implemented. This way, for example, you can integrate a completely different session management system. It makes quick migration and testing the engine with different versions substantially easier.

## 7.9  What jo! achieves

Now that we have discussed the design of jo! we would like to emphasize again what functions it performs:

- jo! is based on a server kit. In this way, we have achieved a clear break between the general server functionality (thread management) and special server technology (web server, servlet engine). This way, it is easy to extend both parts sensibly. In addition jo! implements the I_Service interface. That means that any administration service developed for the server kit can also control jo!.

- jo! implements version 2.1 of the servlet API. The design already includes support for different ServletContexts. Using configuration files you can even define another class for the ServletContext. In addition, it supports the RequestDispatcher interface.

- jo! takes into account the requirement for virtual hosts and supports them in the architecture.

- jo! is entirely defined using interfaces. The classes that fill these interfaces, while in operation, can be changed by modifying a configuration file.

# Servlet method invocation    **8**

**A**s you can see from the example servlets of Chapter 3, it is very difficult to accommodate more than one function in a `servlet`. In the examples we have mostly used the GET method to display pages, while we used the POST method for actions such as sending mail. Often, however, it is not enough to distinguish two operating modes. In order to build an application with servlets, the individual servlets have to be able to provide, or at least have access to, an unlimited number of services. Servlets often serve as mediators between the user and an application: they connect an otherwise unrelated application to a Web server.

Obviously, you will not be able to create hundreds of functions using a single Web server. It makes much more sense to use the servlet to access other servers, each of which always provides a manageable number of functions. It makes sense to be able to associate these components with a servlet. This way, you can build aggregates from standard and special components according to application. A standard component could, for instance, encapsulate access to a database, or the mail API, while a special component implements servlet-specific logic and another component organizes access to non-server-specific business objects.

In order to increase the degree of reusability in different applications, the components have to be compliant with the beans specification (`http://java.sun.com/beans/ docs/spec.html`). For this, we consider it opportune to use the beans event model to achieve the communication between the servlet and the components. All things considered, this process guarantees optimum separation of our components – from the servlet architecture as well as from each other.

In order to make the combined use of resources (databases, external devices, etc.) possible, the components of a servlet must be able to share objects by using a commonly accessible data structure. Just as defined in `HttpSession` (Section 3.9.5), you should be able to notify the bound objects, when they are connected and disconnected. Therefore, each component should be able to send information in the form of an event to another component in the same aggregate.

As several servlets or component aggregates should be able to be share resources between them, there must therefore also exist a context similar to the `ServletContext` in servlet API 2.1. On the other hand, objects bound to the context must be informed if they are connected or disconnected. This function is missing from servlet API 2.1 and requires its own release mechanism.

To sum up, our framework should fulfil the following requirements to improve the servlet API:

- Implement many functions through one servlet.
- Encapsulate functions belonging together, using components.
- Ensure the reusability of standard components through explicit support for aggregates.
- Access functions using through a signal-oriented communication mechanism (events).
- Make collective use of resources on different levels (servlet, components and session).
- Use life-cycle-oriented management of distributed resources.

Package `de.webapp.Framework.SMI` contains the described framework. Analogously to RMI (Remote Method Invocation), SMI stands for Servlet Method Invocation.

## 8.1 Architecture

We would like to clarify which processes are worth putting into practice. A request should be received by a servlet and forwarded to a certain component. This component should process the request and, following this, the requests should be forwarded to another component if necessary.

To work effectively, it is not sufficient to forward the request, i.e. the `ServletRequest` object. A request is only complete when it includes the `ServletResponse` and `ServletContext` objects. As we do not want to forward the three objects belonging together separately, we encapsulate them in an `SMIEvent` (Listing 8.1). Using an `SMIServlet`, which functions as a place for accepting the request, we have to instantiate the `SMIEvent` and then pass it on to the right components. The event is therefore our central communication mechanism. To keep it flexible, it should be as easy as possible to arrange for a servlet to instantiate other event classes which inherit from `SMIEvent`. Therefore we arrange for it to be produced by an `I_SMIEventFactory` that is associated with the `servlet`.

Listing 8.1: The `SMIEvent` class

```
package de.webapp.Framework.SMI;

import java.util.*;

import javax.servlet.*;
import javax.servlet.http.*;

import de.webapp.Framework.ConfigManager.*;

public class SMIEvent extends java.util.EventObject {
/** Values */
```

```
protected Hashtable myValues;
/** The HttpServletRequest object */
protected HttpServletRequest myRequest;
/** The HttpServletResponse object */
protected HttpServletResponse myResponse;
/** The ServletContext object */
protected ServletContext myServletContext = null;
/** Name of the I_SMIEventListener that is to execute the event */
protected String mySMIEventListenerName;

public SMIEvent(Object aSource, ServletContext aServletContext,
HttpServletRequest aRequest, HttpServletResponse aResponse, String
aSMIEventListenerName) {
   super(aSource);
   mySMIEventListenerName = aSMIEventListenerName;
   myRequest = aRequest;
   myResponse = aResponse;
   myServletContext = aServletContext;
   myValues = new Hashtable();
   myValues.put("REQUEST", aRequest);
   myValues.put("RESPONSE", aResponse);
   myValues.put("SERVLETCONTEXT", aServletContext);
}
/** Returns the servlet context. */
public ServletContext getServletContext() {
   return myServletContext;
}
/** Returns the HttpServletRequest object. */
public HttpServletRequest getRequest() {
   return myRequest;
}
/** Returns the HttpServletResponse object. */
public HttpServletResponse getResponse() {
   return myResponse;
}
/** Returns the name of the executing listener. */
public String getSMIEventListenerName() {
   return mySMIEventListenerName;
}
/** Returns a list of the keys. */
public Enumeration getKeys() {
   return myValues.keys();
}
/** Returns a parameter. */
public Object getValue(Object aKey) {
   return myValues.get(aKey);
```

```
}
/** Sets a value. */
public void putValue(Object aKey, Object aValue) {
  myValues.put(aKey, aValue);
}
/** Deletes a value. */
public void removeValue(Object aKey) {
  myValues.remove(aKey);
}
} // End of the class
```

Encapsulation has other advantages in addition to being easy to work with. As there must be a parameter that is used to define which components have to be notified of this event, SMIEvent also has the method getSMIEventListenerName(). The listener name is, in a sense, the address to which the event has to be delivered. It describes the SMIEventListener. In this case, we are talking about a component that implements I_SMIEventListener interface (Listing 8.2), and with which it can respond to SMIEvents.

The fact that the SMIEvent knows the names of its target only partially complies with the beans specification. The alternative would be that, for many events, you would have to define their own event classes, which would each be delivered only to specific, registered listeners. The effort required in this case would far outweigh the benefit, therefore we use universal SMIEvents, which are made specific via their Listenername attribute.

The indirect integration of an event with its listener via a name (Alias) leads furthermore to a stronger separation of the individual components and makes it possible to influence the behaviour of SMI easily, via configuration settings. This, in turn, increases the degree of reusability substantially.

Listing 8.2: The I_SMIEventListener interface

```
package de.webapp.Framework.SMI;

public interface I_SMIEventListener extends java.util.EventListener {

/** Initializes this listener. */
public void init(String aName, I_SMIEventSwitch aSMIEventSwitch);
/** Executes a command. */
public void executeSMIEvent(SMIEvent aSMIEvent);
/** Returns the name of this listener. */
public String getName();
/** Returns the EventSwitch of this listener. */
public I_SMIEventSwitch getSMIEventSwitch();
/** Releases any resources in use. */
public void destroy();
} // End of the interface
```

For passing an SMIEvent on to the right I_SMIEventListener, the SMIServlet

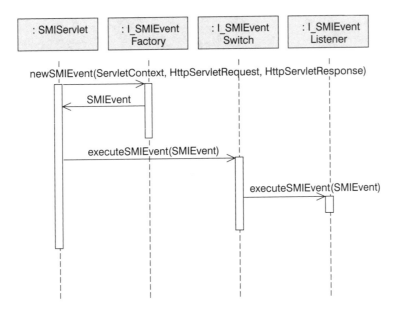

**Figure 8.1** Class diagram for SMI

has an I_SMIEventSwitch. Furthermore, each I_SMIEventSwitch is registered with an I_SMIContext (Fig. 8.1). Therefore, it is possible to divide objects between the I_SMIEventListeners of different I_SMIEventSwitches.

## 8.2 Life cycle

The architecture explained above makes it possible to encapsulate a request and to pass it on to an I_SMIEventListener in the form of an SMIEvent, via an I_SMIEventSwitch (Fig. 8.2). In this case, an I_SMIEventFactory is responsible for telling the event which I_SMIEventListener it is to be passed to. For this purpose, it is useful for the factory to have a configuration which is communicated to it in order to initialize it. Equally, the servlet has to know the name of its I_SMIEventSwitch, which I_SMIEventListeners are registered with it, and to which I_SMIContext the resulting object will belong.

In addition to its role as an interface to the servlet engine, SMIServlet also undertakes the task of producing an instantiation situation which is described using the configuration file. As the servlet has available to it a remotely controlled life cycle (Section 3.4), it makes sense to also make the servlet responsible for dismantling the instances that have been created. Correspondingly, all the interfaces involved have initializing and releasing methods called init() and destroy(). As javax.servlet.Servlet already has a corresponding method, there is no interface for a servlet in the SMI package.

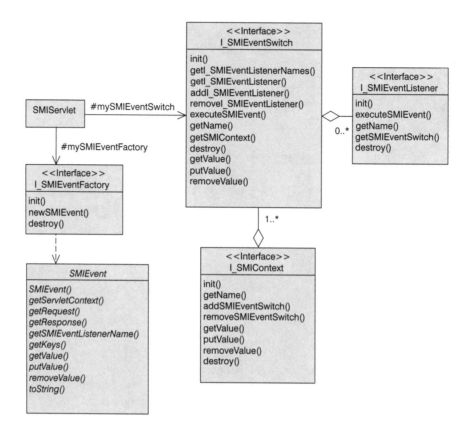

**Figure 8.2**  Basic architecture of SMI

## 8.2.1  Initialization

The creation of the servlet must obviously follow a prescribed sequence (Fig. 8.3). First the `I_SMIEventFactory` is instantiated, then the `I_SMIEventSwitch` and finally the `I_SMIEventListener`. The `I_SMIEventSwitch` must also be registered with its `I_SMIContext`.

As an `I_SMIContext` is shared by several `I_SMIEventSwitches` and `SMIServlets`, it cannot simply be instantiated by the `servlet`. In fact there has to be a check to see whether the context already exists. It only has to be instantiated if it does not exist. Ideally, the engine should take responsibility for administering the context. As it is generally difficult to extend servlet engines, we have to find another way.

The singleton `SMIContextManager` takes over the administration of the contexts. If a context is requested by it, it either returns an existing one, or instantiates it if necessary.

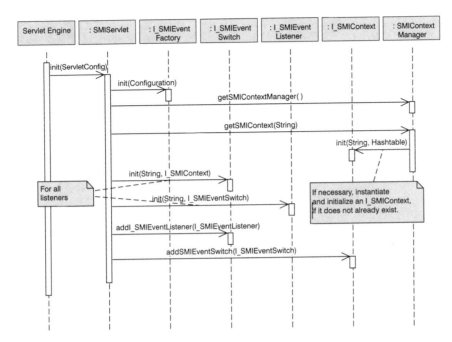

**Figure 8.3** Sequence diagram for the initialization of an SMIServlet

## 8.2.2 Release

The process for releasing I_SMIContexts also differs from the process for releasing the other objects involved (Fig. 8.4). The context cannot simply be released when one of the registered servlets is released. The context can only be released once the last I_SMIEventSwitch registered with I_SMIContext is released. That means that I_SMIEventSwitches have to be removed from their I_SMIContext when their destroy() method is called. Once the last I_SMIEventSwitch has been removed, the I_SMIContext must leave the SMIContextManager and release all the objects bound to it.

## 8.3 Bound objects

An event object is used to inform objects that are created in the HttpSessionBindingListener, I_SMIContextBindingListener or I_SMIEvent SwitchBindingListener interfaces, when they are bound to a session event switch or context, or unbound from it. The possible events are called, accordingly, HttpSessionBindingEvent, SMIContextBindingEvent and SMIEventSwitch BindingEvent. The methods called always have the signature valueBound (<x>BindingEvent) and valueUnbound(<x>BindingEvent):

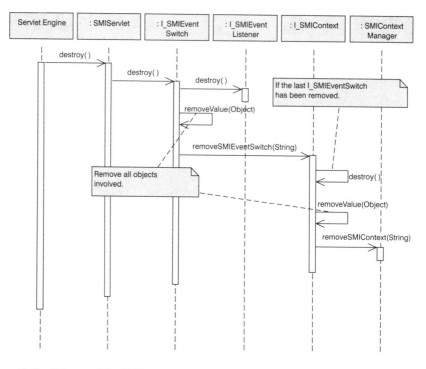

**Figure 8.4** Release of the SMIServlet

Listing 8.3: I_SMIEventSwitchBindingListener interface

```
package de.webapp.Framework.SMI;
public interface I_SMIEventSwitchBindingListener {
  public void valueBound(SMIEventSwitchBindingEvent event);
  public void valueUnbound(SMIEventSwitchBindingEvent event);
} // End of the interface
```

Listing 8.4: I_SMIContextBindingListener interface

```
package de.webapp.Framework.SMI;
public interface I_SMIContextBindingListener {
  public void valueBound(SMIContextBindingEvent event);
  public void valueUnbound(SMIContextBindingEvent event);
} // End of the interface
```

In practice, the interfaces and events shown are particularly useful when a resource should react automatically to its release. For instance, a database connection could automatically close itself as soon as it is disconnected from the I_SMIContext.

## 8.4 Implementation

The model described allows for different implementations and therefore specializations. At the end of the day, we are dealing only with an infrastructure that transports messages. If we want to use this conveniently, it is worth specializing it.

### 8.4.1 Command orientation

The implementation contained in the SMI package uses this method: a request always contains request parameters which are accessible via the `ServletRequest.getParameter(String)` method. The aim is to be able to send a request with a special parameter to our `SMIServlet`. This then makes sure that the corresponding method in an `I_SMIEvent`Listener is executed. To achieve this we define the parameter with the name `Command` to be an alias for a method in an `I_SMIEventListener` (Fig. 8.5).

In order to work comfortably, it is handy to specialize the `SMIEvent`. The command can be accessed easily via the `getCommand()` method. In addition, we also extend the `SMIEvent` by adding methods which allow us to access the session object of the request. We call the resulting class `SMICommand` (Fig. 8.6 and Listing 8.5):

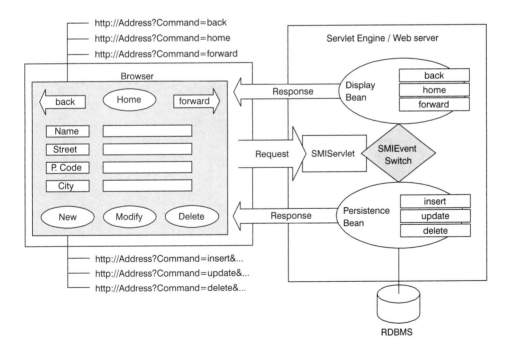

**Figure 8.5** Simplified process for calling a command: `DisplayBean` and `PersistenceBean` are the `I_SMIEventListener`

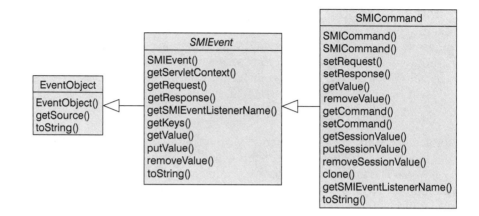

**Figure 8.6** Relationships between the classes `java.util.EventObject`, `SMIEvent` and `SMICommand`

Listing 8.5: The `SMICommand` class

```
package de.webapp.Framework.SMI;

import java.util.*;

import javax.servlet.*;
import javax.servlet.http.*;

import de.webapp.Framework.ConfigManager.*;

public class SMICommand extends SMIEvent implements C_SMI, Cloneable {

/** The command */
protected String myCommand;
/** Default parameter */
protected Hashtable myDefaultParameter;
/** Init parameter */
protected Hashtable myInitParameter;
/** Assignment of commands to listeners */
protected Hashtable myCommand2Listener;

public SMICommand (
     Object aSource,
     ServletContext aServletContext,
     HttpServletRequest req,
     HttpServletResponse res,
     String aCommand,
     Hashtable aValues,
     Hashtable aInitParameter,
     Hashtable aDefaultParameter,
     Hashtable aCommand2Listener
```

```
  ) {
    super(aSource, aServletContext, req, res, null);
    myCommand = aCommand;
    if (aInitParameter != null) myInitParameter =
    (Hashtable)aInitParameter.clone();
    if (aDefaultParameter != null) myDefaultParameter =
      (Hashtable)aDefaultParameter.clone();
    myValues = aValues;
    myCommand2Listener = aCommand2Listener;
    // Overwrite listenername
    mySMIEventListenerName = getSMIEventListenerName(myCommand);
}

// Constructor for creating clones.
public SMICommand (SMICommand aSMICommand, Hashtable aValues, Hashtable
aInitParameter, Hashtable aDefaultParameter, Hashtable aCommand2Listener) {
    super(
      aSMICommand.getSource(),
      aSMICommand.getServletContext(),
      aSMICommand.getRequest(),
      aSMICommand.getResponse(),
      aSMICommand.getSMIEventListenerName()
    );
    myCommand = aSMICommand.getCommand();
    myInitParameter = aInitParameter;
    myDefaultParameter = aDefaultParameter;
    myValues = (Hashtable)aValues.clone();
    myCommand2Listener = aCommand2Listener;
}
/** Sets the HttpServletRequest. */
public void setRequest(HttpServletRequest aRequest) {
    myRequest = aRequest;
    myValues.put("REQUEST", aRequest);
}
/** Sets the HttpServletResponse. */
public void setResponse(HttpServletResponse aResponse) {
    myResponse = aResponse;
    myValues.put("RESPONSE", aResponse);
}
/** Returns a parameter */
public Object getValue(Object aKey) {
    Object value = super.getValue(aKey);
    if (value == null) {
      if (myDefaultParameter != null) {
        value = myDefaultParameter.get(aKey);
      }
```

```
      if (value == null) {
        if (myInitParameter != null) {
          value = myInitParameter.get(aKey);
        }
      }
    }
    return value;
  }
  /** Deletes a value */
  public void removeValue(Object aKey) {
    myValues.remove(aKey);
    if (aInitParameter != null) myInitParameter.remove(aKey);
    if (aDefaultParameter != null) myDefaultParameter.remove(aKey);
  }
  /** Returns the command */
  public String getCommand() {
    return myCommand;
  }
  /** Sets the command. */
  public String setCommand(String aCommand) {
    String oldCommand = myCommand;
    myCommand = aCommand;
    // Set listenername
    mySMIEventListenerName = getSMIEventListenerName(myCommand);
    return oldCommand;
  }
  /** Returns the value of an object that is attached to the session */
  public Object getSessionValue(String aKey) {
    return getRequest().getSession(false).getValue(aKey);
  }
  /** Adds an object to the session */
  public void putSessionValue(String aKey, Object aValue) {
    getRequest().getSession(false).putValue(aKey, aValue);
  }
  /** Deletes an object that is attached to the session */
  public void removeSessionValue(String aKey) {
    getRequest().getSession(false).removeValue(aKey);
  }
  /** Returns a flat copy of the object */
  public Object clone() {
    return new SMICommand(this, myValues, myInitParameter,
myDefaultParameter,
      myCommand2Listener);
  }
  /** Returns the listenername for a command */
  protected String getSMIEventListenerName(String aCommand) {
```

```
        return (String)myCommand2Listener.get(aCommand);
    }
} // End of the class
```

## 8.4.2 Configuration

Just like SMIEvent, the SMICommand has to be instantiated by an I_SMIEventFactory. The class to create the command is called SMICommandFactory. For the instantiation of an SMICommand, the factory interprets a configuration that the SMIServlet passes to it (Listing 8.6). The configuration defines which command is assigned to each SMIEventListener, which of the listener's methods belong to each command, as well as defining which pre-defined (default) values are to be available to the SMICommand.

In addition to this, the configuration file defines which I_SMIEventListeners belong to this servlet. That happens in the first part. After the keyword Listener you can enter the names of listeners in a hash table which, in turn, will be more closely defined by the Class attribute in a hash table. Optionally, you can use the parameters EventFactoryClass and EventSwitchClass to enter the class names of I_SMIEventFactory and I_SMIEventSwitch. The first part of the configuration therefore primarily defines the instantiation situation of the SMI layer.

In the second part we set command-specific default values. That is, to begin with, the standard command DefaultCommand, with which you define what happens when a request contains no parameter with the name Command. In addition, you can use Values to define default values which you can access later, via the SMICommand getValue() method. In the third part we define the commands. A command has to have the attributes MethodName and Listener. Optionally you can, once again, set default values that you can access via getValue(). Fundamentally, the default values in the third part overlap the values set in the second part. The values set in the third part are then in turn overlapped by the parameters of HttpServletRequest. For the sake of convenience, they are always accessible via getValue() – with the difference that all the String arrays are converted into vectors.

Listing 8.6: Example SMI file

```
{
    // Part I: Description of the instantiation situation of the SMI layer
    Listener = {
        PersistenceBean = {
            Class = "de.webapp.Framework.SMICommandListener. PersistenceBean";
        },
        DisplayBean = {
            Class = "de.webapp.Framework.SMICommandListener.DisplayBean";
        }
    };
    // Optional:
    // EventFactoryClass = "de.webapp.Framework.SMI.SMICommandFactory";
```

```
// EventSwitchClass = " de.webapp.Framework.SMI.SMIEventSwitch";
// Part II: Default values for commands
DefaultCommand = "display";
Values = {
  _FollowUpCommand = "display";
  _TemplateName = "/htdocs/index.html";
}
// Part III: Definition of the commands
Commands = {
  display = {
    MethodName = "display";
    Listener = "DisplayBean" ;
  }
  NewObject= {
    MethodName = "getStore";
    Listener = "PersistenceBean" ;
    Values = {
      _TemplateName = "/jsp/object.jsp"
    }
  }
}
}
```

The initialization arguments EventSwitch and Context tell the SMIServlet
which configuration file it needs to interpret. The context has to correspond to an
entry in the Registry.cfg file. Through this relationship the directory in which the
configuration file is stored is determined implicitly. The name of the EventSwitch
should correspond to the name of a file with the extension .smi in this directory. If
we were to interpret both configuration files from Listings 8.7 and 8.8 then the file
/projects/OnlineShop/OnlineShop.smi would also have to be read.

Listing 8.7: Extract from the servlets.properties file

```
...
# OnlineShop
servlet.OnlineShop.code=de.webapp.OnlineShop.OnlineShopServlet
servlet.OnlineShop.initArgs=EventSwitch=OnlineShop,Context=OnlineShop
...
```

Listing 8.8: Extract from the Registry.cfg file

```
{
  ...
  OnlineShop = {
    PATH = "/projects/OnlineShop";
  };
```

```
    ...
}
```

In addition to the SMI definition files there is another configuration file for the SMIContext. You can find it in the same directory as the SMI files. The file has the same name as the context, with the additional file extension con. From OnlineShop for example, we get OnlineShop.con. The class name of the I_SMIContext and default values can be defined in it:

Listing 8.9: Example context definition file

```
{
    Class = "de.webapp.Framework.SMI.SMIContext"
    Values = {
        aKey = "aValue"
    }
}
```

### 8.4.3 SMICommandListener

Once the SMICommand has been generated, it is passed on via the mechanism described above to an I_SMIEventListener (Listing 8.2), by calling its executeSMIEvent() method. Now, there is nothing defined in the interface I_SMIEventListener that would allow the interpretation of a command. For this reason we extend I_SMIEventListener to I_SMICommandListener:

Listing 8.10: The I_SMICommandListener interface.

```
package de.webapp.Framework.SMI;

import java.lang.reflect.*;
import java.util.Enumeration;

public interface I_SMICommandListener extends I_SMIEventListener {
/** Adds an alias for a method */
public void addMethodAlias(String aAlias, String aMethodName) throws
NoSuchMethodException;
/** Removes an alias for a method */
public void removeMethodAlias(String aAlias);
/** Returns all aliases */
public Enumeration getAliases();
} // End of the interface
```

I_SMICommandListener provides methods with which you can administer aliases for method names. The alias in this case stands for a command. It is worth noting that a method can be assigned to different commands in this way, allowing you to separate the mechanism. This would not be possible if the command and the method name were the same.

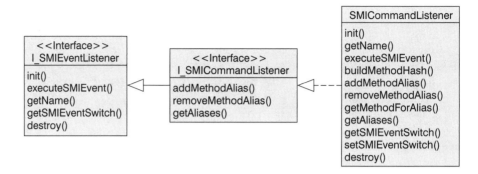

**Figure 8.7** Relationship between I_SMIEventListener, I_SMICommandListener and SMICommandListener

The interface is created using the SMICommandListener class (Listing 8.11 and Fig. 8.7). It provides an automated mechanism for calling the methods. To do this, you use Java's Reflect API (see JDK documentation for the java.lang.reflect package).

Listing 8.11: The SMICommandListener class

```java
package de.webapp.Framework.SMI;

import java.util.*;
import java.lang.reflect.*;

public class SMICommandListener implements I_SMICommandListener,
java.io.Serializable {
/** EventSwitch for this SMICommandListener */
protected transient I_SMIEventSwitch mySMIEventSwitch;
/** Aliases */
protected transient Hashtable myAliases;
/** Method objects*/
protected transient Hashtable myMethods;
/** Name of listener */
protected String myName;
/** Parameters for this CommandListener */
protected Hashtable myParameters;

/** Initializes this listener. */
public void init(String aName, Hashtable aParameters, I_SMIEventSwitch
aSMIEventSwitch) {
  myName = aName;
  mySMIEventSwitch = aSMIEventSwitch;
  myAliases = new Hashtable();
  myMethods = new Hashtable();
  myParameters = aParameters;
  buildMethodHash();
}
```

```
/** Returns the name of the listener */
public String getName() {
   return myName;
}
/** Uses invoke to execute a command. */
public void executeSMIEvent(SMIEvent aSMIEvent) {
   SMICommand aSMICommand = (SMICommand)aSMIEvent;
   Method theMethod = getMethodForAlias(aSMICommand.getCommand());
   if (theMethod != null) {
      Object[] args = {aSMICommand};
      try {
         theMethod.invoke(this, args);
      }
      catch (Throwable t) {
         if (t instanceof InvocationTargetException) {
            throw new SMIEventListenerException
               (((InvocationTargetException)t).getTargetException());
         }
         throw new SMIEventListenerException(t);
      }
   }
}
/** Stores the method objects in myMethods. */
protected void buildMethodHash() {
   myMethods.clear();
   Class[] aSignature = { SMIEvent.class };
   Class[] types;
   Method[] methods = this.getClass().getMethods();
   for (int i=0; i<methods.length; i++) {
      types = methods[i].getParameterTypes();
      if (types.length == 1) {
         if (aSignature[0].isAssignableFrom(types[0])) {
            myMethods.put(methods[i].getName(), methods[i]);
         }
      }
   }
}
/** Adds an alias for a method */
public void addMethodAlias(String aAlias, String aMethodName) throws
NoSuchMethodException {
   Method theMethod = null;
   theMethod = (Method)myMethods.get(aMethodName);
   if (theMethod == null) {
      throw new NoSuchMethodException("There is no method" + aMethodName
         + " in receiver " + this.getClass().getName());
   }
```

```
          myAliases.put(aAlias, theMethod);
      }
      /** Removes an alias for a method */
      public void removeMethodAlias(String aAlias) {
        myAliases.remove(aAlias);
      }
      /** Returns a method for an alias */
      public Method getMethodForAlias(String aAlias) {
        return (Method)myAliases.get(aAlias);
      }
      /** Returns all aliases */
      public Enumeration getAliases() {
        return myAliases.keys();
      }
      /** Returns the EventSwitch for this CommandListener */
      public I_SMIEventSwitch getSMIEventSwitch() {
        return mySMIEventSwitch;
      }
      /** Sets the EventSwitch for this CommandListener */
      public void setSMIEventSwitch(I_SMIEventSwitch aSMIEventSwitch) {
        mySMIEventSwitch = aSMIEventSwitch;
      }
      /** Releases all resources in use */
      public void destroy() { }
    } // End of the class
```

During initialization, SMICommandListener uses buildMethodHash() to create a
hash table of all its methods and their names, which accept an SMIEvent or a subclass
as an argument. Using addMethodForAlias(), assignations of aliases to method
objects can then be registered. That happens during initialization via the SMIServlet.

The main trick for executing all the required commands is coded in the
executeSMIEvent() method. When you call it, the SMIEvent is converted into an
SMICommand (Typecast) and it will be asked for its command using getCommand().

A Method object is found for the command via getMethodForAlias() and executed as an argument with the SMICommand via invoke(). If invoke() fails, the
released Throwable will be encapsulated in an SMIEvent ListenerException. In
the case that an InvocationTargetException is concerned, only the target exception is encapsulated.

As long as SMICommandListener is not extended, this process makes no particular sense – after all, the only method that accepts SMIEvent as an argument is the
executeSMIEvent() method. However, if a class has inherited from SMICommand
Listener, its methods will be automatically registered, and nothing else stands in
the way of its execution via an SMICommand – provided that an alias has been registered for the method.

The use of SMICommandListeners and the entire SMI framework will be demonstrated in detail in the third part of this book. Therefore we have only a small
example here.

## 8.5  DisplayBean

We would like to use the `DisplayBean` (Listing 8.12) as a simple example of an `I_SMICommandListener`. It should interpret the predefined parameter `C_ConfigTemplateName` as a URI, and pass on the request through a `RequestDispatcher`. In order also to be able to access the `SMIEvent` in the addressed resources, the `SMIEvent` is set as an attribute of the request.

Listing 8.12: The `DisplayBean` class from the
`de.webapp.Framework.SMICommandListener` package

```
package de.webapp.Framework.SMICommandListener;

import javax.servlet.*;
import javax.servlet.http.*;
import java.io.*;
import java.util.Hashtable;
import de.webapp.Framework.SMI.*;

public class DisplayBean extends SMICommandListener implements Serializable
{

/** Constants for obtaining the template name from the I_SMIEvent. */
public static String C_ConfigTemplateName = "_TemplateName";
/**
   * Represents a page that has been specified in the _TemplateName
   * command attribute
   * In the request, the command object is stored as an attribute
   * with the key SMIEvent.
   */
public void display (SMIEvent aSMIEvent)
    throws IOException, ServletException {
  aSMIEvent.getRequest().setAttribute("SMIEvent", aSMIEvent);
  String theTemplateName =
  (String)aSMIEvent.getValue(C_ConfigTemplateName);
  RequestDispatcher theRequestDispatcher =
aSMIEvent.getServletContext().getRequestDispatcher(theTemplateName);
  theRequestDispatcher.forward(aSMIEvent.getRequest(),
aSMIEvent.getResponse());
}
} // End of the class
```

The configuration in Listing 8.13 makes sure that the servlet used instantiates the `I_SMIEventListener` `DisplayBean` and assigns two commands to it: `display` and `welcome`. If the servlet is called via the `display` command, you will find the page `/index.html` displayed (Fig. 8.8).

This also happens if no command is entered, as `display` is the `DefaultCommand`. If the `welcome` command is entered, the `DisplayBean` displays the page `/welcome.html`.

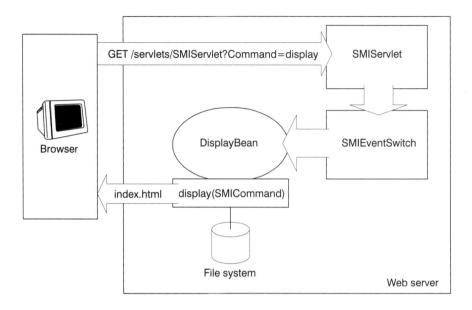

**Figure 8.8**   Execution of the display command with the DisplayBean

Listing 8.13: Example configuration of an SMIServlet for using the DisplayBean

```
{
   // Part I
   Listener = {
     DisplayBean = {
        Class = "de.webapp.Framework.SMICommandListener.DisplayBean";
     }
   };
   // Part II
   DefaultCommand = "display";
   Values = {
     _TemplateName = "/index.html";
   }
   // Part III
   Commands = {
     display = {
        MethodName = "display";
        Listener = "DisplayBean" ;
     }
     welcome = {
        MethodName = "display";
        Listener = "DisplayBean" ;
        Values = {
```

```
            _TemplateName = "/welcome.html"
        }
      }
    }
  }
```

## 8.6  SMI carried further

The implementation of the SMI concept using `SMICommandListener`, as described, is only one of many possibilities. The `de.webapp.Framework.SMI.SMIBean` class, a derivation of the `SMICommandListener`, allows universal application. It makes it possible to call just about any method by configuring defined objects. To allow this, a few more conventions have to be met via the `Command` parameter.

The name of the method to be called is provided by the `MethodName` parameter in the SMI definition file. In addition, we need to define the way in which arguments are to be passed on. We achieve this by using the `_SMIArg<x>` parameter (Table 8.1). Here, the place-holder `<x>` indicates the number of each argument, beginning with `_SMIArg0`. The number of the arguments following each other defines the number of arguments for calling the methods.

Using the `_SMIArgType<x>` parameter, a type can be defined for each argument. All the Java classes with a constructor that expects a `String` as the only argument are permitted. Among others, these include all the basic objects such as `java.lang.Integer`, `java.lang.Double` and `java.lang.Boolean`. The limitation is necessary because the parameter is passed on as a request parameter for the instantiation of the class. The whole class name has to be entered as `_SMIArgType<x>`. If no `_SMIArgType<x>` is entered, then the `SMIBean` interprets the argument automatically as a string.

**Table 8.1**  Possible parameters for `SMIBean`

| Parameters | Meaning |
|---|---|
| `_SMIArg<#>` | Value of argument number `<#>` |
| `_SMIArgType<#>` | Type of argument number `<#>`. The possible classes are, for instance, `java.lang.Integer`, `java.lang.Double`. In addition, the reserved type names `_CommandValue`, `_SessionValue`, `_SwitchValue`, `_ContextValue`, `_CommandObject`, `_SessionObject`, `_SwitchObject`, `_ContextObject` and `_Null` are permitted. |
| `_SMIResultScope` | Defines the area in which the return value of the method called is to be stored. The possible values are `Session`, `Command`, `Switch` and `Context`. |
| `_SMIResultIdentifier` | Defines the key with which the return value is stored. If this parameter is not provided then the standard key `_SMIResult` will be used. |
| `_FollowUpCommand` | Defines the command which should be called after the current command has been executed. |

Often there are situations in which the directly accessible argument types are not sufficient, and in which, for example, an `HttpSession` object has to serve as an argument. This is also possible with the `SMIBean`. As `_SMIArgType<x>` you only have to enter a reserved type name, `_SessionValue`, `_CommandValue`, `_SwitchValue` or `_ContextValue`. The value of `_SMIArg<x>` then serves as the key for the particular data structure. Through this indirect addressing you can pass on the objects themselves, in addition to the values for one of these objects. To do so, you must set one of the types `_SessionObject`, `_CommandObject`, `_SwitchObject` or `_ContextObject`. In the same way, it is also possible to set `null` as an argument. The corresponding argument type is called `_Null`. The general rule is that, for the given argument types, you always call the most specific method (Gosling *et al.* 1997, 313ff.) as defined in the Java language specification.

Naturally, what is interesting is not only the calling of a method, but also its return value. This can be stored in one of these data structures: `HttpSession`, `SMICommand`, `SMIEventSwitch` and `SMIContext`. To do so, you enter one of the `Session`, `Command`, `Switch` or `Context` values as an `_SMIResultScope`. The result of the method that is called will then be stored with the key `_SMIResult`. You can set another key with the parameter `_SMIResultIdentifier`.

In order to be able to interpret the return value, it is possible to set a follow-up command via the parameter `_FollowUpCommand`. Before the follow-up command is executed, the `_FollowUpCommand` parameter is deleted from the command object.

In order to use the `SMIBean`, you have to define whose methods it should call. As a rule, `SMIBean` calls its own methods. That only makes sense when `SMIBean` has been specialized beforehand. In order to call the methods of other objects, you can use the `TargetObject` parameter to set the class of target objects in the SMI definition file. During the initialization of the SMIBeans, the class is instantiated and set as the target object. As a precondition, the target object must have an argument-free constructor. Listing 8.14 shows the configuration of an `SMIBean`, which instantiates a `DisplayBean` as the target object.

Listing 8.14: Example configuration file for `SMIBean`

```
{
  // Part I
  Listener = {
    DisplayBean = {
      Class = " de.webapp.Framework.SMI.SMIBean";
      TargetObject = "de.webapp.Framework.SMICommandListener.DisplayBean";
    }
  };
  // Part II
  DefaultCommand = "display";
  Values = {
    _SMIArgType0 = "_CommandObject"
    _TemplateName = "/index.html"
  }
```

```
// Part III
Commands = {
   display = {
      MethodName = "display";
      Listener = "DisplayBean" ;
   }
   welcome = {
      MethodName = "display";
      Listener = "DisplayBean" ;
      Values = {
         _TemplateName = "/welcome.html"
      }
   }
}
}
```

The implementation of SMIBean offers particularly interesting opportunities for extending it. The SMI2RMIBean (Listing 8.15), derived from SMIBean, interprets the TargetObject parameter as the URL of an RMI object and it is in the position to call methods as long as the argument objects implement the java.io.Serializable interface. The SMI2CORBABean provides a similar component for the CORBA connection. It is only the configuration that is a little different (Listing 8.16). In this way, nothing hinders the generic connection of an Enterprise JavaBeans Server (EJB server), a legacy system or another background server.

Listing 8.15: The SMI2RMIBean class

```
package de.webapp.Framework.SMI;

import java.rmi.*;
import java.util.*;

public class SMI2RMIBean extends SMIBean implements I_SMICommandListener,
C_SMI, java.io.Serializable {

/** Initializes this listener. In doing so, binds the RMI object. */
public void init(String aName, Hashtable aParameters, I_SMIEventSwitch
aSMIEventSwitch) {
   myName = aName;
   mySMIEventSwitch = aSMIEventSwitch;
   myAliases = new Hashtable();
   myParameters = aParameters;
   String theTargetName =
   (String)myParameters.get(_ConfigListenerTargetObject);
   if (theTargetName == null) {
      setTargetObject(this);
   }
   else {
```

```
        try {
          setTargetObject(Naming.lookup(theTargetName));
        }
        catch(Throwable t) {
          throw new SMIEventListenerException(t);
        }
      }
    }
  }
} // End of the class
```

Listing 8.16: The SMI2CORBABean class

```
package de.webapp.Framework.SMI;

import java.util.*;
import org.omg.CORBA.*;
import org.omg.CosNaming.*;

public class SMI2CORBABean extends SMIBean implements I_SMICommandListener,
C_SMI{
/** Helper classes suffix */
public static final String _HelperSuffix="Helper";
/**
   * Initializes this listener.
   * In doing so, binds the CORBA object.
   * In the SMI configuration file there must be an entry
   * that matches the pattern:
   *    ...
   *    Listener = {
   *       myCORBABean = {
   *         Class = "de.webapp.Framework.SMI.SMI2CORBABean" ;
   *         TargetObject = {
   *           Name = "myCORBAObject" ;
   *           Class = "de.webapp.myCORBAObject" ;
   *           ORBInitialPort = "1050" ;
   *           ORBInitialHost = "localhost" ;
   *         }
   *       }
   *    ...
   */
public void init(String aName, Hashtable aParameters, I_SMIEventSwitch
aSMIEventSwitch) {
  myName = aName;
  mySMIEventSwitch = aSMIEventSwitch;
  myAliases = new Hashtable();
  myParameters = aParameters;
  Hashtable theCORBAParameters =
```

```
      (Hashtable)myParameters.get(_ConfigListenerTargetObject);
    if (theCORBAParameters == null) {
      setTargetObject(this);
    }
    else {
      try {
        String theTargetName = (String)
        theCORBAParameters.get(_ConfigName);
        String theTargetClass = (String)
        theCORBAParameters.get(_ConfigClass);
        String theORBInitialHost = (String)theCORBAParameters.get(
          _ConfigORBInitialHost);
        String theORBInitialPort = (String) theCORBAParameters.get(
          _ConfigORBInitialPort);
        Properties props = new Properties();
        if(theORBInitialHost != null) {
          props.put("org.omg.CORBA.ORBInitialHost", theORBInitialHost);
        }
        if(theORBInitialPort != null) {
          props.put("org.omg.CORBA.ORBInitialPort", theORBInitialPort);
        }
        ORB theOrb = ORB.init(new String[0], props);
        NamingContext theNamingContext = NamingContextHelper.narrow(
          theOrb.resolve_initial_references("NameService"));
        NameComponent theNameComponent = new NameComponent(theTargetName,
"");
        NameComponent path[] = {theNameComponent};
        Class theHelperClass = Class.forName(theTargetClass +
_HelperSuffix);
        Class argTypes[] = {org.omg.CORBA.Object.class};
        java.lang.Object args[] = {theNamingContext.resolve(path)};
        java.lang.Object target = theHelperClass.getMethod("narrow",
        argTypes).invoke(null, args);
        setTargetObject(target);
      }
      catch(Throwable t) {
        throw new SMIEventListenerException(t);
      }
    }
  }
} // End of the class
```

## 8.7 SMI summarized

The features of SMI are as follows:

- SMI is an intelligent extension of servlet APIs.
- It allows modular creation of servlet-based applications.
- The genric JavaBeans event is used for direct communication between components.
- Additionally, objects can be made available on different application scopes (`SMIContext`, `SMIEventSwitch` and `SMIEvent`).
- SMI design is motivated by the MVC (Model-View-Controller) Design Pattern and implements parts of the JSP Model 2 architecture from Sun.
- The implementation of interfaces guarantees flexibility and upgradability.
- SMI makes it possible to call Java methods directly via HTTP.

# Java objects in a relational database

**9**

**B**usiness is pushing its way onto the Web with ever-increasing amounts of information. Megabyte- and gigabyte-sized information systems and product databases have to be available quickly, world-wide. Therefore, a business Web site that does not use a database is almost unimaginable today. This necessitates the fastest and easiest approaches available, which allow even complex business processes to be used via the Web. And this is a new challenge for developers.

To fulfil these requirements, it still makes sense to continue administering the data with fast and robust relational databases. But at the same time, Java makes itself a virtual must for achieving a simple, secure and portable implementation of network applications. These considerations result in the need to find the easiest possible way to access relational databases from Java. Inevitably, this leads to JDBC, Java's Database Connectivity (Hamilton *et al.* 1997). This API represents a successful abstract of the various database products. JDBC 2.0 even supports the current version of the SQL3 Standard. As long as the manufacturer can offer 100% pure Java versions of the necessary drivers, currently unsurpassed levels of portability will be guaranteed.

However, JDBC is none too comfortable, especially because it is lacking a real, object-oriented view of the data. Programmers still have to deal with `ResultSets`, columns and rows, although they would much rather work with objects, methods and attributes. What can be done?

We need a framework that lets us save objects in a relational database, reload these objects and specifically search for certain objects. Such saveable objects are called *persistent* objects. Contrary to *transient* objects, they are able to survive past the lifespan of a process. In the WebApp framework, we call these objects `Persistences`. They have the following characteristics: `Persistences` can be saved in a relational database and reloaded at any time. They have an identity and a status. Furthermore, each `Persistence` can be associated with other `Persistences`. Associated `Persistences` can be accessed in just the same way as normal associated objects (Section 9.6).

The persistence framework described in this chapter focuses on saving Java objects in a relational database rather than mapping an existing relational diagram onto Java objects. With the solution given here, we are trying to maintain all the advantages of objects, for the developer, without having to abandon the favourite characteristics of a relational database, its ease of use and low cost.

The persistence framework has to satisfy the following requirements:

- Unique objects at a contact.
- Search for a number of objects with the same characteristics.
- Database queries with SQL.
- Navigation via an object's associations.
- Creating new objects.
- Saving changed objects.
- Memory structures of sets and object nets.
- Supporting transactions.
- Connection to the relational database via JDBC API.
- Temporary saving of objects (caching).
- Easy to extend.

At this point, we would like to remind you that you can find the entire source code on our Web site. We could not include all the details of implementation in this book – there is far too much information – so in this chapter we will concentrate exclusively on the design and the usage.

Before presenting the framework in detail, we would like to give a short basic introduction to relational databases. If you are familiar with this topic, feel free to skip Section 9.1. However, please be sure to read Section 9.2, as in this section we define some work that needs to be done to the database, which is necessary to prepare it for the use of the persistence framework.

In the framework, we use the SQL commands `CREATE`, `SELECT`, `INSERT`, `UPDATE`, and `DELETE`. However, it would be useful to know a bit about the joining expression (`JOIN`) and its modelling in order to have a better understanding of the configuration files which are used to define associations (Date and Darwen 1998, section 11.2).

## 9.1 The basics of relational databases

Relational databases administer data in tables (Heuer and Saake 1997). Each row within a table defines a data record containing data fields consisting of standard data types which we call columns. Anyone who has worked with a spreadsheet before will have no problems. An example for this is given in Table 9.1.

To enable the user to work with the data, a database offers functions which can be used to manipulate these tables. The schema, the table's structure, can be generated and edited. Furthermore, the database – similar to a file system – offers simple operations for generating, editing and deleting the data records in a table.

In fact, a single table could just as easily be saved in a file. The advantage of a relational database versus a file system lies in the fact that, in a relational database, the user can administer many different table structures still having uniform access to the tables.

**Table 9.1**   The 'restaurants' table

| Number | Name | Description |
|--------|------|-------------|
| 123440 | Pizza Don Camillo and Peppone | The Hombruch Pizzeria |
| 123451 | Bruno's Grill | Hot chips and more |
| 123462 | Lung Sing | The Oriental Revelation |

**Table 9.2**   The 'dish' table

| Restaurant number | Dish |
|-------------------|------|
| 123440 | Pizza Inferno |
| 123451 | Pizza Vegetaria |
| 123462 | Pizza Hawaii |

The advantages of relational database systems make themselves felt especially when you need specialized types of access to your tables, requiring a logical analysis of the data fields in different tables. Of course, transaction processing and access speed are additional reasons for using relational database systems (Section 9.1.2). With an additional table defining the dishes offered by each restaurant (Table 9.2) we would, for example, be able to determine which pizza we could order in which restaurant.

To be able to switch between various database products with a minimum of effort, SQL has been defined as a request and definition language for relational database management systems (RDBMS) (Date and Darwen 1998). SQL is defined in the standard SQL/92 published by the ISO and ANSI committees. Furthermore, there is a draft SQL3. Below, we shall give a short explanation of the instructions necessary to understand this book fully.

### 9.1.1   SQL statements

A complete description of SQL would fill many large volumes and would go far beyond this introduction (Date and Darwen 1998, Heuer and Saake 1997). Nevertheless, the basic elements can be learned relatively quickly. Essentially, we can write new files to a database, change and delete them and, of course, also read them again. Below we shall introduce you to the most important commands.

### SQL CREATE *statement*

Before we can save data, we have to create the necessary tables. This can be done with the CREATE statement:

```
CREATE TABLE <Table> (
   <Data field> <Data type>,
   <Data field> <Data type>,
   ...);
```

Exactly as in Java, all commands end with a semicolon. Some manufacturers use the go command, or the final character is implementation-dependent. Case sensitivity is generally irrelevant, but can be configured in some products (i.e. Sybase and Oracle). Our simple restaurant table with Number, Name and Description data types is created with the following statement:

```
CREATE TABLE Restaurant (
  Number INTEGER,
  Name VARCHAR(30),
  Description VARCHAR(255));
```

A table showing the dishes offered by each restaurant is created as follows:

```
CREATE TABLE Dish (Number INTEGER, RestaurantNumber INTEGER, Description
VARCHAR(255));
```

In addition to this simple definition, you can indicate the key fields that identify a data record. Fundamentally, there are two types of keys. The primary key (Primary Key) is a unique characteristic of a data record within a table. The foreign key (Foreign Key), on the other hand, helps to assign a data record to one or more data records in another table. It thus defines a relationship between the data records of two tables. Here, we do not define if it is a 1:1 relationship or a 1:*N* relationship, but only generally define that a relation between certain attributes exists. The **CREATE** statement with these definitions looks like this:

```
CREATE TABLE <Table> (
  <Data field> <Data field type> < Data field extension>,
  ...
  <Data field> <Data field type> < Data field extension>,
  PRIMARY KEY (<List of data fields in the primary key>),
  FOREIGN KEY (<List of data fields>)
    REFERENCES <Name of other table>
    (<List of data fields in the other table>));
```

Therefore, our correct example reads as follows:

```
CREATE TABLE Restaurant (
  Number INTEGER NOT NULL,
  Name VARCHAR(30) NOT NULL,
  Description VARCHAR(255),
  PRIMARY KEY (Number));
CREATE TABLE Dish (
  Number INTEGER NOT NULL,
  RestaurantNumber INTEGER NOT NULL,
  Description VARCHAR(255) NOT NULL,
  PRIMARY KEY (Number),
  FOREIGN KEY(RestaurantNumber) REFERENCES Restaurant(Number) );
```

In addition, with the data field extension you can also define the condition that sets whether a data field can be null or not (not null). In the database, an attribute with the value null has no content. This means that a primary key must never be null. When you set the keys, this is connected with a verification of statement modifications by the database. A data record cannot be deleted if other data records still refer to it.

## SQL INSERT *statement*

You create a new data record with the INSERT statement:

```
INSERT INTO <Table> (<Data field1>,< Data field2>,...)
    VALUES (<Value1>, <Value2>, ...);
```

The sequence of values must correspond precisely with the sequence of data fields.

```
INSERT INTO Restaurant (Number, Name, Description)
    VALUES (1234567,
    'The tasty spinach snack',
    'A vegetarian temptation');
INSERT INTO Dish (Number, RestaurantNumber, Description)
    VALUES (1,1234567,'Pizza Inferno');
```

## SQL UPDATE *statement*

The UPDATE statement changes one or more data records:

```
UPDATE <Table>
    SET <Data field>=<Value>, <Data field>=<Value>,...
    WHERE <Condition> AND|OR <Condition> ... ;
```

Therefore, the data record created above is changed as follows:

```
UPDATE Restaurant
    SET Name = 'The Grand Spinach Gourmet'
    WHERE Number = 1234567 ;
```

## SQL DELETE *statement*

Entries are deleted with the DELETE statement:

```
DELETE FROM <Table>
    WHERE <Condition> AND|OR <Condition> ... ;
```

The following statement will again delete our example data record from the database:

```
DELETE FROM Dish
    WHERE Number = 1 ;
```

The restaurant data record could not be deleted at this point, because a data record of dishes with a reference to the restaurant is still in existence. In this case, you will first have to delete the dishes referring to the restaurant.

### SQL SELECT *statement*

After having created the table, we can now start working with it. For this, you use the SELECT statement to select certain data records from the database.

```
SELECT <Data field>, <Data field>, ...
   FROM <List of tables>
   [WHERE <Condition> [AND|OR <Condition> ...]] ;
```

The conditions are expressions which are used to limit the request to the database. For example, we could search our restaurant database for all restaurants containing a certain part of a name. Apart from identical matches, it is also generally possible to test for non-identical values, such as a certain value range. You therefore can, for example, send the following requests to a restaurant table:

```
SELECT *
   FROM Restaurant;
SELECT Number, Name
   FROM Restaurant
   WHERE Description like '%spinach%' ;
SELECT Number, Name
   FROM Restaurant
   WHERE Number = 1234567;
SELECT t0.Number, t0.Name
   FROM Restaurant t0, Dish t1
   WHERE t0.Number = t1.RestaurantNumber
      AND t1.Description like 'Pizza%' ;
```

The first request searches for all data records in the Restaurant table. Here, the asterisk serves as a wild card for all data fields. In the second request, the search is for the numbers and names of all restaurants whose description contains the word 'spinach'. The third request defines a search for the restaurant with the number 1234. In the fourth request, the search is for all restaurants offering pizza. Here, we have used the aliases t0 and t1 for the two tables. These aliases make it easier for us to assign the data fields used in the request and the result to their corresponding tables. Furthermore, it enables us to separate data fields, with identical names, which are contained in different tables.

### 9.1.2  Transactions

Now we have explained the basic SQL statements, we would like to give a short explanation of the transaction concept. If several commands are used to change a database status or if several users simultaneously access the same database, it is essential to be able to see these commands as an inseparable unit (atomic) to prevent undesirable side-effects such as data inconsistency or a faulty view of the data. This unit is called a transaction.

Transactions are indispensable when it comes to keeping the data stocks (data in the database) in a consistent state. If a command that is part of a transaction cannot be carried out correctly, all other changes that have already been made, owing to this transaction, subsequently have to be undone, without the user having to enter additional commands.

Transactions are supported by all serious SQL databases. Generally, a transaction is opened before each command (BEGIN: this often occurs implicitly, but is implementation-dependent). All subsequent commands are completed by an acknowledgement (COMMIT) or a rollback (ROLLBACK). Unfortunately, the SQL standard does not precisely formulate how transactions are to be managed, which is why different products frequently behave differently (setting of the isolation level). The Finnish database Solid we have used in our examples locks all tables at the start of a transaction so that the data become invisible for any other, simultaneously occurring transaction until completion of this transaction (Fig. 9.1). This also applies especially to the SELECT command. However, it does not always apply to other database products (Dirty Read) (Date and Darwen 1998, 81ff.).

Apart from this, there are a large number of other commands for controlling the database, changing data types, issuing authorizations or administering users. The authorization function assigns the various database users the right to view or change individual tables. If you would like to find out more about this topic, please refer to the corresponding manuals or specialist literature on the topics of SQL and databases (Date and Darwen 1998, Heuer 1992).

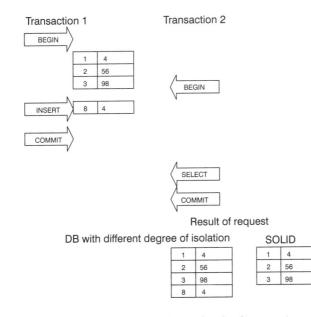

**Figure 9.1**  The various results of different databases for simultaneous transactions

## 9.2 Tables for `Persistence`

For our purpose, which is to be able to save `Persistences` in a relational database, a few additional conventions are required.

### 9.2.1 Generating identity keys

A basic characteristic of objects is their unique identifier. (Booch 1992, Holl and Schorsch 1998). Our persistent objects should have this characteristic as well. In particular, each object should keep this uniqueness throughout all tables. What is the use if the value 12340 defines a restaurant, a supplier and also a person? We would much rather that the identifier clearly shows the type of an object, i.e. its class. With this characteristic, you can achieve very simple and general access to various `Persistences` with just one method. As this identifier is an internal data field, the values have to be determined automatically.

To generate these identity keys, it is necessary to define an assignment of type names to numbers in the database. To ensure there is a different number for each individual object, we will have to save a counter in the database.

As we do not want to save this counter specially each time we create a data record, each connection to the database has to be allocated a certain number of counters at the beginning. To achieve this, we apply the concept of counter accounts.

Here, each connection extracts the lowest account available. If no account is available, an account with the next higher account number is created in the database (Fig. 9.2). For this operation, the connection requires exclusive access to the `AvailableAccount` table, which administers the counter accounts. The following SQL commands create the table and generate the first account:

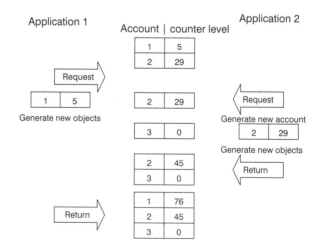

**Figure 9.2** Request for and return of counter accounts for the generation of object identities

```
CREATE TABLE AvailableAccount (
   AccountNumber INTEGER NOT NULL,
   Counter INTEGER NOT NULL);
INSERT INTO AvailableAccount
   VALUES (1, 0);
```

The rules (algorithm) for extracting an account are as follows:

- Use **UPDATE** in all the records of `AvailableAccount` to set all available accounts to read-only.
- Determine lowest account.
- Extract lowest account.
- If lowest and highest account are identical, add a new highest account.
- Extract and delete the lowest account.

If an application has an account, you can allocate the application a unique identifier by simply increasing the counter. As no two account numbers are the same, i.e. all account numbers in the database are unique, an identifier derived from the account number and counter is therefore also unique.

In order to make the most efficient use of the available number range, the account used by a database connection is re-entered into the `AvailableAccount` table after the connection is closed. If the application crashes, the account will be lost, too. Of course, with a bit of effort these accounts can be retrieved. It is imperative that applications running over long periods of time use a larger number range (Section 9.2.3).

## 9.2.2 Encoding the object type

To generate an object identity that fulfils the above requirements we have to add the type information to the account number and counter reading. For this, we use the `TypeNumber` table (Table 9.3). The following SQL command creates this table:

```
CREATE TABLE TypeNumber (
   Type VARCHAR NOT NULL,
   TypeNumber INTEGER NOT NULL);
```

In this table, you define a simple assignment of type names to type numbers. The type names can be any name for classes, class groups or interfaces. After all, they are merely proxy variables or alias names. The same applies to the type number which can be chosen at random. The only condition is that one type number must not be associated with more than one type name.

**Table 9.3**   Assignment of type names to type numbers

| Type | Type number |
| --- | --- |
| Restaurant | 10 |
| Dish | 11 |
| ... | ... |

### 9.2.3 Generating the object identity

The object identity is encoded as follows:

```
<Counter 9-digit><Account 4-digit><Type 3-digit>
```

The values for each counter, account and type are saved individually, right-aligned, in a 16-digit number. The missing digits of each block are completed by an underline character. Currently, we only use numbers.

If the desired number range should prove to be too small, it can be expanded to a different basis by encoding. For example, basis 36 would become possible by adding all the letters (Polar 1998) (most recently also supported by choosing the class `de.webapp.Framework.Persistence.StoreLongOIDAutonumber`). You can of course also extend the character string. The format for identity generation should be defined before the first object is created, as otherwise all subsequent objects and references have to be adjusted accordingly.

### 9.2.4 Preventing unnoticed changes by other applications

Each application has its own independent copy of an object. As there can often be several simultaneous connections to a database, conflicts while saving objects can occur (Fig. 9.3). Problems will arise if several applications modify the same object.

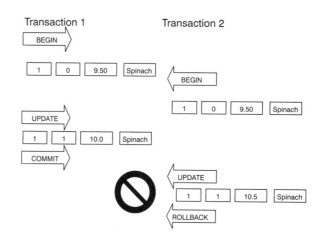

**Figure 9.3**   Conflicting changes arising from other transactions

To enable us to notice previous changes made to the object by another application, each object saves its version number when it has been changed. During a change, each application has to check if it is editing or deleting the correct object version. To arrange this, the `ObjectVersion` data field is added to each table. For each change, the version number increases in increments of one. In addition, an **UPDATE** is always executed with the condition 'AND `ObjectVersion` = `<version value>`'. Changes are made with the following command:

```
UPDATE Restaurant
  SET ObjectVersion = 1,
  Number = 1234567,
  Description = 'The vegetarian temptation',
  Name = 'The Spinach Trap'
  WHERE ObjectIdentifier = '_____1___1_10' AND ObjectVersion=0;
```

Every time an object is changed, all the attributes, with the exception of the identity, are also changed, regardless of whether they have changed or not. A special compensation only uses up memory and computing time. Furthermore, the process used here considerably simplifies command generation and also enables the use of the JDBC `PreparedStatement` command. If the database can support this, the command is translated before being executed, while the values only need to be transferred to the database during execution (Hamilton *et al.* 1997, p. 158).

## 9.3  Definition of the Java objects

When we have previously talked about saving Java objects in a database, we have always defined them as *certain* Java objects. This limitation refers mainly to the fact that, when it comes to attribute types, we consistently use object types instead of scalar or atomic data types because scalar data types would lead to problems with the database value `null`. In a scalar `int`, `double` or `boolean` Java data type, the value `null` is not permitted (Gosling *et al.* 1996, 21ff.). To ensure you did not have to manage without using `null` despite scalar types, you would have to determine a value from the value range of the scalar data type to represent the `null`, for example the value –1 for `int`. However, if you also need exactly the value `null`, you have a bit more of a problem. When real objects are used, a unique value for `null` exists and it can thus be effortlessly displayed in the database.

Table 9.4 contains all the attributes' data types. Here, the object data types have virtually been defined by JDBC. Therefore, for our persistence framework, the tables from our restaurant example would have to be created as follows:

```
CREATE TABLE Restaurant (
   ObjectIdentifier CHAR(16) NOT NULL,
   ObjectVersion INTEGER,
   Number INTEGER NOT NULL,
   Name VARCHAR(30) NOT NULL,
   Description VARCHAR(255),
   PRIMARY KEY (ObjectIdentifier));
INSERT INTO TypeNumber ('Restaurant',10) ;
CREATE TABLE Dish (
   ObjectIdentifier CHAR(16) NOT NULL,
   ObjectVersion INTEGER,
   RestaurantID CHAR(16) NOT NULL,
   Description VARCHAR(255) NOT NULL,
   PRIMARY KEY (ObjectIdentifier),
```

```
        FOREIGN KEY (RestaurantID) REFERENCES Restaurant(ObjectIdentifier));
        INSERT INTO TypeNumber ('Dish',11) ;
```

**Table 9.4**  Representation of the database types for attribute data types

| JDBC type/DB type | Java object type |
| --- | --- |
| BIGINT | java.lang.Long |
| BIT | java.lang.Boolean |
| CHAR | java.lang.String |
| DATE | java.sql.Date |
| DECIMAL | java.math.BigDecimal |
| DOUBLE | java.lang.Double |
| FLOAT | java.lang.Double |
| INTEGER | java.lang.Integer |
| LONGVARCHAR | java.lang.String |
| NUMERIC | java.math.BigDecimal |
| REAL | java.lang.Float |
| SMALLINT | java.lang.Integer |
| TIME | java.sql.Time |
| TIMESTAMP | java.sql.Timestamp |
| TINYINT | java.lang.Integer |
| VARCHAR | java.lang.String |

To make your application easier to use, you will have to change an existing schema. At the moment, there is no way to directly use an existing database. However, there is an easily managed but time-consuming way of migrating the data, by entering into all the tables the data fields ObjectIdentifier and ObjectVersion, together with the corresponding values (Holl and Schorsch 1998). Naturally, all applications – even those previously in existence – then have to generate valid identities and version numbers. This is only rarely worth the effort.

## 9.4  Architecture of the persistence framework

The persistence framework has the task of saving the status of certain objects from an application beyond the lifetime of a process. These objects are called *persistent* objects. Thanks to the persistence framework, persistent objects are represented in a relational database. After it is restarted, the application can therefore again access its persistent objects as if it had never been terminated. The persistence framework is therefore able to save the status of an object, defined by a number of particular attributes, in a database and reload it from there at any time.

In the persistence framework, all the services are made available via the central Store object. With Store you can create new persistent objects, load them from the database and change them. The name Store is an analogy to a warehouse with an assorted range of goods.

Besides `Store`, the `PersistencePeer` and `Persistence` classes make up the base of the persistence framework (Fig. 9.4). Below, we give you a short overview of the roles of these three classes.

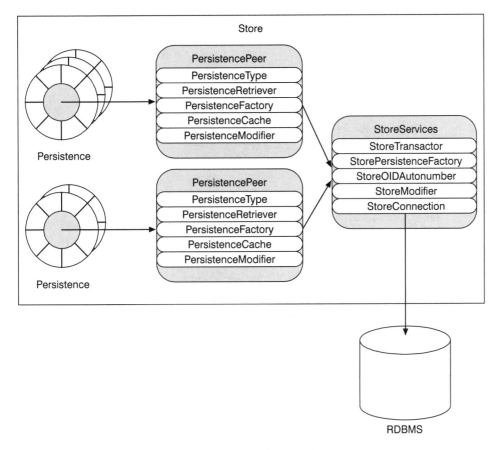

**Figure 9.4**   The components of the persistence framework

`Store` administers all general, *non-type-specific* services. These are:

- `StoreTransactor`, the transaction service;
- `StoreConnection`, the database connection;
- `StorePersistenceFactory`, the non-type-specific factory for persistent objects;
- `StoreModifier`, the non-type-specific service used for deleting, changing and saving persistent objects;
- `StoreOIDAutonumber` or `StoreLongOIDAutonumber`, the non-type-specific services for generating unique object identities.

Apart from this, `Store` creates the type-specific `PersistencePeers`. For every persistent object type, exactly one `PersistencePeer` is in existence. Just like `Store`,

PersistencePeer also arranges for services. However, contrary to Store, its services are *type-specific*. These are:

- PersistenceType metaservice, which is similar to the Reflect API;
- PersistenceRetriever, type-specific search service;
- PersistenceFactory, type-specific factory;
- PersistenceCache temporary memory;
- PersistenceModifier service, used to delete, change and save persistent objects.

Via its PersistenceRetriever search service, a PersistencePeer is able to arrange persistent objects of its own type. These are called Persistences. Each Persistence is represented in the database, where it is manipulated with the methods create(), delete() and update(). Each Persistence can therefore create, delete and update its own representation. In addition, each Persistence knows about its PersistencePeer and, with its help, is able to access the Store with all its services.

### 9.4.1 The class Store

Seen from the outside, Store has the task of creating a connection from an application to the database and encapsulating this connection. It is the central interface of the persistence framework. With its help, services that actually execute the tasks are arranged (Figs 9.4 and 9.5).

Therefore, Store creates the database connection. This connection, StoreConnection, supplies these objects: StorePersistenceFactory, StoreModifier and StoreOIDAutonumber. Once initialized, they work with other services to perform a specific, clearly-defined task.

The StorePersistenceFactory is responsible for all read-only access to the database. It executes the commands for loading table contents. In addition, it generates the corresponding SQL Select command for the requested Persistence type and uses it to access the database with the help of StoreConnection. In conjunction with a type-specific factory, the objects of the result set are created. The exact process is described in the section 'The PersistenceRetriever class' below. It is worth noting here that each Persistence object that comes into the application as a result of a search, has been forced to pass through the StorePersistenceFactory.

The StoreModifier class is used to save changes made to a Persistence in the database. This means that all write access to the database, i.e. insert(), update() and delete(), is processed via this service.

In order to identify each Persistence uniquely, we have the StoreOIDAutonumber which we use to generate this identity. For each new persistent object it generates an ObjectIdentifier, in accordance with the rules described in Section 9.2.3. If the ObjectIdentifier is to be generated in a different way, the class has to be changed accordingly (Appendix B).

To enable you to reload all Persistence objects that have been changed during a transaction, should an error occur, you will need the Transactor. All Persistence objects which reflect the changes to the database, will be registered with the Transactor.

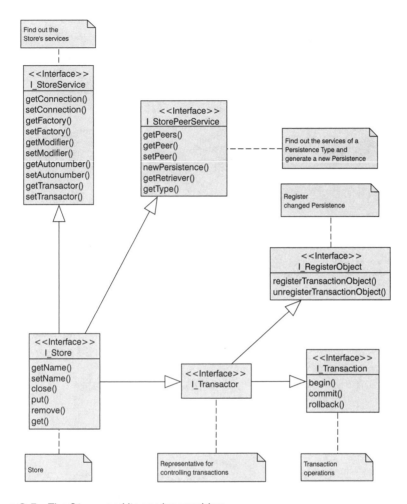

**Figure 9.5** The Store and its service providers

Besides its own services, the Store centrally arranges a PersistencePeer for each Persistence type (Fig. 9.6). The PersistencePeer also arranges services, although its services are limited to a specific type. The PersistencePeer is described in detail in the section 'The PersistenceType class' below. To simplify work with Store, Store is even able directly to determine the actual type-specific type and search service of a PersistencePeer.

A Store entity is created using an object of the type StoreFactory. The StoreFactory is able to instantiate and initialize a Store with the help of a configuration description (Appendix B).

First, the StoreFactory (Fig. 9.7) creates a totally empty Store. Then, it instantiates an object of the Store class for the database connection and passes it on to the objects StorePersistenceFactory, StoreModifier and StoreOIDAutonumber (Fig. 9.8). During initialization of the StoreOIDAutonumber object, the list of types is read and an account to number new Persistences is taken.

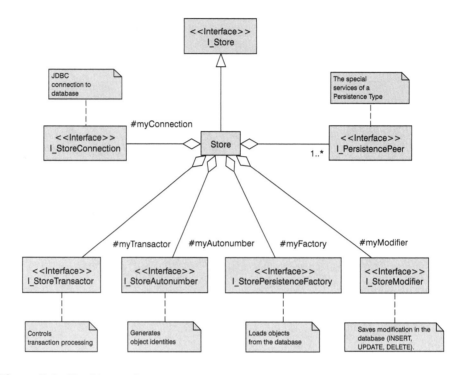

**Figure 9.6**  The Store class

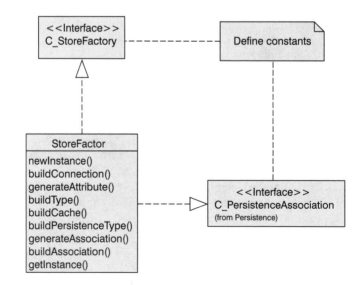

**Figure 9.7**  The StoreFactory class

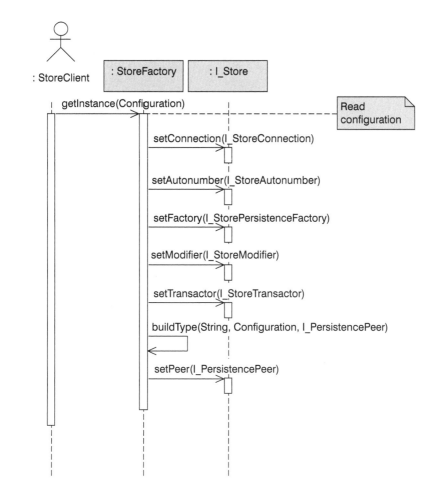

**Figure 9.8**   Generating a store

After the basic services of the Store have been configured, all the PersistencePeers are configured and registered with the Store. To register the PersistenceTypes, two steps are necessary. In the first step, the types with their attributes are created. In the second step, the associations for all PersistencePeers are cancelled. In this way it is even possible to create circular associations without any conflict.

After configuration, the Store is ready for use (Fig 9.8). Each process or each access to one of the Store's Persistences must take place in a synchronized block. This guarantees that only one Thread will use the Store at one time. This is extremely important, especially in a *multithreaded* environment like Java-VM. Also, in order to be able to protect data consistency, a transaction must be initiated before using the Store. The first transaction opens a database transaction. Now you can use as many of the Store's operations as required. To enable you to use partial processes

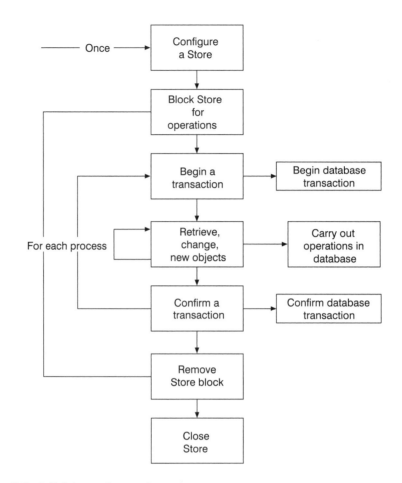

**Figure 9.9** Initializing and accessing a store

efficiently, you can open further transactions. In case of an exception, the whole database transaction is reset (cancelled) and the latest consistent version of the modified object is reloaded from the database. All modifications made during this session will be cancelled (Section 9.1.2).

After all application processes have completed, the `Store` must be closed to release all resources used. If this is not done, the memory clean-up in the `finalize()` method will do this for you. (The garbage collector is a real friend!)

## 9.4.2 The `PersistencePeer`

A `Persistence` is always assigned to exactly one `PersistencePeer`. The `PersistencePeer` provides the central, type-specific services for creating new objects, searching for objects in the database and for saving changes (Fig. 9.10). Furthermore, it includes a type description and a cache. Below you will find a description of the individual interfaces.

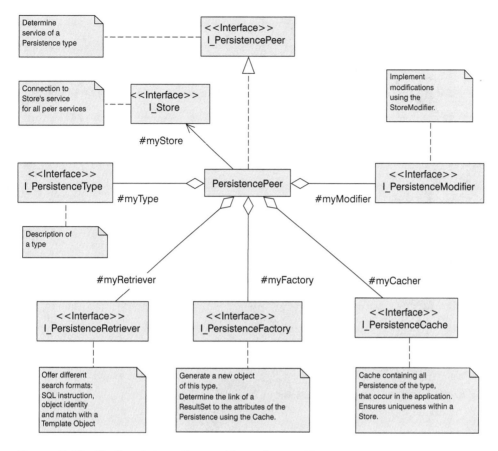

**Figure 9.10**   The `PersistencePeer` and its service providers

## *The* `PersistenceType` *class*

The description of the type of a `Persistence` is a true extension of the Java type system. The type object of a `Persistence` describes its persistent attributes and associations (Figure 9.11). Similar to the Reflect API (`java.lang.reflect`, especially `java.lang.reflect.Method` and `java.lang.reflect.Field`), the descriptive objects `PersistenceAttribute` and `PersistenceAssociation` allow access to concrete associations and attributes. Thus, each `PersistenceAttribute` can access the value of a `Persistence` and a `PersistenceAssociation` object can get a reference object of the association (for more details, see Section 9.6). This type description gives us great flexibility when accessing `Persistence` objects (see the store browser example in Chapter 11).

The term `PersistenceType` itself describes the type of a `Persistence`, and how it is represented in the database, in several ways. Each persistence type has a symbolic name, a table name and a class name. The symbolic name is equivalent to the type name in the `TypeNumber` table, which we have already described in Section 9.2.2.

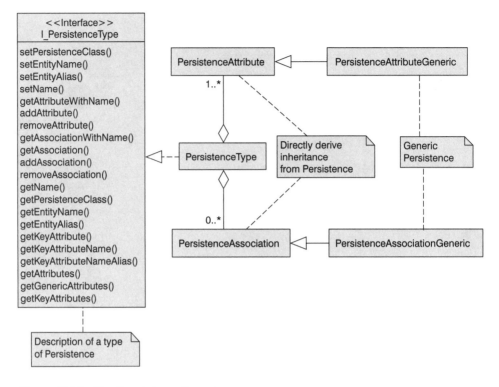

**Figure 9.11**   The PersistenceType class

The table name, also called 'entity', shows the table where a persistent object of this type has been saved. Finally, the class name shows the class that is instantiated in order to create an object of this type.

The advantage of using symbolic names lies in the powerful decoupling of the objects concerned. A Persistence is given its link to a concrete class of a table via its configuration data (Appendix B). This means that the name of the table can also be changed easily. Equally, the class of a Persistence to be instantiated can simply be replaced by a symbolic name. This is especially useful if a class has been specialized retrospectively. In the long term, this method guarantees tremendous flexibility.

### The PersistenceRetriever class

Figure 9.12 shows the PersistenceRetriever class. When searching for Persistence objects, a partial SQL statement is generally used. You could apply the following statements to our restaurant example:

```
WHERE t0.Name LIKE 'Pizza%'
WHERE t0.Name LIKE 'Pizza%' AND t0.Description LIKE '%Spinach%'
```

Here, the table alias t0 represents the actual table names. To link the tables with an SQL joining statement (JOIN), you can enter the desired tables in front of the option

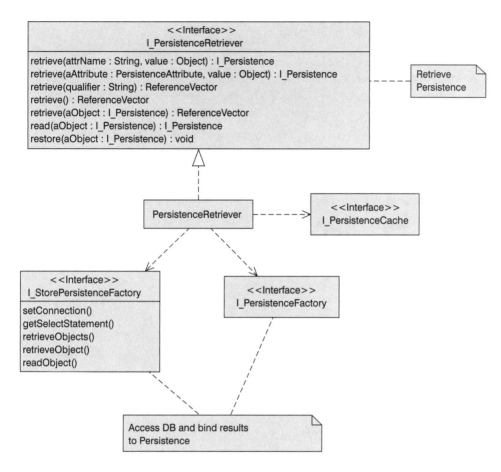

**Figure 9.12**   The PersistenceRetriever class

WHERE. If a number of dishes offered by the restaurant is present in the 'Dish' table, the SQL statement will look like this:

```
, Dish t1 WHERE t0.ObjectIdentifier = t1.RestaurantID AND t1.Description
LIKE '%Pizza%'
```

The comma links the tables in the FROM definition of the SELECT statement. The query is processed via the StorePersistenceFactory.

A qualified query can be carried out with the retrieve() method:

Listing 9.1: The PersistenceRetriever.retrieve(String) method

```
public ReferenceVector retrieve(String qualifier)
    throws PersistenceException
{
    String command;
    if(qualifier != null)
```

```
      command = getSelectStatement() + qualifier ;
   else
      command = getSelectStatement() ;
   I_StorePersistenceFactory theFactory = myPeer.getStore().getFactory() ;
   return theFactory.retrieveObjects(command,myPeer.getFactory()) ;
}
```

If the qualification is missing, the query will find all `Persistence` objects of this type. The `SELECT` statement precedes the qualification. The `getSelectStatement()` method gets the `SELECT` part for its own type from the `StorePersistenceFactory` and temporarily saves this statement for further requests. The complete query statement for restaurants offering pizzas is as follows:

```
SELECT t0.ObjectIndentifier, t0.ObjectVersion, t0.Name, t0.Description
   FROM Restaurant t0, Dish t1
   WHERE t0.ObjectIdentifier = t1.RestaurantID AND t1.Description LIKE
'%Pizza%'
```

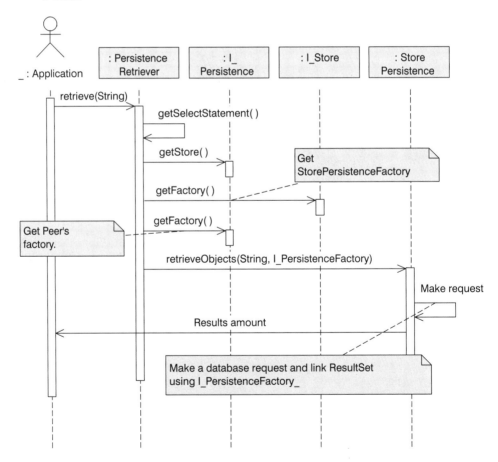

**Figure 9.13** Sequential chart of the `PersistenceRetriever.retrieve(String)` method

The actual request will be triggered by StorePersistenceFactory.retrieve Objects(). Apart from the search command, the factory of the Persistence type will be passed on (Fig. 9.13). After determining the database columns, this factory is responsible for generating the objects.

First, the retrieveObjects(String,I_PersistenceFactory) method checks if a connection exists between the database, the SELECT statement and the PersistenceFactory (listing 9.2). A ReferenceVector is created for the results (see the section on 'Counting references' below). Then, a java.sql.Statement is created via the JDBC Connection and sent to the database. With the help of PersistenceFactory.getObject(ResultSet), a Persistence object is requested for each column of the ResultSet and added to the result set. After all columns of the request have been processed, the Statement is released with close() and the result is returned:

Listing 9.2: The StorePersistenceFactory.retrieveObjects(String, I_PersistenceFactory) method

```
public ReferenceVector retrieveObjects(
   String command,
   I_PersistenceFactory factory )
throws PersistenceException
{
   if (myConnection == null || factory == null || command == null)
      throw new PersistenceException("Search for "
         + command + " not possible" );
   ReferenceVector objects = new ReferenceVector() ;
   Statement statement = null;
   try {
      if(Log.isLog())
           Log.log("START JDBC " + command);
         statement = myConnection.createStatement() ;
         ResultSet rs = statement.executeQuery(command);
         if(rs != null) {
            while (rs.next()) {
               I_Persistence obj;
            obj = factory.getObject(rs);
            if(obj != null)
               objects.addElement(obj);
         }
      }
      if(Log.isLog())
         Log.log("END JDBC result #" + objects.size() +" objects" );
   } catch (SQLException sqe) {
         throw new PersistenceException("Error occurred when binding"
            + command + " command.",sqe);
   } finally {
```

```
        if(statement != null )
          try {
            statement.close() ;
          } catch (SQLException sqe1) {
            throw new PersistenceException(
              "Error when closing " + command
              + " command.",sqe1);
          }
        }
    return objects ;
  }
```

There are alternative search methods. The `retrieve(I_Persistence)` method enables you to find all `Persistence` objects with exactly the same attribute values as the proxy object (template) passed on. Furthermore, with the `read(I_Persistence)` method you can acquire a transient, and therefore no longer saveable, copy of a `Persistence`, or you can change an already existing persistent object to the values saved in the database. If you want to reload a `Persistence` after an unsuccessful transaction, you have to use the `restore(I_Persistence)` method.

The execution of `PersistenceRetriever` shows how the framework makes use of the various services of the `Store` and `PersistencePeer`. Tasks are clearly separated into general and type-specific services.

## The `PersistenceCache` *class*

Figure 9.14 shows the `PersistenceCache` class. There are two reasons why a cache is indispensable in the persistence framework. On the one hand, we would like to avoid accessing the database. Objects that already exist should not have to be

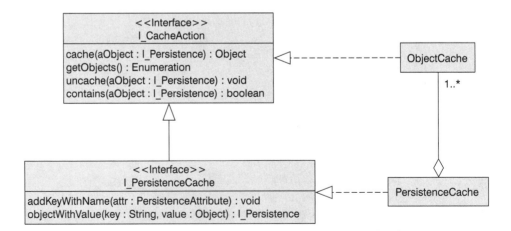

**Figure 9.14**   The `PersistenceCache` class

reloaded from the database. On the other hand, we need to prevent duplicate objects describing one and the same object in the database. Only in this way can we guarantee that changes to the object within an application become immediately visible for all users.

The PersistenceCache class helps to meet these requirements. From the developer's view, it is a representative (proxy) for several ObjectCaches (Gamma *et al.* 1996, Buschmann *et al.* 1996), whereby a separate cache (Listing 9.3) exists for each unique attribute of a Persistence. Each time a Persistence is added to the PersistenceCache, it is entered into the corresponding ObjectCaches.

Listing 9.3: The PersistenceCache.cache(I_Persistence) method

```
public Object cache(I_Persistence aObject)
   throws PersistenceException {
   int i;
   Object theObject = null;
   if(aObject != null) {
      typeCheck(aObject) ;
      for(i=0; i<myKeyCount; i++)
         theObject =
         ((I_CacheAction)myKeyList.elementAt(i)).cache(aObject);
   }
   return theObject;
}
```

Here, the correct type of each Persistence is checked with the typeCheck(I_Persistence) method before the Persistence is transferred into the cache. The shared features of PersistenceCache and ObjectCache are described in the I_CacheAction interface (Listing 9.4).

Listing 9.4: The I_CacheAction interface

```
package de.webapp.Framework.Persistence;

import java.util.Enumeration ;
public interface I_CacheAction {
// Insert Persistence into the cache
public Object cache(I_Persistence aObject) throws PersistenceException ;
// Report all objects in the cache
public Enumeration getObjects();
// Remove object from the cache
public void uncache(I_Persistence aObject) throws PersistenceException ;
// Is object in cache?
public boolean contains(I_Persistence aObject) throws PersistenceException ;
} // End of the interface
```

Listing 9.5: The `PersistenceCache.objectWithValue(String, Object)` method

```
public I_Persistence objectWithValue(String key, Object identifier) {
   ObjectCache keyObj;
   I_Persistence ret = null;
   if(key != null) {
      keyObj = (ObjectCache) myKeyDict.get(key);
      if(keyObj != null)
         ret = keyObj.objectWithValue(identifier);
   }
   return ret;
}
```

With the `objectWithValue(String key, Object identifier)` method you can query the cache for a specific `Persistence` (Listing 9.5). Here, the key chooses which `ObjectCache` will be accessed. With the `identifier` you describe the value of the key. The section that follows describes how the `Persistence` objects are created from the database.

## The `PersistenceFactory` class

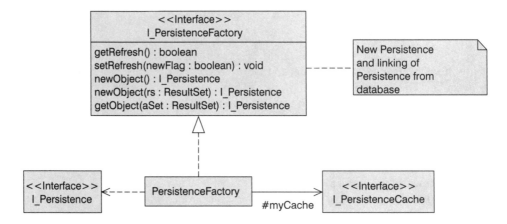

**Figure 9.15**  The `PersistenceFactory` class

Figure 9.15 shows the `PersistenceFactory` class. The factory of a `Persistence` type is responsible for creating new objects of the same type. Here, it is possible to create a completely new `Persistence` or one based on a row taken from a `ResultSet` from the database. The `PersistenceFactory` uses a `PersistenceCache` for binding a `Persistence`. The `Persistence` objects are held in the cache until the application no longer makes any reference to them. The `PersistenceFactory`'s `getObject(ResultSet)` method creates a `Persistence` object from a row taken from a `ResultSet`:

Listing 9.6: The `PersistenceFactory.getObject(ResultSet)` method

```
public I_Persistence getObject(ResultSet rs)
  throws PersistenceException {
  I_Persistence new_Obj = null;
  if(myCache != null) {
    try {
      // Get Key Attribute from first place in ResultSet
      new_Obj = myCache.objectWithValue(
      myPeer.getType().getKeyAttributeName(),rs.getObject(1)) ;
    } catch( Exception e) {
      throw new PersistenceException("Error in binding an object of type "
        + getPeer().getType().getName() + " with the Resultset " + rs
        + "with the cache.",e) ;
    }
    if(new_Obj == null) {
      try {
        new_Obj = newObject(rs) ;
      } catch (PersistenceException pe) {
        throw pe ;
      } catch ( Exception e) {
        throw new PersistenceException("Object "
          + myPeer.getType().getPersistenceClass()
        + " could not be allocated.",e) ;
      }
    }
    myCache.cache(new_Obj);
  } else {
    switch(new_Obj.getObjectState()) {
    case C_Persistence.STATE_PERSISTENT:
    case C_Persistence.STATE_REFERENCEMODIFIED:
    case C_Persistence.STATE_OUTDATED:
      try {
        // Get Version from the second place in the ResultSet
        if(myRefreshFlag &&
          !new_Obj.getObjectVersion().equals(
            (Integer) rs.getObject(2))) {
          if(Log.isLog())
            Log.log("Re-bind object " +
              new_Obj.getObjectIdentifier()) ;
          new_Obj.bind(rs);
        }
      } catch ( SQLException e) {
        throw new PersistenceException(
          "Version access to object "
          + new_Obj + " with ResultSet " + rs
          + " had an error ", e) ;
```

```
          }
          break;
        }
      }
    } else {
      // Create a new object with the ResultSet
      try {
        new_Obj = newObject(rs) ;
      } catch ( Exception e) {
        throw new PersistenceException("Object "
          + myPeer.getType().getPersistenceClass()
          + " could not be allocated ",e) ;
      }
    }
    return new_Obj ;
  }
```

First, the method checks if the `Persistence` already exists in the cache. This is possible because the first column of a `ResultSet` always contains the unique `ObjectIdentifier` which can be used as a key for the cache. If the `Persistence` is not yet present in the cache, a new `Persistence` is generated with `newObject(ResultSet)`. The attributes are bound with the help of the `Persistence.bind(I_PersistencePeer,ResultSet)` method. If the `Persistence` already exists in the cache, the method checks if it has been modified and exists in another version, in order to prevent repeated and unnecessary binding. If no cache exists, a new object is always created.

### The `PersistenceModifier` class

You use the class `PersistenceModifier` (Fig. 9.16) to modify a `Persistence`. When the modification functions `create()`, `update()` or `delete()` are used for the first time, the corresponding `PreparedStatement` is generated by one of the `StoreModifier` class methods `getCreateStatement(I_PersistenceType)` (Listing 9.7), `getUpdateStatement(I_PersistenceType)` or `getDeleteStatement` (`I_PersistenceType`), and saved for future use:

Listing 9.7: The `StoreModifier.getCreateStatement(I_PersistenceType)` method

```
public PreparedStatement getCreateStatement(I_PersistenceType aType)
  throws PersistenceException {
  PreparedStatement stst = null ;
  // Create command
  StringBuffer statement = new StringBuffer("INSERT INTO "
    + aType.getEntityName() + " " ) ;
  generateAttributes(statement,aType.getAttributes()) ;
  statement.append( " VALUES ");
```

```
addParameter(statement,aType.getAttributes().size()) ;
if(Log.isLog())
  Log.log( "Statement " + statement ) ;
try {
  // Pass on values for the command
  stst = myConnection.prepareStatement(new String(statement)) ;
} catch (SQLException sqe) {
  throw new PersistenceException(
    "Command Insert — aTyp " + aType.getName()
    + " could not be carried out ",sqe) ;
}
return stst ;
}
```

The resulting statement for the SQL INSERT statement, for our Restaurant table, looks like this:

```
INSERT INTO Restaurant
  (ObjectIdentifier,ObjectVersion,Name,Description)
  VALUES (?,?,?,?) ;
```

With this SQL statement, you can create a PreparedStatement object via the Store's JDBC Connection and return it to the PersistenceModifier.

Listing 9.8: The PersistenceModifier.create(I_Persistence) method

```
public int create(I_Persistence aObject)
throws PersistenceException {
  myPeer.getStore().registerTransactionObject(aObject) ;
  if(aObject.getObjectIdentifier() == null) {
    I_StoreAutonumber theNumber = myPeer.getStore().getAutonumber() ;
    aObject.setObjectIdentifier(theNumber,
    newObjectIdentifier(aObject)) ;
  }
  if(!myModifier.create(getCreateStatement(),aObject))
    return checkError(aObject) ;
  myPeer.getCacher().cache(aObject) ;
  return DBStateInDB ;
}
```

A Persistence is created with the create(I_Persistence) method (Listing 9.8). Before the status of the Persistence can be saved in the database, it must be registered in the Transactor. Here, the Store serves as a proxy. If no ObjectIdentifier has been set, a new identity will be requested via auto numbering. Now, the StoreModifier is used to save the Persistence in the database. If this is successful, the new Persistence will be accepted in the cache.

Listing 9.9: The StoreModifier.create(PreparedStatement,I_Persistence) method

```
public boolean create(PreparedStatement statement, I_Persistence aObject)
  throws PersistenceException {
  try {
    fillValues(statement,aObject,0) ;
    if(Log.isLog())
      Log.log( "Command create " + statement.toString()
        + " / " + aObject) ;
    statement.executeUpdate() ;
    return statement.getUpdateCount() != -1 ;
  } catch (SQLException sqe) {
    throw new PersistenceException(
      "Command Create — Object " + aObject
      + " could not be carried out ", sqe) ;
  }
}
```

The StoreModifier's create(PreparedStatement,I_Persistence) method enters the concrete attribute values of the Persistence into the pre-set PreparedStatement (Listing 9.8). Then, executeUpdate() is used to send the statement to the database.

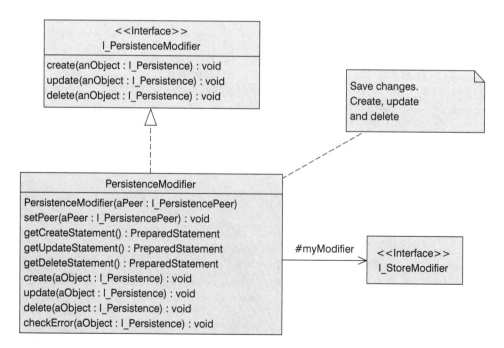

**Figure 9.16**  The PersistenceModifier class

An UPDATE or DELETE statement generates an error message if no line in the database has been modified by the statement, as at least the object version must be increased by one.

### 9.4.3 Persistent Objects

Now we have had a closer look at the administration tools for persistent objects in the last two sections, we would like to deal with the actual persistent objects. Normally, all persistent objects are derived from the superclass de.webapp.Framework.Persistence.Persistence. This class provides the infrastructure which helps to represent business objects in a relational database. It also ensures that the associations with other business objects can be created in a simple way. To ensure efficient work with the objects, they also have a clearly defined status.

### The I_Persistence *interface*

In order to be independent from the Persistence class, all the important characteristics are also defined in the I_Persistence interface (Fig. 9.17). All persistent

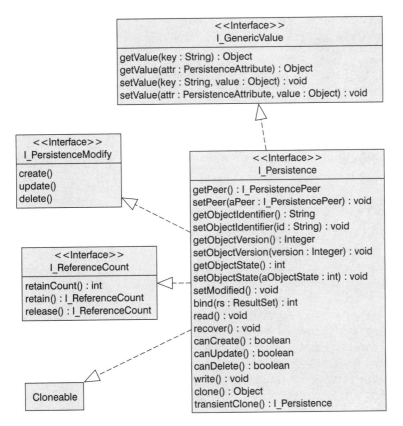

**Figure 9.17** The I_Persistence interface

objects implement the `I_Persistence` interface and thus fulfil the following conditions:

- A `Persistence` has access to its `PersistencePeer` service.
- It has an object identity, object version and a state.
- It can be created by a factory.
- Each of the modification functions `create()`, `update()` and `delete()` (`<op>`) is supplemented by a Hook _method_. This `can<op>()` method can be used to anchor special tests carried out on a `Persistence`, checking its attributes for their consistency before the start of the operation.
- The `clone()` method creates a copy of the object. This copy has not yet been given an identity and has still got the state UNDEFINED (Fig. 9.19).
- The `transientclone()` method creates a complete, transient object.
- The `read()` method reads a current copy from the database. This process is not carried out via the cache. Afterwards, the object is TRANSIENT, unless the object had already been PERSISTENT earlier.
- The `restore()` method is used to undo a transaction and to reload a persistent object from the database. Here, the object is temporarily removed from the cache. This is done so that other potentially existing unique keys will also be correctly taken into account during modification.

Furthermore, the `I_Persistence` interface inherits the methods of the `I_GenericValue` and `I_ReferenceCount` interfaces. The `I_GenericValue` interface offers access to the values of all persistent attributes of a class. This can be achieved on the basis of the attribute name or the attribute description (`PersistenceAttribute`). The second interface, `I_ReferenceCount`, allows you to count the number of references the `Persistence` is used in the application. The functionality will be described in detail in the section 'Counting references' below.

### The `Persistence` class and its derivations

The `Persistence` class fulfils the requirements of the `I_Persistence` interface. The modification methods have been extended to include two additional Hook methods, `before<op>()` and `after<op>()`. In these methods, for example, the functions for changing associations are encoded (Section 9.6.3). If an object is added to an association, the change is followed up accordingly in the methods `afterCreate()` and `afterUpdate()`. During changes, each `Persistence` relies on the `PersistenceModifier` service offered by its `PersistencePeer`.

For the general use of a `Persistence`, the `PersistenceGeneric` class will be used (Fig. 9.18). With its help, it is not necessary to create real Java classes, and then have to change them continually, during the prototype phase of a project. The `PersistenceLink` class supports the modelling of the `Link` classes of an *M:N* association (Section 9.6).

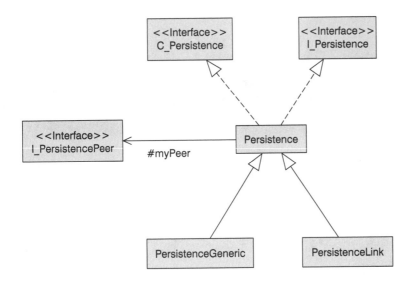

**Figure 9.18** Derivations of the `Persistence` class

## State of `Persistence`

In order to guarantee smooth processing when working with persistent objects, it is necessary to administer their status (Table 9.5 and Fig. 9.19). Basically, you have to distinguish between a `Persistence` that has been saved in the database, so therefore the application merely has a copy of the object, and an object that is exclusively required for the application without ever having been saved in the database. In the first case we are talking about a *persistent* object surviving the application's lifetime.

**Table 9.5** State of a `Persistence`

| State | Description |
| --- | --- |
| UNDEFINED | A `Persistence` has been created in the application. |
| PERSISTENT | The object is located both in the application and in the database. |
| TRANSIENT | The object is located only in the application and will not achieve a `Persistent` state. |
| MODIFIED | The object has been modified in the application and requires an `update()` operation to update the database. |
| REFERENCEMODIFIED | At least one object in an association has been modified in the application and requires a `create()`, `update()` or `delete()` operation to update the database properly. Otherwise, the status will be managed like `MODIFIED`. |
| DELETED | The object is no longer in the database, but the application is still accessing it. |
| UNREFERENCED | The object is still in the application's memory buffer, but there is no real use for the object. Renewed access to this object can lead to problems. |

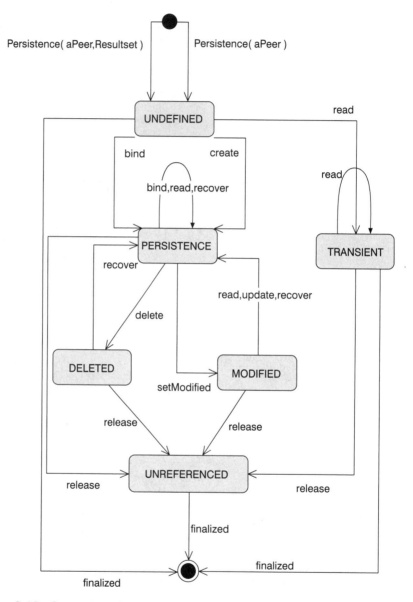

**Figure 9.19** Status chart of a Persistence

In the second case we are talking about a *transient* object whose lifespan is limited to the lifetime of the application.

During creation, the Persistence object always takes the status UNDEFINED. If it is loaded from a database with the help of an I_PersistenceFactory, the bind() method will automatically change it to the status PERSISTENT. However, if a totally new object is created, it will take on the status PERSISTENT only after it has successfully been inserted into the database.

The read() method changes a Persistence to the state TRANSIENT. Apart from this, an object can achieve the status TRANSIENT by creating a copy, by using the transientClone() method. Therefore, a transient object can by all means come from the database, but then changes to it can no longer be recorded there.

A persistent object can be reloaded from the database at any time and changes can be transferred to the database. Here, the modification functions take into account the version used when the object was transferred to the application, in order to ensure that the changes made by other applications are not overwritten by mistake. The framework does not create locks in the database but instead checks if the version is identical, during editing or deleting. If an object is no longer present in the database, the status DELETED is achieved.

Each modification of an attribute should conclude with the method setModified() and set the status MODIFIED for the object. When there is no longer any reference to the object in any application class, the object achieves the status UNREFERENCED (see section 'Counting references' below).

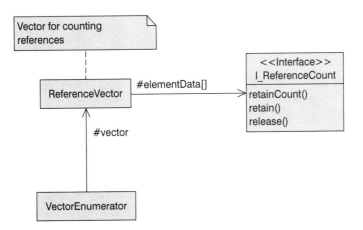

**Figure 9.20**  The ReferenceVector class

## *Counting references*

As the framework enters all `Persistence` objects into a cache, the question arises as to when and how to remove them again. It is recommended that they are removed as soon as they are no longer referenced by other objects, besides the cache itself. Only Java 2 offers a robust mechanism for this behaviour (JDK API documentation for the `java.lang.ref` package). However, as the persistence framework is also required to support JDK 1.1, every `Persistence` object has to count all the references made to it.

In the persistence framework this is achieved using the `ReferenceVector` (Fig. 9.20), which is a reimplementation of the `java.lang.Vector` class. Each object being placed into a `ReferenceVector` has to satisfy the `I_ReferenceCount` interface. It enables a user object to count the references. To do this, each object using a reference counter object has to execute a `retain()` for this object before it can use the counter (Listing 9.10). If the user object no longer requires the reference counter object, it simply releases it with `release()`.

Listing 9.10: The `I_ReferenceCount` interface

```
package de.webapp.Framework.Utilities;
public interface I_ReferenceCount {
// Report counter value
public int retainCount() ;
// Report usage
public I_ReferenceCount retain() ;
// Release an application
public I_ReferenceCount release() ;
// Output for counter
public String toString() ;
}
```

Every time the `ReferenceVector` is changed, this is exactly what happens. As all the results of the `PersistenceRetriever` are saved in a `ReferenceVector`, the user generally does not have to worry about counting the references. When the `ReferenceVector` is released, all reference counter objects are also automatically released.

The `Persistence` class implements the `I_ReferenceCount` interface (Listings 9.11 and 9.12).

Listing 9.11: Implementation of the `Persistence.retain()` method

```
public I_ReferenceCount retain() {
  if( myObjectState != STATE_UNREFERENCED ) {
    if( myReferenceCount >= 0) {
      myReferenceCount++ ;
      if(Log.isLog())
        Log.log(" retain " + getObjectIdentifier() + " "
          + myReferenceCount + " " + myPeer.getType().getName() ) ;
    } else {
      if(Log.isLog())
        Log.log(" retain error in counter" + getObjectIdentifier()
          + " " + myReferenceCount
          + " " + myPeer.getType().getName() ) ;
      throw new PersistenceRuntimeException (
        "The reference counter is less than 0 for object "
        + getObjectIdentifier() + " " + myReferenceCount
        + " " + myPeer.getType().getName() ) ;
    }
  } else {
    if(Log.isLog())
      Log.log("retain error unreferenced"+getObjectIdentifier()
        + " " + myReferenceCount + " "
        + myPeer.getType().getName() ) ;
    throw new PersistenceRuntimeException (
      "The application logic is incorrect. "
      + "An unreferenced object has been referenced again!"
      + getObjectIdentifier() + " " + myReferenceCount
      + " " + myPeer.getType().getName() ) ;
  }
  return this ;
}
```

The `Persistence retain()` method firstly checks if the `Persistence` has already been deleted from the application. If a `retain()` occurs in a `Persistence` object that has the state UNREFERENCED or if the counter shows a negative value, a serious coding error is present. If everything behaves normally, the `myReferenceCount` counter will be increased by 1 and this will be reported using `Log.log()`.

Naturally, release and use are equally protected. Each release decreases the counter by 1. Following the last release, the `Persistence` is actively deleted from the cache of its `PersistencePeer` (Listing 9.12).

Listing 9.12: Implementation of the `Persistence.release()` method

```
public I_ReferenceCount release() {
  if( myObjectState != STATE_UNREFERENCED ) {
```

```
      if(Log.isLog())
        Log.log(" release " + getObjectIdentifier()
          + " " + myReferenceCount + " " + myPeer.getType().getName());
      myReferenceCount-;
      if (myReferenceCount <= 0 && myPeer != null) {
        try {
          if(Log.isLog())
            Log.log(" Release of object "
              + getObjectIdentifier()) ;
          myPeer.getCacher().uncache(this);
        } catch ( PersistenceException e ) {
          throw new PersistenceRuntimeException (
            "Failure to delete object " + this
            + " from cache!",e) ;
        }
        myObjectState = STATE_UNREFERENCED;
        return null ;
      }
    } else {
      if(Log.isLog())
        Log.log( " release error " + getObjectIdentifier()
          + " " + myReferenceCount + " "
          + myPeer.getType().getName());
      throw new PersistenceRuntimeException(
        "The application logic is incorrect."
        + " An unreferenced object has been referenced again! "
        + getObjectIdentifier() + " " + myReferenceCount + " "
        + myPeer.getType().getName() ) ;
    }
    return this ;
  }
```

This way to manage objects certainly requires some getting used to, and is encapsulated in the framework. All reference classes of the framework also encapsulate the counting of references. Therefore its use is completely transparent in the standard application.

## 9.5   A simple example

After having explained the basic structure of the Store, here is our first example. In order to use a persistent object, you have to take the following three steps:

**1** Create a database table.

**2** Enter the object type into the TypeNumber table.

**3** Create a Store configuration file.

In our example, we would like to turn the Restaurant object into a persistent object. The object should have two attributes: Name and Description. Both attributes therefore have to be contained as data record fields in the table to be generated. Furthermore, the attributes ObjectIdentifier and ObjectVersion have to be present in each table that is to be used by a Store  (Section 9.2). The following SQL statement generates the required table:

```
CREATE TABLE Restaurant (
   ObjectIdentifier CHAR(16) NOT NULL,
   ObjectVersion INTEGER,
   Name VARCAHR,
   Description VARCHAR,
   PRIMARY KEY (ObjectIdentifier)
);
```

As described in Section 9.2, the type of an object is encoded in the object identity. For the  Restaurant  table an entry has to be created in the TypeNumber table as follows:

```
INSERT TypeNumber VALUES ('Restaurant', 10);
```

To allow a Store to access this Persistence, the Store configuration file GenericRestaurant.store is required:

Listing 9.13: The GenericRestaurant.store configuration

```
{
Name = "Restaurant" ;
JDBCConnection = {
   DriverClass = "solid.jdbc.SolidDriver" ;
   URLConnect = "jdbc:solid://localhost:1313" ;
   Properties = {
      user = "web" ;
      password = "app" ;
   }
} ;
Types = {
   Restaurant = {
      Type = {
         Name = "Restaurant" ;
         Class= "de.webapp.Framework.Persistence.PersistenceGeneric";
         Entity = "Restaurant";
         EntityAlias = "t0" ;
         Attributes = (
            "ObjectIdentifier",
            "ObjectVersion",
            { Name = "Name" ; Generic = "YES"; },
            { Name = "Description" ; Generic = "YES"; }
         ) ;
```

```
                    }
                  }
               }
            }
```

In it, the connection to a JDBC data source and the `Persistence` types of the `Store` are described. The details of this configuration will be explained in Section 9.6.3 and Appendix B. At this point, you just need to understand that all characteristics of the `Store` and its persistent objects will be described in this configuration. One thing must be noted here: for reasons of simplicity, we will refrain from encoding a specific derivation of the `Persistence` object. Instead we will use the `PersistenceGeneric` object contained in the persistence framework. `PersistenceGeneric` enables you to set and acquire attributes with the help of their attribute names, using universally known methods. For example, instead of `getDescription()` we will use the method `getValue("Description")`. Similarly, instead of `setDescription("a  description")` we are using the method `setValue("Description", "a description")`.

According to its mode, the `GenericRestaurant` program either displays all the restaurants in the database or adds a new one:

Listing 9.14: Test environment for the restaurant example

```java
package de.webapp.Examples.Persistence.Simple;

import java.util.*;
import de.webapp.Framework.ConfigManager.* ;
import de.webapp.Framework.Persistence.* ;
import de.webapp.Framework.StoreFactory.StoreFactory ;
import de.webapp.Framework.Log.Log;
import de.webapp.Framework.Utilities.ReferenceVector;

public class GenericRestaurant{
protected I_Store myStore ;
// Access the Store
public static void main(String args[])
   throws PersistenceException {
   GenericRestaurant theAccess = new GenericRestaurant ("RestaurantStore");
   Integer aCommand = new Integer(args[0]) ;
   theAccess.action(aCommand.intValue(),args);
}
// Construct Store for the Restaurant
public GenericRestaurant(String aStore)
   throws PersistenceException {
   Configuration theStore =
   ConfigManager.getConfigManager().getConfiguration(aStore);
   // Store Config
   myStore = StoreFactory.getInstance(theStore) ;
   if(myStore == null) {
```

```
      Log.log("Could not create Store ") ;
      throw new PersistenceException("Store cannot be configured") ;
   }
}
// Create a new restaurant
protected void newRestaurant (String aName, String aDescription)
   throws PersistenceException {
   I_Persistence newRestaurant = myStore.newPersistence("Restaurant") ;
   newRestaurant.setValue("Name",aName) ;
   newRestaurant.setValue("Description",aDescription) ;
   newRestaurant.create() ;
}
// Find all restaurants for Store
protected void searchAllRestaurant()
   throws PersistenceException {
   ReferenceVector aVector =
      myStore.getRetriever("Restaurant").retrieve();
   for(Enumeration e=aVector.elements();e.hasMoreElements() ; ) {
      I_Persistence aObject=(I_Persistence)e.nextElement() ;
      Log.log("Restaurant/ Name - " + aObject.getValue("Name") +
         " - Description - " + aObject.getValue("Description") );
   }
}
// Carry out a command in a Store
public void action(int aCommand, String[] args) {
   if(myStore != null) {
      // Create environment for access to a Store
      synchronized( myStore) {
        try {
          try {
             myStore.begin() ;
             switch(aCommand) {
             case 0:
                searchAllRestaurant() ;
                break ;
             case 1 :
                newRestaurant(args[1],args[2]) ;
                break ;
             default :
                Log.log("Command " + aCommand + args
                   + " does not exist " ) ;
             }
             myStore.commit() ;
          } catch (PersistenceException e) {
             if(myStore != null)
                myStore.rollback() ;
```

```
                        throw e ;
                    } finally {
                        myStore.close() ;
                    }
                } catch (Exception e ) {
                    e.printStackTrace() ;
                }
            }
        }
    }
} // End of the class
```

The program first generates an instance of `GenericRestaurant`. Here, a `Store` is generated from the `RestaurantStore` configuration. Then, an action is executed with the `action(int, String[])` method (Listing 9.14). In the `action()` method, `synchronized` is used to protect the `Store` from execution by another `Thread` and a transaction frame is provided. Each exception leads directly to the cancellation (`rollback()`) of the transaction. The action '0' displays all existing restaurants and action '1', combined with the arguments 'Name' and 'Description', creates a new restaurant entry.

The following input will create the desired functions:

```
#Display all Restaurants
java -classpath /webapp/lib/webapp.jar;/solid/jdbc/SolidDriver.zip
-DCFGROOT=/webapp/etc/
de.webapp.Examples.Persistence.Restaurant.GenericRestaurant 0
```

In Fig. 9.21 you can see the example display of a program run in which all the restaurants are displayed.

- The `Store` is initialized.
- The transaction starts and the request for all restaurants is executed.
- The database contains the restaurants `Pizza Peppone` and `Pizza Roma`.
- The transaction is completed successfully.
- The program terminates and returns the account.

```
#Add a Restaurant
java -classpath /webapp/lib/webapp.jar;/solid/jdbc/SolidDriver.zip
-DCFGROOT=/webapp/etc/
de.webapp.Examples.Persistence.Restaurant.GenericRestaurant 1 'Pizza Hut
San Francisco'
```

After the `ObjectIdentifier` has been determined, the new `Restaurant` object `Pizza` is written to the database with the help of the **INSERT** command. The transaction is successful. The account, which has now been increased by one counter, is returned to the database (Fig. 9.22).

```
[21.11.1999 17:27:15] - WebApp-Default: begin Transaction jdbc:solid://localhost
:1313
[21.11.1999 17:27:15] - WebApp-Default:  SELECT for Restaurant : SELECT t0.Objec
tIdentifier, t0.ObjectVersion, t0.Name, t0.Description FROM Restaurant t0
[21.11.1999 17:27:15] - WebApp-Default: START JDBCSELECT t0.ObjectIdentifier, t0
.ObjectVersion, t0.Name, t0.Description FROM Restaurant t0
[21.11.1999 17:27:16] - WebApp-Default:  retain _____17__84_10 1 Restaurant
[21.11.1999 17:27:16] - WebApp-Default:  retain _____18__84_10 1 Restaurant
[21.11.1999 17:27:16] - WebApp-Default:  retain _____25__84_10 1 Restaurant
[21.11.1999 17:27:16] - WebApp-Default:  retain _____1__85_10 1 Restaurant
[21.11.1999 17:27:16] - WebApp-Default: END JDBC - result bind #4 objects
[21.11.1999 17:27:16] - WebApp-Default: Restaurant / Name - Pizza Peppone - Desc
iption - the cosy place
[21.11.1999 17:27:16] - WebApp-Default: Restaurant / Name - Pizza Roma - Descrip
tion - Go to italy and eat nice food
[21.11.1999 17:27:16] - WebApp-Default: Restaurant / Name - Pizza Hut New York -
 Description - Big Apple Pizza
[21.11.1999 17:27:16] - WebApp-Default: Restaurant / Name - Pizza - Description
- wonderful
[21.11.1999 17:27:16] - WebApp-Default: commit Transactionjdbc:solid://localhost
:1313

D:\webapp\projects\Examples\bin>
```

**Figure 9.21**   Example display of all restaurants

```
Name:Pizza Hut San Fransisco
Description:eat under the bridge

[21.11.1999 17:38:28] - WebApp-Default:  retain null 1 Restaurant
[21.11.1999 17:38:28] - WebApp-Default: OID for Name Restaurant Class de.webapp.
Framework.Persistence.PersistenceGenericOID : _____1_148_10
[21.11.1999 17:38:28] - WebApp-Default: Statement INSERT INTO Restaurant (Object
Identifier, ObjectVersion, Name, Description) VALUES (?, ?, ?, ?)
[21.11.1999 17:38:28] - WebApp-Default: Statement create solid.jdbc.SolidPrepare
dStatement@199c9916 /
--Type:Restaurant
--Object: (de.webapp.Framework.Persistence.PersistenceGeneric@ad89916 )
--ObjectState: 0
--ReferenceCount: 1
ObjectIdentifier:_____1_148_10
ObjectVersion:0
Name:Pizza Hut San Fransisco
Description:eat under the bridge

[21.11.1999 17:38:28] - WebApp-Default: commit Transactionjdbc:solid://localhost
:1313

D:\webapp\projects\Examples\bin>
```

**Figure 9.22**   Adding a new restaurant entry

## 9.6 Persistent object networks

For the example in the previous section we have deliberately chosen a simple object which was not associated with other objects. However, in real life this is only rarely the case, because each business object generally consists of attributes and associations. An association with reference to a business object is a relationship or an aggregation with another business object. It is possible to define and store hierarchical structures in a database and to use them as an object net in the application. The associations can be defined between various types or tables (Oestereich 1998, 47ff.). In object-oriented programming languages, such relations are generally created via data structures such as `Array`, `Vector`, `Hashtable` and `Collection` or as a simple reference in the case of a 1:1 association.

### 9.6.1 Persistence through serialization

Let us now extend our restaurant example by adding one association. For this purpose, we will associate the restaurant with all the dishes it offers (Fig. 9.23). Furthermore, as an alternative example, we shall compare the use of JDK's serialization mechanism with the use of the persistence framework.

Naturally, the restaurant must have methods to provide information about the dishes it offers. In addition, it makes sense to be able to delete a dish from the menu, or to add a new one to it. Listing 9.15 shows a non-persistent implementation of the two classes `Dish` and `Restaurant`:

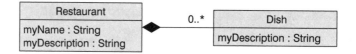

**Figure 9.23**  A restaurant offers many tasty dishes

Listing 9.15: The classes `Restaurant` and `Dish`

```
// ###############################################################
// File: Restaurant.java
package de.webapp.Examples.Persistence.Restaurant.Serial ;

import java.util.Vector ;
import java.util.Enumeration ;
import java.io.Serializable ;

// Restaurant
public class Restaurant implements Serializable
{
    protected String myName ;
    protected String myDescription ;
    protected Vector myDish ;
```

```java
   public Restaurant () { myDish = new Vector () ;}
   public String getName() { return myName; }
   public void setName(String aName ) { myName = aName ; }
   public String getDescription() { return myDescription; }
   public void setDescription (String aDescription ) {
      myDescription = aDescription ; }
   public void addToDish(Dish aDish) {
      myDish.addElement(aDish) ;
   }
   public void removeFromDish (Dish aDish) {
      myDish.removeElement(aDish) ;
   }
   public Enumeration getDish () {
      return myDish.elements();
   }
   public String toString() {
      return "Name: " + myName + "\n" +
         "Description: " + myDescription + "\n" +
         "Dishes:\n" + myDish + "\n" ;
   }
} // End of the class

// ############################################################
// File: Dish.java
package de.webapp.Examples.Persistence.Restaurant.Serial ;

import java.io.Serializable ;

// Dish
public class Dish implements java.io.Serializable {
   protected String myDescription ;
   public Dish () {}
   public String getDescription() { return myDescription; }
   public void setDescription (String aDescription ) {
      myDescription = aDescription ; }
   public String toString() {
      return myDescription + "\n" ;
   }
} // End of the class
```

It is possible for each Restaurant object to use the getDish() method to display all Dishes. To add a new dish to the restaurant you can use the addToDish(Dish) method and delete a less tasty dish with the removeFromDish(Dish) method.

A simple form of persistence is implemented in Java serialization. Using this, it is possible to transform objects that implement the java.io.Serializable interface into a data stream. It is then easy to save this data stream in a Restaurant.serial file and again load it from the file (Listing 9.16). A condition for saving object networks is that all objects involved implement Serializable.

Listing 9.16: Serialization of a restaurant including its dishes

```java
package de.webapp.Examples.Persistence.Restaurant.Serial ;

import java.util.Vector ;
import java.util.Enumeration ;
import java.io.* ;
public class SerialRest {
public static Dish newDish(String aDescription){
  Dish aDish = new Dish() ;
  aDish.setDescription(aDescription) ;
  return aDish ;
}
// Save or load a Restaurant object network
public static void main(String[] argc)
  throws Exception {
  Restaurant aRestaurant ;
  if(argc.length > 0 && argc[0].equals("0") ) {
    aRestaurant = new Restaurant() ;
    aRestaurant.setName("Pizza Peppone") ;
    aRestaurant.setDescription("Quick and tasty") ;
    aRestaurant.addToDish(newDish("Pizza Vegetaria")) ;
    aRestaurant.addToDish(newDish("Pizza Inferno")) ;
    aRestaurant.addToDish(newDish("Pizza Hawaii")) ;

    FileOutputStream f = new FileOutputStream("Restaurant.serial");
    ObjectOutputStream s = new ObjectOutputStream(f);
    s.writeObject(aRestaurant);
    s.flush();
    s.close();
  } else {
    FileInputStream f = new FileInputStream("Restaurant.serial");
    ObjectInputStream s = new ObjectInputStream(f);
    aRestaurant = (Restaurant)s.readObject();
    s.close();
    System.out.println(aRestaurant);
  }
}
} // End of the class
```

First, you use the main(String[]) method to decide if you want to create a new restaurant or display an existing restaurant. When creating a new Restaurant, you enter its name and description. You use the newDish(String) method to create each Dish and add it to the new Restaurant. Finally, the Restaurant's newly created object network, including its Dishes, is written to the Restaurant.serial file with the help of an ObjectOutputStream. Next time this file is called without parameters, this complete object network is read and displayed. Figure 9.24 shows the result of the restaurant serialization.

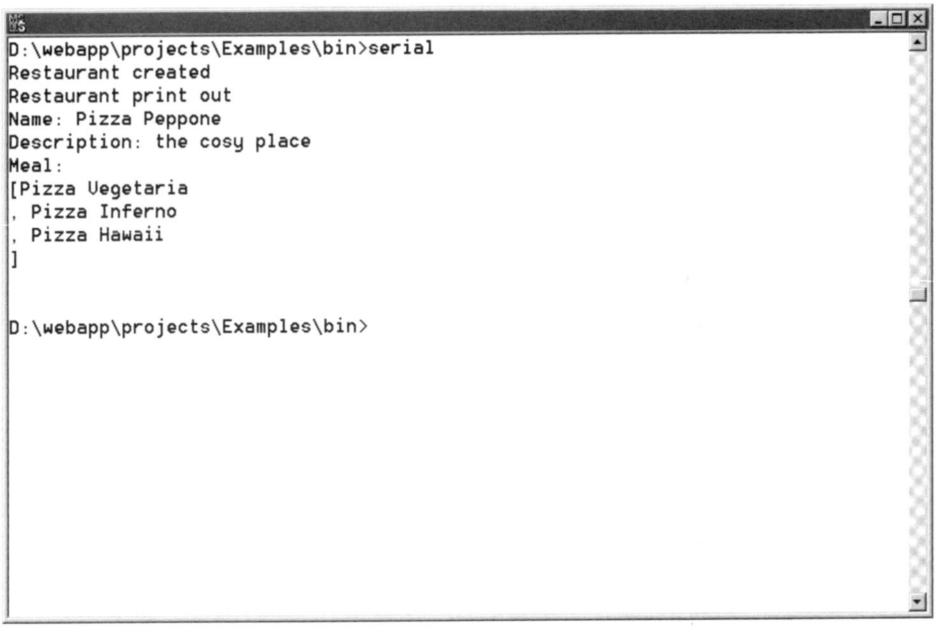

```
D:\webapp\projects\Examples\bin>serial
Restaurant created
Restaurant print out
Name: Pizza Peppone
Description: the cosy place
Meal:
[Pizza Vegetaria
, Pizza Inferno
, Pizza Hawaii
]


D:\webapp\projects\Examples\bin>
```

**Figure 9.24**   Result of restaurant serialization

Although serialized objects are extremely simple to manage, this is counterbalanced by a considerable disadvantage: it is not possible to load object nets only partially when they are really needed.

## 9.6.2  Modelling associations by proxy

Naturally, you can also use the persistence framework to display object nets in a database. To do this, Restaurant and Dish have to be written to two different tables. What is missing here is the link. The solution to this problem lies in the reference classes. They act as proxies for associations and ensure that, if necessary, the Persistence objects concerned are loaded from the database. In the case of associations forming an aggregate, even changes to a dependent Persistence object (i.e. Dish) belonging to an association are saved along with the original Persistence object (i.e. Restaurant) (Fig. 9.27).

Even the question of access has an elegant solution: the 1:1 reference class ToOneReference accesses the database only if the required Persistence is not contained in the cache of the PersistencePeers. The 1:*N* reference class ToManyReference accesses the database only if no Persistence object has been loaded yet. Persistence objects are loaded automatically during the first request to the entity. It also occurs when a Persistence is added to, or removed from, the association. Therefore, if an existing Restaurant would like to add a new Dish to the menu but no Dishes have previously been used for the Restaurant, the existing Dishes are uploaded.

**Table 9.6** Interfaces of the reference classes of the Persistence framework

| Interface | Description |
| --- | --- |
| I_PersistenceReference | Basic interface for all associations. Acquire key value. Access description of the reference. Make a copy. |
| I_PersistenceToOneReference | 1:1 association. |
| I_PersistenceToManyReference | 1:N association. |
| I_PersistenceToManyModifiedReference | 1:N association whose changes are directly taken into account when modifying the Persistence. |
| I_PersistenceModify | Select modification method, create(), update() and delete(). |

Because objects can be related to each other in many different ways, we will have to define a number of interfaces (Table 9.6). The interconnection of these interfaces and their implementation are shown in Fig. 9.25.

It is worth noting the modelling of the 1:N association of an N:M relation (ToManyLinkReference). This type of relation is found, for example, between suppliers and products. One article may frequently be sold by many suppliers. Similarly, one supplier may sell many products. However, when looking at the data, it is generally often only the products offered by a certain supplier or the suppliers of a certain article which are of real interest. In a relational database, such associations are displayed with the help of temporary tables.

In the persistence framework, the ToManyLinkReference class provides the correct view of items and suppliers (Fig. 9.26) and hides the necessary but time-consuming qualification from the user. When a new article is added to the association, a new data record is automatically created in the temporary table SupplierProduct with the keys for Supplier and Products.

The only difference to ToManyReference lies in the qualification of the data records. Generally, the reference classes allow the modelling of randomly qualified associations. In standard cases it is possible to define a static qualification extension. Using the setQualifierExtension(String) method you can set a sorting order 'Order By t0.Description' or a static qualification 'AND Description like "%Pizza%"' in the I_PersistenceToManyReference interface. This would mean in these two examples that the dishes of a restaurant would be alphabetically sorted by their name or that an association existed between restaurants and dishes whose name contained the word 'Pizza'.

For qualification via parameters (generalization of ToManyLinkReference), the basic class ToManyReference offers the refValueQualifier() method. In specialized, qualified associations this method has to be overwritten accordingly. The configuration provides for the entry of a special reference class (Appendix B). Thus, the use of different reference types is almost unlimited.

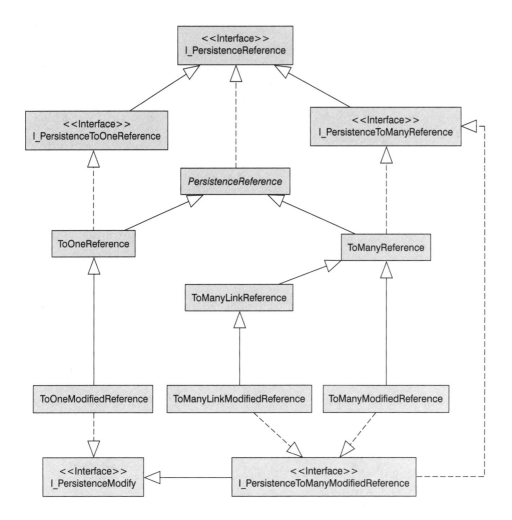

**Figure 9.25** Reference and interfaces of the Persistence framework

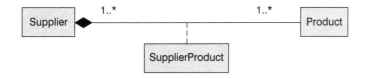

**Figure 9.26** Link class between supplier and product

Reference classes provide an effortless way to navigate through an object network. The objects of an association are only created and bound when they are actually needed by the application. Therefore, the application's memory use is kept under control and its resources are protected. The persistence framework fulfils the common requirements for use within one JVM (Java Virtual Machine).

### 9.6.3 Modelling a persistent object network

As an example, we shall implement the association between `Restaurant` and `Dish`. In comparison with the example in Section 9.5, we have added steps 1 and 5:

**1** Analyze the associations and select the required reference classes.

**2** Create the tables.

**3** Enter the object types into the `TypeNumber` table.

**4** Create a `Store` configuration file.

**5** Code the `Persistence` classes.

First of all, the analysis: for ease of use, all the class attributes are of the type `java.lang.String`. Each `Restaurant` has its own `Dishes` in the shape of a `ToManyModifiedReference` (Fig. 9.27). As mentioned above, this has the result that each change to a `Dish` will also be saved when its `Restaurant` is saved. Each `Dish` is uniquely associated with its `Restaurant` with the help of a `ToOneReference` object.

Because the `Restaurant` table has already been created in Section 9.5, we will not have to do this again – all that remains is to create the `Dish` table with the following SQL statement:

```
CREATE TABLE Dish (
    ObjectIdentifier CHAR(16) NOT NULL,
    ObjectVersion INTEGER,
    RestaurantID CHAR(16) NOT NULL,
    Description VARCHAR,
    PRIMARY KEY (ObjectIdentifier),
    FOREIGN KEY (RestaurantID) REFERENCES Restaurant (ObjectIdentifier)
);
```

Afterwards, we have to enter the type `Dish` into the `TypeNumber` table:

```
INSERT INTO TypeNumber ('Dish',11) ;
```

To define the characteristics of our `Persistence` objects, we have to configure the `Store` (Listing 9.17). We create them in three parts: in part one of the configuration file, only the name of the store is defined. Part two defines a database connection – in this case for a Solid database. Then, the types `Restaurant` and `Dish` are defined in part three.

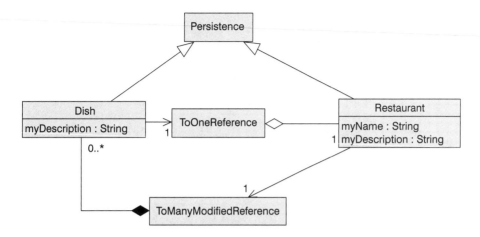

**Figure 9.27**  Modelling the associations with reference classes of the Persistence framework

Listing 9.17: Configuration of the Store for Restaurant and Dish

```
{
// Part I
   Name = "Restaurant" ;
// Part II
   JDBCConnection = {
      DriverClass = "solid.jdbc.SolidDriver" ;
      URLConnect = "jdbc: solid: //localhost: 1313" ;
      Properties = {
         user = "web" ;
         password = "app" ;
      }
      } ;
// Part III
   Types = {
   Restaurant = {
      Type = {
         Name = "Restaurant" ;
         Class = "de.webapp.Examples.Persistence.Restaurant.Restaurant";
         Entity = "Restaurant";
         EntityAlias = "t0" ;
         Attributes = (
            "ObjectIdentifier",
            "ObjectVersion",
            "Name";
            "Description";
         ) ;
         Associations = (
```

```
                          { Name = "Dish" ; Type = "ToMany" ; Modified = "YES" ;
                          ResultType = "Dish" ; Key = "RestaurantID" ;
                          }
                      ) ;
                  } ;
              } ;
          Dish = {
              Type = {
              Name = "Dish" ;
              Class = "de.webapp.Examples.Persistence.Restaurant.Dish";
              Entity = "Dish";
              EntityAlias = "t0" ;
              Attributes = (
                  "ObjectIdentifier",
                  "ObjectVersion",
                  "RestaurantID";
                  "Description";
              );
              Associations = (
                  { Name = "Restaurant" ; Type = "ToOne" ;
                  ResultType = "Restaurant" ; }
              ) ;
              }
          } ;
          }
      } // End of the configuration
```

In contrast to the simple example in Section 9.5, derivations of the
de.webapp.Framework.Persistence.Persistence class are used here instead of
the generic classes. Encoding of the required classes is a bit more involved, but can in
principle be done automatically with the help of a tool. For reasons of speed, true derivations of Persistence should generally be used in preference to generic classes, as
generic classes have to store their attributes in hash tables, whereas true derivations
can directly access instance variables.

Listing 9.18: The Restaurant class as a derivation of Persistence

```
package de.webapp.Examples.Persistence.Restaurant ;

import de.webapp.Framework.Persistence.*;
import de.webapp.Framework.Utilities.ReferenceVector;

import java.sql.* ;

public class Restaurant extends Persistence {
    protected String myName ;
    protected String myDescription ;
    protected I_PersistenceToManyModifiedReference myDishToManyRef ;
```

```
protected Restaurant() {}
// Construction of a new Restaurant
public Restaurant(I_PersistencePeer aPeer)
   throws PersistenceException {
   super(aPeer) ;
}
// Construction of Restaurant from the database
public Restaurant(I_PersistencePeer aPeer,ResultSet rs)
   throws PersistenceException {
   super( aPeer, rs ) ;
}
// Bind the attributes from a result set
protected int bind(ResultSet rs, int offset)
   throws PersistenceException,
   SQLException {
   offset = super.bind(rs,offset) ;
   myName = (String) rs.getObject(++offset) ;
   myDescription = (String) rs.getObject(++offset) ;
   if(myDishToManyRef != null)
      myDishToManyRef.setValue(getObjectIdentifier()) ;
   return offset;
}
// When the identity is changed, it must be matched up
   with the associations.
public void setObjectIdentifier(String identifier) {
   super.setObjectIdentifier(identifier) ;
   if( myObjectState == STATE_UNDEFINED ||
      myObjectState == STATE_TRANSIENT ||
      myObjectState == STATE_UNREFERENCED ) {
      if(myDishToManyRef != null)
         myDishToManyRef.setValue(getObjectIdentifier()) ;
   }
}
// Access the attributes
public String getName() { return myName ; }
public void setName(String aValue) {
   myName = aValue ;
   setModified() ;
}
public String getDescription() { return myDescription ; }
public void setDescription(String aValue) {
   myDescription = aValue ;
   setModified() ;
}
// Access the associations
public void addToDish(I_Persistence aObject)
   throws PersistenceException {
   getDishReference().addToReference(aObject) ;
```

```java
      setReferenceModified() ;
   }

   public void removeFromDish(I_Persistence aObject)
      throws PersistenceException {
      getDishReference().removeFromReference(aObject) ;
      setReferenceModified() ;
   }

   public ReferenceVector getDish()
      throws PersistenceException {
      return getDishReference().getObjects() ;
   }

   public I_PersistenceToManyModifiedReference getDishReference()
      throws PersistenceException {
      if(myDishToManyRef == null) {
        myDishToManyRef = (I_PersistenceToManyModifiedReference)
          getPeer().getType().associationWithName(
          "Dish").newReference() ;
        myDishToManyRef.setValue(getObjectIdentifier());
      }
      return myDishToManyRef ;
   }
   // Synchronization of the associations
   protected void afterCreate ()
      throws PersistenceException {
      super.afterCreate() ;
      if(myDishToManyRef != null)
         myDishToManyRef.create() ;
   }

   protected void afterUpdate ()
      throws PersistenceException {
      super.afterUpdate() ;
      if(myDishToManyRef != null)
         myDishToManyRef.update() ;
   }
   // Delete all associations whose status is MODIFIED.
   protected void beforeDelete ()
      throws PersistenceException {
      getDish();
         myDishToManyRef.delete() ;
      myDishToManyRef = null ;
      super.beforeDelete() ;
   }
   // Copy the object
   public Object clone()
```

```
    throws CloneNotSupportedException {
    Restaurant theRestaurant = (Restaurant) super.clone() ;
    if(myDishToManyRef != null)
      theRestaurant.myDishToManyRef =
        (I_PersistenceToManyModifiedReference)
        myDishToManyRef.clone() ;
    return theRestaurant ;
  }
} // End of the class
```

For each derivation of `Persistence`, three constructors have to be implemented. Although the constructors are public, you should never call them up directly outside a framework upgrade but only use the `Store`'s `newPersistence(String)` method. The default constructor is declared to be protected, to prevent a `Persistence` entity, without a `PersistencePeer`, being created by mistake. The `Restaurant-(I_PersistencePeer)` constructor is used to create a completely new `Persistence` object. In contrast, the `Restaurant(I_PersistencePeer, ResultSet)` constructor is used to create a `Persistence` from the database. With the `bind(ResultSet, int)` method the values from `ResultSet` are assigned to the appropriate attributes.

At this point, there are two critical dependencies. The first one is that the configuration sequence has to correspond exactly with the coding, as the reading of `ResultSet` is position-dependent. The second is that different JDBC drivers do not always have the same mappings of database data types to object data types. Therefore, when switching between databases, the `bind(ResultSet, int)` method can throw up serious problems. These problems frequently occur in conjunction with financial values, integer values and times. Another relatively small problem is the fact that different drivers do not always use the same number of digits after the point (for example, Solid uses two digits after the decimal point, and MS-Access uses four). In Oracle 8.x you have to ensure that each `java.lang.Integer` becomes a `java.sql.BigDecimal`. In the `bind(ResultSet rs, int offset)` method the value of Integer attributes therefore has to be set by `new Integer(rs.getInt(++offset)`.

The `setObjectIdentifier(String)` method has to be overwritten, so that in a new object net the automatically determined object identity of new reference objects can be set accordingly. This means the foreign key is propagated independently. For accessing the attributes, you can use the `get` and `set` methods. The declaration (`protected`) prevents direct access to attributes.

Each reference with the `I_ToManyReference` interface requires the implementation of the four methods shown in Table 9.7. Here, values can be manipulated thanks to the direct access to internal data structures.

In the case of the `Restaurant`, this has been implemented for the association with its `Dishes`. As this association is an aggregation, the association has to be matched up accordingly in the `before<XX>` methods (Listing 9.19, `syncModifiedReference()`). If a `Restaurant` is deleted, all its `Dishes` will be removed, too. According to the application logic, this can either be positive or negative. Every time the association

**Table 9.7**  Methods of a 1:*N* association of a persistence

| Method | Description |
|---|---|
| addTo<Name> | Adds a persistence object to the reference |
| removeFrom<Name> | Deletes a persistence object from the reference |
| get<Name> | Returns all of the reference's persistence objects |
| get<Name>Reference | Returns the reference for special manipulation |

relationship changes, the `setReferenceModified()` method is used to change the status of the `Persistence` object.

Finally, with the `clone()` method, each `Persistence` object can generate a copy of itself. The references of the framework also generate a true copy (see `ToManyReference.clone()`), but without also copying the `Persistence` objects of the reference. Therefore, the dishes of a restaurant will not be copied when a copy of the restaurant is made. Only the main object is duplicated.

Listing 9.19: The `Dish` class as a derivation of `Persistence`

```
package de.webapp.Examples.Persistence.Restaurant ;

import de.webapp.Framework.Persistence.*;
import java.sql.* ;

public class Dish extends Persistence {
   protected String myDescription ;
   protected String myRestaurantID ;
   protected ToOneReference myRestaurantToOneRef ;

protected Dish() {}
// Add a new Dish
public Dish(I_PersistencePeer aPeer)
   throws PersistenceException {
   super(aPeer) ;
}
// Add a Dish that is already present in the database.
public Dish(I_PersistencePeer aPeer,ResultSet rs)
   throws PersistenceException {
   super(aPeer,rs) ;
}
// Bind the attributes from the result set
public int bind(ResultSet rs, int offset)
   throws PersistenceException,
   SQLException {
   offset = super.bind(rs,offset) ;
   myRestaurantID = (String) rs.getObject(++offset) ;
   myDescription = (String) rs.getObject(++offset) ;
```

```
    if(myRestaurantToOneRef != null)
      myRestaurantToOneRef.setValue(myRestaurantID) ;
    return offset;
}
// Access the attributes
public String getDescription() { return myDescription ; }
public void setDescription(String aValue) {
  myDescription = aValue ;
  setModified() ;
}
public String getRestaurantID() { return myRestaurantID ; }
public void setRestaurantID(String aValue) {
  myRestaurantID = aValue ;
  setModified() ;
}
// Access the reference
public I_Persistence getRestaurant()
  throws PersistenceException {
  return getRestaurantReference().getObject() ;
}

public void setRestaurant(I_Persistence aRestaurant)
  throws PersistenceException {
  getRestaurantReference().setObject(aRestaurant) ;
  myRestaurantID = (String) myRestaurantToOneRef.getValue() ;
  setModified() ;
}

public I_PersistenceToOneReference getRestaurantReference()
  throws PersistenceException {
  if(myRestaurantToOneRef == null) {
    myRestaurantToOneRef = (ToOneReference)
      getPeer().getType().associationWithName(
        "Restaurant").newReference() ;
    myRestaurantToOneRef.setValue(myRestaurantID);
  }
  return myRestaurantToOneRef ;
}
// When the data are saved, the keys are matched up for new object nets.
protected void syncModifiedReference()
  throws PersistenceException {
  if(myRestaurantID == null) {
    if(myRestaurantToOneRef != null) {
      I_Persistence aObject = myRestaurantToOneRef.getObject() ;
      if(aObject != null)
        myRestaurantID = (String)aObject.getObjectIdentifier() ;
    }
```

```
      }
    }
    // Synchronization during saving
    protected void beforeCreate ()
      throws PersistenceException {
      super.beforeCreate() ;
      syncModifiedReference() ;
    }

    protected void beforeUpdate ()
      throws PersistenceException {
      super.beforeUpdate() ;
      syncModifiedReference() ;
    }
    // Create a copy of this object
    public Object clone()
      throws CloneNotSupportedException {
        Dish theDish = (Dish) super.clone() ;
      if(myRestaurantToOneRef != null)
        theDish.myRestaurantToOneRef =
          (ToOneReference) myRestaurantToOneRef.clone() ;
      return theDish ;
    }
  } // End of the class
```

The Dish class has a 1:1 association with the Restaurant class (Table 9.8).

**Table 9.8**  Methods of a 1:1 association

| Method | Description |
| --- | --- |
| get<Name> | Returns the persistence |
| set<Name> | Sets the persistence |
| get<Name>Reference | Returns the reference for special manipulation |

Construction, access to the attributes and copying are identical to the Restaurant derivation. However, the association is encoded differently.

Because only a single Persistence object has to be managed by the Reference, the direct methods set and get are used. In the Persistence object, the reference and the foreign key (here RestaurantID) are changed simultaneously. Therefore, the state of the Persistence object has to be set to MODIFIED, using the setModified() method. Selecting the syncModifiedReference() method in the beforeCreate() or beforeUpdate() method causes a synchronization of the foreign key with the reference value. This is especially important if a completely new object network is saved and the object identity of the referenced object is determined only when the network is being saved.

After the rather long definition of the necessary `Persistence` classes, here is the application:

Listing 9.20: Access to a restaurant with the help of the `Persistence` framework

```
package de.webapp.Examples.Persistence.Restaurant;

import java.util.*;
import de.webapp.Framework.ConfigManager.*;

import de.webapp.Framework.Persistence.* ;
import de.webapp.Framework.StoreFactory.StoreFactory ;

import de.webapp.Framework.Utilities.Log;
import de.webapp.Framework.Utilities.ReferenceVector;
import de.webapp.Framework.Utilities.I_WebAppException ;

public class RestaurantTest
{
   protected I_Store myStore ;
// Get Store
public RestaurantTest(String aStore)
   throws Exception {
   ConfigManager.getConfigManager();
   Configuration theStore =
      ConfigManager.getConfigManager().getConfiguration(aStore);
   // Store configuration
   myStore = StoreFactory.getInstance(theStore) ;
   if(myStore == null) {
      Log.log("Store could not be created ") ;
      throw new Exception("Store cannot be configured" ) ;
   }
}
// Create new Dish
protected Dish newDish(String aDescription)
   throws PersistenceException {
   Dish newDish = (Dish)myStore.newPersistence("Dish") ;
   newDish.setDescription(aDescription) ;
   return newDish ;
}
// Generate a Peppone Restaurant
protected void newRestaurantTest()
   throws PersistenceException {
   Restaurant newRestaurant =
      (Restaurant)myStore.newPersistence("Restaurant") ;
   newRestaurant.setName("Pizza Peppone") ;
   newRestaurant.setDescription("Quick and tasty") ;
   newRestaurant.addToDish(newDish("Pizza Vegetaria")) ;
```

```java
    newRestaurant.addToDish(newDish("Pizza Inferno")) ;
    newRestaurant.addToDish(newDish("Pizza Hawaii")) ;
    newRestaurant.create() ;
}
// Find the Peppone Restaurant
protected void searchAllRestaurantTest()
    throws PersistenceException {
    ReferenceVector aVector = myStore.getRetriever("Restaurant").retrieve(
        " WHERE t0.Name = 'Pizza Peppone'") ;
    for(Enumeration e=aVector.elements();e.hasMoreElements() ; ) {
        Restaurant aObject=(Restaurant)e.nextElement() ;
        Log.log("Restaurant / Name - " + aObject.getValue("Name")
            + " - Description - " + aObject.getValue("Description") );
        for(Enumeration
            e1=((ReferenceVector)aObject.getDish()).elements();
            e1.hasMoreElements() ; ) {
            Dish aDish=(Dish)e1.nextElement() ;
            Log.log((String)aDish.getDescription() );
        }
    }
}
// Command branch
public void action(int aCommand, String[] args) {
    if(myStore != null) {
        synchronized( myStore) {
            try {
                try {
                    myStore.begin() ;
                    switch(aCommand) {
                    case 0 :
                        searchAllRestaurantTest() ;
                        break ;
                    case 1 :
                        newRestaurantTest() ;
                        break ;
                    default :
                        Log.log("Command " + aCommand + args
                            + " does not exist" ) ;
                    }
                    myStore.commit() ;
                } catch (Exception e) {
                    if(myStore != null)
                        myStore.rollback() ;
                    throw e ;
                } finally {
                    myStore.close() ;
```

```
        }
      } catch (Throwable e ) {
        Throwable aThrowable = e ;
        while (aThrowable != null) {
          aThrowable.printStackTrace();
          if(aThrowable instanceof I_WebAppException) {
            aThrowable =
                ((I_WebAppException)aThrowable).getThrowable() ;
          } else
            aThrowable = null ;
        }
      }
    }
  }
}
// Start the task
public static void main(String args[])
  throws Exception {

  RestaurantTest theRestaurant = new RestaurantTest("Restaurant Store");
  Integer aCommand = new Integer(args[0]) ;
  theRestaurant.action(aCommand.intValue(),args);
}
} // End of the class
```

The start of the small test environment RestaurantTest (Listing 9.20) creates or displays the restaurant Peppone with all its available Dishes. The Store is configured in the constructor. The action(int, String[]) method enables each desired function. With it, you can synchronize the Store and create the necessary transaction frame. The searchAllRestaurantTest() method searches for the restaurant Peppone with the help of a PersistenceRetriever from the database and writes it to the standard log. The newRestaurant(String, String) method creates a new restaurant Peppone and adds a few Dishes with the help of newDish(String). The restaurant is saved with a single create() command to the new Restaurant object.

## 9.7  Applying Persistence

The application of a persistence framework instead of JDBC generally offers many advantages. For example, it is possible to achieve complete object-oriented encapsulation of the database. Now, the development team requires only one specialist with very good knowledge of SQL. If a persistence framework has been sensibly configured, chances are that you will generally get by without any SQL. This in turn considerably increases portability, extendability and maintainability of applications.

Below is a list of the most important characteristics of the persistence framework:

- Service-oriented architecture.
- All services can be configured and are defined by interfaces.
- Encapsulation of JDBC for accessing tables.
- Configuration of the object-relational representation.
- Use of SQL is limited to formulating qualifications for specific requests.
- Creation of object networks.
- Navigation using associations without the need for knowledge of SQL.
- Generic objects for fast prototyping.
- `null` can be used as a value.
- Flexible and interchangeable identity generator.
- Unification – unique `Persistence` in one `Store`.
- Accelerated speed by using caches.
- Several independent stores in a Java VM.
- Availability of a run-time type description.
- Transaction management.

# Generating dynamic **10**
# HTML pages
# with servlets

N ow that we have laid the foundations for web-based applications with SMI (Chapter 8) and the `Persistence` framework (Chapter 9), we still need to explain how to achieve the processing of dynamic contents on the server. In the past two years there has been a flood of different starting points for the dynamic generation of HTML pages via servlets. Spurred on by Microsoft's Active Server Pages (ASP), the Java community now has the use of JavaServer Pages (JSP), the portable counterpart (Javasoft 1999). The JSP can be implemented in any Web server that has a servlet engine. This has therefore made it very easy to make specific information available on a variety of different operating systems and server environments. JSP is also an elegant solution for formatting the contents. Java is currently used as the script language, and Java beans components are used to encapsulate functions as data.

The end of this chapter introduces programming using JSP. However, first we shall describe and arrange the many other starting points.

## 10.1  Generating HTML pages on the server

Shortly after the publication of the Servlet API 1.0 (1997), Hewlett-Packard (Anders Kristensen) produced HTML in the form of Java classes. For programmers this type of HTML coding is a real pleasure to use. At last they no longer have to struggle with the parameters of certain HTML commands, such as FORM or TABLE. Instead they can use well-formed objects. When it comes to preparing specific, predefined representations quickly, this methodology is unbeatable. However, presenting contents is not usually a programmer's task. It is more often carried out by the designer. Designers require support from the programmers and only take small steps into the depths of a powerful programming language such as Java.

In recognition of this, several very different starting points have been created to achieve the task with specially tailored script languages. Some make it possible to access Java objects, others offer a complete, independent set of language functions and others restrict themselves to simply replacing tags with contents. Deciding which solution is the best in a specific situation very much depends on the content of the project and the various skills of the development team.

The sections that follow give a brief introduction to the various starting points. We have decided to use JSP for the examples in the third part of the book because this path is promoted by Sun and will probably become the standard.

### 10.1.1 HTML programming with Java

In each project, there is the need to format information from a data source. Sometimes there is also a desire to generate simple entry dialogues automatically. For this purpose, the encapsulation of an HTML page into a configurable class is an ideal solution. Here the individual HTML elements are also encapsulated into classes and simply added to the page object.

Each dynamic HTML page which is created in this way must be output from a `servlet`. In Fig. 10.1 you can see an implementation of this kind. In this case, the servlet must already have been translated and registered at the servlet engine. The example originates from the Nexus package (Table 10.1).

The freely available Jetty Web server also supplies an extremely successful HTML package. The encapsulation of all HTML elements makes the programming clear and simple. The `Page` class allows high-level abstraction of an HTML page. The header and body of an HTML page can easily be extended. The methods available to do this, `writeBodyTag(Writer)`, `writeElements(Writer)`, `writeHtmlEnd(Writer)` and `writeHtmlHead(Writer)`, offer sufficient space for manoeuvre. The existing `PageFactory` also allows access to a number of preconfigured HTML pages. In this

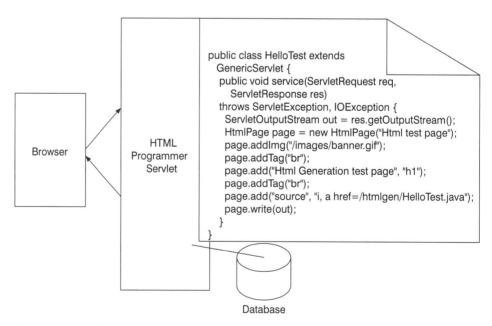

**Figure 10.1** Programming HTML in Java

**Table 10.1**  HTML programming packages

| Package | Link | Comment |
|---------|------|---------|
| HTMLKona | `http://www.weblogic.com/docs/` `examples/htmlkona/htmlexamples.html` | Well integrated in the WebLogic Web Server global concept. Integration of other products e.g. JDBCKona to access databases. |
| Jetty | `http://www.mortbay.com/` | The servlet engine contains a package with Java classes, to program HTML in Java. The source code is very impressive. |
| Nexus | `http://www-uk.hpl.hp.com/` `people/ak/java/` | Can be used independently of the Nexus Web Server. Very simple implementation. |
| SDSU | `http://www.eli.sdsu.edu/java-SDSU/` | Very simple encapsulation. GNU licence. |
| ECS | `http://java.apache.org/ecs/` | The Element Construction Set can use all HTML 4.0 tags and supports XML tags. The flexibility and speed of the objects are impressive. |

way, modules can be developed from pages and the appropriate generic access can be created via an `HTMLDisplayServlet`.

The other packages differ greatly from each other. HTMLKona is the only real product. In many projects it is used together with the BEA WebLogic server. In the other systems, Nexus, ECS, SDSU and Jetty, the source code is supplied. This makes it possible for you to carry out your own modifications (Table 10.1). The ECS system is extremely flexible and gives the programmer a wide-ranging and conceptually well-thought-out package. There is nothing to prevent it also being used commercially.

## 10.1.2  HTML generation with powerful script languages

A completely different path is taken by the products that integrate their own script languages with servlets (Fig. 10.2). Complete and independent languages are usually used here. In such cases the query is passed on via a servlet to the language's interpreter. This then reads the relevant script file and prepares the response.

Two different products in this category are Aspy, which uses JPython, and EcmaScript Page (ESP) (Table 10.2). The common factor is that they both use a complete programming language in addition to HTML and Java.

It is certainly the case that the ESP solution accommodates JavaScript programmers. However, it does not allow access to Java objects. This makes it impossible to use the business logic coded in Java in a useful way. These script extensions only give minimal support to using a clear architecture, as we recommend in this book. The script languages that integrate Java objects are dealt with in the section that follows, and are much more interesting.

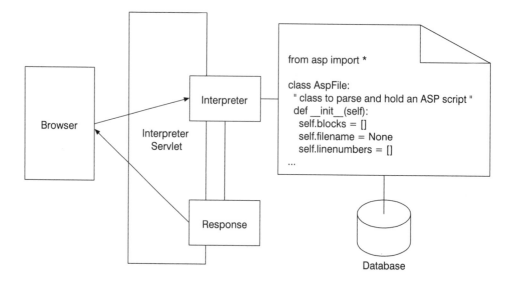

**Figure 10.2** Generating HTML pages using a script interpreter

**Table 10.2** Packages with their own script languages

| Package | Link | Comment |
| --- | --- | --- |
| Aspy | http://www.dstc.edu.au/aspy/src/ | Uses JPython |
| EcmaScript Page (ESP) | http://www.mindspring.com/~rrocha | Based on Fesi, a Java-based EcmaScript interpreter |

## 10.1.3 HTML generation with simple script languages

Instead of defining their own complete language, some products allow direct access to Java objects. This has the advantage that programmers can encapsulate any complex processes in objects, while Web designers only need to access the simple methods of these objects. The target group is therefore Web designers with a knowledge of JavaScript. In addition to the ability to define local variables, the languages offer commands for branching (IF) and iteration (FOR).

The request arguments are provided with either fixed markings (<%REQUEST%> or <%RESPONSE%>) or global variables ($REQUEST or $RESPONSE). As it is possible to access Java Objects directly, any kind of results can be requested and then formatted. This allows you to separate the obtaining and processing of data (see #Result in Fig. 10.3). Even functional objects such as a Mail API or a log output can be accessed directly. Tasks can be elegantly distributed among the members of a team, because the languages support work in parallel. This meets the programmers' desire to encapsulate functionality, and gives the designers enough freedom to be creative.

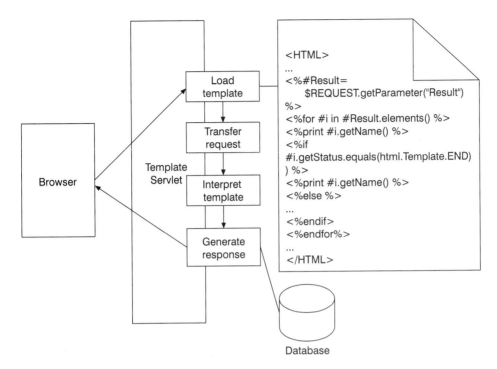

```
<HTML>
...
<%#Result=
    $REQUEST.getParameter("Result")
%>
<%for #i in #Result.elements() %>
<%print #i.getName() %>
<%if
#i.getStatus.equals(html.Template.END)
) %>
<%print #i.getName() %>
<%else %>
...
<%endif>
<%endfor%>
...
</HTML>
```

**Figure 10.3**  Interpretation of a template with access to Java Objects

**Table 10.3**  Packages for Java-based script languages

| Package | Link | Comment |
|---|---|---|
| objectHTML | http://www.factum-gmbh.de/ | Accesses Java objects (attributes, constants and access to methods). Extension of the Reflect API, to access all methods. Optimized interpreter with Parsetree cache. Uses the concept of the formatter for using programs to control the output per object type. Independent of Servlet API [Rossbach and Schreiber 1998ac]. |
| Otembo | http://www.meangene.com/otembo/ | Script language based on a universal tagging concept. |
| WebMacro | http://www.webmacro.org/ | Macro language which is interpreted by a special servlet. |
| FreeMaker | http://freemaker.org/ | An extremely successful macro language under GNU Public Licence (GPL). The implementation uses the Java Collection classes effectively. |
| InstantOnlineBasic | http://www.gefionsoftware.com/ | Uses Includes on the server with special servlets |

The performance of these solutions differs greatly (Table 10.3). All products can access Java objects. It is not easy to integrate Java completely, because some features in the `java.lang.reflect` API are missing. Access to specific signatures only functions if the exact type of an argument is present. If only a sub-class is entered, it is hard to determine the method. It is at this point that objectHTML shows one of its strengths and reveals the weaknesses of many other systems. The formatters are another successful extension of objectHTML. For each type that occurs in an output command (`<%print ... %>`), you can set a function with arguments for formatting. If no special formatting arguments are entered, the `toString()` method is used and the resulting character string is output.

## 10.1.4 Creating HTML by generating Java classes

The absolute winner for generating dynamic HTML pages is using Java as a script language. This development began with the Java Web server 1.1 Page Compilation function at the end of 1997. The next generation was the JavaServer Pages. A special extension to the functionality is that support for Java bean components has been implemented for JSP. Unfortunately the final version of JSP specification 1.1 was not complete when this book went to press. We hope that this will have changed by the time this book is published (`http://java.sun.com/products/jsp`).

A JSP is coded using a mixture of HTML and Java. A few additional markings are enough to separate HTML and Java code from each other. We shall discuss the precise syntax in Section 10.2.1. Generally speaking, you can say that a servlet is generated from each JSP (Fig. 10.4).

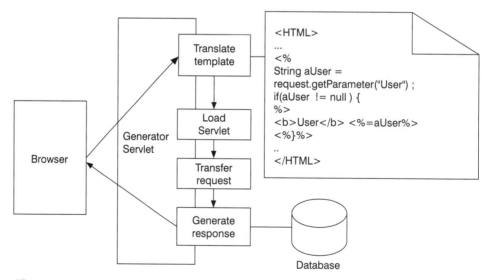

**Figure 10.4** Dynamic generation of a servlet

We can access the servlet parameters, the request (`request`) and the response (`response`), directly in the script. Once the script has been translated, the class is available for all subsequent accesses. It is obvious that this has a significant advantage of speed over the purely interpretative script solutions shown in Section 10.1.3. Table 10.4 shows the variety of resulting solutions.

There are, of course, other products in addition to the reference solution provided by Sun. The outstanding one is definitely the free implementation GNUJSP by Vincent Partington, which accompanied us throughout the development of the WebApp framework. The Live Software company has also implemented an elegant extension with its JRun Scripting Toolkit (JST). Unfortunately, JST is integrated with the JRun Servlet Engine. All JSP implementations are to be combined to form a fast and powerful reference implementation in the Jakarta project, under the management of the Apache group and with the help of Sun (James Duncan Davidson). The advantage of this initiative lies in the complete availability of the source code and the dynamics of free software development. Some of the most important, constantly recurring questions about JSP are answered in the site at `http://www.esperanto.org.nz/jsp/jspfaq.htm`.

All the other systems listed in Table 10.4 are of less importance. For GNU server pages (GSP) you are forced to create code in the old Page Compilation dialect. The only interesting feature is the application expression which has been introduced. Even `ServletFactory` generates servlet classes, which still have to be installed by the user. Unfortunately, the integration of beans is missing entirely. Servc is a small servlet generator and the WebApplication Framework (WeAF) system is based on a script language which makes it easy to integrate JDBC in HTML pages.

## 10.2  JavaServer pages

JavaServer pages are a simple but powerful way of generating HTML pages. The integration of Java beans, which we have already mentioned, is a valuable extension. With them you can use pre-prepared Java components in a JSP. Creating a connection to a database, an RMI server or mail server becomes child's play.

All JavaServer pages are addressed using a `JspServlet`. To do this, you must inform the servlet engine that all the requests that end with `.jsp` should be mapped to this `servlet`. You usually do this via an entry in one of the `mappings.properties`, `rules.properties` or `servlets.properties` files.

Listing 10.1: Example of an entry for GNUJSP in the `servlet.properties` file of jo!

```
# GNUJSP-Servlet 1.0
servlet.gnujsp.code=org.gjt.jsp JSP10Servlet
servlet.gnujsp.initArgs=scratchdir=jsprepository
servlet.gnujsp.aliases=*.jsp
servlet.gnujsp.preload=true
```

This entry means that all the queries to the servlet engine that have the file extension `.jsp` are passed on to the `JspServlet`. When it receives this type of request, this servlet checks whether the class of the requested servlet is already available and loaded. If not, the JSP file is translated, and a new servlet class is created which is usually

**Table 10.4** Packages used to generate Java servlets

| Package | Link | Comment |
|---|---|---|
| JSP – Java Server Pages | http://java.sun.com/products/jsp/ http://developer.java.sun.com/developer/earlyAccess/jsp/ | Reference implementation of JSP1.1. Java as a script language. Is compiled and converted into a servlet. |
| Jakarta | http://jakarta.apache.com/ | Combines the Sun reference implementation of the API 2.2 servlet, JSP1.1 and Apache JServ 1.0 into one uniform version. |
| NewAtlanta | http://www.newatlanta.com | Implementation of JSP 1.0. |
| WebSphere | http://www.software.ibm.com/Web servers/ | Implementation of JSP1.0. |
| GNUJSP 0.9.10 | http://www.klomp.org/gnujsp/ | Implementation of JSP in accordance with the 0.91 specification. Is the most widely used implementation of free software in the world. All information and patches concerning GNUJSP are also published on the site. |
| GNUJSP 1.0 XML | http://www.euronet.nl/~pauls/java/gnujsp/ | Implementation of JSP 1.0 via an XML/DOM (domain object model) |
| GNUJSP 1.0 | http://www.klomp.org/gnujsp/ | A functional JSP 1.0 implementation. |
| RocketJSP | http://www.cyberway.com.sg/~munwai/ | Partially conforms to JSP 1.0 specification. |
| zJSP | http://www.zachary.com/creemer/zjsp.html | Implements the 0.91 specification. |
| PolyJsp | http://www.plentix.org/ | Implements the 0.92 specification. |
| SJSP | http://web.telecom.cz/sator/jsp/index.html | Implements the 0.92 specification. |
| JRun | http://jrun.com | Implements JSP 1.0. |
| JST – JRun Scripting Toolkit | http://www.livesoftware.com/products/jst/index.html | Extension of JSP. Integrated with the JRun engine. |
| ServletFactory (ServletBuilder) | http://www.earlymorning.com | Simple servlet generator (ServletBuilder) based on JSP syntax but without a bean tag. Integrated into ServletFactory, the free Java web server |
| GSP | http://www.bitmechanic.com/projects/gsp/ | Based on the predecessor of JSP; Page Compilation. Own extensions. |
| Servc | http://www.geocities.com/SiliconValley/Pines/3185 | Generating servlets via macros. |
| WeAFJava Web Application Framework | http://www.weaf.com/ | Complete integration of Java. Special tags for JDBC and SQL. |

derived from the HttpServlet class (Chapter 3). This class is then instantiated and initialized. Now the original request (HttpServletRequest) and the response (HttpServletResponse) are passed on to the JspServlet.

In general, a JSP can access the complete range of functions offered by the Java API. This means that all doors are open to the programmers. However, what initially seems to be an advantage becomes a handicap when HTML designers have to work with JSP. Java is simply too powerful. To make things somewhat easier for JSP designers, Sun has created a simple means of integrating Java beans into JSP (Fig. 10.5). Java programmers can make life less complicated for their designer colleagues by presenting them with preprepared components. We strongly recommend you do not directly implement an RMI connection, or the use of the MailAPI within JSP. Instead, you should create standard beans, which simply hide the cumbersome import commands and powerful processes, for this purpose. This makes them much more transparent, and easy to maintain.

One of JSP's important features is that each time a JSP is changed, it is automatically translated again. This is a real blessing at the development stage, at least so long as you do not change your own classes, which are used within JSP. At present, the only safe solution for changing the base classes of a server is to delete all the generated JSP classes. This means, of course, that all JSPs must be translated again for the next request. This type of boot (start-up) phase can lead to long response times and place a heavy load on the server, if several JSPs are required in one HTML page, as often happens when HTML frames with dynamic contents are involved. Attempts are currently being made to find a way of supplying pre-compiled JSP pages. For GNUJSP we developed the JSPExecutor (http://www.webapp.de/).

In the next two sections we shall be dealing with the most important elements of JSP syntax. This is an extremely compact overview. For a more detailed description, you should refer to the JSP specification (JavaSoft 1999).

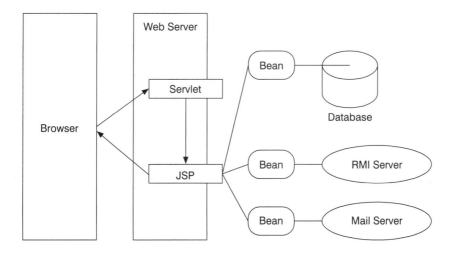

**Figure 10.5** A browser request to JavaServer Pages

### 10.2.1 Syntax of JavaServer pages

The syntax of JavaServer pages has always changed significantly from version to version. Unfortunately, when we delivered the manuscript of this book, the final 1.1 specification was not ready and the JSP 1.0 reference implementation had only just been made available. Despite this we are daring to attempt to give the first complete overview of JSP syntax.

The XML document reflected by the current JavaServer pages specification, 1.0, is not yet final (Table 10.6). It was though, ensured that the previous clear and short `<%...%>` tags remain available (Table 10.5).

To define methods and attributes, the HTML script tag `<SCRIPT runat="server"> </SCRIPT>` has been replaced in favour of a short `<%! %>` tag. The HTML Include syntax (NSCA 1996), used on the server, has been replaced by the practical `<%@ include file="" %>` tag.

In JSP 1.1, the greatest contrasts to all its predecessors are the `page` and `taglib` tags. The `page` tag is used to define all the initialization parameters and globally applicable run-time parameters required for the page. A really well-designed aspect here is the integration of a comprehensive error-handling system, which makes the cumbersome `try-catch` blocks obsolete. Now it is possible to assign an globally applicable error page to each JSP. You can thus control the outputs more effectively using parameters such as buffer size and autoflush. You can also define whether the JSP is programmed in such a way that threads can be used properly. You can create one command file with all the `imports` instruction. You can create and maintain the corresponding list in each JSP whereas previously you could simply use the `include` tag to integrate a commonly used file that contained `import` instructions.

The real innovation lies in the integration of additional special tags, which nowadays make the purely interpreted solutions (Section 10.1) so attractive for HTML designers. The `<%@ taglib .. %>` tag can be used to give each tag its own DTD. To do this, a special class needs to be defined for each tag, for handling the JSP engine. For this purpose there is now a new package, `javax.servlet.jsp.taglib`, which defines the infrastructure needed for a portable implementation of such special classes. You should refer to the JSP specification (JavaSoft 1999) for more detailed information about this integration. We are very interested in its implementation in the various HTML tools and Java development environments. Sun, IBM, BEA and Allaire have also promised to support it.

### 10.2.2 Integrating Java beans in JavaServer pages

The JSP 1.0 specification includes a range of new JSP tags, which encapsulate more complex functions. The `RequestDispatcher`, which was already present in API 2.1, has now been integrated with the `<jsp:include>` and `<jsp:foward>` standard tags. This makes it possible to implement branching and integrations quite easily in one JSP. Therefore, process control can be implemented more directly in the designer/developer team. The `<jsp:plugin>` tag is used merely for the simple HTML integration of applets and beans in the output (Table 10.6).

The integration of preprepared components for the preparation of information is

**Table 10.5**   The standard JSP tags

| Tag | Description | JSP syntax |
|---|---|---|
| Comment in the HTML output | Creates a comment which is retained in the HTML output file. The expressions are evaluated and written to the output. | `<!--comment-->` `<!--comment<%=expression%>-->` |
| Comment in the JSP file | The comment is only retained in the original JSP file. | `<%--comment--%>` |
| Definition | Definition of attributes or methods in the selected script language in the JSP page. | `<%!definition%>` |
| Expression | Contains an expression in the script language of the JSP page. | `<%=expression%>` |
| Scriptlet | Contains a code fragment in the script language of the JSP page. | `<%scriptlet%>` |
| Include instruction | Integration of a file with text or code at the point in time at which the JSP page is translated. | `<%@include file="Path to file"%>` |
| Page instruction | Definition of attributes which apply to the entire JSP page. | `<%@page[language="java"]` `[extends="Package path of the upper class"]` `[import={"Package path of the class"|"Package path.*"},...]` `[contentType={"mimeType[;charset=characterSet]"|"text/html;charset=ISO-8859-1"]` `[session={"true"|"false"}]` `[buffer={"none"|"8kb"|sizeinkb}]` `[autoFlush={"true"|"false"}]` `[isThreadSafe={"true"|"false"}]` `[errorPage="Path to the error page"]` `[isErrorPage={"true"|"false"}]` `[info="text"]%>` |
| TagLib instruction | Definition of a tag library | `<%@tagliburi="URI to the tag's DTD"prefix="Tag'sprefix"%>` |

**Table 10.6** Extended JSP tag used to integrate bean, applet and other servlet resources

| Tag | Description | JSP syntax |
|---|---|---|
| `<jsp:forward>` Transfer to other URI at run-time | A decision is taken within a dispatcher (`Dispatcher` JSP) to define that another JSP, resource or servlet is to be used for the output. | `<jsp:forward page="Context of relative URI" />` |
| `<jsp:include>` Insert contents at run-time. | Static or dynamic contents are added to a page. Only resources in the same application can be used. | `<jsp:include page="Context of relative URI" flush=["true"/"false"]/>` |
| `<jsp:plugin>` Create HTML code for applet or bean | Create HTML instruction for downloading the Java Plugin to execute an applet or bean on the client browser. | `<jsp:plugin`<br>`type={ "bean" | "applet" }`<br>`[code="Object class" ]`<br>`[codebase="Base path for object code" ]`<br>`[name="Name of instance in HTML page"]`<br>`[archive="List of classes archive" ]`<br>`[align={"button"|"top"|"middle"|"left"|"right"}]`<br>`[height="displayHeight"]`<br>`[width="displayWidth" ]`<br>`[hspace="horizontalGutter"]`<br>`[vspace="verticalGutter"]`<br>`[jreversion={"JREVersionNumber"|"1.1"}]`<br>`[nspluginurl="URL to Netscape Navigator Plugin" ]`<br>`[iepluginurl="URL to Microsoft Internet Explorer Plugin" ]>`<br>`[<params> <param name="Name of parameter" value="Value of parameter">+ </params> ]`<br>`[<fallback> Text containing an error message for the user </fallback> ]`<br>`</jsp:plugin>` |

**Table 10.6** *Cont.*

| Tag | Description | JSP syntax |
| --- | --- | --- |
| `<jsp:usebean>`<br>Use of a Java bean | Regulates access to a Java bean. If this is not present in the corresponding context, it is created | `<jsp:useBean`<br>`id="Identity of bean"` |
| `<jsp:getProperty>`<br>Read a bean attribute | Accesses an attribute of a bean and formats the value as a character string. | `scope={"page"\|"request"\|"session"\|"application"}`<br>`{ class="Package path of the class" \|`<br>`type="Package path of the class" \|`<br>`class="Package path of the class"`<br>`type="Package path to interface or class" \|`<br>`beanName="Name of bean"`<br>`type="Package path to interface or class" }`<br>`{ /> \|` |
| `<jsp:setProperty>`<br>Write a bean attribute | Sets an attribute of a bean. To do this the relevant value is generated from the character string for the selected data types. | `<jsp:setProperty`<br>`name="Identity of bean"`<br>`{ property="*" \|`<br>`property="Name of attribute" [ param="Name of parameter" ] }`<br>`property="Name of attribute" />`<br>`value={"character string"\| <%= expression %>" } />` |

extremely efficient. Sun, of course, uses Java beans for this. These are integrated in a page via the `<jsp:usebean>` tags (Listing 10.2).

Listing 10.2: Example of a definition of a Java bean within a JavaServer page

```
<jsp:usebean id="CALENDAR"
    class=" calendar.JspCalendar "
    scope="request" />
<jsp:setProperty name="CALENDAR" property="TimeZone" value="ECT"/>
```

Each JSP bean has a unique name, class and life cycle (Listing 10.5). The (`scope`) `request` mode shows that a bean of this type is created every time a request is made. In session scope the bean is bound to the `HttpSession` of the browser client and then used again for other requests. In page mode the information is merely saved locally for this JSP. Globally, the values in `ServletContext` can be stored or accessed via the `application` scope. The `<jsp:getProperty>` marking makes it possible to access the attributes. Setting the value of a bean attribute is supported by the `<jsp:setProperty>` tag.

We have included the `dates.JspCalendar` bean as an example for the JSP specification. This bean reliably determines all the dates of the request time.

Listing 10.3: Application example of a date bean

```
<HTML>
<HEAD>
  <TITLE>JSP WebApp Time</TITLE>
  <jsp:usebean id="CLOCK" class="dates.JspCalendar" scope="request"
  type="dates.JspCalendar"/>
</HEAD>
<BODY>
<UL>
<LI> Day of the month: <jsp:getProperty name="CLOCK"
property="dayOfMonth"/>
<LI> Year: <jsp:getProperty name="CLOCK" property="year"/>
<LI> Month: <jsp:getProperty name="CLOCK" property="month"/>
<LI> Time: <jsp:getProperty name="CLOCK" property="time"/>
<LI> Date: <jsp:getProperty name="CLOCK" property="date"/>
<LI> Day: <jsp:getProperty name="CLOCK" property="day"/>
<LI> Day of the year: <jsp:getProperty name="CLOCK" property="dayOfYear"/>
<LI> Week of the year <jsp:getProperty name="CLOCK" property="weekOfYear"/>
</UL>
</BODY>
</HTML>
```

Bean attributes must always be enclosed by the appropriate types of quotation marks. An attribute is accessed by entering the bean identifier (`CLOCK`). The example in Listing 10.4 shows that we can create dynamic HTML pages without explicitly using Java. Some people may still remember the `DISPLAY` tag of the 0.92 specification

**Table 10.7**  Standard variables, which are available in a JavaServer Page.

| Implicit objects of a JSP | `<jsp:usebean>` `"scope"` | Type |
|---|---|---|
| `application` | Application | `javax.servlet.ServletContext` |
| `session` | Session | `javax.servlet.http.HttpSession` |
| `config` | Page | `javax.servlet.ServletConfig` |
| `pageContext` | Page | `javax.servlet.jsp.PageContext` |
| `page` | Page | `javax.servlet.jsp.JspPage` |
| `response` | Page | Sub-class of `javax.servlet.ServletResponse` |
| `request` | Request | Sub-class of `javax.servlet.ServletRequest` |
| `out` | Page | `javax.servlet.jsp.jspWriter` |
| `exception` | Page | `java.lang.Throwable` (only available if `isErrorPage="true"`) |

and hope that it will soon reappear in a `Taglib`. Better still would be a formatter concept like the one offered by objectHTML (Table 10.3).

Some objects are offered directly via specific variables to make them easier to handle and make it possible to keep an overview of the situation (Table 10.7).

The syntax of the beans has changed significantly from Version 0.91 through Version 0.92 and to Version 1.0/1.1 of the JSP specification. We are sure that some things will also change before the final publication of Version 1.0/1.1. However, we hope that the fundamental syntactical elements will remain the same. These will be highlighted again in the two examples in the next section.

## 10.2.3  Simple examples of JavaServer pages

We can, of course, use Java to access the date directly without bean integration (Listing 10.3). Nevertheless it is clear that this solution is by no means as elegant as when beans are used.

Listing 10.4: Implementing a JSP to display a date

```
<%page import="java.util.Date" %>
<HTML>
<HEAD>
  <TITLE>JSP WebApp Date Page</TITLE>
</HEAD>
<BODY>
<H1> JSP WebApp Date Page</H1>
Hello WebApper - Today's date is <%= new Date() %>.
</BODY>
</HTML>
```

The `RequestInfoServlet`, which you will have recognized from Chapter 3, can also be formulated as a JSP (Listing 10.8). First of all the request is output (Fig. 10.6).

**Figure 10.6** Servlet snoop as a JavaServer page

This is followed by any header information which is present for every browser request. The output ends with the formatting of the request parameter.

Listing 10.5: Snoop JavaServer page

```
<%page import="javax.servlet.http.HttpUtils, java.util.Enumeration" %>
<HTML>
<HEAD>
   <TITLE>JSP snoop Page</TITLE>
</HEAD>
<BODY>
```

```
<H1>JSP Snoop Page </H1>
<H2>Request for information</H2>
<align=right>Request URL: <%= HttpUtils.getRequestURL(request) %>
<%
   Enumeration e = request.getHeaderNames();
   if(e != null && e.hasMoreElements()) {
%>
<H2>Request Header</H2>
<TABLE>
<TR>
   <TH align=left>Field:</TH>s
   <TH align=left>Value:</TH>
</TR>
<%
   while(e.hasMoreElements()) {
   String k = (String) e.nextElement();
%>
<TR>
   <TD><%= k %></TD>
   <TD><%= request.getHeader(k) %></TD>
</TR>
<%}%>
</TABLE>
<%}%>
<%
   e = request.getParameterNames();
   if(e != null && e.hasMoreElements()) {
%>
<H2>Servlet-Parameter</H2>
<TABLE>
<TR valign=top>
   <TH align=left>Parameter:</TH>
   <TH align=left>Value:</TH>
   <TH align=left>Multiple value:</TH>
</TR>
<%
   while(e.hasMoreElements()) {
      String k = (String) e.nextElement();
      String val = request.getParameter(k);
      String vals[] = request.getParameterValues(k);
%>
<TR valign=top>
   <TD><%= k %></TD>
   <TD><%= val %></TD>
   <TD><%
      for(int i = 0; i < vals.length; i++) {
```

```
            if(i > 0)
               out.print("<BR>");
               out.print(vals[i]);
          }
     %></TD>
  </TR>
<%}%>
</TABLE>
<%}%>
</BODY>
</HTML>
```

# Applications

T he WebApp framework gives us a powerful basis on which we can develop Web-based applications. Despite this comparatively comfortable environment, designing Web applications is not easy, particularly because of the Web browsers as clients and the status-less HTTP. For this reason, in this part of the book we will use three examples to show how applications can be created with the WebApp framework. For this purpose, in Chapter 11 we introduce a generic browser for the Stores described in Chapter 9. Chapter 12 describes an OnlineShop and Chapter 13 shows the development of a browser-based Chat application.

Generally speaking we divide the development process into four phases:

**1** Defining the control flow, business objects and dialogues.

**2** Coding the classes.

**3** Creating the display templates.

**4** Creating the configuration files.

It is important to remember that all the crucial decisions must be made in Phase One. Phases Two, Three and Four are merely production phases, in which the decisions made in Phase One are implemented.

Accordingly, the formal emphasis lies in Phase One. Before coding we create an application case or Use Case diagram (Oestereich 1998, 207ff.) to give an overview of the possible actions. Next we represent this in a process flow diagram for which we use the notation of the state diagrams (Oestereich 1998, 310ff.). Here the SMI commands from Chapter 8 are used as events. In this way we can obtain a list of the commands and a precise overview of the dialogue sequence.

We then create a command table so that we can define the commands and the way in which the application behaves more precisely. This contains a list of the commands, the required parameters and a description of each command's functions.

Now that we have the right tools we can start coding the classes and dialogues. To do this we bear in mind that the application logic and the pure display functions must be kept apart as much as possible (mould, view and control principle). Experience has shown that it makes sense to code the more abstract parts of an application first. Because the application logic is of a more general nature than the HTML pages or

Java Server pages (Chapter 10), which are used to display it, we start by coding the classes (Phase Two). Only after this, in Phase Three, do we code the display elements. In Phase Four we simply add everything together by using the SMI configuration.

Of course, it is not always possible for you to follow exactly the sequence we have recommended. However, this has been a great help to us as a guideline and made it possible for us to create better results more quickly.

The development process we suggest can also be used in other architectures for creating Web-based applications. To achieve this more wide-reaching goal we have particularly emphasized the development process in the examples we use. To this end we have rather neglected error handling and visual implementation, so that the book was not over-large.

# StoreBrowser 11

The first example for the WebApp Framework is a generic browser for Stores, as they are described in Chapter 9. Using this, it is possible to understand the structure of a Store, fill it with initial data and make changes to individual objects. During all this an object-oriented view of the data should be maintained. Figure 11.1 shows the situations in which the StoreBrowser can be used.

This results in the following requirements:

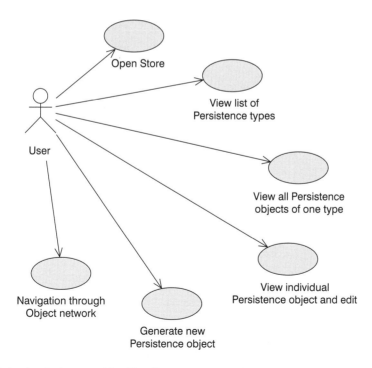

**Figure 11.1**   Applied cases of the StoreBrowser

- Access to any Store.
- Overview of a Store's `Persistence` types.
- Listing all `Persistence` objects of a type.
- Detailed view of a `Persistence` object.
- Create, change and delete objects.
- Navigation via associations.
- User dialogue via a menu.

To meet these requirements we first have to gain a clearer image of the processes that are to be represented.

## 11.1  Control flow

After the StoreBrowser starts, the user should be prompted to enter a Store name (Fig. 11.2). Once this has been done, the next page should show all the object types of this store. Now the user can select one of the types and display a list of all the objects of this type. This list should not only display the attributes of the objects but also references to associated objects. A total of three navigation options should be offered:

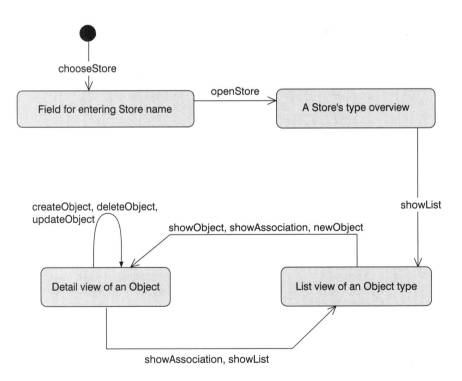

**Figure 11.2**  Simplified control flow diagram of the StoreBrowser

**1** The user should be able to select a `Persistence` object, which is then displayed in detail, and which the user can then process.

**2** A reference should lead directly to an entry dialogue for a `Persistence` object.

**3** Each `Persistence` object, which is associated with one or more other `Persistence` objects, must offer options to navigate to the other objects.

Options one and two would therefore basically lead to the same dialogues, i.e. a detailed view of an object of the type the user has selected. The main difference between them is that, in option one, the user can manipulate an existing `Persistence` object by using the change and delete functions whereas option two only allows the user to create a `Persistence` object. In order not to make the example unnecessarily complicated, we have combined both options in one dialogue.

Option three can lead to two dialogues. In the case of a `ToOne` association, a detailed view of the associated object must be displayed, as in options one and two. In contrast, in the case of a `ToMany` association, a list of the associated object types must be displayed.

The process diagram in Fig. 11.2 shows the required dialogues with the possible events. To make this clearer, we have not included the option of accessing all hierarchically subordinate dialogues via a menu. Figure 11.3 shows the complete diagram. Because Web applications do not have a clearly defined end in the usual sense of the word, neither of the two diagrams has an end status.

Figure 11.3 demonstrates the necessary events of commands, which lead to a change of dialogue. To show this more clearly, Table 11.1 lists the possible commands and their meanings.

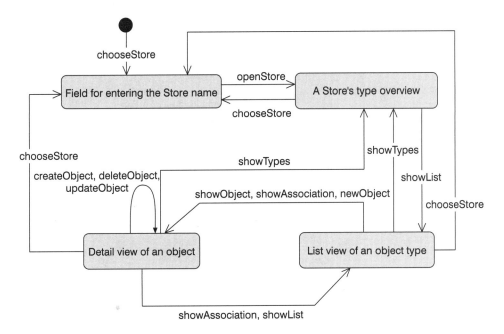

**Figure 11.3**  Complete process diagram of the StoreBrowser

**Table 11.1**  Description of the StoreBrowser commands.

| Command | Parameter | Meaning |
|---|---|---|
| chooseStore | – | Closes a current Store and displays an entry field in which the user can enter the name of an existing Store. Triggers the openStore command. |
| openStore | Store name | Opens a Store and displays its types. If the user selects a type, this triggers the showList command. |
| showTypes | – | Displays an overview of all object types of the selected Store. If the user selects an object type triggers the showList command. |
| showList | Object type | Displays an overview of all objects of one type. The three commands showObject, newObject and showAssociation can be triggered from this dialogue. |
| showObject | Object key and object type | Displays an editable detailed view of an object. The four commands createObject, updateObject, deleteObject and showAssociation can be triggered from this dialogue. |
| newObject | Object type | Displays the entry dialogue for an object. Only the createObject command can be triggered. |
| showAssociation | Association name, ObjectIdentifier of the initial object | Displays an individual associated object or a list of associated objects. See showList and showObject. |
| createObject | Object type | Creates a new object. Then the same options as described under showObject are displayed. |
| updateObject | ObjectIdentifier, attributes | Changes an existing object. Then the same options as described under showObject are available. |
| deleteObject | ObjectIdentifier | Deletes an existing object. Then the same options as described under newObject are available. |

The possible follow-up commands do not include the events which result from menu entries.

## 11.2 Class design

After we have defined which control flow processes the StoreBrowser must implement, we now come to class design. Before we can use a Store, we have to open it. Once it has been used it should be closed again. Now there is the question of which data structure the Store should be stored in while it is being used. Because various StoreBrowser users should be able to view different Stores at the same time without getting in each other's way, we have decided to use the user-specific HttpSession (Chapter 3).

We have also decided to separate the management functions of the Store (open and close) from its manipulation functions and to encapsulate them in their own bean (Chapter 8). We have called the resulting management bean StoreSessionBean (Listing 11.1) and the manipulation bean StoreBrowserBean. Both inherit from SMICommandListener and implement the C_StoreBrowser interface in which all the required constants are defined (Fig. 11.4).

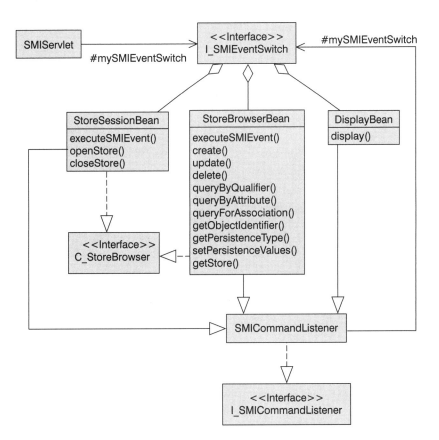

**Figure 11.4** Class diagram of the StoreBrowser

Listing 11.1: The StoreSessionBean class

```
package de.webapp.StoreBrowser;

import de.webapp.Framework.SMI.*;
import de.webapp.Framework.SMICommandListener.*;
import de.webapp.Framework.ConfigManager.*;
import de.webapp.Framework.StoreFactory.*;
import de.webapp.Framework.Persistence.*;

/** Encapsulates the management of a Store in an HttpSession */
public class StoreSessionBean extends SMICommandListener
   implements C_StoreBrowser, C_SMIStore {

/** Passes on an SMIEvent and calls a follow-up command */
public void executeSMIEvent(SMIEvent aSMIEvent) {
   // Run command
   super.executeSMIEvent(aSMIEvent);
   SMICommand aSMICommand = (SMICommand)aSMIEvent;
   // Obtain and run follow-up command
   String followUpCommand =
      (String)aSMICommand.getValue(C_FollowUpCommand);
   if (followUpCommand != null) {
   // Set follow-up command...
   aSMICommand.setCommand(followUpCommand);
   // ... and run it
   getSMIEventSwitch().executeSMIEvent(aSMICommand);
   }
}
/** Instantiates a Store and stores it in the session */
public void openStore(SMICommand aSMICommand)
      throws PersistenceException {
   // Find out name of the Store
   String theStoreName = (String)aSMICommand.getValue(C_StoreName);
   // Obtain the Store's configuration
   Configuration theConfiguration =
      ConfigManager.getConfigManager().getConfiguration(
         theStoreName,
         theStoreName + C_StoreSuffix, true);
   // Instantiate Store...
   I_Store theStore = (I_Store)StoreFactory.getInstance(theConfiguration);
   // ... and store it in the HttpSession
   aSMICommand.putSessionValue(C_Store, theStore);
   aSMICommand.putSessionValue(C_StoreName, theStoreName);
}
/** Closes a Store and removes it from the session */
public void closeStore(SMICommand aSMICommand) throws PersistenceException
{
```

```
    I_Store theStore = (I_Store)aSMICommand.getSessionValue(C_Store);
    if (theStore != null) {
      theStore.close();
      theStore = null;
      // Remove Store from the HttpSession
      aSMICommand.removeSessionValue(C_Store);
    }
  }
}
} // End of the class
```

The StoreSessionBean class consists of only three methods: openStore(SMICommand), closeStore(SMICommand) and executeSMIEvent (SMIEvent). The openStore() method assumes that there is a parameter with the key C_StoreName in the SMICommand. In order to be able to read the configuration of a Store, we assume that a Store's configuration file, used for the 'OnlineShop' application, is present in the configuration directory of the OnlineShop registry entry and that it has the name OnlineShop.store (Chapter 12). If these assumptions are correct, the Store name can be used to read the Store's configuration from the SMICommand and pass on it to a StoreFactory, which instantiates and initializes the Store. The Store and Store name are then saved in the C_Store and C_StoreName keys in the session. Both constants are defined in the C_StoreBrowser interface (Listing 11.2).

Listing 11.2: The StoreBrowser constants are defined in the C_StoreBrowser interface

```
package de.webapp.StoreBrowser;

/** The StoreBrowser's constants */
public interface C_StoreBrowser {

public static final String C_PersistenceType = "_PersistenceType";
public static final String C_PersistenceAttributePrefix = "_PA";
public static final String C_PersistenceOID = "_ObjectIdentifier";
public static final String C_StoreName = "_Storename";
public static final String C_Store = "_Store";
public static final String C_StoreSuffix = ".store";
public static final String C_PersistenceSQLQualifier = "_SQLQualifier";
public static final String C_PersistenceSearchValue = "_SearchValue";
public static final String C_PersistenceSearchAttribute =
   "_SearchAttribute";
public static final String C_PersistenceAssociationName =
   "_AssociationName";
public static final String C_PersistenceResult = "_PersistenceResult";
} // End of the interface
```

The closeStore() method closes the store that was opened with openStore(). To do this, the store is determined from the session, closed using close() and then removed from the session. If this is a store which implements the `HttpSessionBindingListener` interface, it may happen that, when it is removed from the session, another attempt will be made to close the store. As stores can be closed as often as necessary without this causing an error we can safely ignore this process. We leave the store name in the session so that we can access a default value later on if required.

We now only have to explain the `executeSMIEvent()` method: this has been overwritten so that a follow-up command can be run automatically. If a parameter has been defined in the command, with the `C_FollowUpCommand` key (from `de.webapp.Framework.C_SMI`), this is interpreted as a follow-up command and run via `SMIEventSwitch`. This happens after the original command was run via `super.executeSMIEvent()`.

Because the methods in `SMICommandListener` seldom have output functions, it very often happens that a follow-up command is called up to display a result. The same also happens in the `StoreSessionBean`. Opening and closing the `Store` do not lead to any kind of output, because we took the design decision to separate the display and application logic. However, we shall first take a look at the application logic and deal with the display later on (Section 11.3).

Now that we are able to save a `Store` in a session and manage it, we must create the methods for using this `Store`. These are grouped together in `StoreBrowserBean` (Listing 11.3).

Listing 11.3: The `StoreBrowserBean` class

```
package de.webapp.StoreBrowser;

import java.util.*;

import de.webapp.Framework.SMI.*;
import de.webapp.Framework.SMICommandListener.*;
import de.webapp.Framework.Persistence.*;
import de.webapp.Framework.Utilities.ReferenceVector;

/** Bean for accessing a Store that is bound to a session */
public class StoreBrowserBean extends SMICommandListener
    implements C_StoreBrowser, C_SMIStore {

/** Puts a transaction frame round each action and runs a follow-up command */
public void executeSMIEvent(SMIEvent aSMIEvent) {
    SMICommand aSMICommand = (SMICommand)aSMIEvent;
    // Get store from the HttpSession
    I_Store theStore = getStore(aSMICommand);
    // Ensure single access
    synchronized (theStore) {
        try {
            // Start transaction
            theStore.begin();
            // Run command
```

```
        super.executeSMIEvent(aSMIEvent);
        // End transaction
        theStore.commit();
        // Run follow-up command
        String followUpCommand =
          (String)aSMICommand.getValue(C_FollowUpCommand);
        if (followUpCommand != null) {
          aSMICommand.setCommand(followUpCommand);
          getSMIEventSwitch().executeSMIEvent(aSMICommand);
        }
      }
    }
    catch (Throwable t) {
      try {
        // If error occurs, try rollback
        theStore.rollback();
      }
      catch (PersistenceException pe) {
        pe.setThrowable(t);
        throw new SMIEventListenerException(
          "Error during rollback.", pe);
      }
      throw new SMIEventListenerException("Persistence error.", t);
    }
  }
}
/** Creates a persistent object. */
public void create (SMICommand aSMICommand)
      throws PersistenceException {
  // Getstore from the HttpSession
  I_Store theStore = getStore(aSMICommand);
  // Create new Persistence of a particular type
  I_Persistence thePersistence =
    theStore.newPersistence(getPersistenceType(aSMICommand));
  // Set attributes from the request
  setPersistenceValues(thePersistence, aSMICommand);
  // Save Persistence object in the database
  thePersistence.create();
  // Store Persistence object in the command
  aSMICommand.putValue(C_PersistenceResult, thePersistence);
}
/** Changes persistent object permanently. */
public void update (SMICommand aSMICommand)
      throws PersistenceException {
  // Getstore from the HttpSession
  I_Store theStore = getStore(aSMICommand);
  // Get object from the Store on the basis of an ObjectIdentifier
```

```
                    I_Persistence thePersistence =
                      theStore.persistenceWithKey(getObjectIdentifier(aSMICommand));
                    // Set attributes from the request
                    setPersistenceValues(thePersistence, aSMICommand);
                    // Save change in the database
                    thePersistence.update();
                    // Store changed object in the command
                    aSMICommand.putValue(C_PersistenceResult, thePersistence);
                  }
                  /** Deletes persistent object from the database */
                  public void delete (SMICommand aSMICommand)
                       throws PersistenceException {
                    // Get Store from the HttpSession
                    I_Store theStore = getStore(aSMICommand);
                    // Get object from the Store on the basis of an ObjectIdentifier
                    // and delete it
                    theStore.persistenceWithKey(getObjectIdentifier(aSMICommand)).delete();

                  }
                  /** Search using SQL qualifier. */
                  public void queryByQualifier (SMICommand aSMICommand)
                       throws PersistenceException {
                    // Get Store from the HttpSession
                    I_Store theStore = getStore(aSMICommand);
                    // Obtain object type's retriever
                    I_PersistenceRetriever theRetriever =
                      theStore.getRetriever(getPersistenceType(aSMICommand));
                    // Pass on the SQL expression from the
                    // command to the retriever as a request
                    Object theResult =
                      theRetriever.retrieve((String)aSMICommand.getValue(
                        C_PersistenceSQLQualifier));
                    // Store the result of the request in the command
                    aSMICommand.putValue(C_PersistenceResult, theResult);
                  }
                  /** Request an object of a particular type
                  with a particular attribute. */
                  public void queryByAttribute (SMICommand aSMICommand)
                       throws PersistenceException {
                    // Get Store from the HttpSession
                    I_Store theStore = getStore(aSMICommand);
                    // Obtain I_PersistencePeer of the requested type
                    I_PersistencePeer thePeer =
                      theStore.getPeer(getPersistenceType(aSMICommand));
                    // Obtain retriever of the type
                    I_PersistenceRetriever theRetriever = thePeer.getRetriever();
```

```
  // Ask peer for the required PersistenceAttribute
  // via its I_PersistenceType
  PersistenceAttribute theSearchAttribute =
    thePeer.getType().attributeWithName(
    (String)aSMICommand.getValue(C_PersistenceSearchAttribute));
  // Convert the attribute's value into a real object
  Object theSearchValue =
    theSearchAttribute.getObjectForString(
       (String)aSMICommand.getValue(C_PersistenceSearchValue)) ;
  // Starts request with the attribute's value and the attribute
  Object theResult =
    theRetriever.retrieve(theSearchAttribute, theSearchValue);
  // Store result of the request in the command
  aSMICommand.putValue(C_PersistenceResult, theResult);
}
/** Request for associated objects of a given Persistence object. */
public void queryForAssociation (SMICommand aSMICommand)
     throws PersistenceException {
  // Get Store from the HttpSession
  I_Store theStore = getStore(aSMICommand);
  // Get Persistence from the Store on the basis of the ObjectIdentifier
  I_Persistence theObject =
    theStore.persistenceWithKey(getObjectIdentifier(aSMICommand));
  // Obtain the name of the association from the command
  String theAssociationName =
    (String)aSMICommand.getValue(C_PersistenceAssociationName);
  // Obtain descriptive association object
  PersistenceAssociation theAssociation =
    theObject.getPeer().getType().getAssociationWithName(
       theAssociationName);
  // Query associated objects
  I_PersistenceReference theReference =
    theAssociation.getReferenceObject(theObject);
  Object theSearchResult;
  if (theAssociation.getAssociationType() ==
    C_PersistenceAssociation.TO_ONE) {
    theSearchResult =
       ((I_PersistenceToOneReference)theReference).getObject();
  }
  else {
    theSearchResult =
       ((I_PersistenceToManyReference)theReference).getObjects();
  }
  // Store the type of the associated objects in the command
  aSMICommand.putValue(C_PersistenceType,
    theAssociation.getResultType());
```

```
         // Store associated objects in the command
         aSMICommand.putValue(C_PersistenceResult, theSearchResult);
     }
     /** Reads the ObjectIdentifier from the command */
     protected String getObjectIdentifier(SMICommand aSMICommand) {
         return (String)aSMICommand.getValue(C_PersistenceOID);
     }
     /** Reads the PersistenceType from the command */
     protected String getPersistenceType(SMICommand aSMICommand) {
         return (String)aSMICommand.getValue(C_PersistenceType);
     }
     /** Sets the values of a persistent object. */
     protected static void setPersistenceValues(
         I_Persistence aPersistence, SMICommand aSMICommand)
           throws PersistenceException {
         Enumeration e = aSMICommand.getKeys();
         String aValue;
         String aKey;
         while (e.hasMoreElements()) {
           aKey = (String)e.nextElement();
           // If a key begins with a particular prefix ...
           if (aKey.startsWith(C_PersistenceAttributePrefix)
               && aKey.length() > C_PersistenceAttributePrefix.length()) {
             // ... its value is read, ...
             aValue = (String)aSMICommand.getValue(aKey);
             // ... the prefix is removed from the key...
             aKey = aKey.substring(C_PersistenceAttributePrefix.length());
             // ... and the value is assigned to the attribute with the
             // key name
             aPersistence.getPeer().getType().getAttributeWithName(
               aKey).setStringValue(aPersistence, aValue);
           }
         }
     }


     /** Returns a Store from the Session. */
     protected I_SMIStore getStore(SMICommand aSMICommand) {
         return (I_SMIStore)aSMICommand.getSessionValue(C_Store);
     }
} // End of the class
```

All the methods in StoreBrowserBean work with the Store. To ensure this can be done properly, the calls must be synchronized and be carried out in a transaction. For this reason we also overwrite the executeSMIEvent() method in the StoreBrowserBean and wrap a transaction around the call to super.

executeSMIEvent(). In addition to this, we use a synchronized instruction to ensure that the Store cannot be accessed more than once at a time.

We deal with the individual functions required for this in more detail below. As the openStore command is already covered by the StoreSessionBean, we do not have to discuss it any further. The chooseStore command implies the closing of the Store and has also already been described. showList is the next command on the list.

## 11.2.1 showList command

This command should display a list of all the Persistence objects of a type. To do this, the type you require must be passed on to the corresponding method via the SMICommand. We have defined that the type is always referenced via the C_PersistenceType key, and encapsulate the corresponding access to the SMICommand in the getPersistenceType (SMICommand) help method.

In order to get all the Persistence objects of a type from the Store, the I_PersistenceRetriever for the required object type must be called with a blank SQL qualifier. This is exactly what happens in the queryByQualifier() method, provided no qualifier was stored in the C_PersistenceSQLQualifier key, in the SMICommand. The result of the search query is saved in the C_PersistenceResult key in the SMICommand, so that the follow-on commands can access it. We shall do the same with all the other results of search queries.

## 11.2.2 showObject command

The next command, showObject, can only display one single object. Usually you would need the C_PersistenceType type again as well as a C_PersistenceSearchAttribute key name and a C_PersistenceSearchValue key value. A unique ObjectIdentifier would, of course, also be sufficient here because the type is also coded in it. However, we want to select the more powerful functionality because it is more generally applicable. The functionality is provided by the queryByAttribute(SMICommand) method. In detail, this is what happens: Using the object type we can obtain a PersistenceRetriever and the PersistencePeer via the Store. Via the PersistencePeer we obtain the PersistenceType object of this type. As you will remember, PersistenceType describes all the attributes and associations of a Persistence object (Section 9.4.2).

We can also query the PersistenceType for a PersistenceAttribute object based on the value of C_PersistenceSearchAttribute. The obtained PersistenceAttribute object can, in turn, be used together with the C_PersistenceSearchValue for a database query to the PersistenceRetriever. However, before that can happen, the String object referenced by C_PersistenceSearchValue must be converted into an object of the attribute type. Luckily the PersistenceAttribute getObjectForString(String) method is able to do this. At last, we have both the parameters we require together and can query the PersistenceRetriever for the object we are searching for. The result of this request is in turn saved in the C_PersistenceResult key in the SMICommand.

### 11.2.3 showAssociation command

showAssociation, like showObject, is a more complex command. In order to obtain the objects associated with a Persistence, we must first find the object whose associated objects we want to obtain. For this reason, the ObjectIdentifier of the initial object must be part of the request. By using the getObjectIdentifier(SMICommand) help method we can filter this ObjectIdentifier out of the SMICommand and use it to ask the store for our initial object. In addition, the association's name must be stored in the C_PersistenceAssociationName key of the SMICommand. We can use this name to ask the PersistenceType object for a PersistenceAssociation object. This in turn knows a reference object, which has the getObject() or getObjects() method. Depending on whether a ToOne or ToMany association is involved, one of these two methods is run and the result is saved in the C_PersistenceResult key in the SMICommand.

### 11.2.4 createObject command

Next we shall deal with the createObject command. In order to add an object to the store, we must first create a new, empty Persistence object. The store's newPersistence(String) method does this for us. Here the object's type name must be passed on as a parameter. The attributes are then set and the create() method of the Persistence object is called. Unfortunately, although this sounds simple, it is not. We must define which keys are used to describe the values of the individual attributes. We shall define that the attribute key for a Persistence always begins with the prefix C_PersistenceAttributePrefix, to which the attribute name is appended (attached). This makes it possible for us to filter out the attributes we require from all the parameters present in an SMICommand. This is precisely what the setPersistenceValues (I_Persistence, SMICommand) help method does. In addition, it also sets the attribute once it has identified it. After setPersistenceValues() is called, there is nothing to prevent us calling Persistence.create(). We save the newly created object again in C_PersistenceResult. The entire process is coded in StoreBrowserBean.create(SMICommand).

### 11.2.5 updateObject command

The updateObject command is very similar to createObject. The difference between them is that you do not have to create a new object from the store. Instead you only have to modify an existing object. Before you can do this, the ObjectIdentifier of the object you want to modify must be passed on in the SMICommand. To access this easily we shall use the getObjectIdentifier(SMICommand) help method once again. The ObjectIdentifier we get is used to ask the store for the corresponding Persistence, the changed attributes are set with setPersistenceValues(), and then the Persistence's update() method is called. The process described here is implemented by the StoreBrowserBean.update(SMICommand) method.

### 11.2.6  deleteObject command

The last of the modification commands is deleteObject. It is coded in the delete(SMICommand) method and only has two lines. The ObjectIdentifier is used to obtain a reference to the Persistence you want to delete. Its delete() method is then called. In this case there is no need to save a result.

### 11.2.7  Other commands

The remaining commands are newObject and showTypes. On closer inspection you will see that these commands can be carried out by the display(SMICommand) method of the DisplayBean (Section 8.5).

## 11.3  Dialogue and layout

Because it is freely available, we have decided to use Vincent Partington's GNUJSP (now GNUJSP1.0) for display (Section 10.2). To call the JavaServer pages, we shall also use the DisplayBean from Section 8.5. However, first of all we shall plan the design of the display.

### 11.3.1  Importing code fragments

In order to have a starting point for changes to the entire application, we have used the JSP <jsp:include page="path" /> include mechanism. Using this we can add frequently required code fragments via a command in our JavaServer pages.

First of all we define the header and footer of all the pages. Both the relevant code fragments, header.html and footer.html, are printed in Listings 11.4 and 11.5.

Listing 11.4: Code fragment header.html

```
<HTML>
<HEAD>
  <TITLE>StoreBrowser</TITLE>
</HEAD>
<BODY text="#800000" link="#000080" vlink="#000080" alink="#FF0000">
```

Listing 11.5: Code fragment footer.html

```
</BODY>
</HTML>
```

Now we can start with the first dialogue.

### 11.3.2  Dialogue for selecting a Store

To make the Store selection dialogue more user-friendly we expect the name of the store that was opened last to appear automatically in the entry field. To ensure this we must first ask the session for the value of C_StoreName by using the SMICommand. Usually the SMICommand stores the DisplayBean with the SMIEventname as an attribute of the HttpServletRequest. We use this to obtain the command. Next we ask for the Storename and save it in the theStorename local variable which we can later output as a value of the entry field. Alternatively we could also have asked the request object for the session and then asked the session for the name, because we shall mainly be working with the SMICommand. However, we want to remain consistent and not deviate from our usual coding style here.

You should also note that the openStorecommand is hard-coded as a hidden field in the form (Fig. 11.5 and Listing 11.6).

Listing 11.6: Dialogue for entering a Store name: chooseStore.jsp

```
<%@include file="header.html" %>
<%@ page language="java"
import="java.util.*,de.webapp.Framework.Utilities.ReferenceVector,de.webapp
.Framework.Persistence.*,de.webapp.Framework.SMI.SMICommand,de.webapp.
StoreBrowser.C_StoreBrowser" %>
<%
// Obtain command from the request
SMICommand aSMICommand = (SMICommand)request.getAttribute("SMIEvent");
// Get Store name from the session
String theStorename =
    (String)aSMICommand.getSessionValue(C_StoreBrowser.C_StoreName);
%>
```

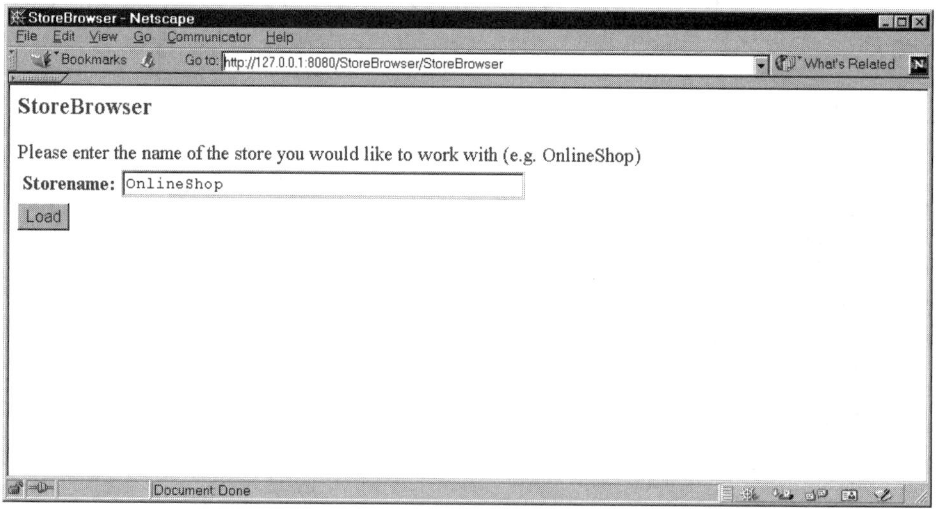

**Figure 11.5** Dialogue for entering a Storename

```
<h3>StoreBrowser</h3>
<form action="StoreBrowser" method="POST">
<input type="Hidden" name="Command" value="openStore">
Please type the name of the Store with which you want to work.<br>
<table>
<tr>
<td><b>Store name:</b></td>
<td>
<input type="Text" name=" <%= C_StoreBrowser.C_StoreName %>" size="40"
value="<%= theStorename %>">
</td>
</tr>
</table>
<input type="Submit" value="Load">
</form>
<%@include file="footer.html" %>
```

### 11.3.3   Type overview

After you open the store it is saved in the session. In the next dialogue we display the type names of this store (Fig. 11.6 and Listing 11.7). This can be achieved by simply iterating the `PersistencePeers` and their `PersistenceType` objects. In order to code the link to the list view correctly, we must pass on each `PersistenceType` as an argument. To do this we use the `C_PersistenceType` constants as the key, as agreed. The dialogue also has a reference to the homepage.

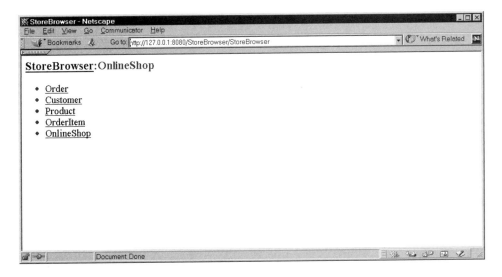

**Figure 11.6**   Type overview dialogue

Listing 11.7: Type overview dialogue: `types.jsp`

```
<%@include file="header.html" %>
<%@ page language="java"
import="java.util.*,de.webapp.Framework.Utilities.ReferenceVector,de.webapp
.Framework.Persistence.*,de.webapp.Framework.SMI.SMICommand,de.webapp.
StoreBrowser.C_StoreBrowser" %>
<%
// Obtain command from the request
SMICommand aSMICommand = (SMICommand)request.getAttribute("SMIEvent");
%>
<!-Display menu with link to Store selection dialogue ->
<h3><a href="StoreBrowser?Command=chooseStore">StoreBrowser</a>:<%=
aSMICommand.getSessionValue(C_StoreBrowser.C_StoreName) %></h3>
<ul>
<%
// Obtain Store from the session
I_Store theStore =
  (I_Store)aSMICommand.getSessionValue(C_StoreBrowser.C_Store);
// Iteration via the PersistencePeers
for(Enumeration e=theStore.getPeers();e.hasMoreElements();) {
  I_PersistencePeer thePeer = (I_PersistencePeer)e.nextElement();
  // Display the type name as link
  out.println("<li><a href='StoreBrowser?Command=showList&"
    + C_StoreBrowser.C_PersistenceType + "="
    + thePeer.getType().getName()
    + "'>"
    + thePeer.getType().getName()
    + "</a><br>");
}
%>
</ul>
<%@include file="footer.html" %>
```

## 11.3.4  List view of an object type

The procedure for outputting the list view is split up into three steps (Fig. 11.7 and Listing 11.8). First the table header text is output, with the names of the attributes and associations. To do this the dialogue uses the store's type description model. Then it iterates through the `C_PersistenceResults` list and outputs all attributes, with key attributes displayed as links to the detailed view of the current object. Then the associations are attached, also as links. The last thing that needs to be output is the link for creating an object.

**StoreBrowser:OnlineShop.**OrderItem

| ObjectIdentifier | ObjectVersion | Amount | Price | ProductID | OrderID | Product | Order |
|---|---|---|---|---|---|---|---|
| 3_182155 | 0 | 1 | 9.00 | 34_84152 | 2_85154 | => | => |
| 3_85155 | 0 | 1 | 11.00 | 34_84152 | 2_85154 | => | => |
| 4_182155 | 0 | 2 | 18.00 | 34_84152 | 2_85154 | => | => |

InsertObject

**Figure 11.7**   Dialogue for viewing a list of an object type: `list.jsp`

## Listing 11.8: Dialogue for creating a list view of an object type

```
<%@include file="header.html" %>
<%@ page language="java"
import="java.util.*,de.webapp.Framework.Utilities.ReferenceVector,de.webapp
.Framework.Persistence.*,de.webapp.Framework.SMI.SMICommand,de.webapp.
StoreBrowser.C_StoreBrowser,java.net.URLEncoder" %>
<%
// Obtain command from the request
SMICommand aSMICommand = (SMICommand)request.getAttribute("SMIEvent");
// Obtain PersistenceType from the request
String thePersistenceType =
   (String)aSMICommand.getValue(C_StoreBrowser.C_PersistenceType);
// Obtain Store from the session
I_Store theStore =
   (I_Store)aSMICommand.getSessionValue(C_StoreBrowser.C_Store);
// Get result of the request for all objects of this type
ReferenceVector theResult =
   (ReferenceVector)aSMICommand.getValue(
     C_StoreBrowser.C_PersistenceResult);
%>
<!- -Display menu with links to store selection dialogue and to types
overview - ->
```

```
<h3><a href="StoreBrowser?Command=chooseStore">StoreBrowser</a>:<a
href="StoreBrowser?Command=showTypes"><%=
aSMICommand.getSessionValue(C_StoreBrowser.C_StoreName) %></a>.<%=
thePersistenceType %></h3>
<table border=1>
<tr>
<%
/* normal attributes ... */
Vector theAttributes =
  theStore.getPeer(thePersistenceType).getType().getAttributes();
for(Enumeration e = theAttributes.elements();e.hasMoreElements();){
  PersistenceAttribute theAttribute =
    (PersistenceAttribute) e.nextElement() ;
  out.println("<th>" + theAttribute.getName() + "</th>");
}
/* ...and the associations */
Vector theAssociations =
  theStore.getPeer(thePersistenceType).getType().getAssociation();
for(Enumeration e = theAssociations.elements();e.hasMoreElements();) {
  PersistenceAssociation theAssociation =
    (PersistenceAssociation) e.nextElement();
  out.println("<th>" + theAssociation.getName() + "</th>");
}
out.println("</tr>");
// Iteration via the results set
for(Enumeration e = theResult.elements(); e.hasMoreElements();) {
  I_Persistence theObject = (I_Persistence)e.nextElement();
  out.println("<tr>");
  for(Enumeration e1 = theAttributes.elements();e1.hasMoreElements();) {
    PersistenceAttribute theAttribute =
      (PersistenceAttribute)e1.nextElement();
    Object theSearchValue theObject.getValue(theAttribute);
    out.print("<td>");
    // Display key attribute as link
    if (theAttribute.isKeyAttribute()) {
      // As the key can contain blanks and special characters,
      // the URL has to be encoded
      String theURL =
      URLEncoder.encode("StoreBrowser?Command=showObject"
      + "&_TemplateName=object.jsp&"
      + C_StoreBrowser.C_PersistenceSearchAttribute + "="
      + theAttribute.getName() + "&"
      + C_StoreBrowser.C_PersistenceSearchValue + "="
      + theSearchValue + "&"
      + C_StoreBrowser.C_PersistenceType + "="
```

```
         + thePersistenceType);
         out.print("<a href='" + theURL + "'>" + theSearchValue + "</a>");
      }
      else {
         out.print(theSearchValue);
      }
      out.println("</td>");
   }
   // Output associations as link
   for(Enumeration e1 = theAssociations.elements();e1.hasMoreElements();) {
      PersistenceAssociation theAssociation =
         (PersistenceAssociation) e1.nextElement() ;
      out.println("<td><a href='StoreBrowser?Command=showAssociation&"
         + C_StoreBrowser.C_PersistenceOID + "="
         + theObject.getObjectIdentifier() + "&"
         + C_StoreBrowser.C_PersistenceAssociationName + "="
         + theAssociation.getName() + "'>=></a></td>");
   }
   out.println("</tr>");
}
%>
</table>
<br>
<%
   // Reference for creating an object of this type
   out.println("<a href='StoreBrowser?Command=newObject&"
      + C_StoreBrowser.C_PersistenceType + "="
      + thePersistenceType + "'>Create Object</a>") ;
%>
<%@include file="footer.html" %>
```

## 11.3.5  Detail view of an object type

The detail view of an object displays its attributes and values as well as its type and store  (Fig. 11.8 and Listing 11.9). To achieve this, the system iterates via the attributes of the type that is to be displayed and, if a C_PersistenceResult is present, the corresponding attribute value is displayed. The ObjectIdentifier and ObjectVersion attributes play a special role here. Unlike all other attributes, these must not be displayed in editable entry fields. In addition, their keys must not begin with the prefix C_PersistenceAttributePrefix which is reserved for changeable attributes. Once the attributes have been output, the references to associated objects are also displayed, just like in the list view. The last things which have to be displayed are the buttons for adding, changing and deleting. However, the last two are only required if an object has actually been displayed.

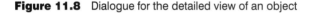

**Figure 11.8** Dialogue for the detailed view of an object

Listing 11.9: Dialogue for the detailed view of an object: `object.jsp`

```
<%@include file="header.html" %>
<%@ page language="java"
import="java.util.*,de.webapp.Framework.Utilities.ReferenceVector,de.webapp
.Framework.Persistence.*,de.webapp.Framework.SMI.SMICommand,de.webapp.
StoreBrowser.C_StoreBrowser" %>

<%
// Obtain command from the request
SMICommand aSMICommand = (SMICommand)request.getAttribute("SMIEvent") ;
// Get result from the command
I_Persistence theResult =
    (I_Persistence)aSMICommand.getValue(C_StoreBrowser.C_PersistenceResult)
;
// Get type
String thePersistenceType =
    (String)aSMICommand.getValue(C_StoreBrowser.C_PersistenceType) ;
// Get Store from the session
I_Store theStore =
    (I_Store)aSMICommand.getSessionValue(C_StoreBrowser.C_Store) ;
// Set value for the menu row
String theOID = null;
if (theResult != null)
    theOID = theResult.getObjectIdentifier();
else
```

```
    theOID= "undefined";
%>
<!-Display menu with links to Store selection dialogue, types overview and
list view ->
<h3><a href="StoreBrowser?Command=chooseStore">StoreBrowser</a>:<a
href="StoreBrowser?Command=showTypes"><%=
aSMICommand.getSessionValue(C_StoreBrowser.C_StoreName) %></a>.<a
href="StoreBrowser?Command=showList&_PersistenceType=<%= thePersistenceType
%>"><%= thePersistenceType%></a>.<%= theOID %></h3>
<form action="StoreBrowser" method="post">
<table border=1>
<tr><th>Name</th><th>value</th></tr>
// Set object's type for createObject
<input type="Hidden" name="<%= C_StoreBrowser.C_PersistenceType %>"
value="<%= thePersistenceType %>">
<%
// Output the attributes
Vector theAttributes =
   theStore.getPeer(thePersistenceType).getType().attributes();
for(Enumeration e = theAttributes.elements();e.hasMoreElements();){
   PersistenceAttribute theAttribute =
      (PersistenceAttribute) e.nextElement();
   String theName;
   Object theValue = (Object) new String("");
   if (theResult != null) {
      theValue = theResult.getValue(theAttribute);
   }
   theName = theAttribute.getName();
   // Attribute name
   out.println("<tr>\n<td>" + theName + "</td>");
   out.println("<td>");
   // If ObjectIdentifier or ObjectVersion are involved, these values
   // must be passed on as hidden fields and users must
   // not be able to edit them.
   // Also, their key must not start with
   // C_PersistenceAttributePrefix, as users must not
   // be able to set these values.
   if (theName.equals("ObjectIdentifier") ||
      theName.equals("ObjectVersion")) {
      %>
      <input type="Hidden" name="_<%=theName%>"
value="<%=theValue%>"><%=theValue%>
      <%
   } else {
      %>
      // Display entry field for attribute
```

```
<input type="Text"
name="<%=C_StoreBrowser.C_PersistenceAttributePrefix%><%=theName%>"
value="<%=theValue%>" size=40>
      <%
  }
  %>
  </td>
  </tr>
<%
}
// Output the associations
Vector theAssociations =
  theStore.getPeer(thePersistenceType).getType().getAssociation();
for(Enumeration e = theAssociations.elements();e.hasMoreElements();) {
  PersistenceAssociation theAssociation =
    (PersistenceAssociation)e.nextElement();
  out.println("<tr>\n<td>" + theAssociation.getName() + "</td>");
  if (theResult != null) {
    out.println("<td><a href='StoreBrowser?Command=showAssociation&"
      + C_StoreBrowser.C_PersistenceOID + "="
      + theResult.getObjectIdentifier() + "&"
      + C_StoreBrowser.C_PersistenceAssociationName + "="
      + theAssociation.getName()+ "'>=></a></td>");
    out.println("</tr>");
  } else {
    out.println("<td>=></td>");
  }
}
%>
</table>
<br>
<input type="Radio" name="Command" value="createObject" checked>Create<br>
<%
// Only display buttons for Delete and Change if
// an object has really been displayed.
if (theResult != null) {
%>
<input type="Radio" name="Command" value="deleteObject">Delete<br>
<input type="Radio" name="Command" value="updateObject">Change<br>
<%
}
%>
<input type="Submit" value="Start Action">
</form>
<%@include file="footer.html"%>
```

### 11.3.6  Displaying associated objects

As we have already mentioned, associations can reference either one, or several, objects. For this reason, depending on the type of association, you should use the list view or the detail view again. Therefore, the JavaServer page `association.jsp` (Listing 11.10) only defines the `C_PersistenceResult` type, then the appropriate `<jsp:include />` is run. Then, `include` is used to pass on the `SMICommand` including `C_PersistenceResult` to the JavaServer page that is providing the display. The `association.jsp` JSP therefore merely has a defining function, and the actual work is carried out by `list.jsp` and `object.jsp`.

Listing 11.10: JavaServer page used to display associations: `association.jsp`

```
<%@ page language="java"
import="java.util.*,de.webapp.Framework.Utilities.ReferenceVector,de.webapp
.Framework.Persistence.*,de.webapp.Framework.SMI.SMICommand,de.webapp.
StoreBrowser.C_StoreBrowser,java.net.URLEncoder" %>
<%
SMICommand aSMICommand = (SMICommand)request.getAttribute("SMIEvent") ;
Object theSearchResult =
   aSMICommand.getValue(C_StoreBrowser.C_PersistenceResult);
if (theSearchResult instanceof ReferenceVector) {
   %>
      <jsp:include page="list.jsp" flush = "true"/>
   <%
} else {
   %>
      <jsp:include page="object.jsp" flush = "true"/>
   <%
} %>
```

## 11.4  SMI – Definition and Configuration

Now we have coded the beans we require and have created the JavaServer pages, the only thing that is missing is the element which joins then together. This role is played by the SMI definition file (Listing 11.11). This file defines the particular call method and particular parameters with which SMI reacts, to a particular command. The follow-on commands are defined here as well. This is usually the `display` command, which is mapped to the `DisplayBean`.

Listing 11.11: The StoreBrowser SMI definition file, `StoreBrowser.smi`

```
{
   // Definition of default values
   DefaultCommand = "Display";
   Values = {
```

```
      _FollowUpCommand = "Display";
      _TemplateName = "chooseStore.jsp";
    }
// Definition of the Listener
Listener = {
   StoreBrowserBean = {
      Class = "de.webapp.StoreBrowser.StoreBrowserBean" ;
   },
   StoreSessionBean = {
      Class = "de.webapp.StoreBrowser.StoreSessionBean";
   },
   DisplayBean = {
      Class = "de.webapp.Framework.SMICommandListener.DisplayBean";
   }
};
// Definition of the commands
Commands = {
   // Display
   display = {
      MethodName = "display";
      Listener = "DisplayBean" ;
   }
   // Display the Persistence types
   showTypes = {
      MethodName = "display";
      Listener = "DisplayBean";
      Values = {
         _TemplateName = "types.jsp"
      }
   }
   // Display list of Persistence objects
   showList = {
      MethodName = "queryByQualifier";
      Listener = "StoreBrowserBean";
      Values = {
         _TemplateName = "list.jsp"
      }
   }
   // Display a Persistence object
   showObject = {
      MethodName = "queryByAttribute";
      Listener = "StoreBrowserBean";
      Values = {
         _TemplateName = "object.jsp"
      }
   }
```

```
// Display an association
showAssociation = {
   MethodName = "queryForAssociation";
   Listener = "StoreBrowserBean";
   Values = {
      _TemplateName = "association.jsp"
   }
}
// Display the Store selection
chooseStore = {
   MethodName = "closeStore";
   Listener = "StoreSessionBean";
}
// Open the Store
openStore= {
   MethodName = "openStore";
   Listener = "StoreSessionBean" ;
   Values = {
      _TemplateName = "types.jsp"
   }
}
// Entry dialogue for a Persistence object
newObject= {
   MethodName = "display";
   Listener = "DisplayBean" ;
   Values = {
      _TemplateName = "object.jsp"
   }
}
// Create a Persistence object
createObject = {
   MethodName = "create";
   Listener = "StoreBrowserBean" ;
   Values = {
      _TemplateName = "object.jsp"
   }
}
// Delete a Persistence object
deleteObject = {
   MethodName = "delete";
   Listener = "StoreBrowserBean";
   Values = {
      _TemplateName = "object.jsp"
   }
}
// Change a Persistence object
```

```
        updateObject = {
          MethodName = "update";
          Listener = "StoreBrowserBean";
          Values = {
            _TemplateName = "object.jsp"
          }
        }
      }
    }
  }
```

To use the StoreBrowser we still have to register it with the servlet engine. As we are using the characteristics of the Servlet API 2.1, we must use a suitable engine. The configuration for jo! looks like the one described in Listing 11.12.

Listing 11.12: StoreBrowser entry in the jo! `servlets.properties` file

```
# StoreBrowser
servlet.StoreBrowser.code/key=de.webapp.Framework.SMI.SMIServlet
servlet.StoreBrowser.initArgs=EventSwitch=StoreBrowser,Context=StoreBrowser
servlet.StoreBrowser.aliases=/StoreBrowser/StoreBrowser
```

At the same time we have used the alias names of the StoreBrowser to define where the JavaServer pages are to be located. In this case, this is the `/StoreBrowser/` directory.

When the Servlet engine starts, the browser is available via the URL `http://<hostname>:<port>/StoreBrowser/StoreBrowser`!

# OnlineShop 12

As the second example for the WebApp framework, we are going to develop an OnlineShop. Here we are going to restrict ourselves to implementing the basic functionality, and we shall not implement any administration components or secure payment.

In an OnlineShop the handler presents its product range to its customers. A customer can then select products from the range and put them into the customer's own virtual product shopping basket, or take them out again. The customer can place an order by clicking with the mouse. To do that, the customer has to tell the handler the customer's method of payment and delivery address. So the customer does not have to do that for every single shopping trip, the handler sets up a customer file for each customer. In order to be able to recover the data from the file, the customer has to enter his or her email address and a password to prove his or her identity.

In this chapter, we describe how to implement an OnlineShop using the WebApp framework. The key functions of our OnlineShop application (Fig. 12.1) are the following:

- Display information about the shop.
- Display the product catalogue.
- Set up a shopping basket for each customer.
- Display the shopping basket.
- Change order later.
- Send and save order.
- Record data for new customer.
- Allow customer login and logout.

## 12.1  Control flow

After calling up the OnlineShop, the user will find a function menu on the left-hand side of the screen, and general information about the shop on the right side of the

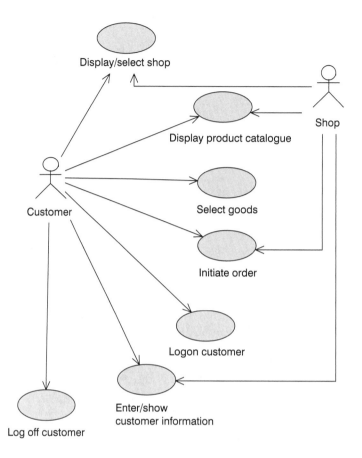

**Figure 12.1** OnlineShop example usage

screen (name, owner, description, etc.) (Fig. 12.2). If the customer has already logged in, then his or her name will appear. If he or she has already put products in the shopping basket, a message will appear to let him or her know.

In the function menu there are entries for calling up product catalogues, for displaying the current product shopping basket and customer data, and for logging the customer in and out. By selecting Start you can always return to the home page of the shop.

If the customer has already chosen the product catalogue, he or she will be able to see a certain number of products per page. This number should be configurable. If the number of products in the catalogue exceeds the maximum number of products per page, then the customer will be able to scroll forwards and backwards through the pages. If the customer chooses a product, the required quantity must be entered. Then, the product will be placed automatically in the customer's shopping basket. Once the customer has placed a product in the shopping basket, he or she can then either confirm the order or return to the catalogue.

Each customer can overview his or her shopping basket at any time with the help

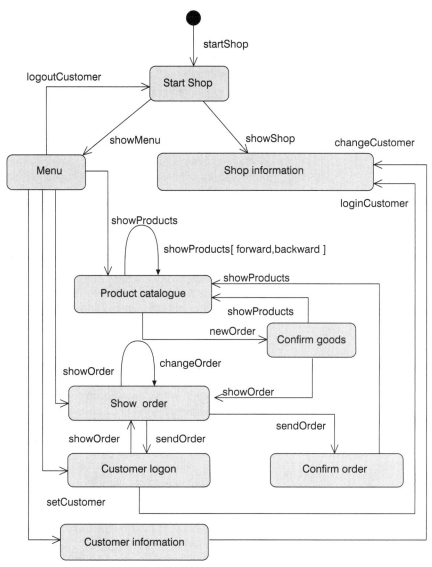

**Figure 12.2** Control flow diagram for OnlineShop

of the function menu. The individual order items can easily be changed. Therefore, the quantity of products ordered can be increased or reduced. Naturally, a product can be removed from the shopping basket entirely. If the customer wants to place other products in the shopping basket, he or she can always return to the catalogue via the function menu.

The order can be sent off only if the customer has logged in. This can happen via the login function, or it will be requested when the order is sent off. When the

**Table 12.1** OnlineShop commands

| Command | Parameter | Meaning |
|---|---|---|
| startShop | – | Start OnlineShop. You will see the commands showMenu and showShop in two separate frames. |
| showMenu | – | Show the menu with options for the commands showProducts, showOrder and showCustomer, loginCustomer, logoutCustomer and startShop. |
| showShop | – | Show information about OnlineShop: name of owner, email address and links to further information. |
| showProducts | Offset | Show product catalogue. The Offset parameter indicates the product from which the display should start. The number of products to be shown in one catalogue page will be set in the servlet configuration. |
| newOrder | Object key of the product, number of products in this order | Display an order with the new order item. If an order is already active, the product will be added to it. The quantity and the price will be stored deposited in the order item. |
| showOrder | – | Show the current order as long as there is one in the shopping basket. Display the total value of an order. |
| changeOrder | Quantity | The quantity of the order can be changed. If quantity 0 is selected, the item will be cancelled. The price will be recalculated with the new quantity. |
| sendOrder | Comment | Remove the current order from the session and generate order and item in the database. When no customer is logged in, request a customer to log in. |
| showCustomer | – | Display of entry dialogue for customer attributes. If a customer is already logged in, then the attributes are displayed so they can be changed. |
| changeCustomer | Customer attributes | If the customer is not registered yet, then a new customer will be set up. Otherwise the attributes of the existing customer will be changed. Before a change is written to the database, the system checks the values in the mandatory fields. |
| loginCustomer | – | Display login dialogue box. |
| setCustomer | Email and password | Log in a customer. If there is an active shopping basket, it is inherited and used. |
| logoutCustomer | – | Log out a customer. If there is an active shopping basket, it expires. |

customer logs in, his or her email address and a password must be entered. Individual delivery and payment parameters are entered in a separate dialogue, and can be changed at any time. If the customer data are changed, the shopping basket is not lost.

Table 12.1 describes all the commands of the OnlineShop in more detail.

## 12.2  Class design

The definition of the OnlineShop procedures yields two kinds of classes: the I_SMICommandListener, which is used for implementing procedures, and the information objects, which form the basis of the OnlineShop.

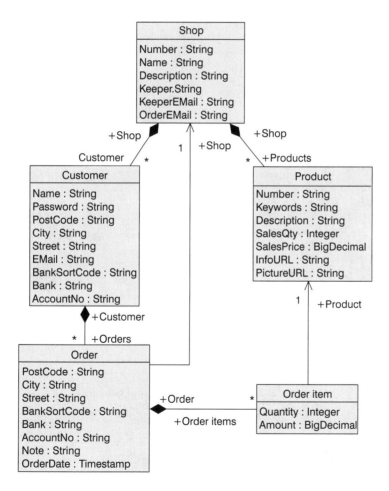

**Figure 12.3**   Business objects used in the OnlineShop

### 12.2.1 Information objects

Now we have to define the information objects involved. These are the OnlineShop, its products, the customers and their orders with the current order items.

- Each OnlineShop has a number of products.
- Each customer is assigned to exactly one shop.
- A number of orders are assigned to each customer.
- Each order has a list of order items containing products (Fig. 12.3).

We use the `Persistence` objects from Chapter 9 as the basis for these simple shop objects. As you do not need to implement special functions for any object, we do not need to code special classes, and fall back on the `PersistenceGeneric` class. That offers the advantage that we can define the attributes and associations of the business objects via a configuration file.

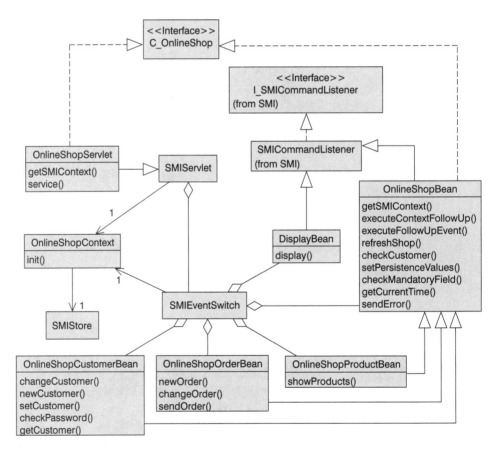

**Figure 12.4** Classes diagram for the components of the OnlineShop

Each OnlineShop has a unique number. With the help of this number, we can arrange for some independent components and database connections for each shop. Although we have restricted ourselves to one shop, in this example, the unique number means that the possibility for extending the functionality easily widening is already built in.

When the customer places an order, the actual delivery address and the bank details of the customer will be stored in the order. To each order you can attach a customer note.

When customer data are changed, unsent orders are changed accordingly. Each order item of an order will be marked by the quantity and the price. The product itself has, in addition to the price and description, a picture and a URL as a link to further information.

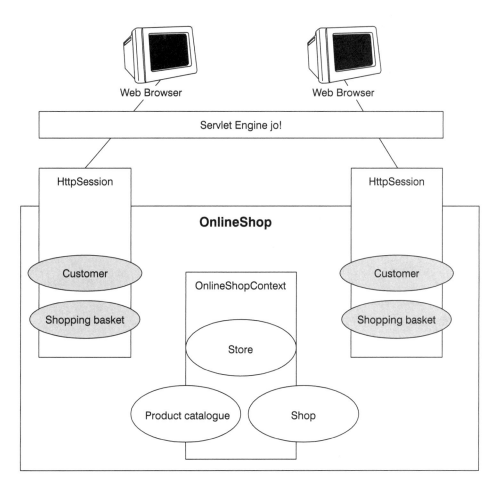

**Figure 12.5** Storage of important information objects for the OnlineShop

## 12.2.2 Components of the OnlineShop

When you first start the OnlineShop you must establish a connection to the database. To do this, we obviously use our store (Chapter 9). As all subsequent beans of the OnlineShop should have access to the information objects, the store will be stored in the OnlineShopContext (Fig. 12.4). As is clear from the definition of the procedure, there are several function groups per customer, product and order. For each of these groups we define a separate bean.

The OnlineShopBean serves as the upper class for our beans. With its derivatives OnlineShopCustomer, OnlineShopOrder and OnlineShopProduct, and the display bean displayBean, it forms the core of the OnlineShop application. The OnlineShopServlet has the task of providing a transaction frame for each access to the OnlineShop and the task of carrying out the necessary synchronization (Listing 12.1).

The shopping basket is implemented using the HttpSession object. For each user of the OnlineShop, a shopping basket and their customer object are held in their session. The product catalogue is stored in the OnlineShopContext, and is therefore accessible to all the customers of the shop (Fig. 12.5).

## 12.2.3 OnlineShopServlet

The OnlineShopServlet is a derivative of the SMIServlet (Chapter 8). It consists only of the two methods getSMIContext() and service() (Listing 12.1). The getSMIContext() method serves as a help method to access the I_SMIContext of the application where there is the instance of an SMIStore, the central data connection of the OnlineShop.

The service() method frames each inquiry made by a customer with an exclusive access to the store. The transaction frame begin() – commit()/rollback() secures all the operations. The command is called in the service() method of the upper class SMIServlet.

Listing 12.1: OnlineShopServlet class

```
package de.webapp.OnlineShop ;

import java.io.IOException;
import javax.servlet.*;
import javax.servlet.http.*;
import de.webapp.Framework.ConfigManager.* ;
import de.webapp.Framework.SMI.* ;
import de.webapp.Framework.StoreFactory.StoreFactory ;
import de.webapp.Framework.Persistence.* ;
import de.webapp.Framework.Utilities.ReferenceVector;
import de.webapp.Framework.Log.* ;

/** Initialization of the Store */
public class OnlineShopServlet extends SMIServlet
    implements C_OnlineShop
```

```
{
/** Get SMIContext of the application via the switch. */
public I_SMIContext getSMIContext()
  { return getSMIEventSwitch().getSMIContext(); }
/** Form transaction frame and secure the Store every time it is accessed.
*/
public void service (ServletRequest req, ServletResponse res)
  throws ServletException, IOException {
  I_Store theStore = (I_Store) getSMIContext().getValue(C_Store) ;
  synchronized(theStore) {
    try {
      theStore.begin();
      super.service(req, res);
      theStore.commit() ;
    } catch (Exception e) {
    try {
      theStore.rollback() ;
    } catch (PersistenceException pe) {
      pe.printStackTrace() ;
    }
    if (e instanceof ServletException) throw (ServletException)e;
    if (e instanceof IOException) throw (IOException)e;
    else throw new ServletException(e.toString()) ;
    }
  }
}
} // End of the class
```

## 12.2.4  The C_OnlineShop interface

The C_OnlineShop interface is used to define all constants used in the OnlineShop.
You have definitions for commands (C_DisplayCommand), parameters for configura-
tions (C_ShopNumber), command transfer parameters (C_FollowUpCommand,
C_CustomerMail), output fields (C_OrderParameter) or mandatory entry fields
(C_CustomerLoginFields) and error messages (C_CustomerNotSet). The interface
and all the constants are marked for this purpose with the prefix C_.

Listing 12.2: C_OnlineShop interface

```
package de.webapp.OnlineShop ;

public interface C_OnlineShop {
// #### Display commands
/** Command for displaying an error page */
public static final String C_ErrorDisplay = "display";
/** Command for display */
public static final String C_DisplayCommand = "display";
```

```java
/** Parameter for follow-up command */
public static final String C_FollowUpCommand = "_FollowUpCommand";
/** Parameter for JSP or HTML page */
public static final String C_Template = "_TemplateName";
/** Name of error page */
public static final String C_ErrorPage = "ShowError.jsp";
/** Name of login page */
public static final String C_LoginCustomer = "customerLogin.html";
/** FollowUp page after login */
public static final String C_LoginCustomerRestartOrder =
    "loginCustomer.html";

// #### Parameter constants
/** Key for ShopNumber */
public static final String C_ShopNumber = "_Shopnumber" ;
/** Default Store name */
public static final String C_DefaultStorename = "OnlineShop" ;
/** Key for name of Store */
public static final String C_StoreName = "_Storename" ;
/** Key for SMIContext */
public static final String C_Context = "_OnlineShopContext" ;
/** Message for error page */
public static final String C_Message = "_OnlineShopMessage" ;
/** Parameter for error page */
public static final String C_Arguments = "_OnlineShopArgumentArray" ;

// #### Session parameters
/** Current order in a session */
public static final String C_Order = "de.webapp.OnlineShop.Order" ;
/** Current customer */
public static final String C_Customer = "de.webapp.OnlineShop.Customer" ;
/** Product in the order */
public static final String C_ProductID = "_ProductID" ;
/** Quantity ordered */
public static final String C_Quantity = "_Quantity" ;
/** Email address of customer */
public static final String C_CustomerMail = "_PAEMail" ;
/** Customer's password*/
public static final String C_CustomerPassword = "_PAPassword" ;
/** Number of item in order that is to be deleted */
public static final String C_DeleteOrderItem = "_DeleteItem" ;

/** Page size*/
public static final String C_PageSize = "_PageSize" ;
/** Product display offset*/
public static final String C_Offset = "Offset" ;

/** Prefix for form fields represented on Persistence attributes */
```

```
public static final String C_PersistenceAttributePrefix = "_PA";

// #### Application key
/** Key for this Store in the OnlineShop application */
public static final String C_Store = "de.webapp.OnlineShop.Store" ;
/** Key for this Shop in the OnlineShop application */
public static final String C_Shop = "de.webapp.OnlineShop.Shop" ;
/** Key for the products of this Shop in the OnlineShop application */
public static final String C_Products = "de.webapp.OnlineShop.Products" ;

// #### Errors
/** Customer not defined*/
public static final String C_CustomerNotSet =
  "The customer has not been defined!" ;
/** Order not defined */
public static final String C_OrderNotSet =
  "There is no order present!" ;
/** Order item's product missing*/
public static final String C_ProductFailed =
  "No product has been assigned to this order item " ;
/** Please enter multiple of sales amount */
public static final String C_Multiple =
  "Please enter multiple of sales amount " ;

// #### Fields and parameters
/** Attributes for parameter exchange between order and customer */
public static final String C_OrderParameter[] = new String[]
  { "BankSortCode", "Bank", "AccountNumber", "PostCode", "Town", "Street" }
  ;
/** Report customer's mandatory fields */
public static final String C_CustomerLoginFields[] = new String[]
  { "EMail", "Password" } ;
/** Customer's mandatory fields */
public static final String C_CustomerFields[] = new String[]
  { "Name", "Password", "EMail", "BankSortCode", "Bank",
  "AccountNumber", "PostCode", "Town", "Street" } ;
/** Entry fields*/
public static final String C_CustomerAddressFields[][] = new String[][];
  { {"BankSortCode", "BankSortCode"},
    {"Bank", "Bank"},
    {"AccountNumber", "AccountNumber"},
    {"PostCode", "PostCode"},
    {"Town", "Town"},
    {"Street", "Street"}
  } ;
/** Display the customer's entry fields */
public static final String C_CustomerInputFields[][] = new String[][]
```

```
    { {"Name *", "Name", "50", "Text" },
      {"EMail *", "EMail", "50", "Text" },
      {"Password *", "Password", "8", "Password" },
      {"PostCode *", "PostCode", "5", "Text" },
      {"Town *", "Town", "50", "Text" },
      {"Street *", "Street", "50", "Text" },
      {"BankSortCode *", "BankSortCode", "10", "Text" },
      {"Bank *", "Bank", "50", "Text" },
      {"AccountNumber *", "AccountNumber", "10", "Text" },
    } ;
} // End of the interface
```

## 12.2.5 OnlineShopContext

When the `OnlineShopContext` is initialized (Listing 12.3 and Section 11.2), the store is configured and initialized, creating the database connection. The name of the store, the page size of the catalogue and the number of the shop will be loaded into it from the context's configuration. The Shop object is loaded from the store, and stored with the store in the context. They are easily accessible there for all beans.

Listing 12.3: OnlineShopContext class

```
package de.webapp.OnlineShop ;

import java.io.IOException;
import java.util.*;
import de.webapp.Framework.ConfigManager.* ;
import de.webapp.Framework.SMI.* ;
import de.webapp.Framework.StoreFactory.StoreFactory ;
import de.webapp.Framework.Persistence.* ;
import de.webapp.Framework.Log.* ;

public class OnlineShopContext extends SMIContext
    implements C_OnlineShop {

// Initialize OnlineShop's Store and select Shop.
public void init(String aContextName, Hashtable aValues)
      throws SMIException {
    super.init(aContextName, aValues);
    // Get Store.
    String theStorename = (String)getValue(C_StoreName) ;
    if(theStorename == null)
      theStorename = C_DefaultStorename ;
    I_Store theStore = null ;
    try {
      ConfigManager.getConfigManager();
```

```
      Configuration theStoreConfig =
        ConfigManager.getConfigManager().getConfiguration(
          aContextName,theStorename,true);
      // Initialize Store
      theStore = StoreFactory.getInstance(theStoreConfig) ;
    } catch (PersistenceException pe) {
      throw new SMIException(pe.toString()) ;
    }
    // Save Store in the context.
    putValue(C_Store,theStore) ;
    // Get Shop.
    String theShopNumber = (String)getValue(C_ShopNumber) ;
    if(theShopNumber == null)
      throw new SMIException("Shop Number not present!") ;
    // Number of products that can be seen at the same time
    String thePageSize = (String) getValue(C_PageSize) ;
    if(thePageSize == null)
      thePageSize = "10" ;
    putValue(C_PageSize,new Integer(thePageSize)) ;
    // Get the Shop from the database.
    synchronized(theStore) {
      try {
        theStore.begin() ;
        // find Shop
        I_Persistence theShop =
          theStore.persistenceWithKey(
            theShopNumber,"OnlineShop","Number") ;
        if(theShop == null)
          throw new SMIException("Shop with Number "
            + theShopNumber + " not found ") ;
        // Save Shop in context.
        putValue(C_Shop,theShop) ;
        theStore.commit() ;
      } catch (Throwable e) {
        try {
          theStore.rollback() ;
        } catch (PersistenceException pe ) {
          throw new SMIException(
            "Shop could not be found!", pe) ;
        }
        throw new SMIException(e) ;
      }
    }
  }
} // End of the class
```

### 12.2.6 OnlineShopBean

The class OnlineShopBean has two functions. First, it defines some help functions for each derivative and second, it implements some general commands.

The refreshShop (SMICommand) method implements complete re-initialization of the OnlineShop. With the help of the sendError (SMICommand) method, all the beans can send an error message. The sendError(SMICommand, Object[]) method allows the passing on of any desired list of parameters as an error description. This is not a pretty way of handling errors, but it is a start.

The executeFollowUpEvent (SMICommand) method leads to the carrying out of a follow-up command, if this is set with the parameter C_Online-Shop.C_FollowUpCommand (see Chapter 11). The executeContextFollowUp (SMICommand) method also stores the OnlineShopContext as a parameter in the command.

The help functions are available to all the derivations of the OnlineShopBean class. You can check with the checkMandatoryField() method whether a dialogue entry's expected arguments have really been passed on with the SMICommand. The setPersistenceValues() method sets the arguments of a command as attributes of a Persistence object. Both checkMandatoryFields() and setPersistenceValues() only use parameters whose key begins with the prefix C_PersistenceAttributePrefix.

Finally, there are the methods checkCustomer() and getCurrentTime(). The first one makes sure that a customer who has already logged in will be recorded in the order. The second one returns the current time.

Listing 12.4: OnlineShopBean class

```
package de.webapp.OnlineShop;

import java.io.*;
import java.util.*;
import java.text.SimpleDateFormat ;
import de.webapp.Framework.SMI.*;
import de.webapp.Framework.Persistence.*;
import de.webapp.Framework.Utilities.*;

/** Upper class of OnlineShopXXXBeans */
public class OnlineShopBean extends SMICommandListener
    implements C_OnlineShop, Serializable {

/** Particular context. */
public I_SMIContext getSMIContext() {
    return getSMIEventSwitch().getSMIContext();
}

/** Set application and follow-up command. */
public void executeContextFollowUp(SMICommand aSMICommand)
      throws OnlineShopException, PersistenceException {
    I_SMIContext theApp = getSMIContext() ;
```

```
      aSMICommand.putValue(C_Context, theApp ) ;
      executeFollowUpEvent(aSMICommand) ;
}

/** Set the value defined in _FollowUpCommand as a command in the context.
*/
public void executeFollowUpEvent(SMICommand aSMICommand)
      throws OnlineShopException {
   String followUpCommand =
      (String)aSMICommand.getValue(C_FollowUpCommand);
   if (followUpCommand != null) {
      try {
         // Set command.
         aSMICommand.setCommand(followUpCommand);
         // Execute follow-up command
         getSMIEventSwitch().executeSMIEvent(aSMICommand);
      } catch( Exception e) {
          throw new OnlineShopException("Call in "
             + getSMIEventSwitch().getName() + " has an error ",e) ;
      }
   }
}

/** Get all Shop's data again! */
public void refreshShop(SMICommand aSMICommand)
      throws OnlineShopException, PersistenceException {
   I_SMIContext theApp = getSMIContext() ;
   I_Store theStore = (I_Store)theApp.getValue(C_Store) ;
   PersistenceGeneric theShop =
      (PersistenceGeneric)theApp.getValue(C_Shop) ;
   // Get Product catalogue.
   I_PersistenceReference aRef =
      theShop.getPersistenceReference("Product") ;
   // Delete product catalogue in memory.
   aRef.clear() ;
   // Get Shop's products again.
   ReferenceVector theProducts =
      (ReferenceVector)theShop.getReference("Product") ;
   theApp.putValue(C_Products,theProducts) ;
   // Delete customers and order
   aSMICommand.removeSessionValue(C_Customer);
   aSMICommand.removeSessionValue(C_Order);
   executeFollowUpEvent(aSMICommand)
}

/** Match up customer with order */
protected void checkCustomer(PersistenceGeneric aCustomer,
```

```
    PersistenceGeneric aOrder)
      throws OnlineShopException,PersistenceException {
      if (aCustomer != null) {
        // Set customer's parameter for the order
        if(aOrder != null) {
          aOrder.setReference("Customer",aCustomer) ;
          for (int i = 0; i < C_OrderParameter.length; i++)
            aOrder.setValue(C_OrderParameter[i],
              aCustomer.getValue(C_OrderParameter[i]));
        }
      }
    }

    /** Set the values of a persistent object. */
    protected void setPersistenceValues(I_Persistence aPersistence,
      SMICommand aSMICommand)
        throws PersistenceException {
      Enumeration e = aSMICommand.getKeys();
      String aValue;
      String aKey;
      while (e.hasMoreElements()) {
        aKey = (String)e.nextElement();
        if (aKey.startsWith(C_PersistenceAttributePrefix)
            && aKey.length() > C_PersistenceAttributePrefix.length()) {
          aValue = (String)aSMICommand.getValue(aKey);
          aKey = aKey.substring(C_PersistenceAttributePrefix.length());
          aPersistence.getPeer().getType().getAttributeWithName(
            aKey).setStringValue(aPersistence, aValue);
        }
      }
    }

    /** Test if the mandatory fields in a form have been filled.
    C_PersistenceAttributePrefix is added to field names */
    protected boolean checkMandatoryField(String aMandatoryFields[],
      SMICommand aSMICommand) {
      String theValue;
      boolean allFilled = true;
      for (int i =0; i < aMandatoryFields.length ;i++) {
        theValue = (String)aSMICommand.getValue(
          C_PersistenceAttributePrefix + aMandatoryFields[i]) ;
        if (theValue == null) {
          allFilled = false ;
          break ;
        } else
          if (theValue.length() == 0) {
            allFilled = false ;
```

```
            break;
        }
    }
    return allFilled ;
}

/** Determine current time in the GMT timezone ECT.
protected String getCurrentTime() {
    TimeZone tz = TimeZone.getTimeZone("GMT");
    SimpleDateFormat dateformat =
        new SimpleDateFormat("yyyy-MM-dd HH:mm:ss");
    dateformat.setTimeZone(tz);
    return dateformat.format(new Date());
}

/** Report error with message*/
protected void sendError(SMICommand aSMICommand, String aMessage)
        throws OnlineShopException {
    sendError(aSMICommand,aMessage,null) ;
}

/** Report error with message and parameters*/
protected void sendError(SMICommand aSMICommand,
    String aMessage, Object[] aArguments)
        throws OnlineShopException {
    I_SMIContext theApp = getSMIContext() ;
    aSMICommand.putValue(C_Context, theApp ) ;
    aSMICommand.putValue(C_Message, aMessage ) ;
    if(aArguments != null)
        aSMICommand.putValue(C_Arguments, aArguments ) ;
    aSMICommand.putValue(C_Template, C_ErrorPage ) ;
    aSMICommand.putValue(C_FollowUpCommand,C_ErrorDisplay);
    executeFollowUpEvent(aSMICommand) ;
}

} // End of the class
```

## 12.2.7 OnlineShopProductBean

The OnlineShopProductBean class has the task of displaying the product catalogue (Listing 12.5). To do so, it uses the single method showProducts. When the
catalogue is first displayed, it will be loaded via the shop object's product association
(see Chapter 9). Then the catalogue is ready for all further inquiries. So that the products can be displayed, they are set as a value of the command (see putValue()).
Furthermore, the Offset parameter, from the request, is attached to the command.
With the help of a call to a follow-up command, the Online-
ShopBean.executeContextFollowUp() method is used to display the catalogue
page, which begins with the Offset item.

Listing 12.5: OnlineShopProductBean class

```java
package de.webapp.OnlineShop ;

import javax.servlet.http.*;
import de.webapp.Framework.SMI.*;
import de.webapp.Framework.Persistence.*;
import de.webapp.Framework.Utilities.*;

/** Display products */
public class OnlineShopProductBean extends OnlineShopBean {

/** Store the Shop's products. */
public void showProducts(SMICommand aSMICommand)
    throws OnlineShopException, PersistenceException {
  HttpServletRequest request = aSMICommand.getRequest() ;
  I_SMIContext theApp = getSMIContext() ;
  I_Store theStore = (I_Store)theApp.getValue(C_Store) ;
  PersistenceGeneric theShop =
    (PersistenceGeneric) theApp.getValue(C_Shop) ;
  ReferenceVector theProducts = null ;
  // Get the Shop's products.
  theProducts = (ReferenceVector)theApp.getValue(C_Products) ;
  if(theProducts == null) {
    theProducts = (ReferenceVector)theShop.getReference("Product") ;
    theApp.putValue(C_Products,theProducts) ;
  }
  // Prepare to output products
  if(theProducts != null && theProducts.size() > 0 ) {
    aSMICommand.putValue(C_Context, theApp ) ;
    String theOffset = request.getParameter(C_Offset) ;
    if(theOffset != null)
    aSMICommand.putValue(C_Offset, theOffset ) ;
    executeFollowUpEvent(aSMICommand) ;
  } else
    sendError(aSMICommand,"the Shop " + theShop.getValue("Name")
      + " has no products! "
      + "<br>Please contact the shop"
      + "management!" ) ;
}
} // End of the class
```

## 12.2.8 OnlineShopOrderBean

The OnlineShopOrderBean class contains all the commands used to change an order (Listing 12.6). A JavaServer page is used to display the data (Listing 12.14).

The newOrder (SMICommand) method shows a new order if there is none in the shopping basket yet (i.e. in the HttpSession), otherwise the existing one is used. A new order item is added to the order via the request parameter. The value of the goods will then be calculated from the quantity and the price of the product, and recorded in the order item's Amount attribute.

You can use the changeOrder (SMICommand) method to change an order item and product quantities can be reduced or increased. After the change, the value of the product will be recalculated. If the quantity of the products is zero, then the item will be deleted.

You can use the sendOrder (SMICommand) method to transfer the order from HttpSession into the database. Before this transfer, the system checks whether the customer, for whom the order is to be posted, has logged in and he or she will be requested to log in if necessary. If the customer has already logged in, then the order will be assigned to the shop and the customer, and the current date is set as order date. After an error-free save to the database, a follow-up command is run which confirms the order.

Listing 12.6: OnlineShopOrderBean class

```
package de.webapp.OnlineShop;

import javax.servlet.http.*;
import java.math.BigDecimal;
import java.sql.Timestamp ;
import de.webapp.Framework.SMI.*;
import de.webapp.Framework.Persistence.*;
import de.webapp.Framework.Utilities.*;

/** Handling orders */
public class OnlineShopOrderBean extends OnlineShopBean {

/** Create order in the customer's session. */
public void newOrder(SMICommand aSMICommand)
      throws OnlineShopException, PersistenceException {
   // Setup
   I_SMIContext theApp = getSMIContext() ;
   I_Store theStore = (I_Store)theApp.getValue(C_Store) ;
   // Does the order exist in the session?
   PersistenceGeneric theOrder =
      (PersistenceGeneric)aSMICommand.getSessionValue(C_Order);
   // Is there a logged-on customer?
   PersistenceGeneric theCustomer =
      (PersistenceGeneric) aSMICommand.getSessionValue(C_Customer);
   // Get order
   if (theOrder == null) {
      // Create new order
      theOrder =
         (PersistenceGeneric)theStore.newPersistence("OnlineOrder") ;
      // Set customer parameter if present.
      if (theCustomer != null)
```

```
        checkCustomer(theCustomer,theOrder) ;
      // Now the order is visible
      aSMICommand.putSessionValue(C_Order,theOrder) ;
    }

    // Create order item for selected product
    String theProductID = (String)aSMICommand.getValue(C_ProductID) ;
    // Determine order quantity.
    int theQuantity =
      new Integer((String)aSMICommand.getValue(C_Quantity)).intValue();
    if (theQuantity < 1) {
      sendError(aSMICommand,C_Multiple) ;
      return ;
    }
    // Create new order item
    PersistenceGeneric theItem =
      (PersistenceGeneric)theStore.newPersistence("OnlineOrderItem") ;
    theItem.setValue("ProductID",theProductID) ;
    theItem.setValue("Quantity",new Integer(theQuantity)) ;
    // Determine amount, if product exists.
    PersistenceGeneric theProduct =
      (PersistenceGeneric) theItem.getReference("Product") ;
    if (theProduct == null) {
      sendError(aSMICommand,C_ProductFailed,
        new Object[]{theOrder,theItem}) ;
      return ;
    }
    BigDecimal theSalesAmount = (BigDecimal)theProduct.getValue("SalesPrice")
    ;
    Integer theSalesQty = (Integer)theProduct.getValue("SalesQty") ;
    if(theQuantity % theSalesQty.intValue() != 0) {
      sendError(aSMICommand,"Quantity entered"
        + theQuantity
        + " is not a multiple of the product quantity " + theSalesQty) ;
      return ;
    }
    // OK, enter the amount.
    theItem.setValue("Amount",
    theSalesAmount.multiply(new BigDecimal(theQuantity /
    theSalesQty.intValue())))) ;
    // Add order item to order
    theOrder.addToReference("OrderItem",theItem) ;
    executeContextFollowUp(aSMICommand) ;
  }
  /** Change the quantity */
  // Delete an order item, if Quantity 0.
```

```java
public void changeOrder(SMICommand aSMICommand)
    throws OnlineShopException, PersistenceException {
  HttpServletRequest request = aSMICommand.getRequest() ;
  String theItem =
    (String)request.getParameter(C_DeleteOrderItem) ;
  if (theItem == null) {
    sendError(aSMICommand,
      "No order item selected for deletion")
    return ;
  }
  int item = new Integer(theItem).intValue() ;
  // Manipulate order.
  PersistenceGeneric theOrder=
    (PersistenceGeneric)aSMICommand.getSessionValue(C_Order);
  synchronized(theOrder) {
    if(theOrder != null
       && theOrder.getObjectState() == C_Persistence.STATE_UNDEFINED) {
      String theQuantity = (String)request.getParameter(C_Quantity) ;
      if(theQuantity == null) {
        sendError(aSMICommand,"No quantity entered");
        return ;
      }
      int quantity = new Integer(theQuantity).intValue() ;
      ReferenceVector theOrders =
        (ReferenceVector)theOrder.getReference("OrderItem") ;
      if( quantity == 0) {
        theOrders.removeElementAt(item) ;
        if(theOrders.size() == 0)
          aSMICommand.removeSessionValue(C_Order) ;
      } else {
        // Get order item and correct quantity and amount.
        PersistenceGeneric theOrderItem = (PersistenceGeneric)
          theOrders.elementAt(item) ;
        theOrderItem.setValue("Quantity",new Integer(quantity));
        PersistenceGeneric theProduct = (PersistenceGeneric)
        theOrderItem.getReference("Product") ;
        // Correct the amount.
        BigDecimal theSalesAmount =
          (BigDecimal)theProduct.getValue("SalesPrice") ;
        Integer theSalesQty = (Integer)theProduct.getValue("SalesQty") ;
        theOrderItem.setValue("Amount",
        theSalesAmount.multiply(
          new BigDecimal( quantity / theSalesQty.intValue()))) ;
      }
    }
  }
```

```
      // Run follow-up command.
      executeContextFollowUp(aSMICommand) ;
}

/** Get the Shop's data again! */
public void sendOrder(SMICommand aSMICommand)
      throws OnlineShopException, PersistenceException {
  I_SMIContext theApp = getSMIContext() ;
  I_Store theStore = (I_Store)theApp.getValue(C_Store) ;
  PersistenceGeneric theCustomer =
      (PersistenceGeneric)aSMICommand.getSessionValue(C_Customer);
  if(theCustomer == null) {
    // No customer logged on => require logon.
    aSMICommand.putValue(C_FollowUpCommand,C_DisplayCommand) ;
    aSMICommand.putValue(C_Template,C_LoginCustomerRestartOrder) ;
    executeContextFollowUp(aSMICommand) ;
    return ;
  }
  // Customer logged on => get active order from session.
  PersistenceGeneric theOrder =
      (PersistenceGeneric)aSMICommand.getSessionValue(C_Order);
  PersistenceGeneric theShop = (PersistenceGeneric)
      theApp.getValue(C_Shop) ;
  // Send order.
  if (theOrder != null
      && theOrder.getObjectState() == C_Persistence.STATE_UNDEFINED) {
    if (theOrder.getValue("ShopID") == null)
      theOrder.setReference("Shop",theShop) ;
    // Set current time
    theOrder.setValue("OrderDate",
      Timestamp.valueOf(getCurrentTime()+".000000000")) ;
    // Set values in Persistence.
    setPersistenceValues(theOrder,aSMICommand) ;
    // Check
    ReferenceVector theItems =
      (ReferenceVector)theOrder.getReference("OrderItem") ;
    if (theItems.size() > 0) {
      // The order is assigned to the current customer
      // and saved.
      theCustomer.addToReference("Order",theOrder) ;
      theCustomer.update() ;
      // Delete the current order from the session.
      // Order now made.
      aSMICommand.removeSessionValue(C_Order);
    } else {
        sendError(aSMICommand,C_OrderNotSet) ;
```

```
        return ;
      }
      executeContextFollowUp(aSMICommand) ;
   } else
      sendError(aSMICommand,C_OrderNotSet) ;
 }
} // End of the class
```

## 12.2.9  OnlineShopCustomerBean

The `OnlineShopCustomerBean` class implements the client management commands. If you want to change the customer data you have to call the
`changeCustomer()` method. It first checks whether all the mandatory fields have
been filled in. If so, then it checks whether the customer has already been registered,
via the entry email address. Then the password is checked. If all the details are correct, the entry values are accepted and stored in the database. Otherwise the method
displays an error message.

The `setCustomer()` method is very similar to the method described above, except
that it registers the customer, without changing the data. After a successful login, the
customer information is transferred into the active order, and any existing follow-up
command is carried out.

The `getCustomer()` help method searches for the customer in the database. It
uses the current shop and the email address as search parameters.

Listing 12.7: `OnlineShopCustomerBean` class

```
package de.webapp.OnlineShop;

import javax.servlet.http.*;

import de.webapp.Framework.SMI.*;
import de.webapp.Framework.Log.Log;
import de.webapp.Framework.Persistence.*;
import de.webapp.Framework.Utilities.*;

/** Implements customer commands. */
public class OnlineShopCustomerBean extends OnlineShopBean {

/** Change a customer's details*/
public void changeCustomer(SMICommand aSMICommand)
     throws OnlineShopException, PersistenceException {
  I_SMIContext theApp = getSMIContext() ;
  I_Store theStore = (I_Store)theApp.getValue(C_Store) ;
  PersistenceGeneric theShop =
    (PersistenceGeneric)theApp.getValue(C_Shop) ;
  PersistenceGeneric theCustomer = null ;
  // Test if the command contains all fields.
  if (!checkMandatoryField(C_CustomerFields,aSMICommand)) {
```

```
        sendError(aSMICommand,
          "Not all mandatory fields have been filled!", C_CustomerFields ) ;
        return ;
      }
      String theMail = (String)aSMICommand.getValue(C_CustomerMail) ;
      // Get customer
      theCustomer = (PersistenceGeneric)
        getCustomer(theStore,theMail,theShop.getObjectIdentifier()) ;
      if(theCustomer == null) {
        // New customer
        theCustomer =
          (PersistenceGeneric)theStore.newPersistence("OnlineCustomer");
        theCustomer.setReference("Shop",theShop) ;
        setPersistenceValues(theCustomer,aSMICommand) ;
        theCustomer.create() ;
      } else {
        // Existing customer
        if(!checkPassword(theCustomer,
            (String)aSMICommand.getValue(C_CustomerPassword) )) {
            sendError(aSMICommand,
              " The customer password "
              + theCustomer.getValue("EMail") + " is incorrect" ) ;
            return ;
        }
        setPersistenceValues(theCustomer,aSMICommand) ;
        theCustomer.update() ;
      }
      // Add customers to the session.
      aSMICommand.putSessionValue(C_Customer,theCustomer);
      executeContextFollowUp(aSMICommand) ;
    }

    /** Set customers. */
    public void setCustomer(SMICommand aSMICommand)
        throws OnlineShopException, PersistenceException {
      PersistenceGeneric theCustomer =
        (PersistenceGeneric) aSMICommand.getSessionValue(C_Customer);
      PersistenceGeneric theOrder =
        (PersistenceGeneric) aSMICommand.getSessionValue(C_Order);
      if (!checkMandatoryField(C_CustomerLoginFields, aSMICommand)) {
        sendError(aSMICommand,
            " Not all mandatory fields have been filled!",
          C_CustomerLoginFields ) ;
        return ;
      }

      String theMail = (String)aSMICommand.getValue(C_CustomerMail) ;
```

```
  // Replace existing customers.
  if(theCustomer != null) {
    if(theMail.equals(theCustomer.getValue("EMail"))) {
      if (!checkPassword(theCustomer,
          (String)aSMICommand.getValue(C_CustomerPassword) )) {
        sendError(aSMICommand,
          "The customer password "
          + theCustomer.getValue("EMail") + " is incorrect" ) ;
        return ;
      }
      // Match up customers and order.
      checkCustomer(theCustomer,theOrder) ;
    } else {
      // Customer has changed.
      aSMICommand.removeSessionValue(C_Customer);
      theCustomer = null ;
    }
  }
  // Set customer for the session.
  if (theCustomer == null) {
    I_SMIContext theApp = getSMIContext() ;
    I_Store theStore = (I_Store)theApp.getValue(C_Store) ;
    PersistenceGeneric theShop =
      (PersistenceGeneric)theApp.getValue(C_Shop) ;
    // Get customer.
    theCustomer = (PersistenceGeneric)
      getCustomer(theStore,theMail, theShop.getObjectIdentifier()) ;
    if (theCustomer != null) {
      if (!checkPassword(theCustomer,
        (String)aSMICommand.getValue(C_CustomerPassword) )) {
          sendError(aSMICommand,
          "The customer password "
          + theCustomer.getValue("EMail") + " is incorrect" ) ;
          return ;
      }
    } else {
      sendError(aSMICommand,
        "You are not a customer yet.<BR>"
        + " Please enter your details in the customer dialogue!" ) ;
      return ;
    }
    // Match up customer with order
    checkCustomer(theCustomer,theOrder) ;
    // Record the customer in the session.
    aSMICommand.putSessionValue(C_Customer,theCustomer);
}
```

```
        HttpServletRequest request = aSMICommand.getRequest() ;
        String theFollowUp = (String)request.getParameter(C_FollowUpCommand) ;
        if(theFollowUp != null) {
            String theTemplate = (String)request.getParameter(C_Template) ;
            aSMICommand.putValue(C_FollowUpCommand,theFollowUp) ;
            aSMICommand.putValue(C_Template,theTemplate) ;
        }
        executeContextFollowUp(aSMICommand) ;
    }

    /** Test a password */
    protected boolean checkPassword(PersistenceGeneric aCustomer,
        String aPassword)
            throws PersistenceException {
        String thePassword = (String) aCustomer.getValue("Password");
        return thePassword != null && thePassword.equals(aPassword) ;
    }

    /** Get the Shop's customer via their email address */
    // This function must be used in a synchronized
    // transaction frame.
    protected I_Persistence getCustomer(I_Store aStore,
        String aMail, String aShopID)
            throws PersistenceException {
        if(aStore == null || aMail == null || aShopID == null)
            return null ;
        // Get the Shop's customer.
        ReferenceVector theCustomers =
            aStore.getRetriever("OnlineCustomer").retrieve(
            " WHERE t0.ShopID ='" + aShopID+ "'" +
            " AND t0.EMail = '" + aMail + "'" ) ;
        if(theCustomers.size() != 1 )
            return null ;
        return (I_Persistence)theCustomers.elementAt(0) ;
    }

} // End of the class
```

## 12.2.10  OnlineShopException, exception definition

For the OnlineShop we need an exception class, the OnlineShopException. When an exceptional situation arises, a new instance of the OnlineShopException is created and the framework or JDK exception is encapsulated in it (Listing 12.8).

Listing 12.8: OnlineShopException class

```
package de.webapp.OnlineShop;

import de.webapp.Framework.Utilities.WebAppException ;

/** Exception for the OnlineShop */
public class OnlineShopException extends WebAppException {

/** Create the exception */
public OnlineShopException() {}
/** Get a description of the error from Throwable. *//
public OnlineShopException(Throwable aThrowable) {
   super(aThrowable) ;
}
/** Set message that describes the exception. */
public OnlineShopException(String aMessage) {
   super(aMessage) ;
}
/** Set message that describes the exception. */
public OnlineShopException(String aMessage,Throwable aThrowable) {
   super(aMessage,aThrowable) ;
}
} // End of the class
```

## 12.3  Dialogue and layout

Now we have thoroughly discussed the components of the application, we can define the dialogue.

### 12.3.1  Importing code fragments

In the StoreBrowser (Chapter 11) we introduced the Server-Side-Includes for header.html and footer.html. These are also used in the OnlineShop.

### 12.3.2  General picture

To display the OnlineShop we have decided to split up the interface into two HTML frames. In the left-hand frame you can find the function menu via which you can call up all the OnlineShop's dialogues (Listing 12.9 and Fig. 12.6). We call this frame overview. In the right-hand frame, which is called info, we display the OnlineShop's dialogues.

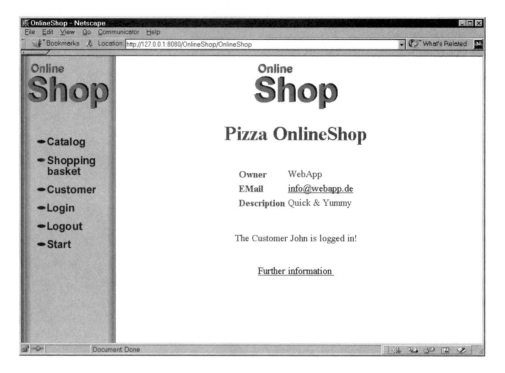

**Figure 12.6**   OnlineShop home page

Listing 12.9: Definition of the frames used for the Shop

```
<html>
<head>
<title>OnlineShop</title>
</head>
<frameset border=0 cols="210, *">
   <frame name=overview src="OnlineShop?Command=showMenu" scrolling="no"
frameborder="0">
   <frame name=info src="OnlineShop?Command=showShop" scrolling="auto"
frameborder="0">
</frameset>
</html>
```

To display the homepage, you use the OnlineShop's showMenu and showShop commands. In the menu you find references to the product catalogue (showProducts), shopping basket display (showOrder), customer information (showCustomer) and customer login (loginCustomer) and logout (logoutCustomer) (Listing 12.10). The Start command reloads the whole shop.

Listing 12.10: OnlineShop functions menu

```html
<html>
<head>
<title>OnlineShop</title>
</head>
<body background="Menu/background.gif">
   <img src="Menu/shop.gif"><br><br><br>
   <a target=info href="/OnlineShop/OnlineShop?Command=showProducts"><img
border=0 src="Menu/catalogue.gif" old="catalogue"></a><br>
   <a target=info href="/OnlineShop/OnlineShop?Command=showOrder"><img
border=0 src="Menu/ShoppingBasket.gif" old="ShoppingBasket"></a><br>
   <a target=info href="/OnlineShop/OnlineShop?Command=showCustomer"><img
border=0 src="Menu/customer.gif" old="Customer"></a><br><br>
   <a target=info href="/OnlineShop/OnlineShop?Command=loginCustomer"><img
border=0 src="Menu/logon.gif" old="logon"></a><br>
   <a target=_top href="/OnlineShop/OnlineShop?Command=logoutCustomer"><img
border=0 src="Menu/logoff.gif" old="logoff"></a><br>
   <a target=_top href="/OnlineShop/OnlineShop?Command=startShop"><img
border=0 src="Menu/start.gif" old="Start"></a><br>
</body>
</html>
```

A simple JSP (Listing 12.11) is used to process the information about the Shop (owner, etc.). The `SMICommand` is extracted from the request. The command provides us with the `OnlineShopContext` and with it access to the shop. Now we have to output the attributes of the shop object. If a customer is logged in, then his or her name is always displayed. In addition his or her shopping basket is displayed, with the number of order items if there is an order.

Listing 12.11: JavaServer Page `ShowShop.jsp`

```jsp
<%@ include file="header.html" %>
<%@ page language="java"
import="java.util.Enumeration,de.webapp.Framework.Utilities.ReferenceVector
,de.webapp.Framework.Persistence.*,de.webapp.Framework.SMI.*,
de.webapp.OnlineShop.C_OnlineShop" %>
<center>
<%
// Get a command.
SMICommand theSMICommand = (SMICommand)request.getAttribute("SMIEvent") ;
I_SMIContext theSMIContext =
   (I_SMIContext)theSMICommand.getValue(C_OnlineShop.C_Context) ;
PersistenceGeneric theShop =
   (PersistenceGeneric)theSMIContext.getValue(C_OnlineShop.C_Shop) ;
%>
<img border=0 src="Menu/shop.gif"><br><br>
```

```
<h1><%= theShop.getValue("Name") %></h1>
<br>
<table>
<tr><td><b>Owner</b></td><td><%= theShop.getValue("Owner") %></td></tr>
<tr><td><b>EMail</b></td><td>
<ahref='mailto:<%= theShop.getValue("OwnerEMail") %>'><%=
theShop.getValue("OwnerEMail") %></a></td></tr>
<tr><td><b>Description</b></td><td><%= theShop.getValue("Description")
%></td></tr>
</table>
<br>
<%
PersistenceGeneric theCustomer=
   (PersistenceGeneric)theSMICommand.getSessionValue(
     C_OnlineShop.C_Customer) ;
if(theCustomer != null) {
%>
<br>Customer <%= theCustomer.getValue("Name") %> is logged on!<br>
<% }
PersistenceGeneric theOrder =
   (PersistenceGeneric) theSMICommand.getSessionValue(
     C_OnlineShop.C_Order) ;
if(theOrder != null) {
   ReferenceVector theOrders = null ;
   try {
     theOrders =
        (ReferenceVector)theOrder.getReference("OrderItem") ;
   } catch ( PersistenceException pe ) {
     throw new ServletException( "ModelError", pe) ;
   }
%>
<br>There is an order with <%= theOrders.size() %> items!<br>
<br>
<% }
String theLink = (String)theShop.getValue("InfoURL") ;
if(theLink!=null) {
%>
<br>
<br>
<a href="<%= theLink %>">Other Information<a>
<% } %>
</center>
<%@ include file="footer.html" %>
```

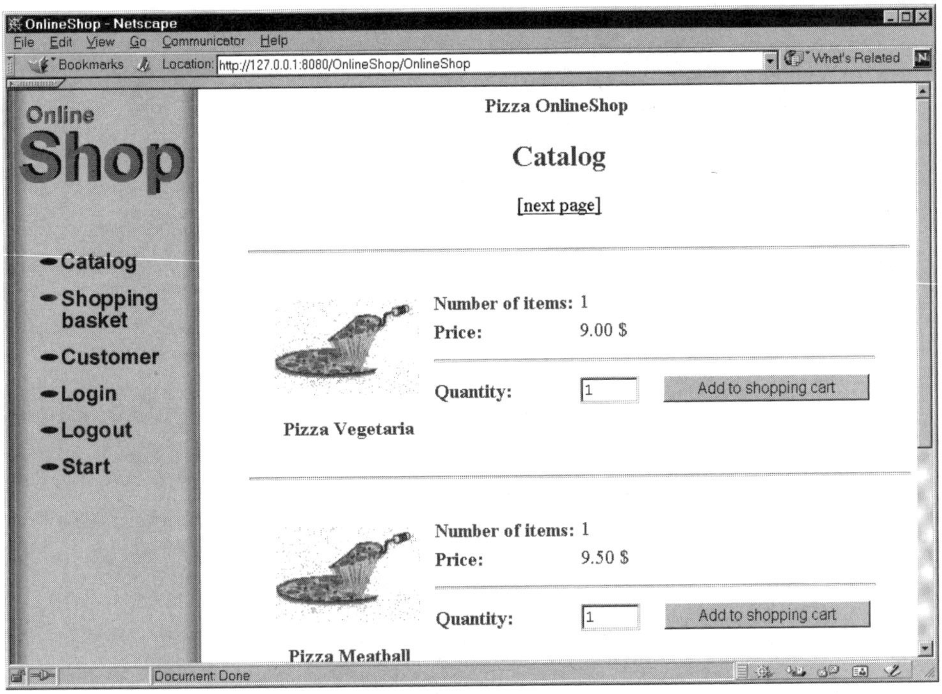

**Figure 12.7** Product catalogue dialogue

## 12.3.3 The product catalogue

The product catalogue will be displayed page by page. The picture of the product is shown on the left in Fig. 12.7, the information about it on the right and the description is below the picture. We can scroll backwards and forwards through the pages of the catalogue.

Once the shop has been determined from the current command (mandatory), the products are requested from the shop (Listing 12.12), and the size of the page and the number of the products are defined. Then a decision is made on whether references are needed for scrolling pages. Finally, the relevant catalogue page is displayed.

Listing 12.12: JavaServer Page ShowProduct.jsp

```
<%@ include file="header.html" %>
<%@ page language="java"
import="java.util.Enumeration,de.webapp.Framework.Utilities.ReferenceVector,
de.webapp.Framework.Persistence.*,de.webapp.Framework.SMI.*,
de.webapp.OnlineShop.C_OnlineShop" %>

<%
// Get command.
SMICommand theSMICommand = (SMICommand)request.getAttribute("SMIEvent") ;
I_SMIContext theSMIContext =
```

```
        (I_SMIContext)theSMICommand.getValue(C_OnlineShop.C_Context) ;
PersistenceGeneric theShop =
    (PersistenceGeneric)theSMIContext.getValue(C_OnlineShop.C_Shop) ;
ReferenceVector theProducts =
    (ReferenceVector)theSMIContext.getValue(C_OnlineShop.C_Products) ;
%>
<center>
The <b><%= theShop.getValue("Name") %></b> Shop
<h2> Shop Catalog</h2>
<%
int thePageSize = 10 ;
int theOffset = 0 ;
try {
  thePageSize =
    ((Integer)theSMIContext.getValue(
      C_OnlineShop.C_PageSize)).intValue() ;
  theOffset =
  Integer.parseInt((String)theSMICommand.getValue(
    C_OnlineShop.C_Offset)) ;
} catch (NumberFormatException nfe) {}
if (theProducts != null && theProducts.size() > thePageSize) {
  if (theOffset > 0) {
    int previous = theOffset - thePageSize;
    out.println("<a href='OnlineShop?Command=showProducts&"
      + C_OnlineShop.C_Offset + "="
      + previous + "'>[previous page]</a><br>");
  }
  if (theOffset + thePageSize < theProducts.size()) {
    int next = theOffset + thePageSize;
    out.println("<a href='OnlineShop?Command=showProducts&"
      + C_OnlineShop.C_Offset + "="
      + next + "'>[next page]</a><br>");
  }
}
%>
<ul>
<%
  if(theProducts != null) {
    for (int i=theOffset; i<theProducts.size()
      && i < theOffset+thePageSize; i++) {
      PersistenceGeneric theProduct =
        (PersistenceGeneric)theProducts.elementAt(i) ;
      int number = theProducts.size()-i;
      String theImage = (String)theProduct.getValue("PictureURL") ;
      if(theImage == null)
        theImage = "Picture/NoPicture.gif" ;
```

```
%>
        <hr>
        <form action="OnlineShop" method="POST">
            <input type="Hidden" name="Command" value="newOrder">
            <input type="Hidden" name="_ProductID" value="
<%= theProduct.getObjectIdentifier() %>">
            <table>
                <tr>
                <td align=center>
                <img src="<%= theImage %>">
                </td>
                <td rowsspan=2 valign=center>
                <table>
                    <tr>
                    <td><b>Number:</b></td>
                        <td><%= theProduct.getValue("SalesQty") %></td>
                    </tr>
                    <tr>
                    <td><b>Price:</b></td>
                        <td><%= theProduct.getValue("SalesPrice") %> DM </td>
                    </tr>
                    <tr><td colspan=2><hr></td></tr>
                    <tr>
                    <td><b>Quantity:</b></td>
                        <td>
                        <input type="Text" name="_Quantity" size="5" value="1">
                            
                        <input type="Submit" value="Add to ShoppingBasket">
                        </td>
                    </tr>
                </table>
                </td>
                </tr>
                <tr>
                <td align=center>
                    <b><%= theProduct.getValue("Description") %></b></td>
                </tr>
            </table>
        </form>
<%
    }
}
%>
</ul>
</center>
<%@ include file="footer.html" %>
```

### 12.3.4 Displaying the shopping basket

When an order arrives in the shopping basket, it will be displayed (Fig. 12.8); and so will the relevant customer information. Before posting the order, one more comment can be attached. In addition, it is easy to change the order items and if this is done, the sums are automatically adjusted (Listing 12.6). If everything is the way the customer wants it, the order can be posted by clicking on the Send order button.

In order to implement the required functionality, the customer and the order will be read from the HttpSession, suitably formatted, and then displayed. The display fields will be determined via constants from the C_OnlineShop interface.

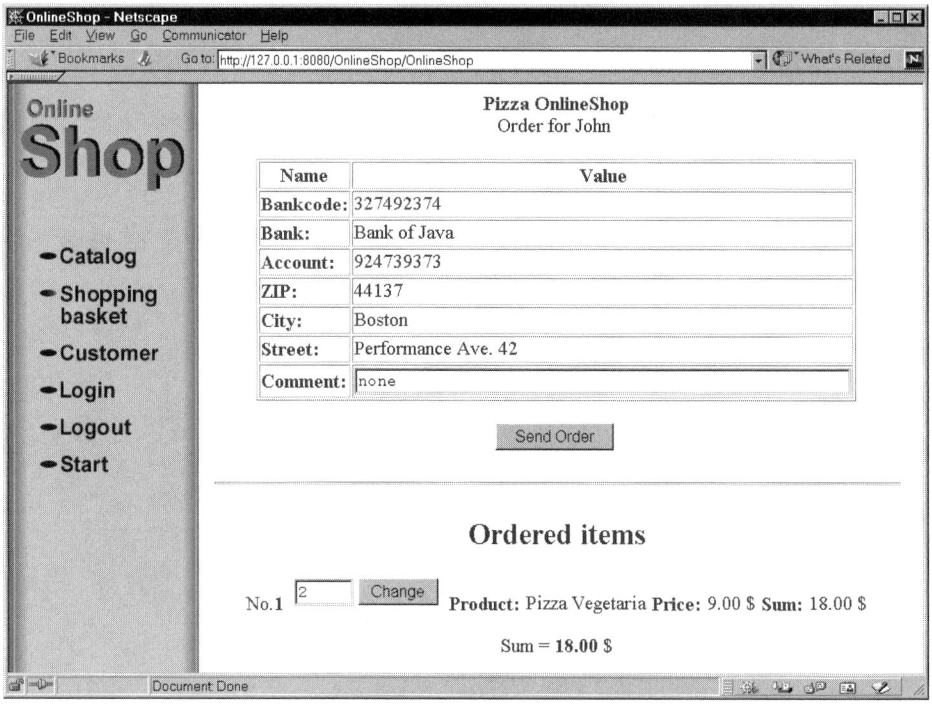

**Figure 12.8** Displaying the shopping basket

Listing 12.13: The JavaServer Page ShowOrder.jsp

```
<%@ include file="header.html" %>
<%@ page language="java"
import="java.util.Enumeration,de.webapp.Framework.Utilities.ReferenceVector
,de.webapp.Framework.Persistence.*,de.webapp.Framework.SMI.*,
de.webapp.OnlineShop.C_OnlineShop, java.math.BigDecimal " %>

<%
```

```
// Get command
SMICommand theSMICommand = (SMICommand)request.getAttribute("SMIEvent") ;
I_SMIContext theSMIContext =
   (I_SMIContext)theSMICommand.getValue(C_OnlineShop.C_Context) ;
PersistenceGeneric theOrder =
   (PersistenceGeneric)request.getSession(
      false ).getValue(C_OnlineShop.C_Order) ;
PersistenceGeneric theShop =
   (PersistenceGeneric)theSMIContext.getValue(C_OnlineShop.C_Shop) ;
PersistenceGeneric theCustomer =
   (PersistenceGeneric)theSMICommand.getSessionValue(
      C_OnlineShop.C_Customer) ;
%>
<center>
The <b><%= theShop.getValue("Name") %></b> Shop
<h2>Shopping Basket</h2>
<%
   if(theOrder!= null) {
      ReferenceVector theOrderItem = null ;
      try {
         theOrderItem =
            (ReferenceVector)theOrder.getReference("OrderItem") ;
      } catch ( PersistenceException pe ) {
         throw new ServletException( "ModelError", pe) ;
      }
      if(theCustomer != null) {
%>
         The order for <%= theCustomer.getValue("Name") %></h2>
   <% } else { %>
         <br>You still need to logon before you
         can place an order!<br>
<% } %>
<br><form action="OnlineShop" method="POST">
<input type="Hidden" name="Command" value="sendOrder">
<%
   for (int i = 0; i < C_OnlineShop.C_CustomerAddressFields.length; i++)
%>
      <input type="Hidden" name="_PA<%= C_OnlineShop.C_CustomerAddressFields
[i][0] %>"
      value="<%= theOrder.getValue(C_OnlineShop.C_CustomerAddressFields
[i][1]) %>">
<% } %>
<table border=1>
<tr><th>Name</th><th>Wert</th></tr>
<%
   for (int i = 0; i < C_OnlineShop.C_CustomerAddressFields.length; i++) {
```

```
%>
<tr>
   <td><b><%= C_OnlineShop.C_CustomerAddressFields[i][0] %>:</b></td>
   <td><%= theOrder.getValue(C_OnlineShop.C_CustomerAddressFields[i][1])
%></td>
</tr>
<% } %>
<tr>
<td><b>Note:</b></td>
<td><input type="Text" name="_PANote" size="50" value='<%=
theOrder.getValue("Note") %>'></td>
</tr>
</table>
<br>
<br>
<input type="Submit" value="Send order">
</form>
<hr>
<br><h2>Order items</h2><br>
<%
   if(theOrderItem != null) {
%>
      <table>
<%
      BigDecimal theTotalAmount = new BigDecimal(0.0) ;
      int i = 0 ;
      for (Enumeration e=theOrderItem.elements();
        e.hasMoreElements();) {
        PersistenceGeneric theItem =
           (PersistenceGeneric)e.nextElement() ;
        I_Persistence theProduct = null ;
        try {
           theProduct =
              (I_Persistence)theItem.getReference("Product") ;
        } catch (PersistenceException pe) {
           throw new ServletException("ModelError", pe) ;
        }
        theTotalAmount =
           theTotalAmount.add(
              (BigDecimal)theItem.getValue("Amount"));
%>
      <tr>
      <td>Nr.<b><%= theProduct.getValue("Number") %></b> </td>
      <td>
      <form action="OnlineShop" method="GET">
        <input type="Hidden" name="Command" value="changeOrder">
```

```
      <input type="Hidden" name="<%= C_OnlineShop.C_DeleteOrderItem %>"
value="<%= i %>">
        <table border=1>
        <input type="Text" name="_Quantity" size="5" value='<%=
theItem.getValue("Quantity") %>'></td>
        </table>
        <input type="Submit" value="Change">
      </form>
      </td>
      <td><b>Product:</b></td>
      <td><%= theProduct.getValue("Description") %></td>
      <td><b>Individual price:</b></td>
      <td><%= theProduct.getValue("SalesPrice") %> DM</td>
      <td><b>Amount:</b></td>
      <td><%= theItem.getValue("Amount") %> DM</td>
      </tr>
<% i++ ;
      } %>
      </table>
      <br>Total amount = <b><%=theTotalAmount%></b> DM<br>
    <% }
    } else { %>
No order active!<br>
<br> Select order items from product catalogue.
<% } %>
</center>
<%@ include file="footer.html" %>
```

## 12.3.5  Displaying customer information

The customer information is displayed in a standard HTML form (Fig. 12.9). All the entry fields are listed in a table. When the customer enters a password, it will be hidden as usual. The customer can change his or her own data by clicking the button.

If the customer wants an overview of the orders, the system sorts all orders in ascending sequence (Listing 12.14).

Listing 12.14: JavaServer Page ShowCustomer.jsp

```
<%@ include file="header.html" %>
<%@ page language="java"
import="java.util.Enumeration,de.webapp.Framework.Utilities.ReferenceVector,
de.webapp.Framework.Persistence.*,de.webapp.Framework.SMI.*,
de.webapp.OnlineShop.C_OnlineShop,java.sql.Timestamp,java.text.
SimpleDateFormat,java.util.TimeZone" %>

<%
```

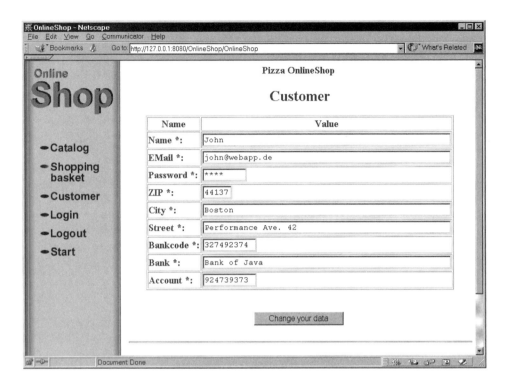

**Figure 12.9** Displaying the customer data

```
SMICommand theSMICommand = (SMICommand)request.getAttribute("SMIEvent") ;
I_SMIContext theSMIContext =
  (I_SMIContext)theSMICommand.getValue(C_OnlineShop.C_Context) ;
I_Store theStore = (I_Store)theSMIContext.getValue(C_OnlineShop.C_Store) ;
PersistenceGeneric theCustomer = (PersistenceGeneric)
  theSMICommand.getSessionValue(C_OnlineShop.C_Customer) ;
PersistenceGeneric theShop = (PersistenceGeneric)
  theSMIContext.getValue(C_OnlineShop.C_Shop) ;
%>
<center>
The <b><%= theShop.getValue("Name") %></b> shop
<br>
<h2>Customer</h2>
<form target=_top action="OnlineShop" method="POST">
<input type="Hidden" name="Command" value="changeCustomer">
<table border=1>
<tr><th>Name</th><th>Value</th></tr>
<%
for(int i = 0; i < C_OnlineShop.C_CustomerInputFields.length; i++) {
  Object theCustomerValue ;
```

```
   if(theCustomer != null)
      theCustomerValue =
         theCustomer.getValue(C_OnlineShop.C_CustomerInputFields[i][1]) ;
   else
      theCustomerValue = null ;
%>
   <tr>
   <td><b><%= C_OnlineShop.C_CustomerInputFields[i][0] %>:</b></td>
   <td><input type="<%= C_OnlineShop.C_CustomerInputFields[i][3] %>"
name="_PA<%= C_OnlineShop.C_CustomerInputFields[i][1] %>" size="<%=
C_OnlineShop.C_CustomerInputFields[i][2] %>" value="<%= theCustomerValue
%>"></td>
   </tr>
<% } %>
</table>
<br>
<br>
<input type="Submit" value="Change your customer data">
</form>
<hr>
<%
   if(theCustomer != null) {
      out.println("<h2>Orders to date</h2><br>") ;
      ReferenceVector theOrders = null ;
      try {
         theOrders =
            (ReferenceVector)theCustomer.getReference("order") ;
      } catch (PersistenceException pe ) {
         throw new ServletException "OnlineShop model has an error!",pe);
      }
      out.println("<table width=70" + "%" + ">");
      out.println("<tr><th align=left><b>OrderDate</b></th>"
         + "<th align=left><b>Note</b></th></tr>") ;
      TimeZone tz = TimeZone.getTimeZone("ECT");
      SimpleDateFormat dateformat =
         new SimpleDateFormat("dd.MM.yyyy HH:mm:ss");
      dateformat.setTimeZone(tz);
      for (Enumeration e = theOrders.elements(); e.hasMoreElements() ;) {
         PersistenceGeneric theOrder =
            (PersistenceGeneric) e.nextElement() ;
%>
   <tr>
   <td><%= dateformat.format(theOrder.getValue("OrderDate")) %></td>
   <td><%= theOrder.getValue("Note") %></td>
   </tr>
```

```
<%    }
      out.println("</table>");
    } else
      try {
        theCustomer =
          (PersistenceGeneric)theStore.newPersistence("OnlineCustomer") ;
      } catch (PersistenceException pe ) {
        throw new ServletException(
          "Could not create new customer! ",pe) ;
      }
%>
</center>
<%@ include file="footer.html" %>
```

### 12.3.6  Logging on a customer

If a customer is already registered, they can identify themself by entering their email address and their password for the system. They do so when they are logging in (Fig. 12.10). The login is implemented with a normal HTML form (Listing 12.15).

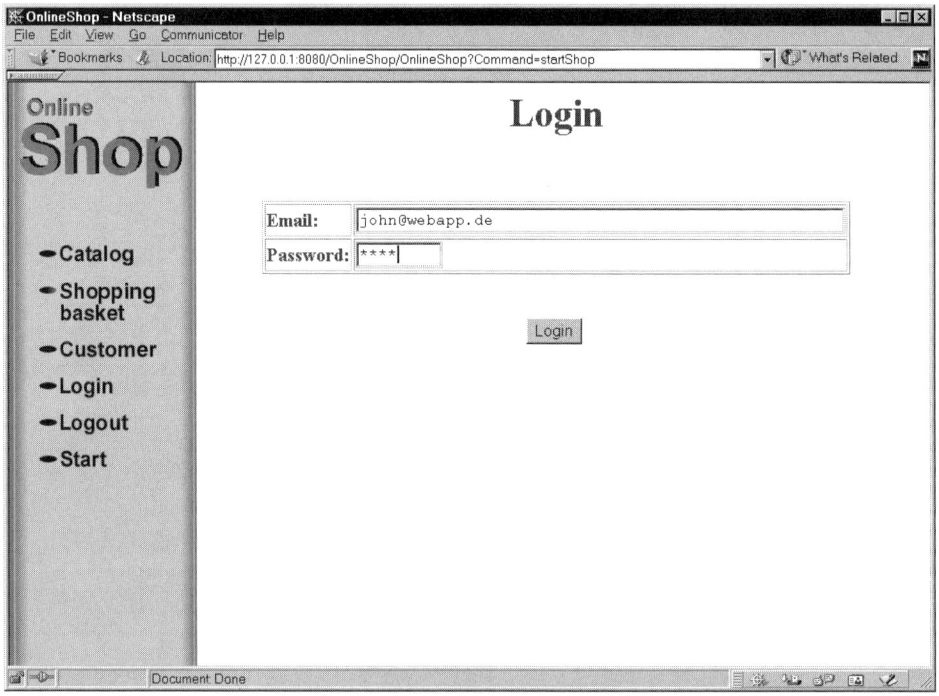

**Figure 12.10**  Customer login

Listing 12.15: Login of a customer with `loginCustomer.html`

```html
<html>
<head>
<title>OnlineShop</title>
</head>
<BODY text="#800000" link="#000080" vlink="#000080" alink="#FF0000">
<center>
<h1>Logon a customer</h1><br>
<form action="OnlineShop" method="POST">
<input type="Hidden" name="Command" value="setCustomer">
<table border=1>
<tr><td><b>Email Address</b></td>
   <td><input type="Text" name="_PAEMail" size="50"></td>
</tr>
<tr><td><b>Password</b></td>
   <td><input type="Password" name="_PAPassword" size="8"></td>
</tr>
</table>
<br>
<br>
<input type="Submit" value="Logon">
</form>
</center>
</body>
</html>
```

If an order is supposed to be posted even if the customer has not yet logged on, it is essential to use a JSP. For these cases we have set up an intermediary login dialogue, which returns to the order display after the valid entry of customer identification.

The trick in this JSP is that the follow-up command is coded in the hidden fields (hidden fields) of the form.

Listing 12.16: Login of a customer if an order is made but no customer is logged on in this HTTP session

```java
<%@ include file="header.html" %>
<%@ page language="java"
import="java.util.Enumeration,de.webapp.Framework.Utilities.ReferenceVector
,de.webapp.Framework.Persistence.*,de.webapp.Framework.SMI.*,
de.webapp.OnlineShop.C_OnlineShop" %>

<%
// Get command.
SMICommand theSMICommand = (SMICommand)request.getAttribute("SMIEvent") ;
I_SMIContext theSMIContext =
   (I_SMIContext)theSMICommand.getValue(C_OnlineShop.C_Context) ;
String theMessage=
```

```
  (String)theSMICommand.getValue(C_OnlineShop.C_Message) ;
Object[] theArguments =
  (Object[])theSMICommand.getValue(C_OnlineShop.C_Arguments) ;
PersistenceGeneric theShop =
  (PersistenceGeneric)theSMICommand.getValue(C_OnlineShop.C_Shop) ;
%>
<center>
<h1>Logon a customer</h1><br>
<form action="OnlineShop" method="POST">
<input type="Hidden" name="Command" value="setCustomer">
<input type="Hidden" name="<%= C_OnlineShop.C_FollowUpCommand %>"
value="display">
<input type="Hidden" name="<%= C_OnlineShop.C_Template %>"
value="ShowOrder.jsp">
<table border=1>
<tr><td><b>Email Address</b></td>
  <td><input type="Text" name="_PAEMail" size="50"></td>
</tr>
<tr><td><b>Password</b></td>
  <td><input type="Password" name="_PAPassword" size="8"></td>
</tr>
</table>
<br>
<br>
<input type="Submit" value="Logon">
</form>
<hr>
</center>
<%@ include file="footer.html" %>
```

## 12.4   SMI – definition and configuration

Once we have coded the specific parts, we integrate them via the configurations. First we have to create the tables in the database. Then we describe the store configuration and the `PersistenceGeneric` objects. The next step is for the commands of the OnlineShop (Fig. 12.2) to be connected with the beans (Fig. 12.4) in an SMI definition file. Finally, the application is registered in jo!, the servlet engine.

### 12.4.1  Store  configuration

Now we create all the database tables. These are based on the OnlineShop table, in which all the shop information is stored. A quick reminder: each shop has a number of products and customers. Each customer can post numerous orders with a large number of order items. Each item is assigned to one of the shop's products. Listing 12.17 shows the required SQL statements.

Listing 12.17: SQL commands for creating the tables for the OnlineShop

```
// Shop
CREATE TABLE OnlineShop (
   ObjectIdentifier CHAR(16) NOT NULL,
   ObjectVersion INTEGER,
   Number VARCHAR(30),
   Name VARCHAR,
   Description VARCHAR,
   Keeper VARCHAR,
   KeeperEMail VARCHAR,
   InfoURL VARCHAR,
   InfoEMail VARCHAR,
   OrderEMail VARCHAR,
   PRIMARY KEY (ObjectIdentifier),
);
INSERT INTO TypeNumber VALUES ( 'OnlineShop', 151 );

// Product
CREATE TABLE OnlineProduct (
   ObjectIdentifier CHAR(16) NOT NULL,
   ObjectVersion INTEGER,
   Number VARCHAR (30),
   Keywords VARCHAR (50),
   Description VARCHAR,
   SalesQty INTEGER,
   SalesPrice DECIMAL,
   InfoURL VARCHAR,
   PictureURL VARCHAR,
   ShopID CHAR(16) NOT NULL,
   PRIMARY KEY (ObjectIdentifier),
   FOREIGN KEY (ShopID) REFERENCES OnlineShop (ObjectIdentifier)
);
INSERT INTO TypeNumber VALUES ( 'OnlineProduct', 152 );

// Customer
CREATE TABLE OnlineCustomer (
   ObjectIdentifier CHAR(16) NOT NULL,
   ObjectVersion INTEGER,
   Name VARCHAR (50),
   Email VARCHAR,
   Password VARCHAR (8),
   PostCode CHAR(5),
   Town VARCHAR (50),
   Street VARCHAR (50),
   Bank VARCHAR,
   BankSortCode VARCHAR (20),
```

```
      AccountNumber VARCHAR (20),
      ShopID CHAR(16) NOT NULL,
      PRIMARY KEY (ObjectIdentifier),
      FOREIGN KEY (ShopID) REFERENCES OnlineShop (ObjectIdentifier)
);
INSERT INTO TypeNumber VALUES ( 'OnlineCustomer', 153 );

// order
CREATE TABLE OnlineOrder (
      ObjectIdentifier CHAR(16) NOT NULL,
      ObjectVersion INTEGER,
      OrderDate TIMESTAMP,
      Bank VARCHAR,
      BankSortCode VARCHAR (20),
      AccountNumber VARCHAR (20),
      PostCode CHAR(5),
      Town VARCHAR (50),
      Street VARCHAR (50),
      Note VARCHAR,
      CustomerID CHAR(16) NOT NULL,
      ShopID CHAR(16) NOT NULL,
      PRIMARY KEY (ObjectIdentifier),
      FOREIGN KEY (CustomerID) REFERENCES OnlineCustomer (ObjectIdentifier),
      FOREIGN KEY (ShopID) REFERENCES OnlineShop (ObjectIdentifier)
);
INSERT INTO TypeNumber VALUES ( 'OnlineOrder', 154);

// order item
CREATE TABLE OnlineOrder item (
      ObjectIdentifier CHAR(16) NOT NULL,
      ObjectVersion INTEGER,
      Quantity INTEGER,
      Amount DECIMAL,
      ProductID CHAR(16) NOT NULL,
      OrderID CHAR(16) NOT NULL,

      PRIMARY KEY (ObjectIdentifier),
      FOREIGN KEY (OrderID) REFERENCES OnlineOrder (ObjectIdentifier),
      FOREIGN KEY (ProductID) REFERENCES OnlineProduct (ObjectIdentifier)
);
INSERT INTO TypeNumber VALUES ('OnlineOrder item', 155) ;
```

Once the tables have been created, we still need to create `OnlineShop.store`, the store configuration file (Listings 12.18 to 12.23). Here you can define the connection to the database in the `JDBCConnection` section. In the connection you integrate the definitions of the business objects, which are always stored in separate files.

Listing 12.18: OnlineShop.store store configuration

```
{
   StoreClass = "de.webapp.Framework.SMICommandListener.SMIStore" ;
   JDBCConnection = {
      // Example configuration
      DriverClass = "solid.jdbc.SolidDriver" ;
      URLConnect = "jdbc:solid://localhost:1313" ;
      Properties = {
         user = "web" ;
         password = "app" ;
      }
   } ;
   Types =
   {
      Shop = #include("Shop.persistence");
      Customer = #include("Customer.persistence");
      Product = #include("Product.persistence");
      Order = #include("Order.persistence");
      OrderItem = #include("OrderItem.persistence");
   }
}
```

Listing 12.19: Definition of the OnlineShop GenericPersistence,
Shop.persistence

```
{
   Type ={
      Name = "OnlineShop" ;
      Class = "de.webapp.Framework.SMICommandListener.SMIPersistenceGeneric";
      Entity = "OnlineShop";
      EntityAlias = "t0" ;
      Attributes = (
         "ObjectIdentifier",
         "ObjectVersion",
         { Name = "Number" ; Generic = "YES" ; Key = "YES" ;},
         { Name = "Name" ; Generic = "YES" ; },
         { Name = "Description" ; Generic = "YES" ; },
         { Name = "Keeper" ; Generic = "YES" ; },
         { Name = "KeeperEMail" ; Generic = "YES" ; },
         { Name = "InfoURL" ; Generic = "YES" ; },
         { Name = "OrderEMail" ; Generic = "YES" ; },
      ) ;
      Associations = (
      { Name = "Product" ; Type = "ToMany" ; Generic = "YES" ;
         Modified = "YES" ;
         ResultType = "OnlineProduct" ; Key = "ShopID" ;
```

```
              QualifierExtension = " ORDER BY t0.Number " ; },
          { Name = "Customer" ; Type = "ToMany" ; Generic = "YES" ;
            Modified = "YES" ;
                ResultType = "OnlineCustomer" ; Key = "ShopID" ; },
        ) ;
        } ;
    }
```

Listing 12.20: Definition of OnlineProduct in Product.persistence

```
    {
        Type = {
          Name = "OnlineProduct" ;
          Class = "de.webapp.Framework.SMICommandListener.SMIPersistenceGeneric";
          Entity = "OnlineProduct";
          EntityAlias = "t0" ;
          Attributes =
          (
            "ObjectIdentifier",
            "ObjectVersion",
            { Name = "Number" ; Generic = "YES" ; },
            { Name = "Keywords", Generic = "YES" ; },
            { Name = "Description" ; Generic = "YES" ; },
            { Name = "SalesQty" ; Generic = "YES" ;
              TypeClass = "java.lang.Integer" ; },
            { Name = "SalesPrice" ; Generic = "YES" ;
              TypeClass = "java.math.BigDecimal" ; },
            { Name = "InfoURL" ; Generic = "YES" ; },
            { Name = "PictureURL" ; Generic = "YES" ; },
            { Name = "ShopID" ; Generic = "YES" ; }
          ) ;
          Associations = (
          { Name = "Shop" ; Type = "ToOne" ; Generic = "YES" ;
            ResultType = "OnlineShop" ;
          }
        ) ;
        } ;
    }
```

Listing 12.21: Definition of OnlineCustomer in Customer.persistence

```
    {
        Type = {
          Name = "OnlineCustomer" ;
          Class = "de.webapp.Framework.SMICommandListener.SMIPersistenceGeneric";
          Entity = "OnlineCustomer";
          EntityAlias = "t0" ;
```

```
    Attributes = (
      "ObjectIdentifier",
      "ObjectVersion",
      { Name = "Name" ; Generic = "YES" ; },
      { Name = "EMail" ; Generic = "YES" ; },
      { Name = "Password" ; Generic = "YES" ; },
      { Name = "PostCode" ; Generic = "YES" ; },
      { Name = "Town" ; Generic = "YES" ; },
      { Name = "Street" ; Generic = "YES" ;},
      { Name = "BankSortCode" ; Generic = "YES" ; },
      { Name = "Bank" ; Generic = "YES" ; },
      { Name = "AccountNumber" ; Generic = "YES" ; },
      { Name = "ShopID" ; Generic = "YES" ; }
    ) ;
    Associations = (
    { Name = "order" ; Type = "ToMany" ; Generic = "YES" ;
      Modified = "YES" ;
      ResultType = "OnlineOrder" ; Key = "CustomerID" ;
      QualifierExtension = " ORDER BY t0.OrderDate DESC" ; },
    { Name = "Shop" ; Type = "ToOne" ; Generic = "YES" ;
      ResultType = "OnlineShop" ; }
  ) ;
  } ;
}
```

Listing 12.22: Definition of OnlineOrder in Order.persistence

```
{
  Type =
  {
    Name = "OnlineOrder" ;
    Class = "de.webapp.Framework.SMICommandListener.SMIPersistenceGeneric";
    Entity = "OnlineOrder";
    EntityAlias = "t0" ;
    Attributes = (
      "ObjectIdentifier",
      "ObjectVersion",
      { Name = "OrderDate" ; Generic = "YES" ;
        TypeClass = "java.sql.Timestamp" ; },
      { Name = "ByLastName" ; Generic = "YES" ;
        TypeClass = "java.lang.Integer" ; },
      { Name = "BankSortCode" ; Generic = "YES" ; },
      { Name = "Bank" ; Generic = "YES" ;},
      { Name = "AccountNumber" ; Generic = "YES" ; },
      { Name = "PostCode" ; Generic = "YES" ; },
      { Name = "Town" ; Generic = "YES" ; },
```

```
            { Name = "Street" ; Generic = "YES" ; },
            { Name = "Note" ; Generic = "YES" ; },
            { Name = "CustomerID" ; Generic = "YES" ; }
            { Name = "ShopID" ; Generic = "YES" ; },
         ) ;
         Associations = (
         { Name = "OrderItem" ; Type = "ToMany" ; Generic = "YES" ;
           Modified = "YES" ;
           ResultType = "OnlineOrderItem" ; Key = "OrderID" ;},
         { Name = "Customer" ; Type = "ToOne" ; Generic = "YES" ;
           ResultType = "OnlineCustomer" ; },
         { Name = "Shop" ; Type = "ToOne" ; Generic = "YES" ;
         ResultType = "OnlineShop" ;}
         ) ;
      } ;
   }
```

Listing 12.23: Definition of OnlineOrderItem in OrderItem.persistence

```
   {
     Type = {
       Name = "OnlineOrderItem" ;
       Class = "de.webapp.Framework.SMICommandListener.SMIPersistenceGeneric";
       Entity = "OnlineOrderItem";
       EntityAlias = "t0" ;
       Attributes = (
          "ObjectIdentifier",
          "ObjectVersion",
          { Name = "Quantity" ; Generic = "YES" ;
            TypeClass = "java.lang.Integer" ;},
          { Name = "Amount" ; Generic = "YES" ;
            TypeClass = "java.math.BigDecimal" ; },
          { Name = "ProductID" ; Generic = "YES" ; },
          { Name = "OrderID" ; Generic = "YES" ; }
        ) ;
     Associations = (
         { Name = "Product" ; Type = "ToOne" ; Generic = "YES" ;
           ResultType = "OnlineProduct" ; },
         { Name = "order" ; Type = "ToOne" ; Generic = "YES" ;
           ResultType = "OnlineOrder" ; }
        ) ;
      } ;
   }
```

## 12.4.2 SMI configuration

Now we have to create the SMI definition file. The content of this file defines which commands will be directed to particular methods, or listeners. In addition, we can define additional standard parameters for each command.

To begin, we set the default command and standard parameters that apply to all commands, and define the listeners with their name and class. These are followed by the command definitions.

Listing 12.24: OnlineShop SMI definition file, `OnlineShop.smi`

```
{
   DefaultCommand = "display";
   Values = {
     _FollowUpCommand = "display";
     _TemplateName = "index.html";
   }
   Listener = {
     OnlineShopBean = {
       Class = "de.webapp.OnlineShop.OnlineShopBean" ;
     },
     OnlineShopProductBean = {
       Class = "de.webapp.OnlineShop.OnlineShopProductBean" ;
     },
     OnlineShopOrderBean = {
       Class = "de.webapp.OnlineShop.OnlineShopOrderBean" ;
     },
     OnlineShopCustomerBean = {
       Class = "de.webapp.OnlineShop.OnlineShopCustomerBean" ;
     },
     displayBean = {
       Class = "de.webapp.Framework.SMICommandListener.DisplayBean";
     }
   };
   Commands = {
     // display
     display = {
       MethodName = "display";
       Listener = "DisplayBean" ;
     } ;
     // Display the Shop
     // Open Frame and display menu and shop information.
```

```
startShop = {
  MethodName = "display";
  Listener = "DisplayBean" ;
  Values = {
    _TemplateName = "index.html" ;
  } ;
} ;
// Display menu.
showMenu= {
  MethodName = "display";
  Listener = "DisplayBean" ;
  Values = {
    _TemplateName = "Menu/Overview.html" ;
  } ;
} ;
// Display Shop information.
showShop= {
  MethodName = "executeContextFollowUp";
  Listener = "OnlineShopBean" ;
  Values = {
    _TemplateName = "ShowShop.jsp" ;
  } ;
} ;
// Display the product catalogue.
showProducts= {
  MethodName = "showProducts";
  Listener = "OnlineShopProductBean" ;
  Values = {
    _TemplateName = "ShowProduct.jsp" ;
  } ;
} ;
// Order
// Accept new order in shopping basket.
newOrder= {
  MethodName = "newOrder";
  Listener = "OnlineShopOrderBean" ;
  Values = {
    _TemplateName = "orderOneProduct.html" ;
  } ;
} ;
// Display current order.
showOrder= {
  MethodName = "executeContextFollowUp";
  Listener = "OnlineShopOrderBean" ;
  Values = {
    _TemplateName = "ShowOrder.jsp" ;
```

```
    } ;
  } ;
  // Change order item.
  changeOrder= {
    MethodName = "changeOrder";
    Listener = "OnlineShopOrderBean" ;
    Values = {
      _TemplateName = "ShowOrder.jsp" ;
    } ;
  } ;
  // Accept order in the Shop.
  sendOrder= {
    MethodName = "sendOrder";
    Listener = "OnlineShopOrderBean" ;
    Values = {
      _TemplateName = "sendOrder.html" ;
    } ;
  } ;
  // Customer's commands
  // Display customer information.
  showCustomer= {
    MethodName = "executeContextFollowUp";
    Listener = "OnlineShopCustomerBean" ;

    Values = {
      _TemplateName = "ShowCustomer.jsp" ;
    } ;
  } ;
  // Change customer.
  changeCustomer= {
    MethodName = "changeCustomer";
    Listener = "OnlineShopCustomerBean" ;
    Values = {
      _TemplateName = "index.html" ;
    } ;
  } ;
  // Display customer's login.
  loginCustomer= {
    MethodName = "display";
    Listener = "DisplayBean" ;
    Values = {
      _TemplateName = "loginCustomer.html" ;
    } ;
  } ;
  // Customer logon.
  setCustomer= {
```

```
                    MethodName = "setCustomer";
                    Listener = "OnlineShopCustomerBean" ;
                    Values = {
                       _TemplateName = "ShowShop.jsp" ;
                    } ;
                 } ;
                 // Customer logoff.
                 logoutCustomer= {
                    MethodName = "refreshShop";
                    Listener = "OnlineShopBean" ;
                    Values = {
                       _TemplateName = "index.html" ;
                    } ;
                 };
              }
           }
```

When the application starts, the store and the shop will be entered in the context for the OnlineShop. To do that, we use the `OnlineShopContext` class. In the `OnlineShop.con` file (Listing 12.25) you can find the necessary definition for the `SMIContextManager` (Chapter 8).

Listing 12.25: `OnlineShop.con` configuration file for the `OnlineShopContext`

```
   {
      Class = "de.webapp.OnlineShop.OnlineShopContext";
      Values = {
         _Storename = "OnlineShop.store";
         _Shopnumber = "1";
         _PageSize = "3";
      }
   }
```

The last definition, the registration at the servlet engine, is still missing. The entry for jo! is described in Listing 12.26.

Listing 12.26: `OnlineShop` entry in jo!'s `servlets.properties` file

```
   # OnlineShop
   servlet.OnlineShop.code=de.webapp.OnlineShop.OnlineShopServlet
   servlet.OnlineShop.initArgs=EventSwitch=OnlineShop,Context=OnlineShop
   servlet.OnlineShop.aliases=/OnlineShop/OnlineShop
```

The OnlineShop should be ready for use after jo! starts using the URL `http://<hostname>: <port>/OnlineShop/OnlineShop`.

In our last example we shall develop a simple web-based Chat room. In this case we also need to define the requirements and procedures. The ways in which the Chat application can be used show what we think Chat should be like (Fig. 13.1). A Chat user should be able to carry out the following functions:

- register him or herself, in order to protect his or her name;
- enter and then leave the Chat-room;
- send messages to selected participants;

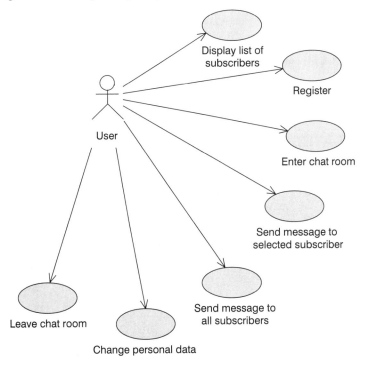

**Figure 13.1** Ways in which the Chat application can be used

- send messages to all participants;
- change personal data (name, password and send colour).

A special feature of this Chat room is that the user need only have access to a browser that is capable of handling frames and Javascript. Java in the form of an applet on the client's system is not necessary.

In order to keep the example simple we are only going to open one chat room now.

## 13.1 Control flow

After starting Chat we first have to display a login dialogue. Here the user can choose whether to log in or to register (Fig. 13.2). To provide the user with information, there is a display listing the people who are currently in the Chat room.

If the user decides to register first, he or she will see a dialogue in which his or her name, password and a send colour must be entered. If the selected name is already taken, or there is another error, an error message will be shown. If the registration is successful, then the user will see a menu dialogue that allows him or her to enter the room, log off, or change the user data. The same dialogue is seen after logging in. Here, a current list of the Chat participants is shown.

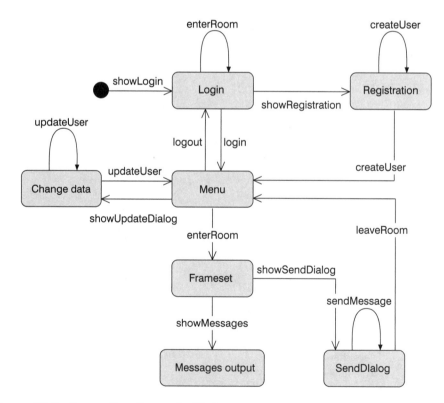

**Figure 13.2** Process flow diagram for Chat

When the user enters the room, the system opens a frameset with two frames. The right-hand frame shows the messages that have been sent. The left-hand frame contains a send dialogue with an entry field, a dropdown list where the user can choose colours, a user list with checkboxes and a `Send` button. In addition, there is also a note in the dialogue which tells the user how to leave the room.

When the user sends a message, the system displays the message in the right-hand frame of all the users whose checkboxes have been ticked by the user who has sent the message. The message will be printed in the colour selected by the user who has sent the message.

Once the user has left the Chat room, he or she will see the menu dialogue. If he or she selects the `Change Data` function, a dialogue is accessed that is similar to a registration dialogue. After successfully changing the data, the user returns to the menu dialogue. From here, he or she can be logged out. Finally, the login dialogue is shown again.

The required commands are listed, in detail, in Table 13.1.

As you were carefully reading through the command descriptions, you probably noticed that we know two types of login. To be able to participate in the Chat at all, users have to authenticate themselves. That means that they have to enter their name and password. If the password is correct, a user has identified him- or herself correctly. That does not mean that the user has entered the Chat room, and participation in Chat is possible only when the Chat room has been entered. Correspondingly, if the user leaves the Chat room, this does not lead to the deletion of his or her authentication. Only actual logout leads to the deletion of authentication.

We differentiate between the two types of login for two different reasons. First, logging in and out is an often-required mechanism, so it is worth while to implement it here, as an example. Second, by separating login from entry to the room, we provide ourselves with a way of attaching additional rooms relatively easily.

## 13.2  Class design

Before we move on to coding, we have to establish which objects are involved in the Chat. It is obvious that the user is there – he or she will be represented by a `User` object that can be stored in a store. In addition we need some objects for controlling the Chat. It seems to make sense to encapsulate the Chat process control (login, logout and authentication) in the `ChatRoom` bean. We also need the `ChatDispatcher` bean, to provide the message-sending mechanism, and the functions for creating and changing the user objects that are provided by the `ChatRegistration` bean. Figure 13.3 shows the Chat classes diagram. The individual classes are presented below.

### 13.2.1  Interface for constants

As we have already discussed in the previous two chapters, Chat also uses an interface for defining the constants. As these are needed in all the following classes, we have already listed the `C_Chat` interface here (Listing 13.1), although some constants will only be explained later.

**Table 13.1**  Description of the commands used in Chat

| Command | Parameter | Meaning |
| --- | --- | --- |
| showLogin | – | A log-in dialogue is shown. The commands whch can be run are enterRoom and showRegistration. |
| showRegistration | – | Shows a dialogue where the user enters personal data. The possible follow-up command is createUser. |
| createUser | Personal data (name, password, send colour) | Creates a user. If an error arises, it is displayed, and the user can enter the data again. If there is no error, the menu dialogue is displayed. The user is now authenticated. Possible commands are showUpdateDialogue, logout and enterRoom. |
| login | Name and password | Authenticates the user. If the name and password match, and if they correspond to a user object, the menu dialogue will be shown accordingly. If that is not the case, an error message is displayed, and the user can re-enter his or her name and password. |
| enterRoom | – | Registers the user in the room. Following that, a frameset is called which opens two frames. The left-hand frame can be accessed with the showSendDialogue command, and the right-hand frame with the showMessages command. |
| showMessages | – | Shows the messages for the user. |
| showSendDialogue | – | Shows a form for sending a message. From this dialogue you can call up the sendMessage and leaveRoom commands. |
| sendMessage | User to whom the last message was sent | Shows the send form as described in showSendDialogue. In addition, there is a cross in the checkbox of the user to whom the last message was sent. Possible follow-up commands are the same as in showSendDialogue. |
| showUpdateDialogue | – | Shows a dialogue for changing the user data. updateUser is the only command that can be run from this dialogue. |
| updateUser | Personal data (name, password, send colour) | Used to change user data. If an error occurs, the entry dialogue will be shown again and the user can enter the data again. If there is no error, then the menu dialogue will be shown. |
| leaveRoom | – | Deletes the registration of the user in the room and leads back to the menu dialogue. Possible actions there are showUpdateDialogue, logout and enterRoom. |
| logout | – | Allows the authentication to expire and leads to the login dialogue. |

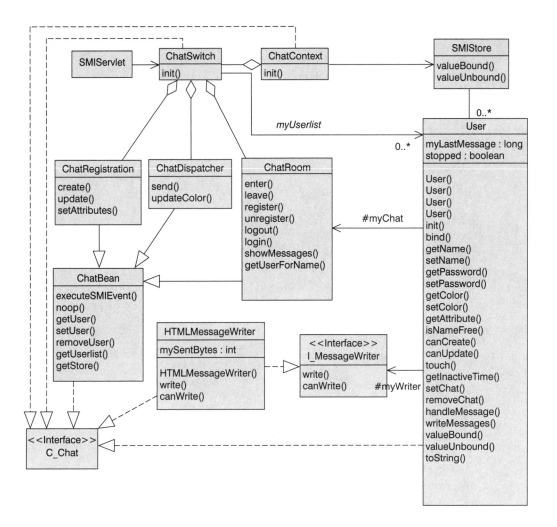

**Figure 13.3** Chat's classes diagram: inherited relationships, the `DisplayBean` and the `HttpSessionBindingListener` and `I_SMIContextBindingListener` interfaces have been omitted

Listing 13.1: The C_Chat interface

```
package de.webapp.Chat ;

public interface C_Chat {

/** Constant for the user */
public static final String C_User = "_User";
/** Constant for the Store */
public static final String C_Store = "_Store";
/** Constant for the StoreName */
```

```java
        public static final String C_StoreName = "_StoreName";
        /** Constant for the DefaultStoreName */
        public static final String C_DefaultStoreName = "Chat.store";
        /** Constant for the user list */
        public static final String C_Userlist = "_Userlist";
        /** Constant for the user name */
        public static final String C_Username = "_Username";
        /** Constant for the password */
        public static final String C_Password = "_Password";
        /** Constant for the password */
        public static final String C_Password2 = "_Password2";
        /** Constant for the colour */
        public static final String C_Color = "_Color";
        /** Constant for the recipient */
        public static final String C_To = "_To";
        /** Constant for the message */
        public static final String C_Message = "_Message";
        /** Constant for "to all" */
        public static final String C_All = "_All";
        /** Parameter for follow-up command */
        public static final String C_FollowUpCommand = "_FollowUpCommand";
        /** Parameter for template for JSP and HTML display */
        public static final String C_Template = "_TemplateName";
        /** Parameter for error messages */
        public static final String C_ErrorMessage = "_ErrorMessage";

        /** Maximum number of bytes that an HTMLMessageWriter
           is permitted to write */
        public static final int C_MaxBytes = 4096;
        /** Maximum length of time before a user is automatically logged off */
        public static final long C_MaxInactiveTime = 1000 * 60 * 15;

        /** colour constants */
        public static final String C_Colors[] = new String[] {
           "#000000", "#ff0000", "#0000ff",
           "#ffff00", "#008080", "#800000",
           "#ff00ff"
        };
        public static final String C_ColorNames[] = new String[] {
           "black", "red", "blue",
           "yellow", "teal", "maroon",
           "fuchsia"
        };

        } // End of the interface
```

## 13.2.2 ChatContext

All beans need to access certain resources. The primary one is the Store, where the user objects are stored. Although we want to develop only one Chat room with just one I_SMIEventSwitch, it makes sense to store the Store in the I_SMIContext. If we later extend Chat by adding more rooms, each with its own I_SMIEventSwitch, these can share the Store. The Store should be opened for the initialization of the I_SMIContext and then closed again when the I_SMIContext is released. To achieve this, we have to do two things. First, we write a class called ChatContext (Listing 13.2) that inherits from SMIContext. It uses its init() method to open the Store and stores it with the key C_Store. Secondly we use an SMIStore from the de.webapp.Framework.SMICommandListener package. If such a store is unbound from an HttpSession, an I_SMIEventSwitch or an I_SMIContext, it will be closed automatically.

Listing 13.2: The ChatContext class

```
package de.webapp.Chat ;

import de.webapp.Framework.ConfigManager.*;
import de.webapp.Framework.SMI.*;
import de.webapp.Framework.StoreFactory.StoreFactory;
import de.webapp.Framework.Persistence.*;
import java.util.Hashtable;

public class ChatContext extends SMIContext implements C_Chat {

/** Open Chat's Store */
public void init(String aContextName,
  Hashtable aValues) throws SMIException {
  super.init(aContextName, aValues);
  // Read Store name
  String theStorename = (String)getValue(C_StoreName);
  // If necessary, use default store name instead
  if(theStorename == null) {
    theStorename = C_DefaultStoreName;
  }
  I_Store theStore = null;
  // Open the Store
  try {
    Configuration theStoreConfig =
      ConfigManager.getConfigManager().getConfiguration(
        aContextName, theStorename, true);
    theStore = StoreFactory.getInstance(theStoreConfig);
  }
  catch (PersistenceException pe) {
    throw new SMIException(pe);
  }
```

```
        // Store the Store as a value in this context
        // with the key C_Store
        putValue(C_Store, theStore);
    }
} // End of the class
```

### 13.2.3 ChatSwitch

Now we have explained how the store is managed, we turn to the users. So we can manage the participants of a Chat, it is necessary to have a list with all the users of the room. This list should be available to all this chat room's I_SMICommandListeners, and is therefore appended to the I_SMIEventSwitch. Similarly to ChatContext, ChatSwitch (Listing 13.3) inherits the init() method from SMIEventSwitch and overwrites it. The user list, a simple hash table, is saved with the key C_Userlist.

Listing 13.3: The ChatSwitch class

```
    package de.webapp.Chat ;

    import de.webapp.Framework.SMI.* ;
    import java.util.Hashtable;
    public class ChatSwitch extends SMIEventSwitch implements C_Chat {

    /** Adds a user list to the switch. */
    public void init(String aSwitchName, I_SMIContext aSMIContext)
        throws SMIException {
        super.init(aSwitchName, aSMIContext);
        putValue(C_Userlist, new Hashtable());
    }
    } // End of the class
```

### 13.2.4 ChatBean

So we can access the user list and the storage easily from our I_SMICommandListener, which we still have not written, we write a class called ChatBean which contains the appropriate methods. In addition, the management of the user object is encapsulated in ChatBean, while the executeSMIEvent() method is overwritten, in order to set the user list as a default value in the SMICommand and so that the follow-up commands can be run automatically. For reasons of performance, we have decided against synchronizing each call to a command with the store object. Instead, we only synchronize the actual manipulations and the reading of data. The consequence of this solution is that the user objects can be changed after they have been read or manipulated and before other threads are output. For our Chat, such behaviour is still acceptable, as it cannot create an inconsistent status for the store.

We still need to explain how the user authentication takes place. Each user is represented via a user object. As long as he or she is also logged in, the user object must be assigned to a certain area. Therefore, the user object must be saved in the HttpSession. We use the setUser() method to do this. In order to obtain the object again, we use getUser(). To remove it from the session we use removeUser(). In all three cases, we use the constant C_User as a key to the HttpSession.

It is also worth mentioning the noop() method. It will be required when the functionality coded in executeSMIEvent() is enough for a command. That is the case, for example, when we want to display the user list.

Listing 13.4: The ChatBean class

```
package de.webapp.Chat;

import java.util.Hashtable;
import de.webapp.Framework.SMI.*;
import de.webapp.Framework.Persistence.*;

/** Base class for subsequent ChatBeans */
public class ChatBean extends SMICommandListener implements C_Chat {
/** Set the user list and run follow-up command */
public void executeSMIEvent(SMIEvent aSMIEvent) {
   SMICommand aSMICommand = (SMICommand)aSMIEvent;
   // Set user list
   aSMICommand.putValue(C_Userlist, getUserlist());
   // Run command
   super.executeSMIEvent(aSMICommand);
   // If required, run follow-up command
   String theFollowUpCommand =
      (String)aSMICommand.getValue(C_FollowUpCommand);
   if (theFollowUpCommand != null) {
      aSMICommand.setCommand(theFollowUpCommand);
      aSMICommand.removeValue(C_FollowUpCommand);
      getSMIEventSwitch().executeSMIEvent(aSMICommand);
   }
}
/** Empty method, used if executeSMIEvent() is good enough */
public void noop(SMICommand aSMICommand) {}
/** Returns the user object from the session */
protected User getUser(SMICommand aSMICommand) {
   return (User)aSMICommand.getSessionValue(C_User);
}
/** Stores a user object in the session */
protected void setUser(SMICommand aSMICommand, User aUser) {
   aSMICommand.putSessionValue(C_User, aUser);
}
/** Removes a user object from the session */
protected void removeUser(SMICommand aSMICommand) {
   aSMICommand.removeSessionValue(C_User);
```

```
    }
    /** Returns the switch's user list */
    protected Hashtable getUserlist() {
        return (Hashtable)getSMIEventSwitch().getValue(C_Userlist);
    }
    /** Returns the I_SMIContext's Store */
    protected I_Store getStore() {
        return (I_Store)getSMIEventSwitch().getSMIContext().getValue(C_Store);
    }
} // End of the class
```

## 13.2.5  Messages

In a Chat, everything depends on sending messages. We want to store these messages as objects, and to reproduce them via the Message class. Each Message knows a sender and a message text (Listing 13.5).

Listing 13.5: The Message class

```
package de.webapp.Chat ;
/** Encapsulates a message */
public class Message {

protected User myFrom;
protected String myText;

/** Constructor */
public Message(User aFrom, String aText) {
    myFrom = aFrom;
    myText = aText;
}
/** Returns the sender */
public User getFrom() {
    return myFrom;
}
/** Returns the message text */
public String getText() {
    return myText;
}
} // End of the class
```

## 13.2.6  User object

Now we have created an infrastructure with ChatContext, ChatSwitch, ChatBean and Message, we still need the User object (Listing 13.8) before we can begin coding I_SMICommandListener.

As the objects of the User class should be stored in a Store, User must implement the I_Persistence interface. Obviously, we do not re-implement I_Persistence, but derive User from Persistence. To obtain a functioning persistent object, we must code the relevant constructors, the bind() method and the access method to the attributes.

Before that, we have to define which attributes User should have. So far we have determined that it should have the attributes name, password and send colour. The corresponding methods are called getName(), setName(String), getPassword(), setPassword(String), getColor() and setColor(Integer). The colours are defined in C_Chat (Listing 13.1).

Whenever we manipulate a persistent attribute, we call up the setModified() method (from Persistence), in order to mark the change of status (Section 9.4.3). In addition, the canCreate() and canUpdate() methods are also important for the persistence to function correctly. In User you make sure that no two different users have the same name.

Besides managing its persistent attributes, each User object also knows further methods for receiving and writing Messages. As our client is a browser, this procedure is not easy to carry out.

In order to be able to write continually in a browser window, the connection has to be kept open. It should not remain so forever, as otherwise the client's storage will overflow. Therefore, once a certain number of characters and messages have been written, writing must stop and a new connection must be established. This procedure ensures that the client can remove old messages from memory.

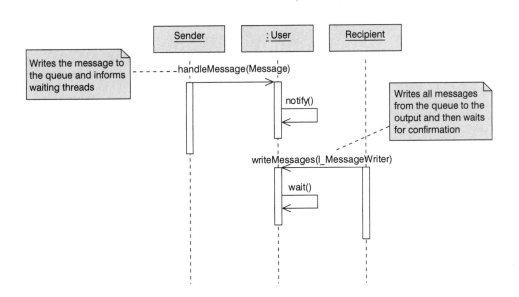

**Figure 13.4** Chat's asynchronous message delivery

Between closing the old connections and opening the new connections, there is a gap in the connection during which no messages can be written. As we do not want to lose any messages, an asynchronous writing mechanism is used (Fig. 13.4).

First `handleMessage(Message)` is used to write messages for a user to the message queue, `myMessageQueue`. Then, if a write thread is waiting in the `writeMessages()` method, it is notified via notify(), and writes the contents of the queue into the user's message frame. If there is no write thread available, nothing happens. If there is one handy, which is to be found in a connection gap, the thread will be allowed to leave the `writeMessages(I_MessageWriter)` method. This way you can create room for a new write thread.

Therefore, the `User` object basically works as a FIFO (first in, first out) buffer into which a thread `inserts` a message via `handleMessage()` and from which another thread removes the messages present there at any time.

As we can already see from the signature of the `writeMessages (I_MessageWriter)` method, you use an `I_MessageWriter` (Listing 13.6) for writing messages. Listing 13.7 shows an implementation of the writer for HTML.

Listing 13.6: The `I_MessageWriter` interface

```
package de.webapp.Chat;

import java.io.IOException;

/** Defines a message writer */
public interface I_MessageWriter {
/** Writes a message */
public void write(Message aMessage) throws IOException;
/** Shows if this I_MessageWriter can still write */
public boolean canWrite();
} // End of the interface
```

Listing 13.7: The `HTMLMessageWriter` class

```
package de.webapp.Chat;

import java.io.*;

public class HTMLMessageWriter implements I_MessageWriter, C_Chat {

public HTMLMessageWriter(Writer aWriter) {
   myWriter = aWriter;
}

protected int mySentBytes;
protected Writer myWriter;

/** Writes a message with the current writer. */
public void write(Message aMessage) throws IOException {
   StringBuffer theOutput = new StringBuffer();
   theOutput.append(aMessage.getFrom().getName());
```

```
      theOutput.append(": <font color=\""
         + C_Colors[aMessage.getFrom().getColor().intValue()]+ "\">");
      theOutput.append(aMessage.getText());
      theOutput.append("</font><p>");
      myWriter.write(theOutput.toString());
      myWriter.flush();
      mySentBytes += theOutput.length();
   }
   /** Checks if the writer can still write. */
   public boolean canWrite() {
      if (myWriter instanceof PrintWriter) {
         ((PrintWriter)myWriter).println();
         return (!((PrintWriter)myWriter).checkError() && mySentBytes <
   C_MaxBytes);
      }
      try {
         myWriter.flush();
      }
      catch (IOException ioe) {
         return false;
      }
      return true;
   }
} // End of the class
```

Finally, we have to consider the relationship of the User object to Chat. As the user is connected to the HttpSession, he or she will automatically be logged out after a certain period of inactivity. Otherwise, he or she can log him- or herself out. That means that the User object and Chat must refer to each other. Therefore, User can use the setChat(ChatRoom) and removeChat() methods to set and remove the association. The counterparts in the ChatRoom are called register(User) and unregister(User) – but more about that later (Section 13.2.9).

We still need to consider what happens when the user is automatically removed from the HttpSession. As User implements the javax.servlet.http. HttpSessionBindingListener interface, it can use the valueBound() and valueUnbound() methods. The User object is therefore notified when it is connected to the HttpSession or when it is disconnected from it. As a result, it is possible for the User object to call up the Chat room unregister(User) method automatically, when it is removed from the session.

We can even take advantage of the mechanism for reference numbers (Section 9.4.3). If the object is connected, we call retain() and increase the internal reference numbers. When disconnecting the object, we call up release().

Listing 13.8: The User class

```
package de.webapp.Chat;

import java.util.*;
import java.io.*;
import java.sql.*;
import javax.servlet.http.*;
import de.webapp.Framework.Persistence.*;
import de.webapp.Framework.Log.*;

/** Chat user */
public class User extends Persistence
    implements C_Chat, HttpSessionBindingListener {
/** User's name */
protected String myName;
/** User's password */
protected String myPassword;
/** User's Send colour */
protected Integer myColor;

/** ChatRoom in which the user is located */
protected transient ChatRoom myChat;
/** Message queue */
protected transient Vector myMessageQueue;
/** Time point at which the last message was sent */
protected transient long myLastMessage;
/** Shows if the asynchronous writing of the message has been stopped */
protected transient boolean stopped;
/** Current I_MessageWriter users */
protected transient I_MessageWriter myWriter;

/** Protected constructor */
protected User() {}
/** Constructor with Peer */
public User(I_PersistencePeer aPeer) throws PersistenceException {
    super(aPeer);
    init();
}
/** Constructor with Peer and ResultSet */
public User(I_PersistencePeer aPeer, ResultSet rs)
        throws PersistenceException {
    super(aPeer, rs);
    init();
}
/** Constructor with Peer, ResultSet and ObjectIdentifier (for MS-Access)
*/
public User(I_PersistencePeer aPeer, ResultSet rs,
```

```
      String aObjectIdentifier)
         throws PersistenceException {
      this(aPeer);
      this.bind(rs, aObjectIdentifier);
   }
   /** Initialization */
   protected void init() {
      myMessageQueue = new Vector();
      myChat = null;
      myWriter = null;
      stopped = false;
   }
   /** Bind a Result Set */
   public int bind(ResultSet rs, int offset)
         throws PersistenceException, SQLException {
      offset = super.bind(rs, offset);
      myName = (String)rs.getObject(++offset);
      myPassword = (String)rs.getObject(++offset);
      myColor = (Integer)rs.getObject(++offset);
      return offset;
   }
   /** Return the name */
   public String getName() {
      return myName;
   }
   /** Set the name */
   public void setName(String aName) {
      myName = aName;
      // Change of status!
      setModified();
   }
   /** Returns the password*/
   public String getPassword() {
      return myPassword;
   }
   /** Set the password */
   public void setPassword(String aPassword) {
      myPassword = aPassword;
      // Change of status!
      setModified() ;
   }
   /** Returns the colour */
   public Integer getColor() {
      return myColor;
   }
   /** Set the colour */
```

```java
    public void setColor(Integer aColor) {
      myColor = aColor;
      setModified() ;
    }
    /** Checks if a user object can be created */
    public boolean canCreate() throws PersistenceException {
      return isNameFree();
    }
    /** Checks if a user object can be changed persistently */
    public boolean canUpdate() throws PersistenceException {
      return isNameFree();
    }
    /** Shows if a name has already been used by another Object */
    protected boolean isNameFree() throws PersistenceException {
      I_Persistence sameName =
        getPeer().getRetriever().retrieve(getAttribute("Name"), myName);
      return (sameName == null || sameName == this);
    }
    /** Help method for obtaining a PersistenceAttribute object
    protected PersistenceAttribute getAttribute(String aAttributeName) {
      return getPeer().getType().getAttributeWithName(aAttributeName);
    }
    /** Gives the user object with a time stamp */
    public void touch() {
      myLastMessage = System.currentTimeMillis();
    }
    /** Reports the time that has passed since
       touch() was last called */
    public long getInactiveTime() {
      return (System.currentTimeMillis()-myLastMessage);
    }
    /** Set the ChatRoom for this user.
       Corresponds to entering the Chat */
    public void setChat(ChatRoom aChat) {
      stopped = false;
      myChat = aChat;
      touch();
    }
    /** Removes the association to Chat. Corresponds to leaving the Chat */
    public void removeChat() {
      myChat = null;
      // Stop asynchronous writing of the message
      stopped = true;
      synchronized (this) {
        // notify waiting write thread
        notify();
```

```
    }
  }
/** Writes a message to the message queue and
    notifies a waiting thread */
public void handleMessage(Message aMessage) {
  myMessageQueue.addElement(aMessage);
  synchronized (this) {
    notify();
  }
}
/** Writes message with the assigned I_MessageWriter, until
    canWrite() returns false or stopped is true */
public synchronized void writeMessages(I_MessageWriter aWriter) {
  // waiting threads that can no longer write
  // (canWrite() == false) the opportunity to leave this method
  // and myWriter = set to null
  notify();
  // If a different writer is still able to function,
  // start an exception
  if (myWriter != null) throw new IllegalStateException();
  // Assign writer
  myWriter = aWriter;
  try {
    // Writing loop
    while(myWriter.canWrite() && !stopped) {
      // Write message queue until empty
      while (myMessageQueue.size() > 0 && myWriter.canWrite()
        && !stopped) {
        Message theMessage = (Message)myMessageQueue.elementAt(0);
        myWriter.write(theMessage);
        myMessageQueue.removeElementAt(0);
      }
      try {
        // Wake up at least every 10 seconds and test
        // if the writer is still working and that the asynchronous
        // writing has not been stopped yet.
        wait(10000);
      }
      catch (InterruptedException ie) {}
    }
  }
  catch (IOException ioe) {
    if (Log.isLog()) {
      Log.log(ioe);
    }
  }
```

```
      // Set writer to null
      myWriter = null;
   }
   /** When binding this object to the HttpSession, increase the reference
   counter */
   public void valueBound(HttpSessionBindingEvent e) {
      if (Log.isLog(C_Log.METHOD)) {
         Log.log("User " + getName()
            + " has been bound to the HttpSession.", C_Log.METHOD);
      }
      retain();
   }
   /** When unbinding this object from the HttpSession, reduce the reference
   counter, log off from Chat and delete the Chat association */
   public void valueUnbound(HttpSessionBindingEvent e) {
      if (Log.isLog(C_Log.METHOD)) {
         Log.log("User " + getName()
            + " has been unbound from the HttpSession.", C_Log.METHOD);
      }
      release();
      if (myChat != null) myChat.unregister(this);
      removeChat();
   }
} // End of the class
```

## 13.2.7  ChatDispatcher

As the first I_SMICommandListener, we are going to deal with the
ChatDispatcher (Listing 13.9). It should map a single command, the
sendMessage. ChatDispatcher, like other I_SMICommandListeners, inherits
from ChatBean. The sendMessage command will be implemented via the send
(SMICommand) method.

First the system checks whether the user wishing to send a message has logged in.
If not, the C_Template value will be set to "notLoggedIn" and the method cancels.
If the user is logged in, then the touch() method is called next, to mark that he or
she tried to send a message. Then the C_To, C_Message, C_All and C_Color
parameters are read from the SMICommand. In the case that the send colour of the
user has changed, the change will be stored persistently.

A Message is instantiated with the data acquired. To deliver it, the
handleMessage() methods of the users to whom the message is addressed are
called.

Listing 13.9: The ChatDispatcher class

```java
package de.webapp.Chat;

import java.util.*;
import java.io.*;

import de.webapp.Framework.SMI.*;
import de.webapp.Framework.Persistence.*;
import de.webapp.Framework.Log.*;

/** Takes responsibility for sending message */
public class ChatDispatcher extends ChatBean implements C_Chat {

/** Sends a message */
public void send(SMICommand aSMICommand) throws PersistenceException {
  // Is the user still logged on?
  User theUser = getUser(aSMICommand);
  if (theUser == null) {
    aSMICommand.putValue(C_Template,
      aSMICommand.getValue("userNotLoggedIn"));
    return;
  }
  // Set time stamp
  theUser.touch();
  // Read parameters from the request
  // theTo contains the ObjectIdentifier of the addressees (recipients)
  String[] theTo = aSMICommand.getRequest().getParameterValues(C_To);
  // theText contains the message
  String theText = (String)aSMICommand.getValue(C_Message);
  // If theToAll != is null, the message is to all recipients
  String theToAll = (String)aSMICommand.getValue(C_All);
  // theColor contains the colour as an integer
  Integer theColor = new Integer((String)aSMICommand.getValue(C_Color));
  if (!theColor.equals(theUser.getColor())) {
    // If required, store colour persistently
    updateColor(aSMICommand);
  }
  // Only send message if it also has addressees (recipients)
  if (theTo != null || theToAll != null) {
    Message theMessage = new Message(theUser, theText);
    if (theToAll==null) {
      // Deliver private messages individually
      // We should always have a copy for the sender
      theMessage.getFrom().handleMessage(theMessage);
      for (int i=0; i < theTo.length; i++) {
        User aUser = (User)getUserlist().get(theTo[i]);
        if (aUser != null && aUser != theMessage.getFrom())
```

```
                aUser.handleMessage(theMessage);
            }
        }
        else {
          // General method for all
          for (Enumeration e = getUserlist().elements();
            e.hasMoreElements();) {
            User aUser = (User)e.nextElement();
            if (aUser != null) aUser.handleMessage(theMessage);
          }
        }
      }
    }
    /** Saves the user object with new colour */
    protected void updateColor(SMICommand aSMICommand)
        throws PersistenceException {
      // Get Store
      I_Store theStore = getStore();
      User theUser = getUser(aSMICommand);
      synchronized(theStore) {
        theUser.setColor(
          new Integer((String)aSMICommand.getValue(C_Color)));
        try {
          theStore.begin();
          theUser.update();
          theStore.commit();
        }
        catch (Throwable t) {
          theStore.rollback();
          if (t instanceof PersistenceException) {
            throw (PersistenceException)t;
          }
          throw new SMIEventListenerException(t);
        }
      }
    }
  }
} // End of the class
```

## 13.2.8 ChatRegistration

The commands used for the manipulation of a user object, createUser and updateUser, should be implemented by the ChatRegistration class. The methods it uses to do so are called create() and update().

In create() you first use newPersistence() to access a blank user object from the Store. This blank user object is then supplied with attribute values via the setAttributes() help method. If everything goes well, create() is used to store the object in the database and setUser() used to store it in the HttpSession. If errors do occur, the entry mask will be reset as C_Template, and an error message will be stored under C_ErrorMessage.update() functions in exactly the same way. Here, however, the object will not be fetched from the store, but instead it is read from the session. Therefore, there is no need to store the object in the session.

Listing 13.10: The ChatRegistration class

```
package de.webapp.Chat;

import java.util.*;
import java.io.*;

import de.webapp.Framework.SMI.*;
import de.webapp.Framework.Persistence.*;
import de.webapp.Framework.Log.*;

/** Manipulating a user object */
public class ChatRegistration extends ChatBean implements C_Chat {
/** Creates a user object and stores it in the HttpSession */
public void create(SMICommand aSMICommand) throws PersistenceException {
  // Get Store.
  I_Store theStore = getStore();
  User theUser;
  // Query Store for new Persistence of type "User"
  theUser = (User)theStore.newPersistence("User");
  // Set attributes and output error message if necessary
  if (!setAttributes(aSMICommand, theUser)) {
    aSMICommand.putValue(C_ErrorMessage,
      "You have entered incorrect details! "
      + "Please try again.");
    aSMICommand.putValue(C_Template, aSMICommand.getValue("failure"));
    return;
  }
  // Save Store
  synchronized(theStore) {
    try {
      theStore.begin();
      theUser.create();
      theStore.commit();
      // Store user in the HttpSession -> ChatBean
      setUser(aSMICommand, theUser);
    }
    // If canCreate() returns false, a
    // PersistenceRuntimeException is initiated.
    // => Output error message.
    catch (PersistenceRuntimeException pre) {
```

```
                     theStore.rollback();
                     aSMICommand.putValue(C_ErrorMessage,
                        "The name you selected has been used already.");
                     aSMICommand.putValue(C_Template,
                        aSMICommand.getValue("failure"));
                  }
                  catch (Throwable t) {
                     theStore.rollback();
                     if (t instanceof PersistenceException) {
                        throw (PersistenceException)t;
                     }
                     throw new SMIEventListenerException(t);
                  }
               }
            }
         }
         /** Save changes to a user object in the database */
         public void update(SMICommand aSMICommand) throws PersistenceException {
            // Read user from the HttpSession
            User theUser = getUser(aSMICommand);
            // If no user is present, output error message
            if (theUser == null) {
               aSMICommand.putValue(C_Template,
                  aSMICommand.getValue("userNotLoggedIn"));
               return;
            }
            // Get Store.
            I_Store theStore = getStore();
            // Set attributes and output error message if necessary
            if (!setAttributes(aSMICommand, theUser)) {
               aSMICommand.putValue(C_ErrorMessage,
                  "You have entered incorrect details! "
                  + "Please try again.");
               aSMICommand.putValue(C_Template, aSMICommand.getValue("failure"));
               return;
            }
            // Save Store
            synchronized(theStore) {
               try {
                  theStore.begin();
                  theUser.update();
                  theStore.commit();
               }
               // If canUpdate() false returns, a
               // PersistenceRuntimeException is initiated.
               // => Output error message.
               catch (PersistenceRuntimeException pre) {
```

```
            theStore.rollback();
            aSMICommand.putValue(C_ErrorMessage,
               "The name you selected has been used already.");
            aSMICommand.putValue(C_Template,
               aSMICommand.getValue("failure"));
        }
        catch (Throwable t) {
            theStore.rollback();
            if (t instanceof PersistenceException) {
               throw (PersistenceException)t;
            }
            throw new SMIEventListenerException(t);
        }
    }
}
/** Sets the attributes of a Persistence and returns false,
    if the values do not make sense */
protected boolean setAttributes(SMICommand aSMICommand, User aUser) {
    // Read values from the command.
    String thePassword1 = (String)aSMICommand.getValue(C_Password);
    String thePassword2 = (String)aSMICommand.getValue(C_Password2);
    String theUsername = (String)aSMICommand.getValue(C_Username);
    Integer theColor = new Integer((String)aSMICommand.getValue(C_Color));
    // Check if they make sense
    if (thePassword1 == null
        || theUsername == null
        || !thePassword1.equals(thePassword2)) return false;
    if (thePassword1.length() == 0
        || theUsername.length() == 0) return false;
    // Set values
    aUser.setPassword(thePassword1);
    aUser.setName(theUsername);
    aUser.setColor(theColor);
    return true;
}
} // End of the class
```

## 13.2.9  ChatRoom

The ChatRoom (Listing 13.11) brings us to the last class we want to describe. It encapsulates all the functions used to manage the room, and it is responsible for authentication as well as for allowing users to enter or leave the room.

Let us begin with authentication. There are two kinds of authentication. The first is when the user registers, as we have already explained when discussing the ChatRegistration class. Alternatively, if the user is already registered, he or she enters his or her name and the password in the login dialogue, and sends the login command. When the command runs, the login(SMICommand) method is called. The first thing checked in that method is whether the user has already been authenticated. If so, the method immediately stops. If the user has not authenticated him- or herself yet, then the C_Username and C_Password parameters are read from the command. Finally, the getUserForName (String) help method is used to ask the store for a User object that matches the names entered. If there is no User registered with the name in the store, or if the password is invalid, then an error message is saved in C_ErrorMessage and the "errorOnLogin" value is set as C_Template. If there is no error, setUser() is used to save the requested user object in the HttpSession. The user is now authenticated.

If the user wants to enter the Chat room, he or she sends the enterRoom command. The command is mapped to the enter (SMICommand) method. In that method there is a check to see if the user has already been authenticated. If not, the value "userNotLoggedIn" is set as C_Template and return is used to leave the method. If an authenticated user exists, then the register(User) method is called. It attaches the User object to the Chat user list and uses setChat(ChatRoom) to associate the Users objects with the Chat. The ObjectIdentifier of the User object is used as a key to the user list.

When the user finds him- or herself in the room, he or she can read the messages in the right-hand frame. The showMessages command is responsible for this. It takes care of calling the method of the same name, showMessages (SMICommand). In that message there is a check to see whether the user has read, passively, for longer than the allowed time. If that is the case, he or she is logged out using logout (SMICommand). The user is no longer authenticated with the system and is no longer registered in the room.

The user can of course leave the room the normal way. To do this, he or she uses the leaveRoom command, which calls the leave (SMICommand) method. In it there is a call to the user's removeChat() method, as well as the unregister(User) method. unregister(User) removes the user from the user list.

The last method we need to explain is logout (SMICommand). As you might expect, it can be called by the logout command. It first calls the leave(SMICommand) method and then removes the user object via removeUser (SMICommand) from the HttpSession.

Listing 13.11: The ChatRoom class

```
package de.webapp.Chat;

import java.util.*;
import java.io.*;

import de.webapp.Framework.SMI.*;
import de.webapp.Framework.Persistence.*;
import de.webapp.Framework.Log.*;

/** Manages the ChatRoom */
public class ChatRoom extends ChatBean implements C_Chat {
```

```
/** Authenticates the user on the basis of name and password */
public void login(SMICommand aSMICommand) throws PersistenceException {
   User theUser = getUser(aSMICommand);
   // Test if the user has already authenticated him- or herself.
   if (theUser != null) {
      if (Log.isLog(C_Log.METHOD,
         getSMIEventSwitch().getSMIContext().getName())) {
         Log.log("User " + theUser.getName()
            + " is already authenticated.", C_Log.METHOD,
            getSMIEventSwitch().getSMIContext().getName());
      }
      return;
   }
   // Read name and password from the SMICommand
   String theName = (String)aSMICommand.getValue(C_Username);
   String thePassword = (String)aSMICommand.getValue(C_Password);
   // Get user from the Store
   theUser = getUserForName(theName);
   // Check if a suitable user object has been found
   if (theUser == null) {
      if (Log.isLog(C_Log.METHOD,
         getSMIEventSwitch().getSMIContext().getName())) {
         Log.log("User " + theName + " does not exist.",
            C_Log.METHOD, getSMIEventSwitch().getSMIContext().getName());
      }
      // Set error message
      aSMICommand.putValue(C_ErrorMessage,
         "No user with the name "
         + theName + " is registered. Please try again.");
      // Set template
      aSMICommand.putValue(C_Template,
         aSMICommand.getValue("errorOnLogin"));
      return;
   }
   // Check user's password.
   if (!(theUser.getPassword()).equals(thePassword)) {
      if (Log.isLog(C_Log.METHOD,
         getSMIEventSwitch().getSMIContext().getName())) {
         Log.log("User " + theName
            + " has entered the wrong password.", C_Log.METHOD,
            getSMIEventSwitch().getSMIContext().getName());
      }
      // Set error message
      aSMICommand.putValue(C_ErrorMessage,
         "Incorrect password. Please try again.");
      // Set template
```

```
          aSMICommand.putValue(C_Template,
             aSMICommand.getValue("errorOnLogin"));
          return;
      }
      // The user exists and has entered the right password.
      // So: store user object in the session.
      // The user is then generally authenticated
      setUser(aSMICommand, theUser);
  }
  /** Calls register(), if the user has authenticated him- or herself */
  public void enter(SMICommand aSMICommand) throws PersistenceException {
      User theUser = getUser(aSMICommand);
      if (theUser != null) {
          register(theUser);
          if (Log.isLog(C_Log.MODULE,
              getSMIEventSwitch().getSMIContext().getName())) {
              Log.log("User " + theUser.getName()
                  + " has entered the room.", C_Log.MODULE,
                  getSMIEventSwitch().getSMIContext().getName());
          }
      }
      else {
          aSMICommand.putValue(C_Template,
              aSMICommand.getValue("userNotLoggedIn"));
      }
  }
  /** This is called to leave the room */
  public void leave(SMICommand aSMICommand) {
      User theUser = getUser(aSMICommand);
      if (theUser != null) {
          // Delete user's association with
          // this chat
          theUser.removeChat();
          // Remove user from the user list
          unregister(theUser);
      }
  }
  /** Deletes the user's authentication*/
  public void logout(SMICommand aSMICommand) {
      leave(aSMICommand);
      removeUser(aSMICommand);
  }
  /** Enter user in the user list */
  public void register(User aUser) {
      // Just in case, check that the user is not already
      // participating in the Chat.
```

```
    if (!getUserlist().containsKey(aUser.getObjectIdentifier())) {
      // Tell the user which ChatRoom they are using.
      aUser.setChat(this);
      getUserlist().put(aUser.getObjectIdentifier(), aUser);
    }
}
/** Remove user from the room */
public void unregister(User aUser) {
    Hashtable theUserlist = getUserlist();
    if (theUserlist != null)
      theUserlist.remove(aUser.getObjectIdentifier());
    if (Log.isLog(C_Log.MODULE,
      getSMIEventSwitch().getSMIContext().getName())) {
      Log.log("User " + aUser.getName()
        + " has left the room.", C_Log.MODULE,
        getSMIEventSwitch().getSMIContext().getName());
    }
    aUser = null;
}
/** Outputs the messages */
public void showMessages(SMICommand aSMICommand) throws IOException {
    User theUser = getUser(aSMICommand);
    // Check if the user has been inactive for longer than the
    // permitted time. If yes, log them out!
    if (theUser != null)
      if (theUser.getInactiveTime() > C_MaxInactiveTime)
        logout(aSMICommand);
    // Test if the user is still logged in
    if (getUser(aSMICommand) == null) {
      aSMICommand.putValue(C_Template,
        aSMICommand.getValue("userNotLoggedIn"));
    }
}
/** Find a user with a particular name in the Store */
protected User getUserForName(String aName) throws PersistenceException {
    User theUser = null;
    // Get Store.
    I_Store theStore = getStore();
    // Read user from the store.
    synchronized(theStore) {
      try {
        theStore.begin() ;
        theUser = (User)theStore.persistenceWithKey(aName,
          "User", "Name");
        theStore.commit() ;
      }
```

```
        catch (Throwable t) {
          theStore.rollback();
          if (t instanceof PersistenceException) {
            throw (PersistenceException)t;
          }
          throw new SMIEventListenerException(t);
        }
      }
      return theUser;
    }
} // End of the class
```

## 13.3 Dialogue and layout

Now we have had a detailed look with the application logic, we now come to the display and management of the Chat.

### 13.3.1 Importing code fragments

Similarly to the other examples, we also use the JSP import mechanism for integrating code fragments in Chat. The fragments to be imported are header.html (Listing 13.12) and footer.html (Listing 13.13).

Listing 13.12: Code fragment header.html

```
<HTML>
<HEAD>
  <TITLE>Chat</TITLE>
</HEAD>
<BODY text="#800000" link="#000080" vlink="#000080" alink="#FF0000">
```

Listing 13.13: Code fragment footer.html

```
</BODY>
</HTML>
```

### 13.3.2 Login dialogue

The Login dialogue (Fig. 13.5) prompts the user to enter his or her name and password, or to register him- or herself, something for which a JavaServer Page is not really needed at all. But the page can do more than that. As part of its standard functionality, users find a list of current users of the same room at the bottom of the page. In brackets, after the name of each user, they can see the length of time that the user in question has been passive, i.e. only reading. In addition, the page can show an error message after an unsuccessful attempt to login, and the login name used at the last login.

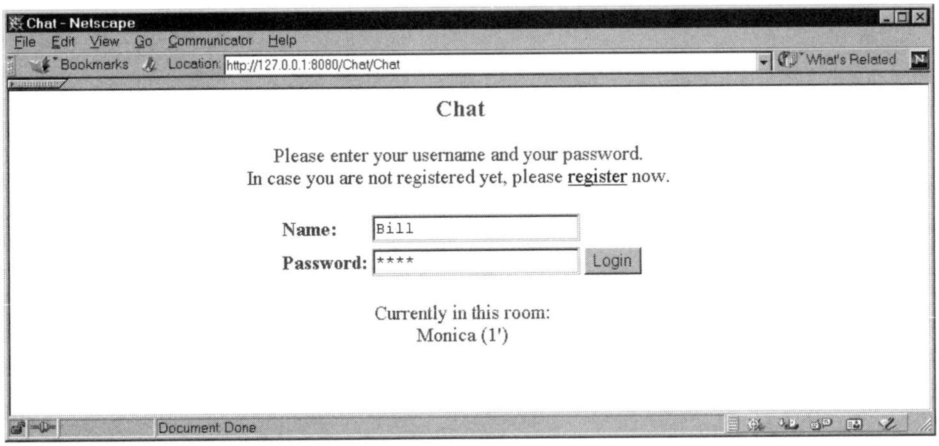

**Figure 13.5**  The Login dialogue

In order to implement all of these features, the SMICommand is now read from the request (Listing 13.14). Next, the command is asked for the user list and an error message, if required. The error message is output immediately, and the user list is displayed at the bottom of the page.

The C_Username and C_Password constants from C_Chat are used to name the Name and Password parameters.

Listing 13.14: Source code for Login dialogue: `login.jsp`

```
<%@include file="header.html"%>
<%@page language="java"
import="de.webapp.Chat.*,de.webapp.Framework.SMI.*,java.util.*" %>
<%
SMICommand theSMICommand = (SMICommand)request.getAttribute("SMIEvent");
Hashtable theUserList =
    (Hashtable)theSMICommand.getValue(C_Chat.C_Userlist);
String theErrorMessage =
    (String)theSMICommand.getValue(C_Chat.C_ErrorMessage);
%>
<center>
<h3>Chat</h3>
<form action="Chat" method="POST">
<input type="Hidden" name="Command" value="login">
<%
if (theErrorMessage != null) out.println(theErrorMessage);
else {
%>
If you have already registered, please enter your user name
and password.
<%
```

```
}
%>
<br>
If you have not already registered, you can do that.
<a href="Chat?Command=showRegistration">here</a>, <p>
<table border=0>
<tr>
<td><b>Name:</b></td>
<td colspan=2><input type="Text" name="<%=C_Chat.C_Username%>" size="20"
value="<%=(String)theSMICommand.getValue(C_Chat.C_Username)%>"></td>
</tr>
<tr>
<td><b>password:</b></td>
<td><input type="Password" name="<%=C_Chat.C_Password%>" size="20"></td>
<td><input type="Submit" value="Logon"></td>
</tr>
</table>
</form>
<p>
Currently, the following users are present in the room:<br>
<%
for (Enumeration e = theUserList.elements();e.hasMoreElements();) {
    User aUser = (User)(e.nextElement());
    long min = aUser.getInactiveTime() / (1000 * 60);
    String idle = String.valueOf(min);
    out.println(aUser.getName() + " (" + idle + "')<br>");
}
%>
</center>
<%@include file="footer.html"%>
```

### 13.3.3  User data dialogue

In Chat there are two dialogues that are used specifically for manipulating the user data: the registration and the change user data dialogue. Both are so similar that we have combined them in the `register.jsp` JavaServer Page (Fig. 13.6 and Listing 13.15). Depending whether the command contains a user object, the user will be shown an Add or a Change dialogue. In the case of a Change dialogue, the current data will be set as default values.

Listing 13.15: Source code for the dialogues for manipulating the user data: `register.jsp`

```
<%@include file="header.html"%>
<%@page language="java"
import="de.webapp.Chat.*,de.webapp.Framework.SMI.*,java.util.*" %>
```

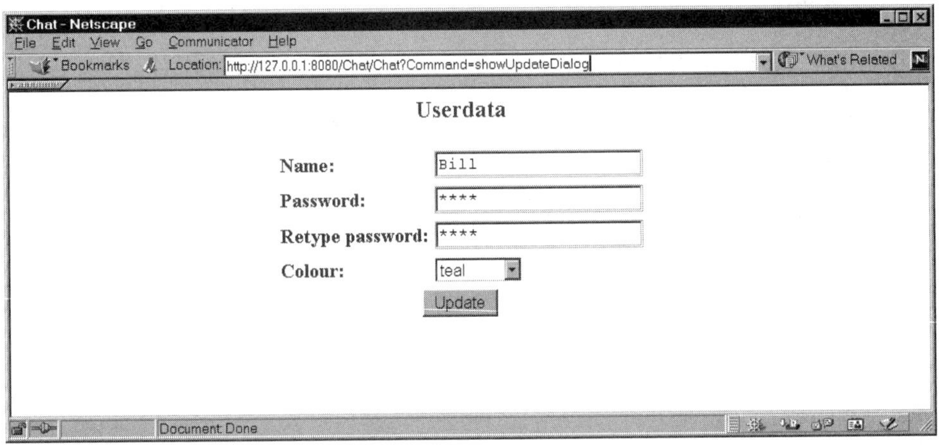

**Figure 13.6** The dialogue for manipulating the user data

```
<%
SMICommand theSMICommand = (SMICommand)request.getAttribute("SMIEvent");
User theUser = (User)theSMICommand.getSessionValue(C_Chat.C_User);
String theButtonLabel = "Create";
String theCommand = "createUser";
String theName = (String)theSMICommand.getValue(C_Chat.C_Username);
String thePassword = (String)theSMICommand.getValue(C_Chat.C_Password);
Integer theColor = null;
try {
   theColor = new Integer((String)theSMICommand.getValue(C_Chat.C_Color));
}
catch (NumberFormatException nfe) {}
if (theUser != null) {
   theButtonLabel = "Update";
   theCommand = "updateUser";
   theName = theUser.getName();
   thePassword = theUser.getPassword();
   theColor = theUser.getColor();
}
if (theColor == null) theColor = new Integer(0);
%>
<center>
<h3>user data</h3>
<%=(String)theSMICommand.getValue(C_Chat.C_ErrorMessage)%>
<form action="Chat" method="POST">
<input type="Hidden" name="Command" value="<%=theCommand%>">
<table>
<tr>
```

```
<td><b>Name:</b></td>
<td><input type="Text" name="_Username" size="20"
value="<%=theName%>"></td>
</tr>
<tr>
<td><b>password:</b></td>
<td><input type="Password" name="_Password" size="20"
value="<%=thePassword%>"></td>
</tr>
<tr>
<td><b>Password (for confirmation):</b></td>
<td><input type="Password" name="_Password2" size="20"></td>
</tr>
<tr>
<td><b>colour:</b></td>
<td>
<select name="_Color">
<%
for (int i=0; i<C_Chat.C_Colors.length; i++) {
  if (i == theColor.intValue()) {
    out.println("<option selected value=\"" + i + "\">"
      + C_Chat.C_ColorNames[i]);
  }
  else {
    out.println("<option value=\"" + i + "\">"
      + C_Chat.C_ColorNames[i]);
  }
}
%>
</select>
</td>
</tr>
</table>
<input type="Submit" value="<%=theButtonLabel%>">
</form>
</center>
<%@include file="footer.html"%>
```

### 13.3.4 Menu dialogue

After logging in, or successfully registering, the user sees the menu dialogue (Fig. 13.7 and Listing 13.16). Here there are three options: enter the room, change user data or log out. All three possibilities are common commands: only the user list at the bottom of the screen requires the use of JSP. The coding here is identical to the Login dialogue (Section 13.3.2).

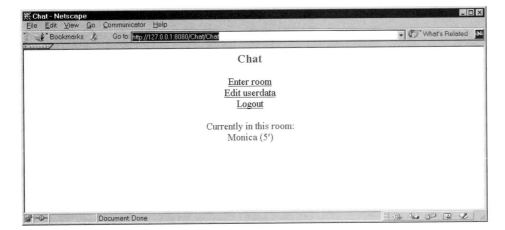

**Figure 13.7** The Menu dialogue

Listing 13.16: Source code for Menu dialogue: `menu.jsp`

```
<%@include file="header.html"%>
<%@page language="java"
import="de.webapp.Chat.*,de.webapp.Framework.SMI.*,java.util.*" %>
<%
SMICommand theSMICommand = (SMICommand)request.getAttribute("SMIEvent");
Hashtable theUserList =
    (Hashtable)theSMICommand.getValue(C_Chat.C_Userlist);
%>
<center>
<h3>Chat</h3>
<a href="Chat?Command=enterRoom">Enter room</a><br>
<a href="Chat?Command=showUpdateDialogue">Edit user data</a><br>
<a href="Chat?Command=logout">Logout</a><br>
<p>
Currently, in this room the following users are present:<br>
<%
for (Enumeration e = theUserList.elements();e.hasMoreElements();) {
    User aUser = (User)(e.nextElement());
    long min = aUser.getInactiveTime() / (1000 * 60);
    String idle = String.valueOf(min);
    out.println(aUser.getName() + " (" + idle + "')<br>");
}
%>
</center>
<%@include file="footer.html"%>
```

### 13.3.5 Frameset

When the user enters the room, the system creates a frameset. The coding is fairly simple – it is pure HTML (Listing 13.17).

Listing 13.17: HTML code for the frameset: `frame.html`

```html
<html>
<head>
<title>Chat</title>
</head>
<frameset cols="50%, *">
   <frame src="Chat?Command=showSendDialog" marginwidth="10"
marginheight="10" scrolling="auto" frameborder="no">
   <frame src="Chat?Command=showMessages" marginwidth="10" marginheight="10"
scrolling="auto" frameborder="no">
</frameset>
</html>
```

### 13.3.6 Send dialogue

The send dialogue displays a mask where the user enters messages (Fig. 13.8 and Listing 13.18). The user can then decide in which colour the message should appear and to whom it should be sent. As the send colour is an attribute of the user, the `request` object must be asked for the command. The command then should be asked for the user. An iteration loops over all possible colours and generates the <option> HTML-tags. Here the user's colour will be marked with the attribute `selected`.

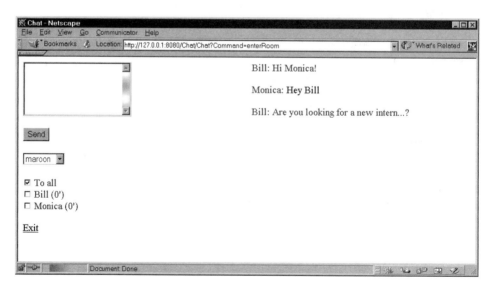

**Figure 13.8**  The Send dialogue

After the colours have been displayed, the system displays the user list with check-boxes. The checkboxes of the users to whom the last message was sent are marked with checked. As the `ObjectIdentifier` of a user is unique, it is used as the value for a checkbox, rather than a name.

At the end of the page we display another note on how to log out.

Listing 13.18: Source code for Send dialogue: `sendform.jsp`

```
<%@include file="header.html"%>
<%@page language="java"
import="de.webapp.Chat.*,de.webapp.Framework.SMI.*,java.util.*" %>

<form action="Chat" method="POST">
<input type=hidden name="Command" value="sendMessage">
<textarea name="_Message" cols=20 rows=5 wrap=soft></textarea>
<p>
<input type=submit value="Send">
<p>
<select name="_Color">
<%
SMICommand theSMICommand = (SMICommand)request.getAttribute("SMIEvent");
Hashtable theUserList =
   (Hashtable)theSMICommand.getValue(C_Chat.C_Userlist);
User theUser = (User)theSMICommand.getSessionValue(C_Chat.C_User);
for (int i=0; i<C_Chat.C_Colors.length; i++) {
   if (i == theUser.getColor().intValue()) {
      out.println("<option selected value=\"" + i + "\">"
         + C_Chat.C_ColorNames[i]);
   }
   else {
      out.println("<option value=\"" + i + "\">"
         + C_Chat.C_ColorNames[i]);
   }
}
%>
</select>
<p>
<%
String[] theTo = request.getParameterValues(C_Chat.C_To);
String[] theAll = request.getParameterValues(C_Chat.C_All);
if (theTo == null || theAll != null)
   out.println("<input type=checkbox name=\"_All\" checked>To all<br>");
else
   out.println("<input type=checkbox name=\"_All\">To all<br>");
for (Enumeration e = theUserList.elements();e.hasMoreElements();) {
   User aUser = (User)(e.nextElement());
   String checked = new String("");
```

```
        if (theTo != null) {
          for (int i=0; (i < theTo.length)
             && (!(checked.equals("checked"))); i++){
            if (aUser.getObjectIdentifier().equals(theTo[i])) {
              checked = "checked";
            }
          }
        }
        long min = aUser.getInactiveTime() / (1000 * 60);
        String idle = String.valueOf(min);
        out.println("<input type=checkbox name=\"_To\" value=\""
          + aUser.getObjectIdentifier() + "\" " + checked + ">"
          + aUser.getName() + " (" + idle + "')<br>");
    }
    %>
    </form>
    <p>
    <a href="Chat?Command=leaveRoom" target="_top">Exit</a>
    <%@include file="footer.html"%>
```

### 13.3.7  Issuing messages

An alternative approach is needed to manage message issue in the way we require. Unlike the other pages, we do not use the normal HTML header, header.html. Instead, we use the outputheader.html file (Listing 13.19). The difference is the refreshWindow() function in the JavaScript. When this function is called, the page is reloaded (refreshed).

Listing 13.19: Code fragment outputheader.html

```
    <HTML>
    <HEAD>
      <TITLE>Chat</TITLE>
    <SCRIPT LANGUAGE="JavaScript">
    <!-
    function refreshWindow() {
      location = "Chat?Command=showMessages";
    }
    //->
    </SCRIPT>
    </HEAD>
    <BODY text="#800000" link="#000080" vlink="#000080" alink="#FF0000">
```

The outputheader.html code fragment is integrated in the messages.jsp file (Listing 13.20) instead of header.html. After the page is called using the showMessages command, the User object is read from the command. Next the user's writeMessages(I_MessageWriter) method is called. Remember that this is the method that writes the messages asynchronously via an I_MessageWriter. As we have to write HTML, we also pass on an HTMLMessageWriter as the I_MessageWriter. This HTMLMessageWriter was initialized with the JavaServer page's PrintWriter. The call to writeMessages() does not return before our HTMLMessageWriter can write no more, i.e. canWrite() returns false. Once it returns, there is a pause of three seconds before the JavaScript function refreshWindow() is called. This ensures that we can deliver all the file to the browser, so that it will not issue any error messages caused by interrupted transmission.

If the call to writeMessage() fails to succeed because of an IllegalStateException we issue an error message.

Listing 13.20: Source code for message display: messages.jsp

```
<%@include file=" outputheader.html"%>
<%@page language="java"
import="de.webapp.Chat.*,de.webapp.Framework.SMI.*,java.util.*" %>
<%
SMICommand theSMICommand = (SMICommand)request.getAttribute("SMIEvent");
User theUser = (User)theSMICommand.getSessionValue(C_Chat.C_User);
try {
    theUser.writeMessages(new HTMLMessageWriter(out));
%>
<SCRIPT LANGUAGE="JavaScript">
<!-
setTimeout("refreshWindow()",3000);
//->
</SCRIPT>
<%
}
catch (IllegalStateException ise) {
%>
You have already logged on.
The display can only be made in one window.
<%
}
%>
<%@include file="footer.html"%>
```

## 13.4  SMI – definition and configuration

Once we have coded the individual parts, we use the configuration to connect them all together. Before we devote ourselves to the SMI definition file, we shall take one more look at the store configuration.

### 13.4.1 Store configuration

First the user table has to be created. Listing 13.21 corresponds to the SQL statements. We use `ChatUser` instead of `User` as the table name, as `User` is a reserved table name in some databases. Once we have created the table, we also add the `User` type and its (arbitrarily selected) type number `600` to the `TypeNumber` table.

Listing 13.21: SQL statements for creating the Chat User table: `Chat.sql`

```
// Table ChatUser
CREATE TABLE ChatUser (
   ObjectIdentifier CHAR(16) NOT NULL,
   ObjectVersion INTEGER,
   Name VARCHAR,
   Password VARCHAR,
   Color INTEGER,
   PRIMARY KEY (ObjectIdentifier)
);
INSERT INTO TypeNumber VALUES ('User', 600);
```

Once the database tables have been created, we just need to create the `Chat.store` Store configuration file (Listing 13.22). For reasons of clarity, we have moved the definition of the User type into the separate `User.persistence` file (Listing 13.23).

Listing 13.22: Store configuration file, `Chat.store`

```
{
   StoreClass = "de.webapp.Framework.SMICommandListener.SMIStore";
   // Example connection data
   JDBCConnection = {
      DriverClass = "sun.jdbc.odbc.JdbcOdbcDriver";
      URLConnect = "jdbc:odbc:webapp";
      Properties = {
         user = "web" ;
         password = "app" ;
      }
   };
   Types = {
      User = #include("User.persistence");
   }
}
```

Listing 13.23: Definition of the User type: `User.persistence`

```
{
   Classes = {
      FactoryClass = "de.webapp.Framework.Persistence.PersistenceFactory
MSAccess";
```

```
    };
    Type = {
        Name = "User";
        Class = "de.webapp.Chat.User";
        Entity = "ChatUser";
        EntityAlias = "t0";
        Attributes = (
            "ObjectIdentifier",
            "ObjectVersion",
            "Name",
            "Password",
            // as Color is not a string, the attribute
            // needs to be defined more accurately.
            {
                Name = "Color";
                TypeClass = "java.lang.Integer";
            },
        );
    }
}
```

## 13.4.2 SMI Definition

Now all we have to do is create the SMI definition file. Its content establishes the interplay between the commands and methods of individual listeners. As we would like to use our own I_SMIEventSwitch, its class name must be defined with the key EventSwitchClass. In addition, we have to create an additional configuration file, Chat.con (Listing 13.24), which defines I_SMIContext. Otherwise everything is the same.

Listing 13.24: Chat SMI definition file

```
{
    // Basic configuration
    EventSwitchClass = "de.webapp.Chat.ChatSwitch";
    // Definition of default values
    DefaultCommand = "showLogin";
    Values = {
        _FollowUpCommand = "display";
        _TemplateName = "login.jsp";
    }
    // Definition of the listener
    Listener = {
        ChatRoom = {
            Class = "de.webapp.Chat.ChatRoom";
        },
```

```
ChatRegistration = {
    Class = "de.webapp.Chat.ChatRegistration";
},
ChatDispatcher = {
    Class = "de.webapp.Chat.ChatDispatcher";
},
DisplayBean = {
    Class = "de.webapp.Framework.SMICommandListener.DisplayBean";
}
};
// Definition of the commands
Commands = {
    // Display
    display = {
        MethodName = "display";
        Listener = "DisplayBean";
    }
    //Display login
    showLogin = {
        MethodName = "noop";
        Listener = "ChatRoom";
        Values = {
            _TemplateName = "login.jsp"
        }
    }
    // Authentication
    enterRoom = {
        MethodName = "enter";
        Listener = "ChatRoom";
        Values = {
            _TemplateName = "frame.html"
            userNotLoggedIn = "notloggedin.html"
        }
    }
    // Display a message
    showMessages = {
        MethodName = "showMessages";
        Listener = "ChatRoom";
        Values = {
            _TemplateName = "messages.jsp"
            userNotLoggedIn = "notloggedin.html"
        }
    }
    // Display the message entry dialogue
    showSendDialogue = {
        MethodName = "noop";
```

```
   Listener = "ChatRoom";
   Values = {
     _TemplateName = "sendform.jsp"
   }
}
// Send message
sendMessage = {
   MethodName = "send";
   Listener = "ChatDispatcher";
   Values = {
     _TemplateName = "sendform.jsp"
     userNotLoggedIn = "notloggedin.html"
   }
}
// Enter the personal data
showRegistration = {
   MethodName = "noop";
   Listener = "ChatRegistration";
   Values = {
     _TemplateName = "register.jsp"
   }
}
// Display dialogue where user changes their data
showUpdateDialogue = {
   MethodName = "noop";
   Listener = "ChatRegistration";
   Values = {
     _TemplateName = "register.jsp"
   }
}
// Create new user
createUser = {
   MethodName = "create";
   Listener = "ChatRegistration";
   Values = {
     failure = "register.jsp"
     _TemplateName = "menu.jsp"
   }
}
// Change a user
updateUser = {
   MethodName = "update";
   Listener = "ChatRegistration";
   Values = {
     _TemplateName = "menu.jsp"
     failure = "register.jsp"
```

```
        }
      }
      // Logout
      logout = {
        MethodName = "logout";
        Listener = "ChatRoom";
      }
      // Login
      login = {
        MethodName = "login";
        Listener = "ChatRoom";
        Values = {
          _TemplateName = "menu.jsp"
          errorOnEnter = "login.jsp"
        }
      }
      // Leave room
      leaveRoom = {
        MethodName = "leave";
        Listener = "ChatRoom";
        Values = {
          _TemplateName = "menu.jsp"
        }
      }
    }
  }
}
```

Listing 13.25: Configuration file for I_SMIContext: Chat.con

```
{
  Class = "de.webapp.Chat.ChatContext";
  Values = {
    _StoreName = "Chat.store";
  }
}
```

Finally, we just need to register with the servlet engine. The entry for jo! is printed in Listing 13.26.

Listing 13.26: Chat entry in jo!'s servlets.properties file

```
# Chat
servlet.Chat.code=de.webapp.Framework.SMI.SMIServlet
servlet.Chat.initArgs=EventSwitch=Chat,Context=Chat
servlet.Chat.aliases=/Chat/Chat
```

The Chat should then be ready for use after being started via the URL http://<hostname>:<port>/Chat/Chat!

# Final comments 14

I n the previous chapters you have seen how to develop Web-based applications using the WebApp framework. We have, of course, used fairly small examples. Despite this we have by no means exhausted SMI's capabilities for modularization. For this reason none of the examples needed more than one `I_SMIEventSwitch` or `SMIServlet`. However, we have demonstrated that an application model such as SMI, based on `Persistence`, can make the development process significantly easier, and create better applications than those developed with servlets and JDBC alone.

The inherent abstraction of the SMIs gives you the ability to control the behaviour of entire applications via configuration files. You can now develop complex Web-based applications which will also have a long life.

The `Persistence` framework has also added considerably to the elegance of the implementation. We have shown you how simple it is to use this framework to program a slimline, object-oriented and Web-based database browser. The amount of code required to implement `Persistence` in the other two examples is also noticeably small.

Part III of this book also demonstrates how a development process model can be used. This simplifies your analyses and can significantly speed up the implementation of your application. In addition it requires that important separation of application logic and display logic, and therefore goes a long way to making your applications future-proof.

We hope that this book has given you a few new insights. We would consider it a sign of its success if we have convinced you to write your applications in a slightly different way in the future.

# ConfigFileReader file format

The name of a file in ConfigFileReader format (Chapter 4) should end with the file extension .cfg. The file itself must comply with the Backus–Naur format (BNF) shown in Listing A.1:

Listing A.1: Backus–Naur format of the ConfigFileReader format

```
body : hashtable
     | vector
literal : STRING
        | INTEGER
        | DOUBLE
        | MINUS INTEGER
        | MINUS DOUBLE
        | TRUE
        | FALSE
object : literal
       | hashtable
       | vector
       | includestatement literal
       | includestatement hashtable
       | includestatement vector
hashtable : OPENCURLYBRACE hashelements CLOSECURLYBRACE
          | OPENCURLYBRACE CLOSECURLYBRACE
hashelements : NAME IS object
             | hashelements NAME IS object
vector : OPENBRACE vectorelements CLOSEBRACE
       | OPENBRACE CLOSEBRACE
vectorelements : object
               | vectorelements object
includestatement : INCLUDE OPENBRACE STRING CLOSEBRACE
```

Here the definitions shown in Listing A.2 apply. Java-compliant comments, commas, semicolons, blank spaces, tabs, etc., are ignored during parsing.

Listing A.2: Definition of the token

```
STRING: any character string
INTEGER: [0-9]+ (whole number)
DOUBLE: [0-9]+\.[0-9]+ (decimal fraction)
MINUS: '-'
TRUE: 'true'
FALSE: 'false'
OPENBRACE: '('
CLOSEBRACE: ')'
OPENCURLYBRACE: '{'
CLOSECURLYBRACE: '}'
NAME: [A-Za-z_][A-Za-z_0-9]* (descriptor)
IS: '='
INCLUDE: '#include'
```

# Options for configuring the Persistence framework

The Persistence framework (Chapter 9) needs a model in order to function correctly. The Store is generated by the StoreFactory, on the basis of a description of the model. One principle of the WebApp framework is that the various different functional areas are defined via interfaces and only form a functioning whole at run-time. The configuration of the Persistence framework takes this principle into account. This means that all the Store and Peer services in the configuration are exchangeable. It is extremely easy to modify them to suit your own services. Naturally enough, StoreFactory also has predefined values.

Therefore, the complete Restaurant.store configuration file, as described in Chapter 9, looks like this:

Listing B.1: Complete configuration of a Store

```
{
    Name = "Restaurant" ;
    StoreClass = "de.webapp.Framework.Persistence.Store" ;
    FactoryClass = "de.webapp.Framework.Persistence.StorePersistenceFactory" ;
    AutonumberClass = "de.webapp.Framework.Persistence.StoreOIDAutonumber" ;
    ModifierClass = "de.webapp.Framework.Persistence.StoreModifier" ;
    TransactorClass = "de.webapp.Framework.Persistence.StoreTransactor" ;
    ConnectionClass = "de.webapp.Framework.Persistence.StoreConnection" ;
    JDBCConnection = {
        // Example connection.
```

**Table B.1**  Store configuration parameters

| Parameter | Optional | Description |
|---|---|---|
| Name | No | Store name |
| StoreClass | Yes | Class of the Store instance<br>predefined value: de.webapp.Framework.Persistence.Store |
| ConnectionClass | Yes | Database connection<br>predefined value: de.webapp.Framework.Persistence.StoreConnection |
| TransactorClass | Yes | Transactor class<br>predefined value: de.webapp.Framework.Persistence.StoreTransactor |
| ModifierClass | Yes | Modifier class<br>predefined value: de.webapp.Framework.Persistence.StoreModifier |
| FactoryClass | Yes | Factory class<br>predefined value:<br>de.webapp.Framework.Persistence.StorePersistenceFactory |
| AutonumberClass | Yes | Class for automatic numbering<br>predefined value:<br>de.webapp.Framework.Persistence.StoreOIDAutonumber<br>for large databases<br>de.webapp.Framework.Persistence.StoreLongOIDAutonumber |
| JDBCConnection | No | Sets the connection parameter of a JDBC connection |
| Types | No | Sets the Persistence types (Table 9.4) |

```
DriverClass = "solid.jdbc.SolidDriver" ;
URLConnect = "jdbc:solid://localhost:1313" ;
Properties = {
   user = "web" ;
   password = "app" ;
}
} ;
Types = {
   Restaurant = #include("Restaurant.persistence") ;
   Dish = #include("Dish.persistence") ;
}
} // End of configuration
```

The JDBCConnection and Types parameters also have other parameters. To set up a JDBC database connection, the JDBC adapter class must be defined by setting the DriverClass parameter. URLConnect is used to enter a special data source of the selected database. Properties is used to describe parameters such as logon.

The Types parameter defines the individual Persistence types of the Store. In the example, the data are split into two separate files.

The Service class entry of the `PersistencePeer` is an optional entry. However, `de.webapp.Framework.Persistence.PersistenceFactoryMSAccess` must be selected as the `FactoryClass` if MS Access is used as a database. Unfortunately the ODBC adaptor in MS Access 97 does not function correctly. It does not allow you to access the same attribute of a `ResultSet` more than once.

The Type entry is a mandatory entry. In particular, it includes a class and the corresponding parameters for mapping to the database tables. All the instructions which are marked as comments (`//`) are optional parameters. Some instructions do not directly refer to the example and are only intended to show the precise position of those types of instruction (`// **`).

Listing B.2: A complete configuration of one `Persistence` object from Restaurant type

```
{
   Classes = {
      PeerClass = "de.webapp.Framework.Persistence.PersistencePeer" ;
      TypeClass = "de.webapp.Framework.Persistence.PersistenceType" ;
      CacherClass = "de.webapp.Framework.Persistence.PersistenceCacher" ;
      RetrieverClass =
      "de.webapp.Framework.Persistence.PersistenceRetriever" ;
      FactoryClass = "de.webapp.Framework.Persistence.PersistenceFactory" ;
      // FactoryClass = "de.webapp.Framework.Persistence.PersistenceFactory
MSAccess" ;
      ModifierClass = "de.webapp.Framework.Persistence.PersistenceModfifier" ;
   }
   Type = {
      Name = "Restaurant" ;
      Class = "de.webapp.Examples.Persistence.Restaurant.Restaurant";
      // ** Class = "de.webapp.
      Framework.SMICommandListener.SMIPersistenceGeneric";
      Entity = "Restaurant";
      EntityAlias = "t0" ;
      Attributes = (
      {
        Name = "ObjectIdentifier";
        Key = "YES";
        MainKey = "YES";
      },{
        Name = "ObjectVersion";
      },{
        // Generic = "YES" ;
        // Key = "YES";
        Name = "Name";
        TypeClass = "java.lang.String" ;
        // Property = "Name" ;
```

**Table B.2** The parameters of a PersistencePeer

| Parameter | Optional | Description |
|---|---|---|
| Classes;PeerClass | Yes | Peer class<br>predefined value:<br>de.webapp.Framework.Persistence.Persistenc<br>ePeer |
| Classes;TypeClass | Yes | Type description class<br>predefined value:<br>de.webapp.Framework.Persistence.<br>PersistenceType |
| Classes;CacherClass | Yes | Cache class<br>predefined value:<br>de.webapp.Framework.Persistence.<br>PersistenceCache |
| Classes;RetrieverClass | Yes | Class for searching for objects<br>predefined value:<br>de.webapp.Framework.Persistence.<br>PersistenceRetriever |
| Classes;FactoryClass | Yes | Class used to create new Persistence objects<br>and to arrange the transformation into a<br>Persistence object from the database<br>predefined value:<br>de.webapp.Framework.Persistence.<br>PersistenceFactory |
| Classes;ModifierClass | Yes | Class used to save changes<br>predefined value:<br>de.webapp.Framework.Persistence.Persistenc<br>eModifier |
| Classes;PeerClass | Yes | Peer class<br>predefined value:<br>de.webapp.Framework.Persistence.<br>PersistencePeer |
| Type;Name | No | Symbolic name of the Persistence (must be<br>present in the TypeNumber table) |
| Type;Class | No | Class which implements this Persistence type |
| Type;Entity | No | Name of the table |
| Type;EntityAlias | No | Alias of the entity in requests |
| Type;Attributes | No | Attribute definition |
| Type;Attributes;<br>Name | No | Attribute name |
| Type;Attributes;<br>Key | Yes | Is the unique key of the table |
| Type;Attributes;<br>MainKey | Yes | Is an attribute of the ObjectIdentifier |
| Type;Attributes;<br>Generic | Yes | Marks generic attributes for the<br>PersistenceGeneric and<br>PersistenceGenericConvertType classes |

**Table B.2**  *Cont.*

| Parameter | Optional | Description |
|---|---|---|
| Type;Attributes; TypeClass java.lang.String | Yes | Attribute type<br>This entry is mandatory if the type is not |
| Type;Attributes; Property | Yes | Name of the attribute in the database |
| Type;Attributes; Field | Yes | Name of the field for the attribute in the class |
| Type;Attributes; GetMethod | Yes | Name of the access method for the attribute |
| Type;Attributes; SetMethod | Yes | Name of the change method for the attribute |
| Type;Associations; Name | No | Association name.<br>Important because this is used for the application and class access methods |
| Type;Associations; Type | No | Cardinality of the relation (ToOne, ToMany, ToManyLink) |
| Type;Associations; Modified | Yes | If this is an aggregate, this parameter must be set to YES. This ensures that the correct reference class is also selected automatically. |
| Type;Associations; ResultType | No | Name of the persistence objects contained in the request result (see Type;Attributes;Name) |
| Type;Associations; Key | No | Name of the key attribute (external key in its own table (1:1) or in the ResultType table(1:N)) |
| Type;Associations; ReferenceClass | Yes | Reference class. Usually the class can be deduced via the association type. |
| Type;Associations; QualifierExtension | Yes | Sets a static qualifier extension, e.g. Order by t0.Name |
| Type;Associations; LinkType | Yes | Sets the link type. This is needed for ToManyLink |
| Type;Associations; LinkLeftKey | Yes | Sets the external key, link to the base table |
| Type;Associations; LinkRightKey | Yes | Sets the external key, link with qualifier parameters |

```
                     // Field = "myName" ;
                     // GetMethod = "getName" ;
                     // SetMethod = "setName" ;
                  },{
                     // Generic = "YES"
                     Name = "Description";
                     TypeClass = "java.lang.String" ;
                  }
                  ) ;
                  // The short form is:
                  // Attributes = (
                  // "ObjectIdentifier",
                  // "ObjectVersion",
                  // "Name";
                  // "Description";
                  // ) ;
                  Associations = (
                  {
                     Name = "Dish" ;
                     Type = "ToMany" ;
                     ResultType = "Dish" ;
                     Key = "RestaurantID" ;
                     // ReferenceClass =
      "de.webapp.Framework.Persistence.ToManyModifiedReference" ;
                     // Modified = "YES" ;
                     // QualifierExtension = " Order By t0.Description" ;
                     // ** LinkType = "SupplierArticle" ;
                     // ** LinkLeftKey = "SupplierID" ;
                     // ** LinkRightKey = "ArticleID" ;
                  }
                  ) ;
               }
            } // End of the configuration
```

Each description of a `Persistence` object is made up of the following parts: services, classes, attributes and associations. One function of the description is to provide the access services for the Store. Another is to supply the services with the parameters required to map to the relational database. The configuration of the `PersistenceType` services for each `PersistencePeer` ensures that a powerful generic description of each type is available at run-time. Basically, there are two different description types. One description is used to define generic `Persistence` objects. The other is used to define `Persistence` objects from direct derivations of the `de.webapp.Framework.Persistence.Persistence` class. In an early phase of a project, a prototype of the business object, based on the generic `Persistence` object `PersistenceGeneric` can quickly be made available. If speed is important, or the semantics of a business object in the application are given greater emphasis, we recommend that real classes are made available.

# Deployment Descriptor's DTD

**A**ppendix C is an extract from Sun's 'Java™ Servlet Specification, V2.2' detailing the DTD of the Deployment Descriptor (which 'conveys the elements and configurations information of a web application between Developers, Assemblers, and Deployers').

The DTD that follows defines XML grammar for a web application deployment descriptor.

```
<!-- The web-app element is the root of the deployment descriptor for a web
application-->

<!ELEMENT web-app (icon?, display-name?, description?, distributable?,
context-param*, servlet*, servlet-mapping*, session-config!, mime-mapping*,
welcome-file-list?, error-page*, taglib*, resource-ref*, security-
constraint*, login-config?, security-role*, env-entry*, ejb-ref*)>

<!--The icon element contains a small-icon and a large-icon element which
specify the location within the web application for a small and large image
used to represent the web application in a GUI tool. At a minimum, tools
must accept GIF and JPEG format images.-->

<!ELEMENT icon (small-icon?, large-icon?)>

<!-- The small-icon element contains the location within the web
application of a file containing a small (16 ×16 pixel) icon image. -->

<!ELEMENT small-icon (#PCDATA)>

<!-- The large-icon element contains the location within the web
application of a file containing a large (32 ×32 pixel) icon image. -->

<!ELEMENT large-icon (#PCDATA)>
```

<!-- The display-name element contains a short name that is intended to be displayed by GUI tools. -->

`<!ELEMENT display-name (#PCDATA)>`

<!-- The description element is used to provide descriptive text about the parent element.>

`<!ELEMENT description (#PCDATA)>`

<!-- The distributable element, by its presence in a web application deployment descriptor, indicates that this web application is programmed appropriately to be deployed into a distributed servlet container. -->

`<!ELEMENT distributable EMPTY>`

<!-- The context-param-element contains the declaration of a web application's servlet context initialization parameters. -->

`<!ELEMENT context-param (param-name, param-value, description?)>`

<!-- The param-name element contains the name of a parameter. -->

`<!ELEMENT param-name (#PCDATA)>`

<!-- The param-value element contains the value of a parameter. -->

`<!ELEMENT param-value (#PCDATA)>`

<!-- The servlet element contains the declarative data of a servlet. If a jsp-file is specified and the load-on-startup element is present, then the JSP should be precompiled and loaded. -->

`<!ELEMENT servlet (icon?, servlet-name, display-name?, description?, (servlet-class|jsp-file), init-param*, load-on-startup?, security-role-ref*)>`

<-- The servlet-name element contains the canonical name of the servlet. -->

`<!ELEMENT servlet-name (#PCDATA)>`

<!-- The servlet-class element contains the fully qualified class name of the servlet. -->

`<!ELEMENT servlet-class (#PCDATA)>`

<!-- The jsp-file element contains the full path to a JSP file within the web application. -->

`<!ELEMENT jsp-file (#PCDATA)>`

<!-- The init-param element contains a name/value pair as an initialization param of the servlet. -->

`<!ELEMENT init-param (param-name, param-value, description?)>`

<!-- The load-on-startup element indicates that this servlet should be loaded on the startup of the web application. The optional contents of these elements must be a positive integer indicating the order in which the servlet should be loaded. Lower integers are loaded before higher integers. If no value is specified, or if the value specified is not a positive integer, the container is free to load it at any time in the startup sequence. -->

**<!ELEMENT load-on-startup (#PCDATA)>**

<!-- The servlet-mapping element defines a mapping between a servlet and a url pattern. -->

**<!ELEMENT servlet-mapping (servlet-name, url-pattern)>**

<!-- The url-pattern element contains the url pattern of the mapping. Must follow the rules specified in Section 10 of the Servlet API Specification. -->

**<!ELEMENT url-pattern (#PCDATA)>**

<!-- The session-config element defines the session parameters for this web application. -->

**<!ELEMENT session-config (session-timeout?)>**

<!-- The session-timeout element defines the default session timeout interval for all sessions created in this web application. The specified timeout must be expressed in a whole number of minutes. -->

**<!ELEMENT session-timeout (#PCDATA)>**

<!-- The mime-mapping element defines a mapping between an extension and a mime type. -->

**<!ELEMENT mime-mapping (extension, mime-type)>**

<!-- The extension element contains a string describing an extension. example: ".txt". -->

**<!ELEMENT extension (#PCDATA)>**

<!-- The mime-type element contains a defined mime type. example: "text/plain". -->

**<!ELEMENT mime-type (#PCDATA)>**

<!-- The welcome-file-list contains an ordered list of welcome files elements. -->

**<!ELEMENT welcome-file-list (welcome-file+)>**

<!-- The welcome-file element contains file name to use as a default welcome file, such as index.html. -->

```
<!ELEMENT welcome-file (#PCDATA)>
```

```
<!-- The taglib element is used to describe a JSP tag library. -->
```

```
<!ELEMENT taglib (taglib-uri, tablig-location)>
```

```
<!-- The taglib-uri element describes a URI, relative to the location of
the web.xml document, identifying a Tag Library used in the Web Application.
-->
```

```
<!ELEMENT taglib-uri (#PCDATA)>
```

```
<!-- The taglib-location element contains the location (as a resource
relative to the root of the web application) where to find the Tag Library
Description file for the tag library. -->
```

```
<!ELEMENT taglib-location (#PCDATA)>
```

```
<!-- The error-page element contains a mapping between an error code or
exception type to the path of a resource in the web application. -->
```

```
<!ELEMENT error-page ((error-code | exception-type), location)>
```

```
<!-- The error-code contains an HTTP error code, ex: 404. -->
```

```
<!ELEMENT error-code (#PCDATA)>
```

```
<!-- The exception type contains a fully qualified class name of a Java
exception type . -->
```

```
<!ELEMENT exception-type (#PCDATA)>
```

```
<!-- The location element contains the location of the resource in the web
application -->
```

```
<!ELEMENT location (#PCDATA)>
```

```
<!-- The resource-ref element contais a declaration of a Web Application's
reference to an external resource. -->
```

```
<!ELEMENT resource-ref (description?, res-ref-name, res-type, res-auth)>
```

```
<!-- The res-ref-name element specifies the name of the resource factory
reference name. -->
```

```
<!ELEMENT res-ref-name (#PCDATA)>
```

```
<!-- The res-type element specifies the (Java class) type of the data
source. -->
```

```
<!ELEMENT res-type (#PCDATA)>
```

```
<!-- The res-auth element indicates whether the application component code
performs resource signon programmatically or whether the container signs
onto the resource based on the principle mapping information supplied by
the deployer. Must be CONTAINER or SERVLET>
```

```
<!ELEMENT res-auth (#PCDATA)>
```

`<!-- The security-constraint element is used to associate security constraints with one or more web resource collections. -->`

```
<!ELEMENT security-constraint (web-resource-collection+, auth-constraint?, user-data-constraint?)>
```

`<!-- The web-resource-collection element is used to identify a subset of the resources and HTTP methods on those resources within a web application to which a security constraint applies. If no HTTP methods are specified, then the security constraint applies to all HTTP methods . -->`

```
<!ELEMENT web-resource-collection (web-resource-name, description?, url-pattern*, http-method*)>
```

`<!-- The web-resource-name contains the name of this web resource collection. -->`

```
<!ELEMENT web-resource-name (#PCDATA)>
```

`<!-- The http-method contains an HTTP method (GET | POST |...) -->`

```
<!ELEMENT http-method (#PCDATA)>
```

`<!-- The user-data-constraint element is used to indicate how data communicated between the client and container should be protected. -->`

```
<!ELEMENT user-data-constraint (description?, transport-guarantee)>
```

`<!-- The transport-guarantee element specifies that the communication between client and server should be NONE, INTEGRAL, or CONFIDENTIAL. NONE means that the application does not require any transport guarantees. A value of INTEGRAL means that the application requires that the data sent between the client and server be sent in such a way that it can't be changed in transit. CONFIDENTIAL means that the application requires that the data be transmitted in a fashion that prevents other entities from observing the contents of the transmission. In most cases, the presence of the INTEGRAL or CONFIDENTIAL flag will indicate that the use of SSL is required. -->`

```
<!ELEMENT transport-guarantee (#PCDATA)>
```

`<!-- The auth-constraint element indicates the user roles that should be permitted access to this resource collection. The role used here must appear in a security-role-ref element. -->`

```
<!ELEMENT auth-constraint (description?, role-name*)>
```

`<!-- The role-name element contains the name of a security role. -->`

```
<!ELEMENT role-name (#PCDATA)>
```

`<!-- The login-config element is used to configure the authentication`

method that should be used, the realm name that should be used for this application, and the attributes that are needed by the form login mechanism. -->

```
<!ELEMENT login-config (auth-method?, realm-name?, form-login-config?)>
```

<!-- The realm-name element specifies the realm name to use in HTTP Basic authorization. -->

```
<!ELEMENT realm-name (#PCDATA)>
```

<!-- The form-login-config element specifies the login and error pages that should be used in form based login. If form based authentication is not used, these elements are ignored. -->

```
<!ELEMENT form-login-config (form-login-page, form-error-page)>
```

<!-- The form-login-page element defines the location in the web app where the page that can be used for login can be found. -->

```
<!ELEMENT form-login-page (#PCDATA)>
```

<!-- The form-error-page element defines the location in the web app where the error page that is displayed when login is not successful can be found. -->

```
<!ELEMENT form-error-page (#PCDATA)>
```

<!-- The auth-method element is used to configure the authentication mechanism for the web application. As a prerequisite to gaining access to any web resources which are protected by an authorization constraint, a user must have authenticated using the configured mechanism. Legal values for this element are "BASIC", "DIGEST", "FORM", or "CLIENT-CERT". -->

```
<!ELEMENT auth-method (#PCDATA)>
```

<!-- The security-role element contains the declaration of a security role which is used in the security-constraints placed on the web application. -->

```
<!ELEMENT security-role (description?, role-name)>
```

<!-- The role-name element contains the name of a role. This element must contain a non-empty string. -->

```
<!ELEMENT role-name (#PCDATA)>
```

<!-- The security-role-ref element contains the declaration of a security role reference in the servlet's code. The contents of the role-name element is that of the String used in the servlet code to specify a role. The role-link element specifies that this coded role should be linked to a role described by the security-role element. -->

```
<!ELEMENT security-role-ref (description?, role-name, role-link)>
```

<!-- The role-link element is used to link a security role reference to a defined security role. The role-link element must contain the name of one of the securiy roles defined in the security-role elements. -->

```
<!ELEMENT role-link (#PC-DATA)>
```

<!-- The env-entry element contains the declaration of an application's environment entry. This element is required to be honored on in J2EE compliant servlet containers. -->

```
<!ELEMENT env-entry (description?, env-entry-name, env-entry-value?, env-entry-type)>
```

<!-- The env-entry-name contains the name of an application's environment entry. -->

```
<!ELEMENT env-entry-name (#PCDATA)>
```

<!-- The env-entry-value element contains the value of an application's environment entry. -->

```
<!ELEMENT env-entry-value (#PCDATA)>
```

<!-- The env-entry-type element contains the fully qualified Java type of the environment entry value that is expected by the application code. The following are the legal values of env-entry-type: java.lang.Boolean, java.lang.String, java.lang.Integer, java.lang.Double, java.lang.Float. -->

```
<!ELEMENT env-entry-type (#PCDATA)>
```

<!-- The ejb-ref element is used to declare a reference to an enterprise bean. -->

```
<!ELEMENT ejb-ref (description?, ejb-ref-name, ejb-ref-type, home, remote, ejb-link?)>
```

<!-- The ejb-ref-name element contains the name of an EJB reference. This is the JNDI name that the servlet code uses to get a reference to the enterprise bean. -->

```
<!ELEMENT ejb-ref-name (#PCDATA)>
```

<!-- The ejb-ref-type element contains the expected java class type of the referenced EJB. -->

```
<!ELEMENT ejb-ref-type (#PCDATA)>
```

<!-- The ejb-home element contains the fully qualified name of the EJB's home interface. -->

```
<!ELEMENT home (#PCDATA)>
```

<!-- The ejb-remote element contains the fully qualified name of the EJB's remote interface. -->

```
<!ELEMENT remote (#PCDATA)>
```

<!-- The ejb-link element is used in the ejb-ref element to specify that an EJB reference is linked to an EJB in an encompassing Java2 Enterprise Edition (J2EE) application package. The value of the ejb-link element must be the ejb-name of an EJB in the J2EE application package. -->

```
<!ELEMENT ejb-link (#PCDATA)>
```

<!-- The ID mechanism is to allow tools to easily make tool-specific references to the elements of the deployment descriptor. This allows tools that produce additional deployment information (i.e. information beyond the standard deployment descriptor information) to store the non-standard information in a separate file, and easily refer from these tools-specific files to the information in the standard web-app deployment describtor. -->

```
<!ATTLIST web-app id ID #IMPLIED>
<!ATTLIST icon id ID #IMPLIED>
<!ATTLIST small-icon id ID #IMPLIED>
<!ATTLIST large-icon id ID #IMPLIED>
<!ATTLIST display-name id ID #IMPLIED>
<!ATTLIST description id ID #IMPLIED>
<!ATTLIST distributable id ID #IMPLIED>
<!ATTLIST context-param id ID #IMPLIED>
<!ATTLIST param-name id ID #IMPLIED>
<!ATTLIST param-value id ID #IMPLIED>
<!ATTLIST servlet id ID #IMPLIED>
<!ATTLIST servlet-name id ID #IMPLIED>
<!ATTLIST servlet-class id ID #IMPLIED>
<!ATTLIST jsp-file id ID #IMPLIED>
<!ATTLIST ser-file id ID #IMPLIED>
<!ATTLIST init-param id ID #IMPLIED>
<!ATTLIST load-on-startup id ID #IMPLIED>
<!ATTLIST servlet-mapping id ID #IMPLIED>
<!ATTLIST url-pattern id ID #IMPLIED>
<!ATTLIST session-config id ID #IMPLIED>
<!ATTLIST session-timeout id ID #IMPLIED>
<!ATTLIST mime-mapping id ID #IMPLIED>
<!ATTLIST extension id ID #IMPLIED>
<!ATTLIST mime-type id ID #IMPLIED>
<!ATTLIST welcome-file-list id ID #IMPLIED>
<!ATTLIST welcome-file id ID #IMPLIED>
<!ATTLIST error-page id ID #IMPLIED>
<!ATTLIST error-code id ID #IMPLIED>
<!ATTLIST exception-type id ID #IMPLIED>
<!ATTLIST location id ID #IMPLIED>
<!ATTLIST resource-ref id ID #IMPLIED>
<!ATTLIST res-ref-name id ID #IMPLIED>
```

```
<!ATTLIST res-type id ID #IMPLIED>
<!ATTLIST res-auth id ID #IMPLIED>
<!ATTLIST security-constraint id ID #IMPLIED>
<!ATTLIST web-resource-collection id ID #IMPLIED>
<!ATTLIST web-resource-name id ID #IMPLIED>
<!ATTLIST http-method id ID #IMPLIED>
<!ATTLIST user-data-constraint id ID #IMPLIED>
<!ATTLIST transport-guarantee id ID #IMPLIED>
<!ATTLIST auth-constraint id ID #IMPLIED>
<!ATTLIST role-name id ID #IMPLIED>
<!ATTLIST auth-method id ID #IMPLIED>
<!ATTLIST basic-auth id ID #IMPLIED>
<!ATTLIST form-auth id ID #IMPLIED>
<!ATTLIST form-login-page id ID #IMPLIED>
<!ATTLIST form-error-page id ID #IMPLIED>
<!ATTLIST mutual-auth id ID #IMPLIED>
<!ATTLIST ejb-ref id ID #IMPLIED>
<!ATTLIST ejb-name id ID #IMPLIED>
<!ATTLIST ejb-type id ID #IMPLIED>
<!ATTLIST ejb-home id ID #IMPLIED>
<!ATTLIST ejb-remote id ID #IMPLIED>
<!ATTLIST ejb-link id ID #IMPLIED>
```

# Figures

# Appendix  E

# Tables

# Listings

# Bibliography

Behme, Henning; Mintert, Stefan (1998): *XML – In der Praxis*. Bonn: Addison-Wesley.

Berners-Lee, Tim (1989): *Information Management. A Proposal*. http://www.w3.org/History/1989/proposal.html.

Berners-Lee, Tim; Fielding, Roy; Frystyk, Henrik (1996): *RFC 1945 – Hypertext Transfer Protocol – HTTP/1.0*. http://www.cis.ohio-state.edu/htbin/rfc/rfc1945.html.

Booch, Grady (1992): *Object Oriented Analysis and Design*. 2nd edition, Redwood City: Benjamin/Cummings.

Buschmann, Frank; Meunier, Regine; Rohnert, Hans; Sommerlad, Peter; Stal, Michael (1996): *A System of Patterns*. Bonn: John Wiley & Sons.

Campione, Mary; Walrath, Kathy (1997): *Das Java Tutorial*. 1st edition, Bonn: Addison-Wesley.

Coplien, James O.; Schmidt, Douglas C. (1995): *Pattern languages of Program Design*. Reading, Addison-Wesley.

Cornell, Gary; Horstmann, Cay S. (1996): *Java bis ins Detail*. 1st edition, Hanover: Verlag Heinz-Heise.

Cox, Brad J.; Novobilski, Andrew J. (1991): *Object Oriented Programming*. Addison-Wesley.

Date, Chris J.; Darwen, Hugh: *SQL – Der Standard*. Bonn: Addison-Wesley.

Eilebrecht, Lars (1998): *Apache Web-Server*. 2nd edition, Bonn: International Thomson Publishing.

Farley, Jim (1998): *Java Distributed Computing*. Sebastopol, CA: O'Reilly.

Fielding, Roy; Gettys, Jim; Mogul, Jeffrey; Frystyk, Henrik; Masinter, Larry; Leach, Paul; Berners-Lee, Tim (1999): *Hypertext Transfer Protocol – HTTP/1.1*. http://www.rfc-editor.org/rfc/rfc2616.txt

Flanagan, David (1997): *JAVA Examples in a Nutshell*. Sebastopol, CA: O'Reilly.

Fowler, Martin; Scott, Kendall (1998): *UML konzentriert*. Bonn: Addison-Wesley.

Gamma, Erich; Helm, Richard; Johnson, Ralph; Vlissides, John (1996): *Entwurfsmuster – Elemente wiederverwendbarer objektorientierter Software*. Bonn: Addison-Wesley.

Gosling, James; Joy, Bill; Steele, Guy (1996): *Java – Die Sprachspezifikation*. 1st edition, Bonn: Addison-Wesley.

Hamilton, Graham; Cattel, Rick; Fisher, Maydene (1997): *JDBC Database Access with Java*. Reading, MA: Addison-Wesley.

Heid, Jörn (1998): *Servlets als CGI-Alternative*. In: *iX* **11**, page 64.

Heid, Jörn (1998): *Serverseitiges Scripting mit JSP*. In: *iX* **11**, page 68.

Heid, Jörn (1997): *Kettenreaktion, Servlets als CGI-Ersatz*. In: *iX* **11**, page 166.

Heuer, Andreas (1992): *Objektorientierte Datenbanken*. Bonn: Addison-Wesley.

Heuer, Andreas; Saake, Günther (1997): *Datenbanken*. Königswinter: International Thompson Publishing.

Holl, Matthias; Schorsch, Stefan (1998): *Objektidentität und Altdaten.* In *ObjektSpektrum* No. 6, Sigs.

Hughes, Merlin; Hughes, Conrad; Shoffner, Michael; Winslow, Maria (1997): *Java Network Programming.* Manning.

Hunter, Jason; Crawford, William (1998): *JAVA Servlet Programming.* Sebastopol, CA: O'Reilly.

JavaSoft (1998): *Java Development Kit API 1.2.* http://www.javasoft.com/products/jsp.

JavaSoft (1999): *JavaServer-Pages – Specification 1.0 und 1.1.* 1999, http://java.sun.com/products/jsp.

Klute, Rainer (1998): *Mehr als Applets.* In: *iX* **11**, page 60.

Krishnamurthy, Balachander; Mogul, Jeffrey C.; Kristol, David M. (1998): *Key Differences between HTTP/1.0 and HTTP/1.1.* 1998, http://akpublic.research.att.com/library/trs/TRs/98/98.39/98.39.1.body.ps.

Lea, Doug (1997): *Concurrent Programming in Java.* Reading, Massachusetts: Addison-Wesley.

Lemany, Laura (1997): *Castanet.* Indianapolis, IN: Sams Net.

Merkle, Berhard (1997): *RMI: Verteilte Java-Objekte.* In: *iX* **12**, page 130.

Moss, Karl (1998): *Java Servlets.* New York, NY: McGraw Hill.

Musciano, Chuck; Kennedy, Bill (1997): *HTML – Das umfassende Referenzwerk.* Sebastopol, CA: O'Reilly.

NCSA (1996): *Server Side Includes.* http://hoohoo.ncsa.edu/docs/tutorials/ includes.html.

Oestereich, Bernd (1998): *Objektorientierte Softwareentwicklung mit der Unified Modeling Language.* 4. edition, Munich/Wien, R. Oldenbourg Verlag.

Orfali, Robert; Harkley, Dan; Edwards, Jeri (1996): *The Essential Distributed Objects Survival Guide.* John Wiley & Sons.

Orfali, Robert; Harkley, Dan (1997): *Client/Server Programming with Java and CORBA.* New York: John Wiley & Sons.

IBL: Company (1998): Various publications on modelling object-relational mappings. http://www.ibl.de.

Reese, George (1997): *Database Programming with JDBC and Java.* Sebastopol: O'Reilly.

Rossbach, Peter; Schreiber, Hendrik (1997): *Suns JavaServer 1.1.* In: *iX* **12**, page 70.

Rossbach, Peter; Schreiber, Hendrik (1998a): Reference *objectHTML.* http://www.factum-gmbh.de.

Rossbach, Peter; Schreiber, Hendrik (1998b): *Server-Programmierung in Java.* In: *Java Spektrum* 3, page 42.

Rossbach, Peter; Schreiber, Hendrik (1998c): Tutorial *objectHTML.* http://www.factum-gmbh.de.

Rossbach, Peter; Terfloth, Axel; Mimberg, Dirk (1998): *Whitepaper PerFACT.* http://www.factum-gmbh.de.

Richard, Stevens, W. (1990): *Unix Network Programming.* 10th edition, Englewood Cliffs, NJ: Prentice-Hall.

Vlissides, John M.; Coplien, James O.; Kerth, Norman L. (1996): *Pattern languages of program design.* Reading, MA: Addison-Wesley.

Wilkinson, Nancy M. (1995): *Using CRC Cards.* Sigs Book.

Wirfs-Brock, Rebecca; Wilkerson, Brian; Wiener, Lauran (1990): *Design Object Oriented Software.* Englewood Cliffs, NJ: Prentice-Hall.

# Index